THE THEORY OF
KNOWLEDGE AND
EXISTENCE

' It matters little whether the ether really exists; that is the affair of metaphysicians. The essential thing for us is that everything happens as if it existed, and that this hypothesis is convenient for the explanation of phenomena. After all, have we any other reason to believe in the existence of material objects? That, too, is only a convenient hypothesis.'

POINCARÉ
(Halsted's translation).

THE THEORY OF
KNOWLEDGE AND EXISTENCE

By

W. T. STACE, Litt.D.

LECTURER IN PHILOSOPHY IN PRINCETON
UNIVERSITY

GREENWOOD PRESS, PUBLISHERS
WESTPORT, CONNECTICUT

Originally published in 1932
by the Clarendon Press, Oxford

First Greenwood Reprinting 1970

Library of Congress Catalogue Card Number 70-109852

SBN 8371-4343-8

Printed in the United States of America

PREFACE

THE title of this book would seem to indicate that it takes for its provinces both epistemology and metaphysics. First and foremost, however, it is an essay in epistemology. But the theory of knowledge which it advocates has implications regarding the nature of existence. Whether these implications are held to belong to metaphysics will depend upon how metaphysics is defined—itself a difficult problem. I have, however, followed two principles in this matter. I have, firstly, dealt only with those questions regarding the nature of existence the answers to which seemed to be necessarily bound up with my epistemological premises, and which, therefore, I could not avoid without leaving my work a torso. I have nowhere sought them out for their own sakes. Secondly, I have rigidly avoided any problem which I should regard as belonging to 'transcendental' metaphysics. My standpoint throughout is strictly empirical. This will be found more fully explained in the text. I would only add here that this exclusion of transcendental questions is not to be regarded as due to a contempt for them, or to an opinion adverse to their claims upon the human spirit. My view rather is that empiricism and transcendentalism do not clash (as has been commonly supposed), but are simply aiming at different ends, each of which may be quite legitimate. And as the inquiries on which this book is engaged are empirical inquiries, it appeared right to exclude transcendental issues.

One advantage at any rate it is worth while to claim for this procedure. When philosophers discuss transcendental problems, such as the ultimate nature of Reality with a capital R, or the first cause of the universe, there is apt to be at least the suspicion that they are setting riddles to which there is no answer, that the solution of these problems is beyond the reach of the human intellect altogether, that they are 'too high for us', or that at any rate any answers which we may give are mere speculations and guesses which go beyond any data of evidence available to us. I do not say that this suspicion is well founded. To make such an assertion would be already to give an opinion on a transcendental question. I say only that the suspicion exists in many minds. But nothing of the sort applies to any of the questions discussed in this book. 'What do we mean by saying that a proposition is *true*? What is the nature of truth?' 'Is there any logical ground for believing that objects exist when no one is perceiving them, and if not, what is our justification for believing it?' 'What is the function of reasoning in knowledge?' 'What is the relation of presentations to real objects?' 'Are presentations in any sense "mental"?' There cannot be the slightest ground for thinking that the answers to these questions are beyond the reach of human intellect. They may be very difficult and puzzling. Perhaps there will never be general agreement about them. But at least every one of them is such that there is in its own nature no reason at all why it should not be completely solved by the ordinary methods employed by intelligence on other subjects. There is no more reason to say that they are beyond us than there would be to say the same of the problems of physics and astronomy. Epistemology, as I view it, is an empirical science.

A certain kinship of spirit will be recognized, I think, between my work and that of two very diverse personalities, I mean Poincaré and Vaihinger. But Poincaré was not a philosopher in the technical sense at all, nor had he any definite epistemology. His writings—which are a quarry rather than a building—are remarkable for their wealth of inspiring intuitions, thrown out almost at random, and for the profound knowledge of mathematics and the sciences which informs them throughout. Though not a philosopher, his ideas are deeply suggestive from the point of view of philosophical construction, and he has already exercised a deep influence. Vaihinger, who is a professional philosopher, emphasizes the importance of fictions in the development of human knowledge, and my work makes contact with his at this point. Nevertheless his whole approach to the problem of knowledge, as well as his conclusions, are quite different from mine.

I have to state that there is a certain inconsistency between the conclusions now reached in my chapter on the categories and some remarks on the same subject which appear in my book *The Meaning of Beauty*. That book was concerned with aesthetics, and problems relating to the categories were quite subsidiary. It did not then appear necessary to examine them in detail. I allowed myself to adopt more or less traditional views about the nature of the categories which now, on a more thorough scrutiny for the purposes of epistemology, I believe to be wrong. Only very slight changes, however, would be required to bring what I there wrote into line with what I now think and the views expressed in this book. And these changes would in no way affect the essentials of the aesthetic theory which it was the purpose of that book to set forth.

It will be noticed that much more space has been devoted in this book to the analysis of the elementary forms of knowledge, such as are possessed even by quite uneducated people—'common knowledge', as I call it—than to the advanced knowledge contained in mathematics, the sciences, and the other learned disciplines. There are two considerations which are pertinent to this matter. Firstly, it is the foundations of knowledge, its early beginnings, its primary data, which need the most careful scrutiny. It is precisely in them that the principles which govern all the rest will be found. If we go wrong here, we shall be wrong all through. Especially will this be the case with a theory, such as ours, which attempts to exhibit knowledge as an *evolution* from lower to higher stages, from rudimentary beginnings up to its supreme achievements in science and philosophy. The task which I have set myself resembles very closely that which was undertaken in the philosophy of Descartes. The attempt of Descartes went awry at the very start. I have tried to learn this lesson. For this reason Chapter VI is perhaps the most important in the book. Therein the first steps of the mind's advance from its original data are analysed. Therein the fundamental axioms or assumptions which lie at the root of our whole knowledge of the physical world are laid bare, and their logical character, justification, order, and development are—for the first time, I believe—rationally defined.

Secondly, my equipment is in any case insufficient to enable me to deal adequately or at length with mathematics and the sciences. I cannot claim anything more than a very elementary and popular knowledge of either. I will say no more than that I have contributed on these subjects what little I could, and that I hope others, more competent than I am, will be induced to treat more adequately the difficult problems of which I have merely touched the fringe. Some of these problems are now pressing in upon us with great insistence, and have certainly not yet been adequately discussed. Here are two examples taken at random. What is the bearing of Heisenberg's Principle of Indeterminacy, which apparently attributes contradictory qualities to the electron, upon epistemology and logic? Would it be over-audacious to suggest that, if the modern theory of the atom and the laws of logic come into conflict, it is likely to be the theory of the atom, and not the laws of logic, which will have to be modified? And again, am I right in suggesting, as I have in the text, that the common talk about humps and hills in space-time which push the planets into curved courses—whether the genuine authorities on relativity or the mere popularizers are responsible for it—as much implies an anthropomorphic, animistic, unscientific, superstitious concept as did the old conception of 'force'; and that the cause of this error is the almost universal confusion, which infects even men of science and philosophers, between questions of the 'how' of things and questions of their 'why'? And is it not plain that, although formulae may be devised for calculating *how*, i.e. in what paths, the planets and other heavenly bodies move, yet not all the Newtons and Einsteins of the world can tell us any more of *why* they follow these courses than is contained in the proposition 'they move in that way because that is the way in which they move'?

Notwithstanding that the philosophy of this book is based on no expert knowledge of the sciences, I would venture to suggest that it is definitely the outcome of the scientific *spirit* of the present day, and that it may be found to supply the philosophical foundation best suited to the superstructure of modern physics. An instructive correspondence was recently published in *The Times* newspaper regarding the difficulties involved in the conception of an 'expanding universe'. Sir James Jeans, who took a leading part in the discussion, referred to the old Berkeleian identification of *esse* with *percipi* as helpful to modern science. He also spoke of space as a 'framework' partly constructed by the human mind. I cannot but take encouragement from the fact that the philosophy here presented provides, as I believe, a detailed justification of these views.

I have done my best to see that what I have written on mathematics and the sciences, whatever may be thought of the philosophy of it, is not marred by serious mathematical or scientific errors. To this end I asked Dr. C. D. Broad, of Trinity College, Cambridge, to look through the sheets of the chapter on mathematical knowledge (except the last few pages, which he has not seen) and the sections on space-time and gravitation. This he most kindly did, and I owe a great deal to his criticisms and suggestions. He is not, of course, in any way responsible for any of the opinions expressed, and if there are any actual errors in my statements, they are to be attributed solely to my failure to take advantage of his kind help to the full. Not only do I owe a debt of gratitude to him, but also to Mr. H. L. Reed, the Principal of the Royal College, Colombo, Ceylon, who assisted me by allowing me to profit by his knowledge of mathematics and the theory of relativity and to talk over with him various points in connexion with these particular parts of my book before I wrote them.

W. T. S.

CONTENTS

I. KNOWLEDGE AS A VALUE 1
II. BACK TO DESCARTES 14
III. THE GIVEN 31
IV. THE CONCEPTS OF THE GIVEN . . . 48
V. THE WORLD OF THE SOLITARY MIND. . 65
VI. THE CONSTRUCTION OF THE EXTERNAL WORLD 95
VII. FACT, CONSTRUCTION, AND HYPOTHESIS . 149
VIII. THE DISCOVERY OF OTHER MINDS . . 169
IX. SPACE AND TIME 199
X. CONCEPTS OF THINGS 241
XI. MATHEMATICAL KNOWLEDGE . . . 258
XII. CATEGORIAL KNOWLEDGE . . . 289
   1. Being 294
   2. Existence 297
   3. Quality 300
   4. Unity and Plurality 303
   5. Identity and Diversity 304
   6. Substance 311
   7. Possibility 316
   8. Causality 321
   9. Reality and Unreality 325
  10. Relation 334
      Conclusions 335
XIII. LOGICAL KNOWLEDGE 340
XIV. SCIENTIFIC KNOWLEDGE 375
   1. Evolution 375
   2. The Atomic and Electric Theories of Matter . 377
   3. The Geological and Astronomical Past . . 385
   4. Einstein's Space-Time 389

CONTENTS

    5. Gravitation—Newton and Einstein . . . 396
    6. Ptolemaic and Copernican Astronomy . . . 404
    7. The Ether of Space 409
    8. The Subconscious 411

XV. HISTORICAL KNOWLEDGE. PHILOSOPHICAL KNOWLEDGE. THE PROBLEM OF TRUTH AND ERROR 414

XVI. CONCLUSION 443

INDEX 449

CHAPTER I
KNOWLEDGE AS A VALUE

IT is commonly said—and I think with truth—that the great scientific fact of the nineteenth century was the establishment of the theory of biological evolution. This theory has influenced all branches of thought, not excepting philosophy. We have had, of course, our philosophies of 'creative' and 'emergent' evolution. But I think that a deeper and more far-reaching influence has been visible in the theory of knowledge. Knowledge, like all other human things, has grown up in the struggle for existence. And this reflection has led to the belief that the structure of knowledge and its inner nature, like the structure of the physical organism, has been determined by biological needs. Bergson, William James, Vaihinger, and the pragmatists have emphasized different aspects of this view. And it has come to be thought that, in one way or another, knowledge is the handmaid of practical activity.

This was a new thought in philosophy, a thought which was not to be found in the classical systems of pre-evolution days. For Plato and Aristotle, for Berkeley, Hume, and Kant, knowledge was something—though they hardly considered its historical origin explicitly—which, for all any one could say to the contrary, might have come into existence with a bang, ready made and complete. It was regarded as wholly theoretical, and its theoretical character kept it in a water-tight compartment separated completely from the practical activities of life. Hints and shadowy glimpses of the opposite view may no doubt be found here and there scattered among the pages of the earlier philosophers. But the conception of knowledge as dependent for its structure and even for its validity upon biological needs could not, in the absence of the theory of evolution, penetrate deeply into the marrow of their systems.

This new thought is likely to be abiding in its influence. The theory of knowledge can never return to its pre-evolution attitude. Any epistemology which in the future does not reflect, at least in some measure, the new insight, is likely to stand self-condemned as unscientific. The philosophies of Bergson and the pragmatists may well be no more, in the forms in which their authors have shaped them, than transient phenomena, symptoms of the passing age. They contain much that is not likely to remain for long acceptable to the scientific mind. But the influence of the thought that action at least in some measure governs knowledge will spread and will become incorporated in the philosophies of the future.

It frequently happens that the originators of a new idea ride it to death, and bring it, for the time being, into disrepute. And this, I fear, has been the tendency of the more extreme among the pragmatists. They have so subordinated knowledge to action that they have destroyed the basis of knowledge. And this has been instinctively perceived by the plain unphilosophical man who conceives that the definition of truth as any belief which 'works' is likely to lead to fantastic results. It would seem, therefore, that a balanced and sane examination of the issues is one of the chief needs of to-day in the theory of knowledge.

For knowledge has been conceived in the past as a *value*. I use the word value here in a special sense, and as practically equivalent to what some philosophers have called 'absolute value'. We commonly speak of food, money, clothes, houses, health, or anything else which we desire, as possessing value. But in the special sense in which I am electing to use the word they do not possess it. When it is said, in common parlance, that such things have value for us, it is meant only that they are things after which we strive because they satisfy our various needs and desires. It is true that the exact psychology of the matter has been the subject of much dispute. But the statement just made is good enough for our present purposes. In addition to the many things which we happen to desire and strive after there exist a few things which we feel are more exalted, and which we *ought* to strive after, whether in fact we do so or not. Common examples are goodness, beauty, and truth or knowledge. (There is a distinction between truth and knowledge, but that may be neglected for the moment.) The value of these things is believed to differ from the values of all other things in that there is in them an inherent rightness or excellence which imposes upon us an 'ought', an *obligation* to pursue and strive after them. Some people like meat; others prefer fish. But whichever your preference may happen to be, you do not assert that your preference is 'right' and the opposite liking 'wrong'. You do not think that all men 'ought' to prefer fish or meat as the case may be. You do not think that it is their duty to strive after meat or fish. These are matters of taste. *De gustibus* . . . But we *do* think that we 'ought' to prefer the good, the beautiful, and the true, to the evil, the unbeautiful, and the false. It is not here a matter of personal taste, but of one thing being inherently and in itself more excellent than another. The possession of this quality is what I here call value. And from this point of view I say that goodness, beauty, and knowledge possess, or are believed to possess, value; but that butter, eggs, clothes, houses, and the like do not possess it. It will readily be seen that by value I mean much the same as what is commonly meant by the word 'ideal'. Most people would admit that truth is an ideal. But no one would assert that butter is.

Now what I said was that, in the past, knowledge has generally been regarded as a value in this sense. It has been thought of as being an end in itself, as being valuable even when it cannot be shown to have any practical utility. Or at least it has been thought that if a proposition is true, it still remains true even if the knowledge of its truth is useless. That truth is something independent of our wishes and our needs; that it is an august ideal to be sought after even though it might be disastrous to our aspirations; that truth is truth whether we like it or not; that it remains what it is whether it forwards or hinders the success of our practical undertakings; these thoughts have seemed to men to possess genuine validity. And they stand in unyielding contradiction to the theory of knowledge as completely subordinated to action.

One question seems to have been insufficiently pondered by the upholders of the extreme pragmatic view. If knowledge has no purpose except action, what then is the purpose of action? The consideration of this question would carry them outside the bounds of epistemology into the sphere of ethics, which is perhaps not their strong point. And yet they cannot decline the issue. For it is they who have connected knowledge to action. It is they who have insisted that the two cannot be separate. And it is too late therefore to protest that ethical considerations must be given no weight in the theory of knowledge.

We need not inquire what answers may or may not have been given to this question. There is only one answer which is really consonant with the premisses of pragmatism. The justification of knowledge, they tell us, is success in action, and its value—though they do not always say this—is a survival value. The criterion of right thinking is the successful satisfaction of biological needs. Will not the criterion of right action be also biological success? And will not moral ideas have no more than a survival value? Right action, we shall have to think, can only be defined as action which in the long run satisfies human desires. And what are these desires? Not the desire for knowledge, and not the desire for moral goodness. For to think this would be to argue in a circle. If moral conceptions only come into existence for the purpose of satisfying human desires, then those desires (which are the aim and end of life) must be prior to and independent of moral conceptions. And the same applies to knowledge. If knowledge is *only* an instrument, then it is not an end. What other ends can be suggested? The satisfaction of our aesthetic desires? But no one is likely to say that the desires for the satisfaction of which knowledge and morality have been evolved in the struggle for existence are the aesthetic desires. And certainly that is not the answer commonly given by pragmatism.

What desires, then, are left? None, so far as I can see, except the brute desires of the body. I am far from wishing to decry as low or contemptible the body and its desires. They have their proper place in life, and an honourable place it is. But what I wish to point out is that theories of knowledge and ethics which reduce both truth and morality to a striving after the satisfaction of the non-spiritual desires destroy completely the conception of value which was explained above. Knowledge, in that case, has no aim except to help towards success in action; and action has no aim except the satisfaction of desires. And since these desires cannot be the desires for truth, goodness, or beauty, they can only be the desires for food, sex, health, wealth, power, and the like. These must be our sole ideals, these the final aim and justification of our lives. But I say that to admit this is to destroy all value and to make life purposeless.

I am not trying to befog the issue by appealing to human vanities and prejudices. On the contrary, I am trying to make the issue clear. The unqualified acceptance of successful action as the sole criterion of truth will destroy, not only truth, but moral and aesthetic values as well. If reason, logic, and science lead to this conclusion, we must loyally accept it, even though it devastate our hopes and our ideals. We cannot support comfortable delusions. But even this very assertion proclaims belief in truth as an ideal, as an end in itself which is independent of mere success in action. Whether reason, logic, and science do in fact lead to this conclusion is, however, not yet clear, and is precisely the question to be examined. And therefore we must have the issue clear to start with. *Either there must be some other criterion of true knowledge besides that of success in action, or else we must submit to the destruction of all values and ideals* and admit that our life has no higher purpose than the satisfaction of our desires to go on living, to live softly, pleasantly, or powerfully. If value is destroyed there can, of course, be no higher or lower in anything in life. For all judgements of 'higher' and 'lower' are judgements of value. Man will be no higher than the brute. Beautiful art will be no higher than eating and drinking. Socrates will be no better than the pig. It is idle to reply that 'higher' and 'lower' can be interpreted in terms of success in action, that the higher is the more successful, and so on. For to equate rightness with mere success is contrary to any genuine conception of rightness. And I fail to see how Socrates was more successful than the pig. The pig at least drinks no hemlock, is more successful in his efforts at survival than that!

Of course it may be possible to take up for the moment the position that the function of knowledge is success in action, but that action itself is or ought to be governed by some absolute end other than mere success or survival. We might try to adopt, for example, some realistic theory of goodness as an objective quality of the external world (or of the internal world) on a par with qualities of things such as redness, spatiality, or other such. But in the first place such a position would not be consistent. For our belief in the existence of objective qualities would itself be a piece of knowledge which would have to be explained as a function of practical activity. And secondly, such a position is obviously one in which philosophy could not rest. The inevitable outcome of taking successful activity as the sole criterion of truth is to make it also the sole criterion of morals. We may set up some such half-and-half philosophy as a temporary dam against the value-destroying flood. But the flood will carry it away.

It is conceivable that we might be compelled to admit that our values are delusions based upon our conceit, our false hopes, our vanity. If so, it would be unphilosophical any longer to uphold them. But it is equally unphilosophical not to be clear about the issues, not to realize all the logical implications of the theory which we are discussing. And the logical conclusion from that theory—be it true or false—is the destruction of all values. We must either give up our belief in value, or we must find some criterion of truth which is not wholly dependent upon practical activity. We cannot have it both ways. It is not any tenderness for delusive human hopes, but a simple regard for logical consistency and for a genuinely scientific view of the world which compels us to face the dilemma.

That truth is something to be sought for its own sake,

and not for its practical utility, is a belief which has been the spur of science and philosophy in the past. Great discoveries have for the most part been made in those civilizations in which the disinterested pursuit of truth, regardless of practical issues, has been an honoured ideal. And if this spirit should die, it is probable that science would die with it. In such civilizations as that of India knowledge for its own sake is not highly valued. Neither philosophical nor scientific problems are thought out for their own sakes *as* problems. Indians have never puzzled their heads, as the early Greeks did, about the motions of the heavenly bodies or their physical composition. Their only interest in the stars was *astrological,* i.e. they were only concerned to know whether the stars had any *practical* influence on life. If Europeans had been similarly practical-minded, astronomy would never have been born. It is the same in philosophy. The European is anxious to solve philosophical problems for their own sakes. Hence the wealth of European philosophical thought. The Indian only values philosophical knowledge if it can be put to practical use in freeing the soul from 'the wheel of things', in attaining Nirvana, union with Brahma, or some other such self-regarding end. And the result of this attitude is that science has never come into existence at all, and that philosophy, which has never separated itself properly from religion, has, after a brief early career, stagnated for centuries. And the people—in spite of Yoga philosophies and the like—have remained steeped in ignorance, error, and superstition.

These considerations show, at any rate, that belief in truth as one of the genuine values is deep-set in the human spirit. They show also that this belief has been of service to the human race, from which it would seem to follow that on pragmatic grounds it ought to be regarded as true! It *may,* nevertheless, be a delusion. But it is at least not a recommendation to a philosophy that it flies in the face of man's deepest ideals and aspirations. And when one remembers that the pragmatic view of knowledge has been belauded by some of its followers on the very ground that it enables man to have faith, through the 'will to believe', in his own ideals, the ironical nature of the position becomes clear. We have been told that since truth is what works, we can repose faith in our religious and moral aspirations if we find that they assist us in life. The delusive character of this hope should now be clear. It proposes to support our values by first destroying them.

We had thought that in some way moral activity was good and right because it is rational, because reason validates it. But we cannot have it both ways. If practical action validates reason, as these philosophers would have us think, then reason cannot validate practical action. If rational knowledge has no validity except as a guide to successful action, then the validity of right action cannot be founded on reason. On the pragmatist view reason has for its end action. And action has for its end what? Nothing, so far as I can see, except the satisfaction of desire. And then value disappears.

The same point may be put otherwise. According to the pragmatist view, if it is followed to its logical conclusion, not only truth but all values are for the sake of action. What then is action for the sake of? The answer is an absolute blank. But the opposite view is possible, and does not leave us with a blank at the end of our inquiries. This view consists in asserting that instead of value being for the sake of action, action is, on the contrary, for the sake of value. Our lives are then no longer purposeless. Knowledge is not something that has no meaning and no value except in so far as it helps us to ward off dangers, to obtain food, to keep on living our useless lives. It is a real ideal to strive for. Art is not to be sought after merely because it satisfies some idle and transient desire which is of such a nature that we should be just as well off if (like the pig) we did not have the desire at all. Art too is something to live for. Moral goodness is not the mere success of the species in the wearisome and fatuous business of keeping alive, a means to an end which is in itself purposeless, but it is an aspiration to an end which is really and genuinely higher and better than the lives we are leading. We live and strive for the absolute ends of truth, beauty, and goodness. We are not artists, saints, scientists, and philosophers merely in order to live. Much easier and probably pleasanter to live by being pork butchers. But we live, even the pork butchers among us, in the hope of becoming artists, saints, scientists, and philosophers. Such a view validates value, just as the pragmatist view destroys it.

If it is true, as I have urged elsewhere, that truth and reason lie at the heart of both beauty and moral goodness; and that truth is rational thinking, beauty rational feeling, and goodness rational action, then it is clear that in epistemology lies the whole crux of man's spiritual situation. We have to look to the theory of knowledge either to validate or to condemn not only truth-value, but moral and aesthetic values as well. And the question upon which this whole problem of man's spiritual life turns is this. Has rational knowledge, has truth, any justification apart from its use as a guide to successful action? If it has, then man's spiritual life is founded on a rock. If it has not, then all human ideals are vain.

I said at the beginning of this chapter that any future epistemology which fails to incorporate the thought that the development and structure of knowledge have been in some measure determined by biological needs, i.e. by the practical problem of living, must stand self-condemned. The pragmatic view rests upon a genuine insight, embodies a truth not again to be ignored with impunity. It is not therefore a simple question of finding arguments to dispute the pragmatic view in the interests of human values. The problem is rather to found an epistemology which reconciles the two sides of the dilemma, which gives due weight to the pragmatic element in knowledge without condemning knowledge to fatuity.

And we can see at once that the apparent contradiction is not absolute. Because knowledge has a biological value, it does not follow that it has no other value. Because its origin is in biological needs, it does not follow that it ends in them. It is an ancient and venerable insight that the essence of a thing, and its value, are not to be determined by any considerations regarding its historical origin and development. The flower is something other than the mud and dung out of which it grows. And I trust that I shall not be mistaken for a supporter of sacraments and superstition if I remind the reader that even the theologian is logically entitled to urge that, even if his sacrament had its historical origin in crude magic and cannibalism, this does not necessarily condemn it as false. Morality may have come into being through the struggle for existence and the biological advantages of co-operative effort. But it does not follow that morality is nothing but intelligent selfishness. Selfishness may at first have dictated to us a policy of fair treatment to others as well as to ourselves. And we may *afterwards* have come to see that the unselfishness which was thereby engendered is good *in itself*, apart from the selfish motive which was its origin. We may well believe that out of the stress and struggle of living, out of the evolution of life, there have emerged values which transcend their lowly origins. This may be true both of knowledge and of the other values. And a detailed examination of the structure of knowledge may perhaps support this view.

It will be objected perhaps that in the foregoing discussion we have not allowed a sufficiently wide interpretation of the pragmatist point of view. In order to do it anything like justice, one must not attach too narrow a meaning to such words as 'action', 'useful', 'working', which so constantly appear in its vocabulary. One must not think that 'action' is confined to purely *practical* activities. Thinking itself, even when purely theoretical, is an action. The manipulation of the retort by the chemist, the adjustment of the telescope by the astronomer, even when they are directed to the making of discoveries apparently remote from the common affairs of life, are yet 'actions'. The 'useful' is not merely that which satisfies our lower physical or other desires, but rather that which is instrumental towards *any* desired end, including ideal ends such as knowledge for its own sake. A mathematical device is 'useful' if it helps to solve the problem with which the mathematician is concerned, notwithstanding that this problem may have, or appear to have, no practical bearing of any kind. Similar remarks apply to the conception of what 'works'. Einstein's theory of relativity 'works' if it solves the problem which it is intended to solve. The proposition 'Queen Anne is dead' is true and 'works' because it fits in with the evidence, and to believe it does not bring about any untoward practical or theoretical consequences.

We must certainly bear in mind these admirable professions of intention. But the position appears to be as follows: (1) If the narrower interpretation is given to the terms which we have just been discussing, if knowledge is conceived as relative to *practical* activities, then pragmatism may remain self-consistent, but at the cost of destroying the concept of value. (2) If the more extended meanings suggested in the last paragraph are given to the pragmatist's stock words, then pragmatism becomes self-contradictory, and will be compelled to admit the reality of a truth which is independent of action and independent of any kind of usefulness.

The first of these two propositions has, I think, been made abundantly clear. And not very much argument is necessary for the demonstration of the second. For the protest against giving too narrow a meaning to the terms, and the movement towards widening the meaning, arise from the desire to do to the conception of knowledge as a value a lip service which is really inconsistent with the essentials of pragmatism. Pragmatist writers tell us that knowledge, like anything else, can be treated as an end in itself. But this needs analysis. Suppose that the proposition P is true. On pragmatist principles this can *only* mean that its truth consists in the fact that it constitutes a successful means to some end *other than its own truth*. True propositions cannot be defined as propositions which are successful in being means to truth. Such a definition is circular and self-contradictory. It makes truth dependent on truth. In effect it makes truth absolute and self-dependent and independent of being a successful means to anything. It is therefore inconsistent with pragmatism. When it is said, therefore, that knowledge may be made an end in itself, all that the pragmatist can consistently mean by this assertion is that the knowledge of the proposition P may as a matter of psychological fact be treated by individual minds as an end in itself, but that its truth, whether it is so treated or not, still depends entirely upon its being useful as a means to some end *other* than itself. Truth is not true 'in itself'. It is only true as subserving some end other than truth, i.e. some end which is not theoretical but practical. So we come back to the same old position. If pragmatism defines truth in terms of purely practical ends, it destroys value. If it attempts to rise above this and to admit knowledge as a value, it is self-contradictory and destroys itself.

So we see pragmatism doing what we are all apt to do when we have been so unfortunate as to take up a false position. It attempts to maintain itself by twisting. It takes up first a position based on the concepts of practical activities, biological needs, &c. It soon begins to feel this position uncomfortable because it is dimly perceived to be inconsistent with any belief in value. It therefore tries to shift its position while nevertheless using the same words. It endeavours somehow to foist into its conceptions of the 'useful', of 'what works', and of what leads to successful 'action', the quite alien conceptions of the *theoretic* value of truth, of knowledge as an end in itself, and so on. Hence arises that loose, ambiguous, and elusive use of such words as 'useful' and 'works' which has always been characteristic of pragmatists. The ambiguity of language is used to conceal the essential inconsistency of thought. And if we try to tie down the meaning of the terms to anything definite, the pragmatist will at once complain that he is 'misunderstood', that our interpretation of his terms is too narrow, &c.

But we began by admitting that the pragmatic point of view contains a genuine insight. The insight is that the structure and even the validity of knowledge must have been moulded in some way by practical needs in the course of the evolution of the species. We have to work out a *sane* theory of truth, a theory which includes this insight while at the same time avoiding the errors of pragmatism. It is time that the less irresponsible elements in the philosophical world began to seek out a satisfactory theory, a theory which must be characterized by judgement and balance, and not by paradox and cheap cleverness.

CHAPTER II
BACK TO DESCARTES

WE sometimes speak of knowledge as if it were a body of truths existing independently of any human brain. Speaking in this way we say that mathematics is a part of knowledge, and that $2+2=4$ is a proposition in mathematics. We speak of philosophy in the same way. It is a body of thought. It exists historically in various movements. It has developed. It takes this direction or that.

To speak in this way is very convenient. But it is, after all, only a manner of speech. Knowledge actually exists only as a number of psychic events in the minds of knowers. Philosophy only exists in the philosophical thoughts of individual thinkers. Philosophy in general is an abstraction, like humanity. Humanity only exists as actual men, philosophy as actual processes of thought. There is your philosophy and my philosophy. There are also the philosophies of Smith, Jones, and Robinson. Philosophy in general is only the aggregate of all these, or else an abstraction from them.

My philosophy, then, must take its rise within my own mind, must begin, develop, and end there. I may, of course, borrow it from others. It need not be original. Or it may consist of new thoughts which no one ever had before me. But in either case it is equally a process which begins and ends solely within my own mind.

Its starting-point must be within me. Now it will generally be admitted by all schools of thought that philosophy must in some sense take its rise from experience. To which I pose at once the crucial question: *whose* experience? And there can only be one answer. Each individual thinker must necessarily base his own philosophy on, and understand the philosophies of others in terms of, his own individual experience. I must begin philosophizing from my experience, you from yours.

Philosophers and men of science are apt to talk of

experience as if it were impersonal, as if there were but one experience, and as if it were something which exists independently of experiencing minds. This, like 'knowledge', and 'philosophy', is no doubt a quite legitimate abstraction which serves the purposes of thought. But an abstraction it is. Abstraction is the work of thought, however. It is the end-result of a process, not the beginning. Hence an impersonal and independent experience is not the proper starting-point of philosophy. It is not a datum.

The concretes from which the abstraction of an impersonal experience is made can only be the individual experiences of each of us. It is here that we have to begin. And this reduces itself to the position that each of us must perforce take as the ultimate premiss of his philosophy nothing except his own individual experience. For each of us is, in some sense, shut up within his own mind. We can only interpret the experiences of others, when they are communicated to us, by translating them into terms of our own experiences. When you speak of 'red', I can only understand this by interpreting it in terms of my own perceptions of red. I cannot directly see *your* red. I can only see my own and suppose that yours is like it. And this supposition is itself a result of thought, not a datum.

In general each mind is at first only aware of its own experience. And it never to the end has any *direct* awareness of the experiences of others. All such knowledge is indirect and derivative. It is the result of a process, and is not given.

I am aware, of course, that some philosophers assert that we know of the existence of other minds by a direct apprehension of them. We shall have to consider this assertion, and what it means, very carefully in the sequel. Whatever it may mean, however, I do not think it can be held to contradict the position here taken up. It will hardly be alleged that I can ever directly see your sensation of redness any more than I can feel the pain in your leg. Even telepathic communication proves nothing to the contrary. Suppose that X thinks of a number, and that this number is flashed telepathically into the mind of Y.

It is still true that Y is aware of it only as a part of *his own* experience, not as a part of X's. Telepathy, if it is a reality, proves no more as regards our present point than does ordinary communication by speech. By speech, too, an idea is transferred from one mind to another, but this means that a similar idea is generated in the second mind, not that numerically the same and identical idea exists in both minds. Each, after all, can only apprehend his own private experience, and is shut off from all others. And it is to be observed, finally, that even if we are aware of other minds by direct apprehension, that awareness is still to each of us a part of his own private experience. X's direct perception of Y's mind, if it exists, is just as much a part of X's individual experience as is his direct perception of red.

The necessity of philosophizing in terms of one's own experience may further be illustrated by inquiring how in fact we understand the philosophies of other thinkers. Kant asserted that geometrical axioms are necessarily true. We are not here concerned with whether this opinion is correct, but with the question how we understand it. And it is obvious that each of us can only understand it by testing it in his own private mental experience. He will ask himself the questions: 'Do I find the axioms self-evident? Do they appear necessary to *me*? Do they compel *my* mind?' And when philosophers speak of sensations, perceptions, thoughts, judgements, and the like, we can only understand the meanings of such words by thinking of them in terms of our own sensations, perceptions, thoughts, and judgements. Unless I were myself a creature of volitions I should find it an impossibility to understand what philosophers mean when they speak of volitions.

Every mind is, in this sense, a self-enclosed monad. And philosophy must take its rise for each of us, not in some generalized experience, but in the individual experience of each mind. We shall advance to a generalized experience later. The point is that we have to realize that it *is* later. We have to arrive at it as the result of a process.

This is the truth which underlay the famous method of

Descartes. He realized that every philosophy must begin from the I and work outwards. But unfortunately he at once became entangled in unjustified metaphysical assumptions about the nature of the ego and fallacious arguments about the external world. Because we begin with individual experience we are not to make any assumptions about the nature of personality nor of reality. The question which we are discussing is one of logical order and procedure. Our *method* must be to begin with the immediate data of the individual's experience, the given element in his knowledge, and working upwards from that basis, to attempt to see how the organized development of knowledge has arisen on that foundation. We shall assert nothing whatever about the metaphysical nature or status of the given element. We shall assert only that it is a logical ultimate, an absolute premiss to knowledge, at which therefore we must begin our inquiries and our arguments.

It will soon become evident, as our inquiry proceeds, that given certain elementary data to start with, the mind creates out of these materials the whole structure of knowledge. We have already had occasion in this chapter to observe the difference between the original data and later elaborations. We have remarked that an impersonal and independent experience is not a datum; that the belief that your red is similar to my red is not a datum. These are later developments, the results of thought working upon its materials. And it will be part of our task to trace out how they arise.

Obviously our first step must be to sort out and separate the given elements of knowledge from the rest. If we are to begin with the data and proceed thereafter to the rest, we must first have a clear idea of what the data are. We can then make an attempt to see in what manner the mind builds on this foundation, and what principles govern its procedure.

Perhaps it will be objected that such a method is bound to have metaphysical implications, and that our hope of adopting a method without entangling ourselves in such implications is a vain one. But this objection misrepresents our hopes. No doubt it is true that every method has its implications. We neither can nor do we desire to escape that necessity. On the contrary, what we desire is to hit upon the right method, the correct beginning, and then to draw out what necessarily follows. Admittedly all depends upon the beginning and the method. That is an argument for beginning in the right place and proceeding in the right manner. It is not an argument against beginning at all. And if it were a valid objection to our method, it would be equally valid against any method whatever.

And where else can we begin except with the given element in the individual experience of each of us? Consider any piece of knowledge taken at random, for example, that Sirius has a companion star which is a 'white dwarf'. Obviously this belief involves some general knowledge of astronomy, of the nature of double stars, of what is meant by 'white dwarfs', &c. It is an elaborate mental product. Now we may be asked two relevant questions regarding this product; firstly, how it arose, and secondly, how it is justified. These are two separate problems, but they are intimately connected. To solve either of them we must necessarily go back in the last resort to such given and immediate mental elements as the sensations which we receive through starlight striking the eye, the sensations of the colour patches which constitute the spectrum, and the like. On such immediate sense data is all our astronomical knowledge built.

This is accurate, however, only for an astronomer. He may get knowledge direct from the colour bands of the spectrum. But those of us who are not astronomers and do not know how to handle the spectroscope cannot do this. Our knowledge that Sirius has a 'white dwarf' companion is based upon the fact that the astronomer told us so, and that we think we have good reason to trust his opinion. In that case our knowledge goes back to the sound sensations which we received when we heard the astronomer lecture. Those sound sensations are among the data on which we built our knowledge. But the journey from the beginning in sound sensations to the end, i.e. belief in the 'white dwarf' companion of Sirius, is a very long, difficult, and intricate one. For example, one of the stations through which we have to pass on the way is belief in the existence of another mind, that of the astronomer. But enough has been said to make it clear that, however we come by an astronomical belief, whether by our own researches or otherwise, the knowledge of each of us rests in the last resort upon the colour patches, sounds, and so forth, in *his own* experience.

It is not to be concluded that sensations are the only given elements of knowledge. That would be entirely false. They are, however, the most obvious of such elements and were taken for that reason as illustrations of our point. Our point was this. Whether the question before us be that of the historical origin and development of our knowledge, or that of its logical foundation, in either case we have to find the starting-point in the 'given'. How did our knowledge of the stars historically originate? From looking at the stars, i.e. from light sensations. What is the logical foundation of that knowledge? Again the light sensations from which all astronomical inferences arise.

Our method, then, will be to begin with an account of the given. This we shall attempt in the next chapter. We shall then endeavour to show by what steps knowledge has advanced beyond the given to something like its present state.

At once we shall be asked whether what we propose to trace out is the logical or the historical development of knowledge. For these, it will be said, are two very different things. It is one thing to inquire how the Greeks came to discover that the square on the hypotenuse of a right-angled triangle is equal to the sum of the squares on the other two sides. It is another thing to inquire how Pythagoras proved this proposition.

Our answer must be that we are concerned essentially with the logical development of knowledge, and that to unfold its history is not our business. That must be left to psychology, anthropology, or whatever is the appropriate empirical science. And yet we shall urge that the difference of the logical from the historical, however plain it is in theory, may be, and often is, exaggerated in practice. The two are *in fact* intertwined. The logical is in the last resort the marrow of the historical.

But postponing this latter point for later consideration, and concentrating for the moment only on the logical issue, we may say that our method will be as follows. We shall take our starting-point from the given. For the given can neither be explained nor disputed. It is *there*. And not even the most ingenious sophist can deny that it is there. He may dispute the existence of the world, or of the ego. But he cannot dispute the existence of the sensation of red when he has that sensation. This shows that the given is the logical foundation of knowledge, whatever may be its historical beginning. The given is what is *certain* in knowledge, what cannot be disputed. And it is immediate, not the result of a logical process. It is therefore the only possible logical foundation of knowledge.

We shall next ask ourselves what can be deduced from the beginning. Granted that the given is certain (whatever the given may be), what is the next step? What are the inferences by which, one after another, we build up and justify the elaborate structure of knowledge?

It will be seen that our method is the same as that of Descartes. But unfortunately Descartes took as his ultimate certainty, his datum, his starting-point, what is anything but a primal certainty, the ego as a substance. And he proceeded at once to make deductions regarding the external world which were fallacious. His method was correct, and rested on the most fundamental insight in modern philosophy. His application of the method was a series of blunders from the very outset.

We shall take as our beginning not the ego, but the given. I see a green patch before me. A foundation of knowledge, an indisputable certainty, is this simple experience of the green patch. *Not* the ego which is supposed to experience it, but the experience itself.

But what about the steps which are to follow? Descartes assumed that they must all be logical *inferences*. Now one of the first lessons which we shall learn is that from the given *nothing* about the external world can be *inferred*. (We can infer, I believe, something about the existence of other minds and their contents. But I am now speaking only of our knowledge of the external world.) Certain elementary acts of abstraction and conception, which we shall call 'the concepts of the given', will be found to be logically possible. But they will amount only to the classification of what is given. They merely enable us to arrange the elements of the given in helpful patterns. They do not enable us to advance to any kind of objective existence superior to the bare given. We cannot, for example, advance by any process of inference from the bare momentary experience of the green patch to the belief in the independent existence of a permanent external green *object*. We shall find, if we rely on logical inference alone, that we can never reach that point. We shall find ourselves shut up, each within his own private world of phantasms, and unable to get out of it. The wonderful fabric of knowledge can never, as Descartes thought it could, be built up in that way. By his method of inferences we shall begin with the given, and shall stay there for ever. We shall find that any inferences which have been supposed to lead from the private given to the public world of science and knowledge are utterly fallacious.

Shall we then conclude that our method is wrong? Shall we conclude that the mind has not actually started from the private experience of each individual and worked outwards? Shall we throw this overboard and hunt about for some other starting-point and method? By no means. For we shall find that there are other logical steps possible besides inferences, namely, *mental constructions*. We shall see that these mental constructions are the great instrument by means of which knowledge has advanced from its starting-point to its present state. It will be found that logical inferences are apt to be subordinate to them, to be no more than a means of co-ordinating our constructions, of ensuring that they are consistent with themselves and with one another.

That constructions are common in the higher reaches of science has long been suspected. That they permeate all knowledge, even in its most rudimentary stages, that no ordered world of any kind would be possible without them—this, I think, has not yet been realized.

We cannot yet say what is the logical nature of construction. Nor is it possible at this stage to solve the all-important problem of what is the criterion by which a true construction is distinguished from a false one, or to know what constructions can legitimately be embodied in knowledge and what cannot. These are matters for our future study. But glancing ahead from our beginning we may say this: we shall not expect to advance from the bare given even to the common belief in an external world, in the existence of objects, without the use of logical constructions which are quite other than inferences. We shall find that the material which is given to the mind is surprisingly meagre, and that out of this material it has built, by means of constructions, the entire universe.

It was because he did not understand this that Descartes failed. He could not advance one step from his beginning by legitimate inferences. And so, since he was unaware of the mind's use of imaginative constructions, he attempted to advance by means of illegitimate inferences, fallacies.

And yet what we are to study will be primarily the *logical* nature of the procedure of the mind, not merely its psychological development in time. For the construction, though it is to be sharply distinguished from inference, yet has its own logical structure, which we shall have to study. We shall begin at the logical beginning, the given. We shall attempt to advance to belief in an independent external world. We shall detail the steps by which this advance is made, and shall find that they are constructions; although, when once constructions are set up, inferences from them and between them come into play. We shall attempt to follow the mind further in its journey, beyond the common belief in an external world to more advanced scientific and philosophical knowledge. And we shall hope that by these means light will be thrown both upon the nature and structure of knowledge and upon its validity.

We have stressed the logical character of the mind-process which we are about to study and have distinguished it sharply from psychological and historical development. This is essential to our purpose. And yet it must be recognized that the historical is in many cases based upon and follows the logical. We must believe that in such cases each mind actually in some sense goes through all the logical stages required to arrive at a belief, though this process is implicit, unconscious. This assertion seems to require both explanation and defence; which I will now do my best to give it.

If we are asked, 'Why do we believe that there is an external world?' the question may have two meanings. It may mean 'What valid reason is there to believe it?' The question then concerns the logical steps which justify the belief. Or it may mean 'What is the psychological history of the belief?' Now what I wish to assert is that the psychological way in which a belief is actually reached is often identical with the logical way (notwithstanding that the two aspects are rightly distinguished), or in other words that the mind has actually arrived at its belief by a process of reasoning which is identical with that which it would adopt if it had to justify its belief. This is not always true. For example the Greeks may have known empirically the truth of the theorem of Pythagoras before Pythagoras discovered its logical proof. But in many important cases, and especially in the kind of cases we shall be dealing with in the next few chapters, it appears to me to be true.

How do I know that the world is round? Because the astronomer says so. This is clearly an account primarily of the psychological origin of my belief. And yet, assuming that I do not know enough science to understand the astronomer's reasons, his authority becomes validly *my* reason. I argue, 'The astronomer is a clever fellow who understands these matters. He says the world is round. Therefore that is probably true, and I will believe it.' This is a perfectly sound logical justification of my belief so far as it goes, though it does not carry certainty. Thus the answer, 'because the astronomer says so' really gives both the logical and the psychological origins of my belief. They are in this case identical.

Similarly the answer which we give to such a question as 'Why do we believe in an external world?' is likely to combine both the logical and the historical aspects. The actual workings of each mind in arriving at the belief will be that particular mind's reasons, valid or invalid, for accepting that belief. And if we find that the logical path which leads from the given to the belief in an external world is a plain and open one, there is no reason why that path should not be the one which the human mind has actually followed in history. But its thoughts and reasonings will have been implicit and unconscious. No one except a philosopher has ever explicitly asked and attempted to answer the question why we believe in an external world. The plain man will probably think the question simply silly. Yet the logical train of thought which the philosopher makes explicit may well be precisely that which has lain, deeply buried, in the subconscious mind of the race these many ages. I believe that, in a sense, mind developing from its animal to its human stage must actually have gone through the reasonings and arguments, the inferences and constructions, which I shall elaborate in the coming chapters. I believe that Pithecanthropus and his successors thought out these syllogisms, gradually constructed these beliefs. And if this seems fantastic, this impression will vanish when the statement is understood. The primitive savage or half animal mind must have had these mental processes unconsciously within it. But it was not *aware* of them. It had not the brains to understand its own thought.

It is no longer possible to believe in a complete hiatus between the mind of the animal and the mind of man. If we accept the theory of evolution we have to believe that the one shades off into the other. That reason is the exclusive possession of man, that there are no beginnings of it to be found in the animal mind, is itself an irrational view to put forward. A great advance there certainly has been, but I should say that that advance has consisted, not in the acquisition of reasoning as a new power in man, but in the conscious realization of it. Reasoning is implicit, unconscious, in the animal mind. It has become partially explicit and conscious of itself in man, so that reasonings which previously went on in the darkness have now emerged into the full light of consciousness. This is the same as saying that the essential advance of man on the animal consists not in his rationality but in his self-consciousness.

Reason in the animal world is not a rare exception. It is not a question of hunting out marvellous stories of unusual animal sagacity. Unconscious reasoning takes place in the daily operations of the lives of at least the higher animals, as for example in their acts of vision. The brute recognizes objects by sight. It also sees things at a distance and judges the distance for the purposes of a spring, or to regulate its movements. But the operations of sight are well known to involve trains of logical operations. Both recognition of objects and judgement of distances necessitate inferences which are often wrongly drawn, so that the organism makes a mistake of some kind. The mistake is not in the immediate apprehension, but in the inference from it. The mind of the brute therefore argues and infers. But the brute is not aware of its own reasonings. The reasoning is implicit, unconscious.

There is nothing remarkable in this. We can trace in ourselves innumerable unconscious reasoning processes similar to those which we assert in the brute. Human beings, though capable of conscious and explicit reasoning, also reason unconsciously. We do so in the phenomena of vision. We do so in all the manifold trifles and details of daily life. From the faintest flicker of the eyelid of our friend we infer that he is angry or hurt. But we may have seen the flicker of the eyelid without noticing it, and have made the inference without being aware of it. Unconscious reasonings are frequently mistaken by the credulous for 'intuitions', and are then regarded with great awe. And this mistake is the foundation stone of much muddled philosophical thinking and of whole systems of erroneous philosophy.

The reader will be aware of the controversy as to whether we come to know the existence of minds other than our own by direct apprehension or by inference from bodily behaviour. Without at the present stage going into the merits of the dispute (which we shall have to do afterwards), one can see that those who believe in inference from bodily behaviour must refer to unconscious and implicit inference. No one supposes that the human child, growing out of infancy, solemnly and consciously goes through the steps of an argument by analogy before coming to the conclusion that his mother is alive and conscious. The reasoning, in all save philosophers, is unconscious and instinctive. But it is perfectly reasonable to hold that the argument by analogy from human behaviour is not only the logical justification of our belief in the existence of other minds, but is also its psychological source. In fact if we rule out the theory of direct apprehension, no other psychological source except an unconscious inference seems possible, and we are compelled to think that the oft-described argument by analogy from bodily behaviour is actually, though unconsciously, gone through by every mind as it develops. I am not trying to pre-judge the issue as to how we discover other minds. I am merely trying to show that unconscious reasoning in the matter must always have been believed in by those philosophers who accepted the usual inferential theory, and that it is not, therefore, a revolutionary or novel suggestion.

The aim of this discussion has been to show that, although the distinction between logical and historical order is a real and important one, yet they do not always lie apart, but quite frequently coincide. Logic is the soul of history. And much that has just been said of our knowledge of other minds may very well be true also of our knowledge of the external world. In the following chapters we shall attempt to trace out the logical steps by which the mind, starting from what is given, arrives at and justifies its belief in an external world. But this logical process may be also the psychological history of our beliefs. The individual and the race may actually reach this belief by passing subconsciously through these stages of argument. If so, the process of the child-mind in infancy will be not unlike the development of the embryo which, in the womb, traverses the stages of earlier evolution. What we shall lay down here, therefore, is not a set of barren sophisms, the solution of idle academic puzzles. It is the process of thought which the human race, and every individual mind, must actually have pursued. It claims to be, not the ingenious logic-chopping of an idle philosopher, but the laying bare of the living tissue of human thought, the ideal history of the human mind.

As already stated, the progress from the given to belief in an external world will not be found to be a series of inferences, but a series of mental constructions. The adoption of this view will cut out the appeal to 'primitive belief' and 'instinctive belief' which is relied upon by some realist writers. They perceive that our belief in an external world cannot be justified by any valid inference from what is given in consciousness. They are unwilling to subscribe to the view that it must therefore be a mental construction. And as they can accordingly give no rational account of it whatever, or show it as the result of a logical process of any kind, they are compelled to set it down as primordial, given from the beginning, and call it an instinctive or primitive belief. But this is mere mystery-mongering. A primitive belief is no more than a belief which we have held for a long time, and it may as likely as not be false. Nor is it reasonable to point to instinct as a source of our opinions in such matters. An instinct is some kind of tendency to action, directed perhaps towards an end which is not realized in consciousness. It is impossible to see how it can be a valid source of any beliefs except perhaps blind prejudices. At any rate to *justify* one's beliefs by an appeal to instinct does not seem to be a course which either science or logic could approve.

It is an ancient and sound insight that we can have no knowledge of the outside physical world save through the physical senses, that there is nothing in mind which was not in sense. It is true that mystics claim to have knowledge of divine things by the medium of some kind of super-sensuous intuition. But no one has yet claimed that we have knowledge of chairs and tables through such a source. And if it is admitted, as surely it must be, that our knowledge of the external world can only come to us through sense, or through what the mind makes out of sense-material, then everything we believe about the external world must be either (1) a mental report of what is directly given, or (2) an abstraction from what is given, or (3) an inference from what is given, or (4) a mental construction.

Those who appeal to primitive belief must argue as follows: 'Our belief in an external world is not a mere report of the given. It is not a mere abstraction. For the 'object' is not a common element in the sensuously given, but something more than is given, something which lies behind the given as its supposed cause or ground. Nor is it an inference from the given. For it is generally admitted that all such inferences are invalid. Therefore it must be a belief of mysterious origin, a primitive or instinctive belief, of which no further account can be given, and of which no logical justification is possible'. But this is no more than the unphilosophical appeal to intuition. In opposition to this, our argument will be as follows: 'Our belief in the external world is not a mere report of the given. It is not an abstraction nor an inference. Therefore there is only one thing it can be, namely, a mental construction.'

We can cut away appeal to 'primitive belief' and 'intuition' by the application of Occam's razor. Why, when we can give a rational and logical account of a belief as a mental construction, need we assume these mystical sources?

We have spoken here chiefly of our belief in an external world. That is the first problem we shall have to face, and perhaps it is the most difficult. But it is far from being the only problem. We begin with the bare given. We pass from this by a somewhat difficult passage to belief in an independent external world, the common world of objects, 'things', &c. From that we shall have to pass on to the more advanced knowledge contained in science. But the method which we have outlined will cover our investigations in the whole field of knowledge. All truth, all knowledge, we shall find, takes its origin from the given, is built thereon as a fabric of interwoven constructions, inferences, and abstractions. The constructional element in especial will be found to permeate all knowledge from the bottom to the top.

Our method is empirical, and the philosophy to be expected in these pages will be an empirical philosophy, in accordance with the English tradition.

In medical science the word 'empirical' is loosely used as importing knowledge gathered from experience without any understanding of underlying causes. It is then opposed to 'deductive'. But for us the word 'empirical' is opposed, not to deductive, but to 'transcendental'. I mean by empirical that which does not attempt to transcend the bounds of experience. I mean by transcendental that which does attempt to do so.

Geometry, although it is wholly deductive, is an empirical science because it takes from experience its subject matter—spatial magnitudes and figures—without question. But a branch of knowledge which sought to get behind the space which we experience and to explain it as a form of our perception, or as the self-limitation of an infinite mind, would be transcendental.

Epistemology is an empirical science on a par with biology. Biology examines the structure of the organism, and the functions of its parts. Epistemology will examine the structure and functions of knowledge in an exactly similar spirit. But the essential point in which its empirical character comes out is this. It takes the data of experience —colour patches, sounds, and other sense data—for granted without seeking to inquire into their transcendental origins. I am now seeing a green patch. That is for epistemology an ultimate fact. Epistemology does not seek to know, as a transcendental philosophy would, how and why the data of sense have arisen, whether, for example, they are the projections of a cosmic mind into individual experiences (whatever that may mean), or whether they are the results of 'divine imagining'. It does not seek to know whether the existence of the green patch which I am now seeing is rational, or can be deduced from the Idea of the Good. It simply takes the green patch for granted as a fact.

It is a common mistake to suppose that an empirical philosophy and a transcendental philosophy necessarily contradict one another. This is not so, although it is true that they are apt to be somewhat opposed in spirit. They might perfectly well exist side by side. They do not usually contradict one another because they are not on the same ground. They are concerned with different problems. There is nothing in Kant's 'transcendental aesthetic' which contradicts anything in geometry, mechanics, or any other science which deals with space or time. Or at least this was true in Kant's time. And if the reader happens to believe, with Hegel, that the world of sense issued out of the womb of an Absolute which consists of pure thought, or if he believes with Plato that it is a copy of the world of forms, there will be nothing in this book with which he need necessarily quarrel. Our empirical philosophy simply does not deal with these problems. It takes the world of sense, or at least the sense data, the colour patches, sounds, &c., out of which the world of sense is constructed, as ultimate facts of experience, and does not seek to go behind them.

CHAPTER III
THE GIVEN

OUR first step must be to disentangle the given from the later developments of knowledge, to take stock of the given as our starting-point. It must not be forgotten, however, that *the* given is itself an abstraction, an end-result of thought which cannot, therefore, be a beginning. For it is a concept generalized from the various givens of different individuals. It is in the same position as that independent and impersonal experience which we saw in the last chapter to be abstracted from the individual experiences of us all. The true starting-point, of course, is not *the* given, but *my* given. Each mind being self-enclosed must begin its philosophical journey from its own given.

As has already been pointed out, there is no certainty even that the givens of two different minds are similar. How do we know that the sensation of red colour is the same in any two minds? We have no guarantee that it is so. Your red colour, instead of being similar to mine, may possibly resemble what I should call a toothache. Or our sensations may even be wholly incommensurable. Your sensations may be such that I cannot even conceive them. They may be such that if I could somehow come to feel them they would be to me completely new experiences, unlike anything known to me before.

That we speak familiarly to each other of our sensations proves nothing to the contrary. The fact that when we both look at a tree we agree that it is green does not prove that your green is the same as my green. It proves that the formal relations among my sensations correspond to the formal relations among your sensations. Agreement of relations, unaccompanied by agreement of content, is sufficient to make communication possible. A simple illustration will make this clear. Suppose you tap out a message to me in sounds in the Morse code, and I understand it. It does not follow from this that sound to me is the same as sound to you. For I should equally have understood the message if I had received it in light signals in Morse. And there is therefore nothing to prove that what I felt was not a sensation which you would call light, or in other words that my sound is not like your light and vice versa; or that the content of my sensation-series in Morse is not wholly unlike anything in your experience.

To speak as yet of *the* given, then, assuming that there is one given for us all, is to go ahead much too fast. It jumps at least two steps. The first is the step to the belief that our givens are similar. The second is the step constituted by the abstract concept based on this similarity as common quality of the many givens. We have to begin at the beginning. And the beginning for me is *my* given.

It would be pedantic, however, to proceed from this point exclusively in the first person singular. And I shall not hesitate to speak, as is ordinarily done, of *the* given; just as we, who no longer believe in the daily revolution of the sun round the earth, still speak of the sunrise. The reader will bear in mind that this is no more than a convenience of speech, and that the actual starting-point which we are discussing in this chapter is the particular given of a particular individual, i.e. what each of us will call 'my' given. It will also be understood that in speaking of *the* given we are making no illicit assumptions regarding the similarity of our different givens, a question which we shall have to discuss later.

The word given presents an ambiguity which we must first of all clear up. It may mean either the metaphysical given or the logical given. The former is the given as conceived by Kant, who supposed that the matter of the object is 'given' from the outside, from the side of the thing-in-itself, while the form is contributed by mind. This meaning rests upon and implies the dualism of mind and object. In this sense given means something which is metaphysically different from mind, essentially non-mental, literally 'given' to the mind as a present from an outside source.

Here, in our present study, we must clear our minds of

THE GIVEN

any such metaphysical presuppositions and theories. Not that it is our business to declare them false or in any way to adjudicate on them. We are not concerned with that. They may, for all we know, be either false or true. All we have to say about them here is that they are no proper *starting-point* for philosophy; that they are not involved in our conception of the given; and that if our method of beginning with the given caused us unwarily to entangle ourselves in any such assumptions, we should inevitably suffer the fate of Descartes, whose very first steps from his beginning were fallacious.

The given for us does not imply any metaphysical theory as to its own status. We are to consider, not the metaphysical given of Kant, but the logical given. By the logical given is meant anything that is necessarily taken as given or granted, as logically ultimate and indisputable, in an argument; that which we cannot doubt because we cannot go behind it; that which possesses primitive and absolute certainty, and which is therefore the necessary logical beginning of argument.

Perhaps we might successfully hit off the difference between the metaphysical and the logical givens by saying that the former is given in the sense of 'presented' or 'gifted'; while the latter is given in the sense of 'granted in argument'. A gift or present is something not originally mine, but handed over to me from the outside. And this idea is stressed in the metaphysical given, while it is entirely irrelevant to the logical given.

A little later on we shall find ourselves in agreement with Kant to the extent that we shall assert that the given is passive, while the mind's dealing with it is active. But this is a subsequent empirical observation which is in no sense implied in our conception of the given as such. It is not part of, or implied in, the definition of the given. We are not as yet concerned with it. As for Kant's view that the given is given from the outside, from the external thing-in-itself, any such idea is quite foreign to our philosophy. For us, on the contrary, the externality of the given is not something aboriginally 'there', on which the mind works, but something which is itself constructed by mind. This will appear in the sequel.

The most obvious given elements of experience consist in images or presentations. My awareness of red is an ultimate indisputable fact. I may *interpret* it as a red flower or as a danger signal or in various other ways. I may *explain* it on idealistic or on materialistic theories. These interpretations and these explanations, because they go beyond the given, may all be erroneous. They depend on inferences which may be mistakenly drawn. But the given element itself, the bare awareness of red, is a fact about which there can be no mistake or dispute. It is a true datum or beginning.

Presentations may or may not arise specifically from the senses. The sensation of red colour may be received through the eye, or it may be part of a dream image or hallucination. It is important to understand that the images of hallucination and dream are just as much part of the given as are sense presentations. There does not, in fact, appear to be any *intrinsic* difference between a dream image and what we afterwards learn to call an image of physical reality. Any suggestion that we can distinguish the dream image by its being paler, less vivid, or less clear, is quite illusory. The difference is *extrinsic*, residing in the relations of the image with contiguous experience. We classify one image as real the other as unreal according to the nature of these extrinsic relations. This classification involves concepts, and is therefore not given. Hence under the general heading of presentations or images I include (1) all sense presentations, colours, sounds, odours, tastes, smells, muscular sensations, &c.; (2) all images of hallucination, dream, illusion, or memory, which have the same immediate or given character as sense presentations.

By presentations we are not, of course, to understand 'objects', whether objects in dream or in reality. The inkpot before me is not a presentation. It is a complex of presentations, concepts, and ideal constructions. We do not arrive at objects until a much later stage in our philosophizing. Objects are not given. We are at present at the very beginning of our thinking, and have got no further than colour patches, disconnected sounds, and the like.

It will serve to illustrate the extreme meagreness of the given if we consider in a little detail what any one of the senses actually gives us. We will choose for this purpose the sense of sight, because sight undoubtedly supplies normal people with more of the raw material of knowledge than any other sense. It is the least meagre source of the given. And it is also the sense which is most easily observed and understood by most of us.

What we actually see, then, is nothing except moving and changing patches of colour. It is disputed whether or not these colour patches are flat and two-dimensional, so that the third or depth dimension has afterwards to be discovered or constructed. Since Berkeley's time the most common opinion has been that sight by itself gives only a flat plane. Some more recent writers, however, have attempted to prove otherwise. They think that depth is immediately given. This attempt has been, in my opinion, without success, and I shall adopt the opinion of Berkeley on this matter. But I do not wish to interrupt the discussion of the given at this point by a controversial argument, and I shall therefore postpone the full discussion of the question till we reach the chapter on space and time. For the present I shall assume as true the opinion that the visual given is flat and without depth.

There being no depth, the colour patches do not lie at a distance from us out in space, but appear to lie right up against the eyes. Strictly speaking this is inaccurate because it implies that the mind distinguishes what is close up against the eyes from what is far away, i.e. that it has a sense of depth. What is really intended, however, is that the mind at this stage has no sense of depth at all. It is aware of the colour patches, but is not aware that they lie at any distance, either small or great, out in space.

The mind *constructs* depth and distance. And long practice and experience enable us to read them into what we see, so that they appear as if they were given. But if we leave aside these results of mental elaboration, we find that all sight actually presents us with is a world like a picture, flat without depth.

It will be evident that the given of sight includes both extension-spread and duration-spread. But this is very far from saying that it includes space and time. It will be well to make this distinction clear. In the first place the extension-spread which is part of the given is two-dimensional only. It only exists, moreover, within the visual field of our colour patches. It does not extend away indefinitely beyond the immediately presented experience. It is bounded by what we see at the moment. Infinite or indefinitely continued space is a later construction.

It is also most important to notice that empty space is not given. Empty space cannot be sensed. It is a mental construction. It involves three dimensions, and it also involves the extension of space beyond the colour field. If it be suggested that a two-dimensional empty space can be sensed as that which intervenes between two colours on the flat surface of the given, the suggestion will be negatived by a moment's thought. What intervenes between two colours is invariably another colour. Up against the wall of my study are two tables several feet apart. The sophisticated mind believes that there is empty space between the two tables. But all that can actually be *seen* between them is the colour of the wall behind them. And the colour of the wall is not *seen* as behind them, but as lying in the same flat plane as that in which they lie. Between the stars we see the blue-black colour of the sky. Black colour is no doubt the mere absence of light. But it appears in consciousness as a positive colour sensation. The space between the stars is not seen as empty space, but as a flat blue-black surface.

Spatial *shape*, so far as it is two-dimensional, i.e. outline, is given. For the colour patches have outline. But the extension-spread of the given has absolutely no geometry. The elaboration of geometry is a long subsequent operation of the abstracting mind. Even our description of extension-spread as two-dimensional is inaccurate. For its two dimensions are the result of sophistication. They belong to our *view* of the given, not to the given itself. The given has nothing more than undefined spread. This spread is in all directions on the flat surface. The conception of two directions at right angles to one another, serving as co-ordinates for measurements, is the result of later analysis and thought. And the same is true of all geometrical conceptions.

The colour patches change. They move from side to side. They pass out of the field of vision altogether. They flicker, fade, grow brighter or darker, appear and disappear, increase or decrease in size. These changes we afterwards interpret as due to various causes. We think that the movement of the patches from left to right, and then their disappearance outside the edge of the field of vision, is due to our turning our heads round. Or we explain the decrease in size of the patch as due to its receding from us into the distance. Or we think that the change in outline of one of the patches is due to some other object intervening between us and it, and cutting part of it off from view. But all these explanations belong to the stage of sophisticated thought. They are not given. For we have before us not objects, but only the colour patches. None of these explanations of the changes of the colour patches could possibly occur to the aboriginal mind moving exclusively on the level of the given (supposing that such a mind could exist). To such a mind there could be no such thing as a head to be turned round. For there would be no objects. Our bodies are not given to us *as* bodies. They are merely part of the kaleidoscope of colours which we sense. And they are not, except after considerable experience of movement, specially connected with ourselves. My hand lies on the table in front of me. No grounds are *given* for supposing that this pinkish colour patch, which I afterwards come to interpret as my hand, is part of me. Afterwards, for a variety of reasons later to be examined, I come to regard it as specially attached to me, as part of 'my' body. But this is a result of thought and experience. It is not a beginning, not a given. The hand is originally merely an indifferent part of the colour world which floats chaotically around me. It might as well be regarded as part of the table on which it lies. Nor again could the aboriginal mind explain the decrease in the size of a colour patch as due to its receding from him. For the idea of depth, or spatial distance along the line of vision, has as yet no existence.

The movements and changes of the colour patches make it clear that the given has duration-spread, and that the relation of 'before and after' is given. This duration-spread stands to the developed conception of time in much the same relation as the rudimentary extension-spread of the colour patches stands to the developed conception of space. Duration-spread is not the 'even flow' of Newton, any more than extension-spread is the space of Euclid. Duration-spread is not infinite and endless. There is no empty time, and no future time, in the given. The future is clearly an expectation which arises only as a result of reflection on the present and the past.

Enough has been said to indicate the general character of the given of sight. Similar accounts might be written for the other senses. From hearing we receive a medley of sound patches. They have no extension-spread, but they have duration-spread, and exhibit such temporal relations as 'before and after' and 'between'.

Touch is, of course, a most important sense in the development of spatial concepts. Passing one's hand over a flat surface gives rise to both tactile duration-spread and extension-spread. The genuineness of the extension has been doubted. It has been thought that the extensional parts must be successive, or in other words that tactile space must be simply time. But recent psychology of the blind shows that this is a mistake.

The formal relations to which extension- and duration-spread give rise, such as 'between', 'before and after', &c., are given. All the elementary and primitive spatial and temporal relations are given.

Thus it would be a mistake to suppose that presentations and images make up the whole of the given. It also includes relations of various kinds. The most important are (1) relations of position in the extension-spread, such as 'to the left of', 'between', and the like; (2) relations of position in the duration-spread, such as 'before and after'; and (3) the profoundly important relations of *resemblance* and its opposite. But this does not profess to be a complete list of given relations.

It is sometimes supposed that all relations are in some special sense the work of thought and cannot, therefore, be given. The given is in that case conceived as the bare and utterly formless matter of sensation. Form is supposed to be contributed by mind, and includes relations. This is the Kantian standpoint. It may or may not be legitimate. But I only mention it here in order, by excluding it from our discussion as irrelevant, to avoid confusion in our thinking. To introduce it here as an objection to our view that some relations are given would be to confuse the metaphysical with the logical given, and completely to fog the issue. Relations may, for all I know to the contrary, be the creation of a cosmic and transcendental mind. In that case they are doubtless not part of the metaphysical given, i.e. of that which is supposed to be contributed from outside the mind by the thing itself. But they are still part of the logical given with which we are here concerned. For they are still ultimate primordial facts of our experience which we cannot get behind and which stand logically at the beginning of all inquiry as premisses. The same distinction must be made, not only for relations, but also for space and time, and even for presentations themselves. Even if we were to admit with Kant that space and time are the work of mind, and so not metaphysically given, yet extension-spread and duration-spread are none the less logically ultimate in our experience, and belong to the logical given. Again, colour patches and images generally have been held by some philosophers, such as Berkeley, to be subjective 'ideas'. But those who hold this view need not deny that such presentations are logical givens. Thus in general the various phases of the idealist-realist controversy do not concern us in our present discussion, and can be left out of account as having no bearing upon our statement that some relations are given.

It will be noted that I say only *some* relations. For it is not asserted that all relations are given. Some are undoubtedly mental constructions or the results of such constructions. Such, for example, is the relation of substance and accident, the construction of which we shall discuss on a later page.

If two colour patches in the given are both red, then the relation of resemblance between them is also given. So is the relation of unlikeness between a red and a green, or in general any relations of likeness and unlikeness. It is sometimes said that resemblance is dependent upon the comparison of two presentations, and that comparison involves a comparing mind. But this only means that in order to *notice* the resemblance a mind is necessary. And the same is true of the bare presentations themselves. In order to become aware of the resemblance a comparing mind is no doubt necessary. In order to become aware of red colour a perceiving mind is necessary. No doubt only minds can be aware either of presentations or resemblance relations. But the relation, like the presentation, is given.

We have spoken so far only of that kind of given which later becomes the basis of our knowledge of the external world. This consists of sense presentations, what we may call physical relations, &c. It must not be overlooked, however, that we possess knowledge of the internal world of the self, and that this knowledge must also take its start in a given of some kind. The greater part of our knowledge, whether in history, science, art, or any other branch, is concerned with the external world. The immense preponderance of human knowledge looks outward. All the sciences, except psychology, the most junior of them all, have portions of the external world for subject-matter. I suppose that at least ninety-nine out of every hundred articles in the *Encyclopaedia Britannica* deal

THE GIVEN

with things in the external world. Only a few scattered psychological or philosophical articles deal with mind.

It is perhaps natural in these circumstances that a theory of knowledge should have a tendency to dwell on our knowledge of the external world more than on self-knowledge. Yet we cannot ignore the latter. Not only has it its legitimate place in knowledge, but, as we shall see, it is interwoven with knowledge of the external world in such a manner that the latter would be impossible without it. Knowledges of the outer and inner worlds are interdependent. We must therefore inquire what is the starting-point of self-knowledge, what is the given on which it is based.

It must be made clear at the outset that the ego, conceived as some kind of transcendental unity, is not given. As Hume long ago observed, when we look into ourselves we perceive volitions, emotions, ideas, and the like, but never the *I* which *has* them. It is no part of our intention in this chapter to discuss metaphysical theories of the nature of the self. But what we have to note regarding all such theories is that the knowledge which they purport to contain is always derivative, never given. These theories are philosophical constructions of the sophisticated mind. They are never pure reports of the given.

The internal given, then, does not include any pure ego. But it includes all the *acts* of what has been called the empirical mind. I become aware of myself by becoming aware of my activities such as thinking and feeling. And the sense of the I as distinguished from the not-I is based upon the perception of myself as active in contradistinction from the not-I as passive. The distinction between active and passive is the fundamental basis of the division of the world into internal and external, mind and matter.

Suppose there could exist a mind, wholly innocent of sophistication, aware only of the fleeting images and presentations in the world of the given. Suppose it shut off from communication with other minds and unaware of their existence. Could such a mind become aware of itself? and if so, how? Now in the first place, according to the views here adopted, it could not be aware of the external world in the sense in which sophisticated knowledge is aware of it. It would see before it a phantasmagoria of moving colour patches. It would hear sounds and receive sensations from the other senses. It would not think that the colour patches continued existing when they disappeared from its own vision, or the sounds when they vanished from its hearing. It could have no possible reason to think so. It would therefore have no conception of a world independent of, and existing apart from, its own presentations. It would thus be living in a world of private dreams.

It might be argued that such a mind could not be aware of itself, since self-knowledge can only come into existence when the self is contrasted with the external world. But I do not think this view is correct. Knowledge of self does not depend on prior knowledge of the world as independent and external. On the contrary, as we shall see, knowledge of the world as independent and external depends immediately on our knowledge of other selves, and therefore ultimately on our knowledge of our own selves. And our self-knowledge depends on the contrast, not between mind and what is independent of mind, but between activity and passivity. Before me is the moving stream of colour patches, the private world of phantasms. The logically original act of consciousness is awareness of these, not of myself as a self. But what happens next? I am looking at a green patch. Growing tired of it I begin to look at the adjoining red patch. In doing so I have not only moved my eyes. I have also performed what must be regarded as my first conscious *act*. I have focused *attention* first on one thing, then on another. After this, perhaps, I notice the resemblance between a number of different red patches. I thereupon form the concept 'red'. This again is an activity, the activity of abstraction and conception. Next, I find that I dislike one presentation and desire another. Emotional and volitional activities come into being and are noticed.

It is these activities of the mind which form the given

THE GIVEN

on which all self-knowledge is based. And it is important to realize that they are ultimate unanalysable *data*, genuine starting-points, in the same sense as presentations. Just as the red colour before my eyes is an ultimate fact of consciousness, so the acts of mind, attention, conception, willing, &c., are ultimate facts of consciousness. The science of psychology, or any other possible knowledge of mind by itself, starts from these as a basis, as an ultimate premiss, just as all physical sciences start from the basis of physical sensations as their ultimate premisses.

When we regard the activities of mind as given, we are of course taking them as objects. The mind thinks. And it can also watch itself thinking. It is when it makes its actions the objects of its attention that they are apprehending as being 'there', as given.

As contrasted with its activity in conception, judgement, attention, volition, the mind is, in pure sense presentation, wholly passive. The green patch lies in front of me. It is *there*. Its being there is no act of mine. I do nothing to make it appear. I am not, as a rule, even aware when it is going to appear. When it does appear I merely accept it. I am purely receptive of its appearance. No doubt an act of mental attention is involved in continued perception, as also a whole series of muscular activities which centre on the object. But these activities are easily distinguished from the content of the sensation itself. The attention is an activity which falls on *my* side. The green colour itself is not an activity, and falls therefore, on the side of the not-I.

The green patch, further, is independent of my consciousness in the sense that my consciousness does not control it. Its presence, its movements, its disappearance or replacement by a red patch, all these happen, or may happen, independently of me, independently of my wishes, thoughts, or feelings. They *happen* in my consciousness. This is a character of the not-I in general.

Thus the primitive world of the given divides itself into two halves, (1) what I do, the activities of my consciousness, and (2) what I suffer, what happens in my consciousness independently of me or of any of my activities.

The latter cannot be attributed to 'me'. It is something distinct from me and my acts. The former is the world of the I, the latter the world of the not-I.

The world of the not-I is at this stage independent of mind in the sense just explained, i.e. as being not an act of the mind and not subject to its control. But it is not as yet independent in any other sense. That it 'exists' apart from the mind, that it goes on existing when the mind is not aware of it, or that it exists for other minds, such thoughts cannot emerge at this stage, and are much later developments.

It will be noted that the characters of the not-I which we have mentioned above belong as much to the presentations of dream or hallucination as they do to the presentations of sense. The dream-mountain is as passive and as independent of my conscious activities as is the 'real' mountain. The dream-mountain falls on the side of the not-I. It is only at a later stage that it is again distinguished from the presentations of 'reality' and is condemned as 'subjective'.

The independence of the given is only another aspect of its passivity. It is independent for the very reason that there is no sign of my activities in it. Hence the only element of distinction between the I and the not-I which is given at the start, the only distinction which is a datum, is that between activity and passivity. This distinction, I say, is itself given. For the mind is immediately aware of its own activities—thoughts, feelings, volitions—*as* activities. This active character of mental life is just as much immediately presented as is the redness of red. The absence of any such activity on the part of presentations constitutes an immediately given contrast, and causes the primitive world to fall at once into the two halves, the I and the not-I.

It will be well to notice that for the consciousness of the distinction between them to arise there is not necessary any recognition that the presentation is either 'mental' or 'non-mental', that it is 'inside' or 'outside' the mind; and that the application of such epithets to it is probably quite meaningless, and is certainly not implied in the idea of the

THE GIVEN

not-I itself. Nothing is implied except passivity. That alone is the essence of the not-I. Statements that the objects which we see and hear are 'mental' or are not 'mental', that they are 'outside' the mind or 'inside' it, that they are 'ideal' or 'real', are all of them mere metaphysical theories which we *afterwards* weave. They are not reports of the given. They have no part in the original world of the given which we are considering. They are constructed, and how they come to be constructed is part of our problem.

We may now sum up our conclusions. Our assumption —to be justified by the course of our inquiries—is that the mind starts from certain fundamental data, which we call the given, and that it builds upon these data the whole fabric of knowledge by means of constructions and inferences between constructions. It is thus essential to our method to get clear about our starting-point, to separate what is given from what is not given. What is not given we have then to explain as construction or inference.

The given falls into two parts, that part which lies at the basis of our knowledge of the external world, and that part which lies at the basis of our knowledge of ourselves. The latter consists of our own mental activities, such as knowing, thinking, willing, feeling, attending. The former includes (1) presentations, meaning thereby the images of sense, of dream, hallucination, or delusion, which have not as yet become differentiated and distinguished from one another; for the differences between them are not given, but subsequently elaborated. The given of the external world also includes (2) duration-spread and extension-spread, and (3) certain relations, not only those involved in duration-spread and extension-spread, but also such relations as resemblance.

As a general account of the given this must suffice for our purposes, though making no pretence at being exhaustive. But there are two supplementary observations which it seems desirable to make before we pass on. The first is to avoid a misunderstanding. It is not intended, of course, that pure awareness of the given, without any thought element whatever, is ever an actual psychological state of either man or animal. Such pure awareness is an abstraction. In every state of consciousness there must be at least some minimal conceptual element. Such a minimal thought element will be studied in the next chapter under the name of the concepts of the given. It is difficult to conceive of any actual consciousness which would not involve at least some vague *recognition*, not of course of objects, but of sensory elements such as colour. Such recognition will involve the concepts of the given, and will to that extent go beyond pure awareness, pure passivity. Our contention must be, therefore, firstly that pure awareness, though it never exists unalloyed, is nevertheless a distinguishable element in knowledge and is the *logically* prior element; and secondly, that the most primitive actual consciousness, though it must contain some implicit or unconscious conceptual element, will yet approximate to pure awareness, and will approximate the more closely to that limiting state the more primitive and undeveloped it is. So that something not very far removed from pure awareness must have been the historical as well as the logical beginning.

Our second observation concerns the relation of knowledge to action. The given is independent of the will. The red patch is red, and its being so is not the result of our conations or of any kind of mental activity on our part. We cannot by any act of will alter red to blue. Outside my window is a tropical garden. I cannot alter this to a London street by a mere wish. The given has the hardness and unyielding character which is attributed to *fact*. Pure given and pure fact are identical. The given is precisely that which exists prior to and independently of any activity of the mind. The utmost that the mind can do is to build the fabric of knowledge on it as a foundation. It is possible (and we shall see later that it is true) that the mind may have before it more than one alternative way in which it may construct the fabric of knowledge, and that it may choose at its pleasure or convenience between them. But the foundation of the given it cannot alter. It is *there*.

Hence the extreme pragmatic view that knowledge has no function and no justification save that which it finds in action is not born out here at the starting-point of knowledge. This is sometimes expressed by saying that the pragmatic view fails to explain what is called 'fact'. In respect of what is given the mind is not free to apprehend what it likes. One can imagine circumstances in which the belief 'This is blue' might be much more useful than the belief 'This is red'. But if in fact the object is red, we cannot accept the belief that it is blue, however useful it would be to do so. Knowledge in its more advanced stages may perhaps possess some measure of freedom. We have yet to discuss that question. But it is not free here at the beginning. Nor can it ever, even in its highest flights, shake itself free from the given, which it contradicts only at the risk of being false. *Knowledge is everywhere tied to the given.* That is a first principle of epistemology.

This principle applies not only to that elementary kind of knowledge which consists in mere reports of the given, such as 'This is red'. It is true of knowledge throughout. The most elaborate and advanced scientific hypothesis must agree with the facts. If such a hypothesis leads to the prediction 'A will be red', and in fact A turns out to be blue, then we shall have to amend or give up our hypothesis. What contradicts the given or anything that is inferred from the given cannot be true. It is in this sense that all knowledge, even the most advanced, is tied to the given.

CHAPTER IV
THE CONCEPTS OF THE GIVEN

THE starting-point of knowledge is *my* given. And my given consists in the phantasms and appearances which occupy consciousness within my self-enclosed ego. In order to advance to knowledge of a public external world, it is necessary for me to issue forth from the privacy of my own ego into communication with other minds. The solitary mind, without the co-operation of other minds, can never come to the knowledge of an objective world. Its world will remain a private world of dreams. Hence the first great step forward towards knowledge is the substitution of a public external world for the private world of each ego. But before this great step is taken, is any knowledge possible? Is it possible for the solitary mind, shut up within itself, to elaborate even a rudimentary kind of knowledge? If so, it is clearly necessary that we should describe such knowledge in its correct sequence. The question will be discussed in this chapter. And we shall find that such knowledge, elementary though it be, is logically possible. It consists in what we shall call the concepts of the given.

No knowledge whatever is possible without concepts. We are as yet far from the kind of knowledge which is embodied in scientific laws and generalizations. And we need not consider it here. Let us examine any of the most rudimentary pieces of knowledge we can come at, and we shall find it conceptual. Not only such elementary judgements as 'This is red' involve concepts, but even the bare recognition of sensations such as might be expressed by the ejaculatory 'Red'! is conceptual, since it involves the classification of sensations.

Conceptual thought is the instrument with which the mind works upon the given. The given in itself is a chaos of presentations and presented relations. This chaos the mind reduces to order by means of its concepts. The mind

THE CONCEPTS OF THE GIVEN 49

is the builder of the cosmos, and its bricks are the varied elements of the given.

The fact of there being concepts does not admit either of explanation or of further analysis. It is a *given* fact. We cannot say how or why the mind conceptualizes. That it does so is an ultimate fact. Conceptuality is the fundamental nature of thought which we *find*, and which we have to accept with 'natural piety'. All we can do is to begin at the beginning by studying first those concepts which form the logical starting-point of knowledge.

We must not be confused by the fact that the concept has two aspects, can be looked at in two different ways. It is the mind's instrument for dealing with the given. And it is also itself part of the given. We may view concepts along with volitions, feelings, emotions, &c., as the ultimate given elements of mental life. We are then looking at concepts from the outside and treating them as objects. Thus objectively viewed they are part of the given because they cannot be explained or analysed, but are ultimate data. But subjectively the concept is an instrument which the mind uses on the given. The concept sorts out the given and arranges it in order. And it may deal with itself as part of the given of mental life in this way. The psychologist classifies concepts. He is then using the concept (viewed as an instrument) to classify concepts (viewed as part of the given).

The logically first kind of concepts are what I shall call the *concepts of the given*. Let us remind ourselves that the mind at this earliest stage of its thinking is not confronted with objects or 'things'. It is confronted by the pure given, i.e. by sense-presentations, dream-images, hallucination-images, extension-spread, duration-spread, and a few relations. The 'thing' or object is as yet far ahead in the journey of knowledge. It has not yet been constructed.

The mind, therefore, cannot at this stage make to itself concepts of objects such as 'house', 'star', or 'man'. Much less can it generalize about houses, stars, and men. It has to begin with the concepts of sense-presentations, images, and the like. The earliest concepts are therefore concepts such as 'red', 'blue', 'loud', 'odour', 'between', 'after', 'bitter-tasting', &c. And these are what I call the concepts of the given.

No doubt such concepts are constructions in the sense that they involve the activity of the mind. They are actively thought, not passively given. But they are not constructions in the technical sense in which I propose to use that term in this book. We have not yet reached examples of genuine constructions. We shall meet them first in the mind's advance from its private dream-world to a public external world of objects. We shall then see that this advance involves a leap beyond the given. It involves an extension of the given beyond itself by means of constructs or fictions. The mind has to introduce elements which are *not* given. No such addition of new or invented matter is involved in the concepts of the given. They contain no element which is not itself given, except the activity of thought itself. We shall not call them constructions, therefore, and shall avoid the use of that word except in the technical sense later to be introduced.

All that is necessary for the coming into being of the concepts of the given is that the mind should notice the resemblances and differences which occur among the elements of the given. All concepts whatever are founded upon the fact of a resemblance. This is true even of the later and more advanced types of concept. But here we are concerned only with the concepts of the given. All that is involved in the concept 'red' is that the mind should notice the resemblance of two or more red patches, and should identify the red in them. *How* the mind does this is a question which cannot be asked. The *fact* that it does so is ultimate and unanalysable. It is itself given.

The reader (who is of course an acute logician) may object that it is possible to have concepts of classes with only one member to each class, or with no members at all; and that therefore the concept as such cannot be founded, as here suggested, on the resemblance of two or more things or appearances. 'Red elephant', for example, is a class with no members. 'Planet inhabited by men' may

THE CONCEPTS OF THE GIVEN

perhaps be a class with only one member. But these are hair-splitting refinements of later thought. The original concepts of the mind could not have come into existence without the comparison of two similar things, and such comparison is the logical foundation of the concept. The concept 'red' could never have become separated from the sensuous perception of red, thought would never have emerged from sensation, without such comparison. If we have the concept of a class with only one member, this at least implies the *possibility* that there might be other members possessing the common characters of the class. Mathematicians insist that 0 is a number. But this number could never have been discovered unless there had been something in the world to count, something to give us the previous conceptions of the numbers 1, 2, 3. . . . In the same way concepts of nil-classes or of singular classes presuppose classes of at least two members. Therefore the comparison of two or more presentations is the logical basis of concepts. If this is admitted we can proceed with the argument which the acute logician interrupted.

The red patches are given, and the relation of resemblance between them is given. And the concept 'red' contains nothing except these elements. There is nothing in this concept which the mind has *assumed*, or introduced out of its own stores. There is nothing except what has been actually *seen*, actually perceived by the senses. To arrive at the concept there is necessary, of course, the mental act of comparison. But the act of comparison does not involve that the mind in making the concept *adds* any element to the given, and then takes that addition to be a part, not of itself, but of the object. This occurs in the true 'constructs' of the mind which we shall study later, but not in the concepts of the given. These latter have nothing in them except what is itself given.

It is for this reason too that we take the concepts of the given to be the logically *first* kind of concepts. They are possible to the solitary mind which has no knowledge either of other minds or of a public external world of objects. They are the only kind of knowledge which is so possible, and therefore they constitute the beginning, the first step, of knowledge. They involve too the smallest possible element of mental elaboration. They are the closest to bare awareness of the given. They depart from it by a hair's breadth. They differ from such bare awareness only in being of the nature of thought, in being conceptual. But they involve no inferences, no hypotheses, no fictions, and no genuine world-building. The concepts of 'things' and objects which we meet with later, 'house', 'man', 'star', are logically subsequent to the concepts of the given, because (1) they involve concepts of the given, and could not come into existence unless the concepts of the given had come into existence first; and because (2) they involve that the mind actually adds to the given by means of imaginative constructions.

Needless to say, concepts of sense-presentations are not the only kind of concepts of the given. In the first place, such a concept as 'red' might be derived as easily from the experiences of dream or hallucination as from the experience of what we afterwards come to call the real. Secondly, concepts of the given include concepts of those relations which are themselves given. 'Resemblance' is a concept of the given. So is 'unlikeness'. So again are such durational concepts as 'before' and 'after', and such extensional concepts as 'beside', 'above', 'between', &c. (but 'between' is gathered both from duration-spread and from extension-spread). But we must be careful here not to fall into the mistake of supposing that these last-mentioned concepts are the advanced spatial and temporal concepts of geometers and mathematicians. Nothing like space or time has yet come on the scene. We have only extension-spread and duration-spread. We may see a red patch between two blue ones. When the same conjunction occurs again on another occasion, we compare the two experiences, and note the resemblances of the relations, and we have the concept 'between'. This does not involve a three-dimensional space, nor an empty space, nor a space extending beyond the actual field of presentations. Much less does it involve any recognizable geometry.

THE CONCEPTS OF THE GIVEN 53

Not only concepts of particular qualitative presentations, such as 'red', 'loud', 'sweet', fall under the head of the concepts of the given, but even more general concepts such as 'colour', 'sound', 'odour', 'taste', 'sensation'. This may at first sight seem surprising. For it is customary to arrange concepts like a pyramid, the less general at the bottom, the more general at the top. Arranged in this way, we should have 'red', 'green', 'blue', 'bitter', at the bottom, and the general concepts 'colour', 'taste', 'smell', above these. And still higher in the pyramid above 'colour' and 'taste', would come the even more general concept of 'sensation'. It might seem, then, that the more general concepts are farther away from the given than the less general ones, and should not be lumped together with them, but should be made to constitute a second stage, a later advance, in knowledge.

There is no objection to counting two stages instead of one, if the reader so desires. I shall allow him to arrange his concepts in pyramids or any other pretty figure that takes his fancy. But it still remains true that the so-called higher concepts, the more general ones which are placed high up in the pyramid, may still be concepts of the given in the sense here defined. Any concept is a concept of the given if it can be formed direct, without any intermediate steps, from a comparison of two or more elements of the given. There is nothing in such concepts beyond what is given, except the mental act of comparison. There is no hypothesis, assumption, or other addition by the mind to the given. The mind observes two red patches, observes the resemblance of red to red, and frames the concept 'red'. The mind observes two patches, one red, the other green. It notes a certain resemblance between them, a common something which binds them together and distinguishes them from sounds, tastes, &c., and so frames the concept 'colour'. There is nothing in this concept except the given resemblance. Moreover the concept is formed directly from the experience of the given without any intermediate logical steps. The concept 'colour' is not dependent, as the pyramid theory is apt to assume, on the more specific concepts such as 'red' and 'green'. To prove this, we will consider a mind confronted by a number of colour patches no two of which are of the same colour, a mind whose experience is entirely limited to one red, one green, and one blue patch. Such a mind would have difficulty in framing the concepts 'red', 'green', and 'blue', because to frame the concept 'red' normally requires the presence of at least two reds, and so with the other colours. But such a mind could without difficulty notice the resemblance between the red, green, and blue patches which is connoted by the word 'colour', and could therefore frame that concept independently of the lower concepts.

The fact is that the pyramid arrangement of concepts is by no means logically essential. It is merely an arrangement which we choose because it is convenient for certain purposes which we need not discuss here. We could form the 'higher' concepts without first having framed the lower.

It may be true that to note the general resemblance between blue and green and red is more difficult, requires a more practised and alert mind than to notice the resemblance between red and red. The latter resemblance is more obvious than the former. But that is a psychological, not a logical, difficulty. It may also be true that as a matter of historical fact, men actually framed the lower concepts first, and then with the practice and skill thereby attained, went on to notice the more general and less obvious resemblances which give rise to the higher concepts. But all this is not to the point. The resemblance between red and green, though less obvious, is just as much *given* as the resemblance between red and red. And the general concept of 'colour' is therefore a concept of the given.

The same remarks obviously apply to such general concepts as 'sound', 'odour', 'taste', as distinguished from the concepts of particular kinds of sounds, odours, and tastes. Indeed the truth of what is here urged is perhaps more plain in regard to such presentations as those of taste than it is in the case of visual presentations. For it does not appear that the mind would experience any special difficulty in noting the general resemblance between differing tastes, and so forming the generic concept of 'taste', even before it had compared sweet with sweet or bitter with bitter to form the particular concepts of those special kinds of taste.

Even such a very general and pervasive concept as that of 'quality' is really a concept of the given, provided it is not taken in the sense of quality inhering in 'things'. In this latter sense it is a cognate of the concept of 'substance and accident', and belongs to a much later and more sophisticated stage of thought. It is not then a concept of the given. It is rather a metaphysical theory about things, or at least implies a background of such theory. But if, eschewing these advanced ideas, quality is taken in its simplest possible sense to mean only that general resemblance which colours, sounds, tastes, bear to one another, without any metaphysical implication of an underlying substance, it is then a concept of the given.

It makes no difference whether a concept of the given is formed from comparison of a sense-presentation with another sense-presentation, or with a memory-image, hallucination-image, or any other. The phenomena of memory no doubt present somewhat mysterious features. That, however, is not our present problem. From the point of view at which we now are the image which stands before the mind in memory is simply part of the given. It exhibits all the features of givenness, and the distinction between memory-images and actual sense-presentations is not relevant to our present inquiry.

Concepts of the given elements of mental life are, of course, to be included among concepts of the given. Thus the concepts of 'concept', 'sensation', 'volition', 'emotion', are concepts of the given.

We have represented the concepts of the given as the earliest step in our knowledge. There are two possible misunderstandings to be avoided here. Firstly, it is not meant that the concepts of the given are necessarily first in historical or psychological order. It is meant that they are logically first. How knowledge began in the history of the race is a problem the solution of which is probably lost in the mists of past ages, notwithstanding that biological and anthropological inquiries may possibly throw some light upon the subject. How it begins in the history of each individual, by what stages the human infant progresses towards knowledge, is a question the fringe of which the psychologist, whose special business it should be, has scarcely yet touched. It is likely enough that his researches in the future may prove that knowledge begins simultaneously at a number of different points. He certainly will not discover that the infant explicitly and clearly frames such a tenuous and abstract concept as 'quality', or indeed any clear concepts at all, before it has any idea of 'things'. But we need not concern ourselves with these questions. Although we have urged that the psychological order of events frequently follows the logical order, it would be the height of absurdity to suppose that this is always the case. And where the two orders diverge, our business is with the logical only. We are here inquiring what knowledge would logically be possible to a self-enclosed mind which had not yet arrived at the knowledge either of 'things' or of other persons. Such knowledge, we must hold, is the logical beginning of all knowledge, since each of us must necessarily begin with his own self-enclosed experience. Looked at from this point of view it is clear that the logically first element of knowledge is the concepts of the given. They are presupposed by the later concepts of 'things', and more obviously by the still later forms of knowledge embodied in generalizations and scientific laws. One could not understand the mineralogical laws which govern the formation and distribution of rubies unless one had first the idea of what rubies are. And the knowledge of what 'ruby' means presupposes the recognition of the sense-qualities red, hard, and the like. And we shall find that whereas the concepts of the given imply nothing more than a simple act of comparison between two or more givens, e.g. between two red patches, the concepts of 'things' on the other hand

THE CONCEPTS OF THE GIVEN

imply this and *also* a great deal of additional mental construction.

The second misunderstanding which we have to avoid goes hand in glove with the first. It is not meant to be alleged that this first stage of knowledge ever exists by itself as a separate psychological state. It is not asserted that there are minds in existence, either human or subhuman, which know the concepts of the given, but do not know 'things', and have no other kind of knowledge. What is here asserted is, firstly, that within any given psychologically normal state of knowledge, the element which we have called the concepts of the given can be logically distinguished from the other ingredients. And secondly, that it is logically prior to any other kind of knowledge. A solitary mind, cut off from all communication with other minds, and living in its private world of phantasms, could not conceivably rise to the knowledge of external 'things'. It could know nothing of a common public world. But it could frame the concepts of the given. They are therefore the first steps which the solitary mind makes towards knowledge.

We need not concern ourselves overmuch with the formal question of what kind of *judgement* can be based on the concepts of the given. Knowledge, it may be urged, consists in judgements. This is not anything different from saying that it consists in concepts. For a concept can always be translated into a judgement, concept and judgement being but two forms or aspects of a single unitary mental activity. What kind of judgements, then, can the solitary mind, possessed of no concepts save those of the given, make? Bearing in mind that the question is not as regards psychological possibilities, I can see no reason why such judgements as 'This is red', 'This is loud', or even 'This colour is red', 'This sound is loud', should not be possible. If it be urged that 'this' is an impossible conception at this stage, since it implies a world of objects, I should dispute this view. 'This' merely signifies whatever occupies the focus of attention, and if taken in that sense is itself a concept of the given. Even the bare ejaculation

'Red!' is an implicit judgement the logical meaning of which is 'This is red'. Hence there seems no reason to doubt that the concepts of the given constitute genuine knowledge, however meagre.

We must now turn to the important question whether there is any evidence, in the rudimentary kind of knowledge which we are discussing, of its subordination to action; or of its validity being constituted by its practical usefulness. We may begin with a remark which is really of general application to all knowledge. The doctrine of evolution renders it probable that all knowledge, and therefore the elementary kind of knowledge involved in the concepts of the given, has been developed for practical reasons in the struggle for existence. No doubt intelligence grew because it was found to give its possessor an advantage over less intelligent competitors. No doubt knowledge would never have come into existence if it had not been for its practical value. And certainly these facts will have left their mark on the structure of knowledge. But it does not follow that knowledge *is* nothing but whatever belief happens to be practically helpful. Because knowledge of truth is useful, and has been evolved solely because it is useful, it does not follow that whatever is useful among our beliefs is true. To find out whether the pragmatic test is or is not the sole determinant of the validity of knowledge, we must examine the structure of knowledge at each of its several stages. And we will now proceed to do this for the first stage of knowledge, the concepts of the given.

The pure given itself is admittedly independent of our wills, is not fashioned by us to meet our practical needs. It is the concept which, during the last thirty or more years, has received the special attention of those philosophers who most vociferously insist that knowledge has no validity except that which it borrows from action. It is the concept which, we have been told, has been so exclusively evolved for practical ends that it does not truly serve the theoretical purposes of knowledge. It is the concept

THE CONCEPTS OF THE GIVEN 59

which is supposed, by one of the leading philosophers of this way of thinking, to mislead us and distort the truth, so that 'intuition' has to be called in to repair the damage. Indeed the main battle of modern philosophy, which is the battle of reason against various forms of 'intuition' and irrationality, rages round the concept.

In studying the concepts of the given we are studying the original fountain and source of conceptual knowledge. We are at the very beginning. It is here, therefore, that we should begin our study of the relation of concept to action. Whatever we find at this stage is bound to have an important influence on the whole of our inquiry.

Wherever the relation of resemblance holds, even partially, between any two elements of the given, there is possible a concept of the given. A *class* can be based on *any* resemblance. And as any given element will stand in numerous relations of resemblance to numerous other elements, a single element may therefore be a member of many different classes. The red patch before my eyes is not only a member of the class 'red'. It not only resembles the neighbouring red patch, but it also resembles green in being a 'colour'. It even resembles a sound or odour in being a 'sensation'. In general, any given may fall into numbers of different classes. And since the number of different resemblances which may be observed to hold within the general field of the given will be indefinitely large, the number of possible concepts of the given is also indefinitely large.

It is here, if anywhere, as it seems to me, that the pragmatic factor will exert its influence. For the mind, confronted by the possibility of a very large number of concepts, and being unable to make use of them all, is compelled to *select*. What will be the motive of its selection? On what principle will it use some and neglect others? It is certainly logically possible that its selection might be made in the theoretic interest of pure knowledge. But though this is a logical possibility, no one who considers the question will accept it as a fact. For the ideal of pure knowledge has come into existence very late in the history of the race. Even now it is real only for a few men of science, scholars, and philosophers—a mere drop in the ocean of humanity. For the vast masses of men knowledge is almost solely an instrument of practical activity. And that those concepts which, being logically presupposed by all others, must have come into use in the very first glimmerings of the dawn of knowledge, should have been selected on theoretical grounds is a manifest absurdity. One is impelled to the conclusion that, as a matter of fact, selection must, throughout the greater part of the history of the race, have been made in the interests of action. The mind will have selected those concepts which are likely to be useful to it in the control of experience.

Consider, for example, the colour concepts. The number of distinguishable shades of colour is not unlimited, but is very large. Colours shade off into one another. And not all shades of colour have names. But the conceptualization of colour will depend upon the use each particular person makes of it. For certain crude purposes a simple classification into red, blue, green, and yellow may suffice. The loving labourer in flower gardens will require a more elaborate classification, and the artist a still higher discrimination of shades.

To the primitive man the resemblance between red and red, the concept 'red', is important. In the recognition of objects, the search for food, the flight from danger, colour will be in a thousand ways an important clue. But the subtle and tenuous resemblance between a colour and a sound which gives rise to the very abstract concept of 'quality', will be useless to him. It may, however, become very useful to those in a more advanced state of society whose interests necessitate the use of more abstract concepts.

There is a resemblance between a star and the sharp point of a thorn. Both are material points. And we might on this basis classify thorns and stars together. But though this would be logically defensible, it would be useless in practice, and this resemblance will therefore be ignored. Primitive men will class thorns with thorns as hurtful to the bare feet, and he will class stars with stars as giving him a faint light at night to guide his steps. In general the mind will select the useful resemblances and make concepts of them, and will ignore the useless ones.

But although to this extent the pragmatic test will be operative even in this first stage of knowledge, it will be noted that it acts among the concepts of the given as a criterion of usefulness and not of truth. A concept of the given will be true if based on an existing resemblance, false otherwise. And if this is admitted, the further point must be pressed home that such a concept may be true even though useless. Among the innumerable resemblances which exist we select those which will be useful to us in our practical activities and ignore the rest. But the ignored resemblances are just as real, and to note them would be just as true. To compare a thorn-point to a star may be useless, but is nevertheless a correct comparison, and a concept or judgement based on it would be 'true'.

It is most important to note that the bare concept of the given does not contain that element of *prediction* which has been stressed as characteristic of the concept in general by some modern pragmatist writers.[1] It is pointed out by such writers that our concept of an object, say an apple, has as part of its meaning the fact that certain presented experiences are the signs of possible future experiences. For example, I see the red appearance of the apple. I do not actually *see* that it is an apple at all. All I see is a red round patch with certain characteristic markings and shades of light. I *interpret* this visual appearance in the light of past experience as an apple. This means that I take the characters which I have actually perceived (the red round colour patch) as a sign of the possibility of experiencing those other characters of an apple which I have not as yet perceived in the present instance. The red round appearance is a sign that *if* I bite the object I shall experience a sweet taste; that *if* I open up the interior of the object I shall experience a whitish visual appearance,

---

[1] See, for example, *Mind and the World-Order*, by Clarence Irving Lewis.

and so on. Opposite me as I write is a shiny yellowish surface. I interpret this to myself by applying to it the concept 'wall', i.e. I believe it to be the wall of my study. This means, among other things, that I take the yellowish appearance to be a sign that *if* I stretch out my hand I shall experience the tactile sensation of resistance or hardness. Thus the recognition of an object by means of the application to it of a concept always involves, and in fact consists in, a prediction of possible future experience.

This *predictive* character of the concept is used by some writers as evidence of the complete subordination of knowledge to action, and of the truth of the general attitude of pragmatism. For it is pointed out that this predictive character is found wherever objects are conceptualized, and that it is in this way that the concept becomes a guide to action. I only know how to act if I can predict that *if* I do thus and thus, I shall experience such and such results. The concept enables me to do this. And this, and nothing else, is the function of the concept. The concept which successfully guides action is true. The concept which misleads action is false. Knowledge generally, therefore, is to be judged by whether it leads to successful action or not.

It cannot be doubted that concepts of objects have this predictive character, that they do guide action in this way, and that knowledge has in fact been developed in the struggle for existence as an instrument of practical action. But in suggesting that this predictive character is essential to a concept and is the sole ground on which its validity can be judged, *the pragmatists appear to have overlooked the concepts of the given*. For, unlike the concepts of *objects*, the concepts of the given do not possess this predictive character. The recognition of any object as what it is —an apple, a star, a philosopher—means that I read into the presentation a great deal more than is *now* actually presented. Into the presentation of the round red appearance I read the sweetness, the white interior, of the apple. But nothing of this kind occurs at the level of the concepts of the given. The concept 'red' implies nothing beyond the fact that the mind has noted the resemblance of this red to that red. The mind does not in such a case interpret. It does not predict, or add, or introduce anything from the outside. The concepts of the given are therefore, *in themselves*, useless as guides to action. Of course they become useful when they are taken up to form parts of concepts of objects. Thus in the recognition of an apple the concept 'red' becomes a sign of other possible experiences. But by itself the concept 'red' indicates nothing whatever beyond itself. This is the same with all the concepts of the given. In themselves they do not possess any predictive characters, and are not in any way guides to action.

Perhaps the point is clear enough, but still I will put it in yet another way. To say of a certain visual appearance 'This is an apple' is to make various predictions of possible future experience which may guide action. But to say simply of the same appearance 'This is red' predicts nothing at all, and cannot in itself help action in any way. *And yet it is true*. Therefore its truth cannot reside in its utility.

In other words, the assertion that concepts are predictive is not universally true. It is only true of *some* concepts. Therefore this character cannot be the ground of the validity of conceptual thought in general. For no one will dare to assert that the concepts of the given are not perfectly valid concepts. They possess truth. And this truth they possess quite apart from any predictivity or utility, which they do not in themselves possess.

It will not avail to reply that in combination with other concepts the concepts of the given are useful. This we already know. No doubt the concept 'red' helps in the recognition of an 'apple', and the concept 'apple' of course is predictive and utilitarian. But the concepts of the given can logically exist without any knowledge of objects. It is knowledge of *objects* which is predictive. Therefore the concepts of the given can exist and be valid without any such connexion with concepts of objects as renders them useful.

This conclusion is profoundly significant. Not only does it show that perfectly valid concepts are possible whose validity cannot be identified with usefulness. But it is also clear that all later knowledge depends on such concepts, and that therefore, whatever influence practical activities may exert on the development of later knowledge, it is not the sole determinant. All knowledge, therefore, depends in the last resort upon a class of concepts which are valid apart from any pragmatic rest of validity. The fount and origin of knowledge, which is here in the concepts of the given, has a validity independent of any usefulness. This conclusion about the beginning must inevitably influence profoundly our further study of knowledge.

It will be clear, I think, that even here we have not overlooked the genuine insight which we admitted at the outset to be embodied in the pragmatic point of view. But among the concepts of the given utility does not constitute truth. It does no more than guide the mind's selection, from among innumerable concepts, of those most likely to be helpful to mankind. Concepts of the given are, *in themselves*, without any utility value. They acquire utility only as parts of concepts of 'things'. Their truth is independent of utility. But those which, when taken as parts of concepts of things, are useful, will be selected by the mind to form part of its everyday armoury of concepts.

CHAPTER V
THE WORLD OF THE SOLITARY MIND

PHILOSOPHERS as a rule take fright at the bare mention of solipsism. Immediately it comes in sight they shy to one side like a horse frightened of a piece of paper. It is common to read in their writings arguments such as the following: 'Such and such a line of thought will lead us into solipsism. *Therefore* we must avoid that line of thought since it must be wrong.' And with that unphilosophical attitude they are satisfied, never calmly facing the issue. They think that to admit that the solipsist position must be the initial position of the mind is an admission which will get them into difficulties. They *dislike* the idea. It arouses, perhaps, unpleasant feelings of loneliness and futility. Their objections are not based on any rational thought, but upon this emotional dislike or fear. Here, for example, is a passage from a lecture by Mr. C. C. J. Webb on *Our Knowledge of One Another* which has recently been issued.

> I have a recollection of hearing the late Lord Balfour remark in the course of a philosophical discussion that he found it very difficult to deny 'solipsism' to be our original condition, but no less difficult to see how, if it were so, we could ever get out of it. The second difficulty appears to me insuperable, but as to the former I cannot believe that solipsism is a position that any one was ever really in.

'Found it very difficult to deny' are tell-tale words. They plainly indicate that there is a desire to deny it. In other words the question is not being viewed in the dry light of reason, but the wishes and feelings of the thinker are being allowed to dictate the conclusion. Lord Balfour felt *forced* to admit that the initial position of the mind is solipsism, but *feared* nevertheless to look the thought in the face. And Mr. Webb assumes without any argument that it cannot be accepted, and seems to think that the fact that one does not like the idea is a sufficient reason for its rejection.

But philosophy, as I understand it, necessitates our following reason *to the end*. And if one is going to be frightened of the conclusions to which reason points, if one is going to philosophize half-way, and only so long as one likes the results, one might as well give up philosophizing altogether. Why not, then, rest in 'common sense' or in 'primitive belief' or in blind prejudice, and so sleep in peace untroubled by philosophic doubts?

It seems to me that we ought to take philosophy seriously, loyally following wherever she leads. And I believe that any one who is prepared to follow reason absolutely, with no reservations, will be compelled to accept the philosophy to be developed in the next two chapters. I claim that it alone is the true rationalism. But as human nature is such that men will not follow reason, I predict that in fact very few will accept it, and that most will comfort themselves with some vain delusion imposed upon them, not by their reason, but by their hopes or fears. But for my part I shall proceed uncompromisingly to the end.

It is evident that, however we may wish otherwise, we cannot, if we are honest, escape the conclusion that the initial position of every mind must be solipsistic. By this I do not mean that I shall remain in the belief that I alone exist. I think on the contrary that there is very good reason to believe in the existence of other minds. That is a question which I shall discuss in Chapter VIII. But in the meanwhile I assert that each of us must *begin* from within his own consciousness. Belief in other minds is not a datum.

That I am, to start with, only aware of *my own* thoughts and experiences, appears to be self-evident. Since it is the true beginning, it is clear that it cannot be an inference from anterior data, since in that case those anterior data would themselves constitute the beginning. We cannot *prove* the solipsist position in the sense of deducing it from some other position. But we can establish it by pointing out the given facts which *constitute* the position. This we have already to a large extent done, and nothing more is necessary here except once more to summarize those facts. They are as follows.

I cannot experience anything except *my own* experience. I can see my red, but I can never see yours. I can feel a pain in my leg. But I can never feel the pain in your leg. I can feel my emotion, but not yours. Even if your anger infects me, so that I feel it in sympathy with you, it is yet, in so far as I feel it, *my* anger, not yours. I can never be you, nor you me. I cannot see through your eyes, nor you through mine. Even if you can telepathically transfer a mental state, say an image, from your mind to mine, yet, when I become aware of it it, is then *my* image and not yours. Even if, as some think, I can directly perceive your mind, without having to infer it from your body, still this perception of your mind will then be to me *my* perception, *my* experience.

All knowledge, all philosophy, must be based upon experience. And from whose experience can I begin except from my own? Whatever belief I hold on whatever subject must be either a datum of *my* consciousness or else an inference or mental construction which *I* base upon *my* data. If I accept a scientific belief on your authority, this belief must be an inference which *I* make from the sounds (words) I hear you utter, and from *my* belief in your repute as a scientific authority. Whatever I believe rests in the end upon the data of my own consciousness. Therefore all knowledge must have had its beginning in my own self-enclosed personal experience. This original solipsism is utterly unescapable except by prejudice or by refusing to see it. Philosophers blink the fact or gloss it over. But we shall begin here and loyally accept whatever results may follow.

We shall have to make further study of the world of the solipsistic or solitary mind, the world which the mind would inhabit but for its acquired communication with other minds. For it must be remembered that the solitary mind is no mere legend of a consciousness which may or may not have existed in remote past ages. It is true that we look upon it as, in a sense already explained, an historical as well as a logical beginning. But the solitary mind is also a present fact. For it is the mind of every one of us stripped of all accretions of knowledge, and pushed back upon its absolute foundation. The mind which is here described, and whose world is here discussed, exists here and now embedded in the consciousness of every one of us. It is true that the mind of every one of us contains, and is, *much more than this*. But this it is at least. This is the underground foundation of the building. And the foundation is not abolished or rendered a legend by the building of the upper stories. It is still there. So, too, the world of the solitary mind is not an unreal or imaginary world. It is the world which every one of us inhabits even now, though we have *added* many riches of existence to it.

In the concepts of the given the mind revealed the first activity of its thought. They were the first advance of the mind beyond the bare given. They were definitely *thought*, as distinguished from mere awareness or receptiveness. But these concepts could never lead the solitary mind out of itself, out of the grotto of its private phantasms, into the public world of external things. The mind might go on living alone, in its world of insubstantial colour patches and sounds, without any consciousness of the outward world of real things. The concepts of the given could never help it. They would enable it to recognize 'red', to distinguish 'red' from 'blue', to group colours under a different head from sounds, and so forth. But that is all. To get from this stage to that of consciousness of the real external world will clearly require some quite new activity of the mind. And it must be our aim to discover that activity.

But before describing the detailed steps by which the mind passes outwards to a belief in a public external world it will be well to see more clearly where it at present stands, and to measure the distance which it has to travel in that passage. What is the distance between our starting-point and our goal? Our starting-point is the given, along with its special and elementary concepts. And the given means for each individual his own given. My given is not your given. Nor am I yet aware of your given or even of your existence. The existence of other minds is not itself part of the given. It is a later discovery. And therefore each mind must be, at its starting-point, completely solitary. It is aware of its colour patches, its sounds, scents, and tastes. These are its aboriginal world. They come and go like the images in a dream. It is unaware of anything else. It has no knowledge of the existence of any other mind. It has no knowledge of the existence of external objects in so far as these differ from mere presentations.

In what respects external objects differ from mere presentations is precisely the point upon which it is now desired to fix attention. For the world from which we start is a world of mere presentations. Yet we all of us come to believe in a world of external objects or 'things'. Before we attempt in the next chapter to ascertain how the mind reaches that belief, we had better first settle what the belief involves. How does a public external world of real objects differ from a world of mere presentations?

The distinguishing characters of such a world appear to be three. Objects such as tables and chairs and mountains differ from mere presentations in the following respects: (1) They have an *independent* existence. And by this use of the word independent I mean that they are believed to exist even when they are not presented to any consciousness. And (2) they are not private to my personal consciousness but are parts of a common world of knowledge which is shared by a multitude of minds. Finally (3) they exist for more than one of the senses. The *same* thing may be seen, touched, smelt, tasted, and heard. Mere presentations belong only to one sense. For example, the visual presentation, obviously, can only be seen.

The world of the original solitary mind differs from the world of 'things' in every one of these respects. (1) The solitary mind has no reason to think that its presentations go on existing after they have ceased to appear to itself. The mind sees a green patch. When that disappears it will seem that it has ceased to exist. That it should go on existing when it is no longer being perceived is a belief which would never occur to the solitary mind, because it would be a quite unnecessary hypothesis, not needed to account for any of the experiences of that mind. It is a belief which belongs essentially to the stage of the knowledge of 'things'. It may seem self-evident to *us*, sophisticated and advanced in knowledge as we are, that the table on which I am writing will not go out of existence when I turn my back on it. But as a matter of fact it is not self-evident at all. We have come to think of it as self-evident because it has been firmly fixed in our minds as a belief for possibly hundreds of thousands of years. Just as Euclid's axiom of parallels, which is not self-evident, yet seemed so to many people out of long custom in believing it. A mere presentation flickers and goes out and ceases to exist. The natural belief, which the mind would take for granted unless it had special reason to think otherwise, would be that anything ceases to exist when it is not being perceived. We shall show as we proceed that the mind comes to have special reason to think otherwise as soon as it gets into communication with other minds and attempts to co-operate with them in establishing a common world. But the solitary mind, of course, has not reached that stage. For it, therefore, there exist only presentations which go out of existence as soon as they pass out of perception. Hence belief in the persistence of 'things' and their independence of being perceived is the first essential mark of our belief in an external world of objects, and distinguishes it from the world of the solitary mind.

The world of the solitary mind is (2) not public property. For the solitary mind is not even aware of the existence of other minds. Other people exist for it, if at all, merely as moving colour patches among other similar colour patches. Awareness of these patches does not involve awareness of the existence of the minds which we afterwards come to think of as existing behind them. But belief in an external world of things involves essentially that we think that what is there for me is there for other minds too. This table is there. I regard it as a real object.

THE WORLD OF THE SOLITARY MIND 71

This means that I believe that other minds can also see the table there. If I saw the table and no one else could see it, if it was thus private to my consciousness, I should conclude that it was an hallucination or in some way unreal. This shows that the belief that objects are *public*, not private, is an essential part of our belief in an external world. And this is the second way in which it differs from the world of the solitary mind.

Finally (3) the world of the solitary mind differs from the public world of objects in that it has not yet identified the objects of the different senses. I see the table and I also touch it. For the solitary mind at the beginning of its career the touch sensation and the sight sensation have nothing to do with one another, exist in wholly distinct universes. For the developed mind which believes in an external public world they have become conjoined as two presentations or 'qualities' of the same object. If I saw a table but could get no touch sense of it, if when I put out my hand to feel the table my hand went through it, I should conclude that I was dreaming or insane. And this shows once more that the identification of the objects of the different senses is an essential characteristic of our belief in the existence of an external world, a characteristic which is missing from the world-view of the solitary mind.

Thus, to recapitulate, the solitary mind is in the beginning confronted with its own given. It alone exists, solitary and solipsist in its world of presentations. This world of presentations is wavering, unsolid, and impermanent. The colour patches of which it largely consists come and go, flicker and fade. It is true that the mind has learnt to recognize similar presentations when they recur. It recognizes a red colour as red. It distinguishes it from other colours. It distinguishes colours from sounds. But in spite of this, nothing is permanent in its world. And above all it has no idea that anything goes on existing when it is not being perceived.

It is necessary to insist repeatedly upon this latter point. Let us imagine that what *we* know to be a green book is passed before the eyes of the solitary mind. To that mind this event will present itself simply as the appearance and disappearance of a green patch. When once it has gone out of sight the solitary mind has no reason whatever for supposing that it still continues in existence. While it is being perceived the only reason for believing in its existence is the fact of its being perceived. When that reason is removed why should its continued existence be contemplated? Even if the book is brought back into view a second time, this will be explained by the solitary mind as the appearance of *another* green patch similar to the first. It is not necessary, in order to explain the facts, to introduce the hypothesis of the *identity* of the two patches and their continued existence between appearances. This, as we shall see, becomes necessary as soon as a society of minds attempts to establish a common world. But it is quite unnecessary now when there is only one mind in the world. The view that nothing exists except what is actually being perceived and while it is being perceived, and that if what *we* should call the 'same' things reappear, this is due to the appearance of different but similar colour patches, is quite sufficient to explain all the facts in the world of the solitary mind. Hence it is evident that the solitary mind has no idea that anything exists unperceived by it.

This implies that for the solitary mind the *esse* of things which we afterwards regard as belonging to the external world is identical with their *percipi*, or if we prefer to translate this jargon into English, that their very existence is constituted by the fact of being perceived. Not that the solitary mind is capable of consciously making such an identification. For in order to make an identification of the two terms their difference must first have been realized. And the mind has not so far realized the difference. The differentiation of *esse* and *percipi* results from holding the beliefs that what is perceived persists in existence when we are not perceiving it, and that it exists for other minds. But neither of these insights has as yet dawned upon the solitary mind. Both are constructions which belong to a later stage of knowledge. Hence the identity of existence

THE WORLD OF THE SOLITARY MIND

with being perceived is for the solitary mind primary and implicit.

I am afraid we cannot escape being dragged by these statements into the arena of the famous idealism versus realism controversy. Our final attitude to that controversy cannot be defined at this stage of our inquiry. But certain preliminary conclusions may be reached. The question, however, presents itself to us in a somewhat different form to that in which it is usually agitated by idealists and realists. They ask whether the completed 'thing', the chair, the table, or what not, is real or ideal. But for us the 'thing' is a mental construction still to be reached in the future. We have before us no completed objects but only the flitting presentations of the solitary mind. And the question for us is concerning the status of these original data of the mind. And it is surely here that the question ought to be asked, here in the factory of the mind where the raw materials of what is to become the external world are on view, not later when that complicated product, the object, has been constructed.

I will first endeavour to state in a brief form the preliminary conclusions which I shall reach in this chapter, and I will then discuss and defend them. The conclusions which I shall reach in this chapter are the following:

(1) The solitary mind, or in other words the mind of every one of us when stripped of all the knowledge it has acquired, is confronted with a phantasmagoria of private presentations. It cannot be aware that these presentations continue to exist when it is not perceiving them. This knowledge is not a datum, and is impossible until the solitary mind gets into touch with other minds and begins in collaboration with them to construct a common or public world.

(2) The solitary mind, further, cannot be aware of any distinction between the *esse* and the *percipi* of its presentations. It cannot, for example, draw any distinction between 'blue' and 'awareness of blue'. This distinction is not a datum, but a later construction.

(3) The solitary mind cannot be aware of the existence of any permanent object beyond or behind the presentations. For example, when a penny is rotated in a certain way, it appears circular at one angle, then becomes more and more elliptical, and lastly appears as a narrow rectangular band. The solitary mind is aware of these various presentations or 'sensa', as they have been called, but not of the one unchanging 'real' penny which is supposed to lie behind them or in them. Such knowledge of permanent objects is not a datum but a later construction.

(4) Later knowledge of all the points referred to in the last three paragraphs is a *result* of the construction of a common world by a society of minds. One of the first steps in this construction consists in inventing the fiction that a presentation can persist in existence when it is not being perceived. We shall see in the sequel why and how this assumption is made, and we shall see that it is no unusual procedure for the mind to invent fictions of this kind, but that it is of a piece with the whole procedure of knowledge and science. For the moment our point is that as soon as this assumption of the continued persistence of presentations after perception of them has ceased has been made, it then becomes necessary to distinguish between *esse* and *percipi*, since it is clear that the *esse* of an unperceived presentation cannot consist in its *percipi*. This distinction once made is afterwards extended from unperceived presentations to perceived ones, so that we have *now* come to think even when we are looking at a blue patch that the 'blue' is something different from the 'awareness of blue'.

(5) To the question whether the presentation is 'mental' or 'non-mental' we shall reply that this question is itself meaningless, and that the dispute which is supposed to centre round it is a mere quarrel over words.

(6) It may be asked whether the presentation is dependent or independent on *perception*. I shall answer that the only sense in which a presentation can be independent of perception is when it exists unperceived. But an unperceived presentation, for example a green colour when

THE WORLD OF THE SOLITARY MIND

no one is looking at it, is not a datum, and is unknown to the solitary mind. It is a later construction. In the pure presentation as such the *esse* is identical with the *percipi*. In this identity there is no room either for the relation of dependence or for that of independence.

(7) It may be asked whether the presentation is dependent or independent on *mind*. The presentation is part of the passive not-I, and is therefore distinct from the mind, which consists in the activities of thought, attention, &c. Since they are not identical, relations of dependence or independence might possibly exist. But dependence may mean either causal dependence, or logical dependence, or the dependence of part on whole in the part-whole relation. There is no reason to regard presentations as caused by the mind, and their logical dependence cannot be satisfactorily established. And to ask whether the presentation is part of the mind would appear to have no meaning. It is identical with the question whether the presentation is 'mental', a question which has already been declared meaningless.

I would preface my detailed observations under these heads with the general remark that it is impossible to establish our position firmly until, in the next chapter, we have shown in detail how the mind constructs a public world. If we can show that, starting from a world in which there is no distinction between *esse* and *percipi*, the mind must necessarily construct a world in which that distinction exists, and if we can also show in what manner it is reasonable to suppose that this construction has occurred, this will render antecedently probable our present conclusions about the nature of the world before that construction takes place. Thus it is hoped that the conclusions of the present chapter and those of the next chapter will mutually reflect light upon one another.

Our first position is one which has already been explained, and is merely repeated here in order to give a complete list of our preliminary conclusions. The solitary mind has no reason to think that its presentations exist when they are not perceived by it. When the green book is passed before the eyes, and then taken away, the disappearance of the green patch will be for the solitary mind its ceasing to exist. Even when the green book is again placed before the eyes, the mind will have no reason to think that the green patch has continued in existence in the interval between its two appearances. The natural and obvious explanation of the facts will be that there have been two different green patches, alike no doubt in colour and shape, but none the less not identical, and that in the blank interval between the two appearances there had been no green patch in existence. The identification of the two appearances as the 'same', and the supposition that the existence of this one thing was continuous between them, is a position which is certainly not self-evident, and cannot be a datum for the mind in its original contact with the world. It is a position which must have been in some way 'arrived at' after starting from the beginning. We shall find that, as it cannot be regarded as an inference from any datum, it must be considered a construction.

It is only when two or more minds meet and begin to compare notes that they will enter upon this construction together. The first glimpse of it begins to appear when we find that another mind continues to perceive the green patch after we ourselves have ceased to do so. How do we know that any object exists when we are not perceiving it? Surely the first step towards this knowledge is obviously taken when we make the discovery that some other mind was perceiving that object while we ourselves were not. The detailed steps of this development will be set out in the next chapter. But this much I have anticipated in order to make clearer the view here adopted that the solitary mind could have no reason to believe in the continued existence of its presentations after perception of them has ceased. It only begins to have reason for doing so when it attempts to establish, along with other minds, a public external world.

Any other view seems to me quite impossible. I, as a sophisticated mind, believe that the green patch goes on

THE WORLD OF THE SOLITARY MIND

existing when I am not perceiving it. This belief must be either a datum, or an inference, or a mental construction. It is clearly not an inference, for there is nothing from which it could be validly inferred. From the existence of a green patch *now* (which I know because I see it) I cannot possibly infer the existence of the green patch yesterday or to-morrow. Such an argument would be a simple *non sequitur*, a fallacy into which no one could fall who clearly understood the steps, or rather lack of steps, of the argument.

My view, therefore, is that the belief is a construction. The only other possible alternative is that it is a datum. If it is asserted that this belief could be known to the solitary mind, i.e. to the mind before any construction takes place, this can only mean that the belief is a datum. It must be supposed that the mind in some way *directly perceives* that the presentation goes on existing when no one is perceiving it. This, however, is an absurdity. The green patch appears to me, and then disappears. At which moment is it that I perceive that it goes on existing after it has disappeared? Do I perceive this while it is still appearing to me? If so, this means that I *now* directly perceive the *future*, i.e. that I perceive what is not there to be perceived. Or do I perceive it after the green patch has disappeared? This means that while no green patch is appearing to me I yet perceive the existence of the green patch. Whichever alternative you choose will be equally absurd. The whole position that the belief which we are discussing is a datum is affected by a contradiction. For it implies that it is possible to perceive an existence which is by hypothesis unperceived.

We must conclude, then, that our belief in unperceived existence is not a datum, is not an inference, and must be a mental construction. It does not belong to the aboriginal state of the mind. It was not 'always there'. It has somehow been arrived at. It was unknown to the solitary mind.

Our second position is that for the solitary mind the *esse* of a presentation is its *percipi*, and that such a mind could not be aware of the distinction between *esse* and *percipi*. This means, of course, that even for us the pure presentation, if we strip it of all the accretions with which thought has enriched it, if we strip it of all that has been acquired during the development of mind, does not contain within itself the distinction which we are discussing. It means that even for us there is no distinction between 'blue' and 'awareness of blue', except such distinction as we ourselves have introduced by means of our mental constructions. It means, in fine, that the distinction is not given, nor immediately perceived, and cannot be explained as the object of a 'primitive belief'.

Prima facie this follows from our previous position that the solitary mind cannot know that its presentations continue in existence when not perceived. For such a mind *esse* and *percipi* are simultaneous and coterminous. The existence of the presentation begins at the moment its perception begins. And existence and perception also end at the same moment. So that existence and perception are like two straight lines the two ends of which coincide. Two such lines are identical and there is no distinction between them. And *esse* and *percipi* are likewise identical and without distinction. There is no existence without being perceived and no being perceived without existence. *Esse* and *percipi* completely coincide, and why then should the mind distinguish between them? It is different for us as sophisticated minds. For us *esse* and *percipi* do *not* coincide, since we believe that our presentations continue existing unperceived, and it is precisely because of this discrepancy that we are compelled to distinguish between the two. We have come to believe that things exist when no one is perceiving them. But obviously such an existence, which lies altogether outside perception, cannot be the same as being perceived. If my office desk exists during the night when no one is conscious of it, its *esse* cannot at *that* time be its *percipi*, since it has no *percipi*. We therefore have a reason for distinguishing *esse* from *percipi*. But the solitary mind has no reason whatever to do so. When it says 'This green patch exists', it can mean nothing except 'This green patch is being perceived by me'. The two expressions will have *for it* no difference of meaning.

If this is not admitted then we shall have to suppose that the distinction between *esse* and *percipi* exists intrinsically and primordially in the presentation itself, that the distinction is *given* from the beginning. For it must be either given, inferred, or constructed. It is generally admitted that it cannot be inferred. For from what could it be inferred? My view is that it is a construction. But if we do not admit this, we must suppose that it is given. And in that case our knowledge of it must be a direct perception. In other words it must be possible to look at the green patch and distinguish its *esse* from its *percipi* just as one may by simple inspection distinguish its shape from its colour.

But nothing can be plainer than that no such 'existence' can be perceived. When I look at the green patch, what do I perceive about it? I can perceive that it is green, that it has a certain shape, possibly that it moves or changes in some other way. These are characters which I actually *see*. But apart from these can I *see* its existence? Can I perceive an existence which is distinct from its greenness, its motion, its shape, its other visible qualities? Such an existence is a pure abstraction. It may be for some purposes a legitimate abstraction. But as an abstraction it cannot be perceptible to the senses, it cannot be given.

A number of arguments have been urged against the view here adopted. It has been widely asserted that in the experience of 'awareness of green' we distinguish between the awareness and the green. The awareness is an activity of our minds. It is 'mental'. The green is not.

It is quite true that we do make this distinction between our awareness and that of which we are aware. But in my view this distinction is itself the result of the mental construction of the external world. Because the belief that there is an external world independent of mind, and that this external world is composed of independent objects which are green, hard, spatial, and so on, is ingrained in us, has become part of our very blood, we think of green as something distinct from our awareness of it. I do not assert that to think this is erroneous. On the contrary I shall assert that it is true. But this is because truth itself is largely composed of mental constructions. The view that the distinction which we are discussing is a mental construction does not imply that it is false. But if it is asserted that the distinction exists apart from mental construction, that it is primordial and essential to consciousness as such, then this assertion is false. For it is equivalent to the view that the distinction is given. And we have seen that it cannot be given.

If we can in imagination withdraw ourselves back into the world of the solitary mind, if we can think of ourselves as each, where he must have logically started, shut up within his own private world, we shall see that in such a world no distinction between green and awareness of green could ever have arisen. It has evidently arisen as a result of the belief that green goes on existing when I do not perceive it. Because I believe that the green tree is there when no one is looking at it, I am compelled to think that the green tree is not the same as my awareness of it. But I came to believe that it goes on existing when I am not aware of it as a result of a train of thinking the details of which will be explained in the next chapter. One of the first steps in this train of thinking is the discovery that other minds are seeing the tree when I am not. Because *you* see it while I am asleep I am forced to the view that it exists when I do not perceive it. This is one of the first steps in the building up of the construction of an independent existence. This construct is therefore dependent upon my awareness of the existence of other minds. But the solitary mind in its private world is not aware of the existence of other minds. And therefore it cannot be aware of the independence of its objects, or of the distinction between green and awareness of green which that independence implies. In other words the distinction is not intrinsic to the presentation as such.

Realist writers on this point seem to put the cart before

the horse. They think that the independence or 'non-mental' character (whatever that may mean) of the object can be deduced from the existence of the distinction between green and the awareness of green. The truth is that this distinction is made as a result of the mental construction of the independence of the object. We first construct that independence, and then argue 'Because green is to be regarded as existing apart from, and therefore independently of, my awareness, therefore the green and the awareness must be thought of as distinct from one another'. Consequently it is illicit thereafter to deduce the independence of the object from the existence of the distinction, a proceeding which is nevertheless a hot favourite among realists.

Those who think that the distinction is not constructed, but primordial or given, may urge in favour of their view that the awareness is an *activity* of the mind, whereas the green of which we are aware is a pure passivity. I think the former of these two statements is mistaken. Pure awareness is not an activity. The mind, when it is active, *does* something to the object. For example, the acts of abstraction and conception—genuine mental acts these—alter the object by cutting away a part of it and considering only the other part. The act of comparison between two objects involves distinguishing between them while at the same time linking them together. The act of attention *selects*. But pure awareness as such appears to me to be wholly lacking in activity. It is purely passive. That is why, if you stare blankly at one object for a long time, eschewing thought, and avoiding the activity involved in shifting the attention backwards and forwards from one point to another, you will rapidly become unconscious. Pure awareness, without any of the characteristic activities of mind added to it, is equivalent to unawareness, unconsciousness. It is, of course, an abstraction similar to pure sensation. It cannot exist by itself. So that just because the mind when it approaches to pure awareness ceases to be active, it at the same time ceases to be conscious. For the essence of mind, the essence of the 'mental', is activity.

The impression that awareness is an activity which can therefore be distinguished from that of which the mind is aware is probably the result of confusing attention with awareness. In all ordinary sense perception we select our object and concentrate attention on it. Hence awareness is always accompanied by attention. If the attention wholly ceased it is probable that the mind would lapse into unconsciousness at once. Attention is a mental activity. Hence the confusion to which I have referred is not an unnatural one. When we introspectively examine any particular piece of awareness we invariably find the mind active in it. We *feel* this activity within ourselves very strongly. We fail to see that this is not the activity of awareness, but of the attention which always accompanies it. And we are therefore apt to dismiss as absurd the suggestion that awareness is not a mental activity. To this confusion I attribute the famous assertion of the realists that the distinction between green and awareness of green is intrinsic and primordial.

No doubt it follows from the position which I am here adopting that awareness is not a part of mind at all, but is in some way 'non-mental', which will no doubt appear at first as a curious result. Nevertheless I accept it, except that I am of opinion that the adjective 'non-mental' is misleading and inappropriate. As has already been pointed out, the mind distinguishes between itself as active in attention, conception, abstraction, inference, and thought generally, and on the other side the pure passivity of the presentation. This is the only real basis for any distinction between the I and the not-I, the 'mental' and the 'non-mental'. Now if we say that the awareness of the presentation *is* the presentation, that there is no intrinsic distinction between green and awareness of green, then of course it follows that the awareness (which is only another word for the presentation itself) is part of the not-I, is 'non-mental'.

Thus our point of view agrees with realism to this extent, that it abolishes any intermediatory 'idea' between the mind and its object. The mind, for us as for the realists, sees its object, or rather sees its presentation, direct. It stands face to face with it. And this is a profoundly important point of contact.

No doubt it appears strange to speak of an awareness as if it were not part of the mind at all, but rather of the external world. But the reader has perhaps by now forgotten that it is not *we* who speak thus, but rather the solitary mind. For *us*, sophisticated as we are, there *is* a distinction between awareness and that of which we are aware. And when, as a result of our mental construction of an independent external world, we have made that distinction, we then begin to regard that of which we are aware, the presentation, as belonging to the independent world, and the awareness as belonging to us, to our consciousness. That has become our natural point of view. And bearing in mind that, since 'truth' includes not only the aboriginal given but also all that has been added on to it by means of legitimate mental constructions, it will be seen that it is the 'true' point of view. And it is therefore natural that when we penetrate back into the dim prehistory of the mind, when we speak from the point of view of the solitary mind as we are now doing, there should result turns of expression, modes of viewing things, which are apt to strike *us* now, as sophisticated minds, with a kind of shock owing to their essential strangeness. It is thus that we experience a sense of strangeness when we hear that for the solitary mind awareness is not a part of consciousness, but of the not-I.

That the distinction between the awareness and the presentation itself is not made by the solitary mind, is not aboriginal, but is dependent on the discovery of other minds and the subsequent construction of a *public* world, is borne out by a circumstance to which attention has been pointedly drawn by those very writers who differ from our view. It has been pointed out that in the case of visual presentations we very easily make the distinction between the awareness and that of which we are aware; but that in the case of bodily sensations such as headache we do not make this distinction. We think that there is a green object as well as an awareness of green. But we do not ordinarily conceive that there is a 'headachy object' as well as a feeling of headache.¹ This difference between sight and bodily sensation has been found inexplicable by those writers who have pointed it out. But it is precisely what we should expect from the point of view here advocated. For the world of sight is a public world, the world of headaches and other bodily sensations a private world. You and I believe that we both see the same green object. But we never suppose that we feel the same identical headache. Hence the world of sight comes to be regarded as an independent world which, because you are aware of it even when I am not, does not depend for its existence on *my* being aware of it. Therefore in the case of sight we distinguish green from our awareness of green. We are compelled to do so by the fact that the green which is supposed to exist when I am not aware of it must clearly be different from my awareness. This distinction then extends itself from the green of which I am not aware to the green of which I am aware. Here too I begin to suppose that there must be a distinction between the green and the awareness of the green. So in the visual world the distinction becomes universally established and taken for granted. But in the world of bodily sensations no such necessity is felt, and no such distinction established, because I never suppose that you feel the same headache as I do, much less that you feel it when I am not aware of it. Thus the difference between the visual world and the world of headaches in this respect is exactly what we should expect if, as our theory holds, the distinction between a presentation and our awareness of it is not intrinsic or primordial, but is a product of our construction of a public world.

It is also argued that we have a 'primitive faith', an 'instinctive belief', in the existence of an independent external world, and therefore in the reality of the distinction between *esse* and *percipi*. This is also sometimes called an 'animal faith'. In some form or other, explicit or tacit,

¹ See C. D. Broad's *Scientific Thought*, p. 254 et seq.

it seems to be relied on by most realists. And necessarily so. They are compelled to rely on some such weak shift. For they have to admit that the existence of an independent external world cannot be proved, i.e. that it is not a valid inference from our presentations. The various appearances of the penny as I rotate it are the only existences of which we have *direct* evidence. That these appearances go on existing after we cease to perceive them, or that they existed before we began to perceive them, can never be proved. That there exists behind the varying appearances a single unchanging 'real' penny can also never be proved. It is admitted on all hands that this is so, and that any supposed inferences to these beliefs would be fallacious. The obvious conclusion is that these beliefs are mental constructions. But as this would destroy the preconceived notions of realism, it is alleged instead that we know of the existence of the independent world by means of a 'primitive belief' or by 'faith'. Thus Dr. Broad says: 'The belief that our sensa are appearances of something more permanent and complex than themselves seems to be primitive, and to arise inevitably in us with the arising of the sensa. It is not reached by inference, and could not logically be justified by inference.'[1]

Such an attitude is contrary to the rationalism, the determination to follow whither reason leads us *to the end*, to take philosophy seriously, which we in this book have adopted as our ideal. Philosophy cannot, in my opinion, accept as gospel the deliverances of primitive instinctive belief any more than it can accept the mysterious unmediated revelations of the mystic. And a 'primitive instinctive belief' is, I venture to assert, no more than a euphemism for an obstinate prejudice. We believe that there is an independent world. Granted. Is this true, and why? 'Because we have a primitive belief in it', say these philosophers. But this is only saying over again that we believe it, which we knew before. We believe it because we believe it. This is a poor position for a philosopher to take up!

[1] *Op. cit.*, p. 268.

By a 'primitive belief' is meant, I presume, simply a belief which people have held for a very long time. It may have been accepted by our semi-human ancestors of a million years ago. It may have so ingrained itself into our race that a tendency to believe it has become hereditary, and has only to be awakened in each new individual by the faintest suggestions from his fellows. For it is by no means certain that we have not 'innate ideas' at least to the extent that we have inherited through hundreds of thousands of years certain *tendencies* of thought and feeling. Even though our belief in an independent world is of this kind, it does not follow that we ought to accept that fact as its sufficient justification. We might be compelled to accept on nearly similar grounds as a 'primitive belief' the view that the earth is a flat disk.

Not, of course, that we dispute the truth of the belief in an independent external world. Nor do we dispute that, as a matter of psychological fact, that belief may have become in the course of long ages practically instinctive. But it is utterly absurd to give this as the *logical* origin of the belief, or as its justification. Our point of view would appear more reasonable and philosophical. It is that as the belief in question admittedly cannot be an inference from our direct experience, it must be a mental construction. It is 'true', because, as will be proved later, truth includes mental constructions. To explain it as a 'primitive belief' is merely to give it the status of an unaccountable prejudice. I am prepared to give it a better justification than that, and to exhibit it as part of a rational scheme of knowledge founded on mental constructions which are legitimate because governed by rational laws. This point of view has, of course, to be developed and justified in the rest of this book.

The assertion that our belief in an independent world 'arises inevitably in us with the arising of the sensa' seems to be quite unjustified. Either it means that the belief is held by people without proper ground, as a prejudice—a statement which may be psychologically true, but is philosophically worthless. Or it means that the belief is 'inevitable' in the sense that it is a 'necessary' truth like the axioms of geometry. But no one is likely to assert this view seriously in an age which scouts the former supposed necessity of the axioms of either Euclid or any other geometer, and which finds it difficult to accept belief in even logical necessity.

The assertion that the belief 'arises in us with the arising of the sensa' must mean, if it means anything, that the independence of the object is *given*, that it is directly perceived by the senses. But we have already seen clearly that this is false.

Finally our view has to meet the following argument. If green and the awareness of green are the same thing, then since awareness of green is a mental state, green must be a mental state. In that case what is green is the state of mind itself. Hence the awareness of green must be a green state of mind. The perception of a square must be a square state of mind, and so on. This, it is supposed, will embarrass us very much. For to speak of the mind itself, or of its contents, as green, square, &c., would seem to smack of materialism—indeed to commit us to a wholly materialistic view of the mind.

In reply we may point back to what has already been said on the supposed 'mental' character of our awareness of presentations. For the solitary mind the awareness is *not* mental, for no awareness of green exists apart from the green itself. The awareness is only distinguished from the green, set up as an entity on its own account, and classed as 'mental' *after*, and as a result of, the construction of a public external world. Before that construction has been made, the awareness is not a mental state. It is identical with the presentation, which is itself not a mental state, but a part of the not-I. (We shall see this more clearly when we discuss a little later in this chapter the supposed 'mental' character of the presentation.) Therefore the argument that our point of view implies the existence of a green state of mind falls to the ground. After the construction has been made, on the other hand, the distinction between the awareness and that of which it is aware comes into being, and therefore once more the argument does not arise.

Our third and fourth positions are that the solitary mind cannot be aware of the existence of any permanent object beyond or behind the presentations, and that our belief in such objects, as also our belief in the existence of unperceived presentations and in the distinction between *esse* and *percipi*, are later mental constructions. These views have been fairly well explicated in the course of our discussion already, and it is unnecessary to say much more here. They cannot, of course, be fully established until we have shown in the next chapter how these mental constructions come to be made. But in the meanwhile we may recapitulate their essential foundations briefly as follows. It is clear that what the mind is immediately aware of is the presentations or sensa, and *nothing else*. It cannot perceive the supposed permanent 'real' objects which these are believed to represent. Nor can it perceive presentations existing unperceived. This is the absolute foundation of our position. The next step consists in the realization that from these immediately perceived data no logical inference of any kind can be drawn as to the existence of unperceived presentations or 'real' objects. I think this is admitted by all competent philosophers of all schools. Nor can one even suggest what kind of inference could possibly be put forward as fulfilling the necessary conditions. Therefore unless one is prepared to rely on a mysterious 'primitive belief' or 'animal faith' one is compelled to conclude that our beliefs on these subjects must have been constructed by the mind itself. Reliance on 'primitive beliefs' is totally irrational and incomprehensible, and is a mere 'chucking up the sponge' on the part of philosophy. Hence we must explore the path which seems to be opened up by the suggestion that our beliefs on these matters are mental constructions.

Our next position concerns the question whether presentations are 'mental' or not. The adjective seems to me wholly inappropriate, and it is my conviction that those who discuss the question are not themselves clear as to what they mean by the word mental. For what can be meant by either asserting or denying that a green patch is mental?

There are apparently two possible meanings which might be attached to such language. Firstly, we have seen that the mind distinguishes its own activities from what it passively suffers, and that the activities constitute the I, the passivities the not-I. This distinction, which is made even by the solitary mind, is the only true distinction between 'mental' and 'non-mental', and in this sense it is quite clear that the green colour or other presentation is non-mental. And this is, I believe, the only intelligible sense in which the question can be asked and answered.

But this does not appear to be quite what is meant by those who agitate the problem. If they urge that the presentation is mental they appear to mean that it has that quality which causes the images of dream, hallucination, or delirium, to be regarded as mental or 'subjective'. And in distinguishing the mental from the non-mental they apparently have at the back of their minds the difference between dreams and veridical perception. A dream is a series of private presentations. The world of veridical perception is a world of common or shared presentations. The dream is popularly supposed to be in some way a 'mental' phenomenon, whereas the real world is regarded as 'non-mental'.

Now the essential differences between the presentations of dream and of veridical perception are that the former are private and in some ways lawless, while the latter are shared in common by many minds and are subject to the general laws of physics. In other words the differences are extrinsic to the presentations themselves. They consist in the relations of the presentations to each other and to other things outside themselves. There are no intrinsic differences. The dream-images cannot be discriminated because of their paler or less vivid appearance. We only know them as dreams when we cannot fit them into the common world shared by us and by other conscious beings. It follows that when people speak of dreams as in some special way mental they must be referring to their character as private. It does not appear to be their character as lawless which is important here. For that is very much less obvious to the plain man than is their private nature. And one is led to the conclusion that 'mental', when applied to dreams and other non-veridical perceptions, really means nothing more than private, as distinguished from shared.

If mental means nothing beyond private then of course the presentations of the solitary mind are mental. But for my part I protest that this language is misleading and erroneous, and that the doctrine of the 'mental' character of our presentations is meaningless.

The mistake begins when we call dreams mental. Since there is no intrinsic difference between dream-images and those of veridical perception, therefore both are mental or else neither are. But this is not realized. The habit of calling dreams mental has sprung up because it is falsely supposed by the unphilosophical that there *is* some intrinsic difference between dreams and veridical perception. The presentations of veridical perception are (quite rightly) classed as 'real' or as belonging to the physical world. Those of dream are classed (quite rightly) as 'unreal' and as excluded from the physical world. The unreal then becomes confused with the totally different conception of 'error'. And as error is undoubtedly in some way peculiar to mind, and produced by mind, the unreal entities of the dream are then classed as mental. This seems to be something like the psychological history of the erroneous usage by which dreams are classed as mental while veridical percepts are classed as non-mental, whereas it is clear that in respect of being mental or otherwise they both stand on exactly the same footing.

The popular error then gets transferred from vulgar thought into philosophy. Since dreams are supposed to be mental, and since their essential distinctive character is really their privacy, hence the same word 'mental' gets attached to any presentation which is private, and therefore to the pure presentation as such, or, as we have called it, the presentation of the solitary mind. The presentations of every mind at the beginning, before that mind enters upon, and takes its part in, the public world, must be private. And therefore, according to the erroneous usage which we are reviewing, they must be mental. And since all presentations, even those of veridical perception, are ultimately, when isolated and taken out of their context in the public world, private to each individual, therefore all presentations may come to be represented as mental.

This confusion has, of course, been powerfully helped along by Berkeley's misuse of the word 'idea'. This word, for him, covered presentations. The word as properly understood refers to thoughts or activities of the ego of some kind. Hence if you call a presentation an idea, you tacitly imply that it is of the nature of thought, of the nature of the I, and so mental. This is of course the very opposite of the truth, since the presentation is essentially passive and belongs to the not-I. And it is probable enough that Berkeley was himself misled into this confusion by that same popular error as to the difference between dreams and veridical perception which we have just discussed.

Thus the discussion whether presentations are mental or non-mental, as this discussion is usually conducted, is simply meaningless. I see a green patch. I say that it is green, that it is circular, that it is increasing in size, that it is moving from left to right. All these terms mean something. But now if you inquire whether the green patch is mental, what do your words mean? When you are pressed as to what you mean, you will have to say one of two things. Either you mean by calling it mental that it belongs to the activities of the I, and not to the passivities of the not-I, in which case what you are saying is manifestly untrue. Or you mean that it is private as distinguished from common or public, in which case you are merely using the word 'mental' in a stupidly erroneous sense.

It is equally meaningless to inquire whether the green

patch is 'inside the mind' or 'outside' it. One can see that an object which exists unperceived might be metaphorically described as outside the mind. This is no more than a metaphor, but is unobjectionable as such. But to discuss whether the pure presentation as such, when it is being perceived, is inside or outside the mind, seems to me, so far as I can judge, the same as discussing whether it is mental or non-mental. The discussion takes for granted a distinction in kind between the presentations of veridical perception and those of dream, and supposes that the former may be outside the mind and non-mental, while the latter are inside it and mental. The one thing that is clear, however, is that the two stand on precisely the same footing. If the green patch which I see in veridical perception is outside my mind, then so is the green patch of my dream. If the green patch of my dream is inside my mind, then so is the green patch of veridical perception. The whole discussion rests on the false distinction between the supposed mental character of dreams and hallucinations and the supposed extra-mental character of veridical perception. When once it is seen that this distinction is illusory, that the difference between dreams and 'real' presentations is extrinsic, consisting in their relations with their contexts, and not intrinsic, then it must also be seen that the whole discussion is meaningless.

Our last two positions refer to the question of 'independence', and may be quite shortly expounded. The *esse* of the pure presentation is neither dependent nor independent on its *percipi*. The relations of dependence and independence involve the presence of two distinct terms to be related. But the *esse* and the *percipi* of the green patch as it exists for the solitary mind are not two things, but one. They are identical. Automobiles are not dependent on motor-cars. Nor is Jack dependent on John. Where there is identity, there is no room for relations of dependence or independence.

But this cannot be said of the relation between *esse* and mind or knowledge generally. My mind consists in my thoughts and mental activities. It is the I. The presentation is part of the not-I, and is clearly not identical with the I. And it may therefore be asked whether the presentation is dependent, or independent, on mind. This question may have several meanings.

The questioner may be referring to *causal* dependence. If so, the plain answer to the question is that there is no ground whatever for asserting that presentations are caused by minds. The causes of a presentation seem to be always previous presentations, or at least the causes seem always to fall within the not-I. The cause of the sound of thunder is not my mind, but is the lightning. Neither my will nor my thinking has anything to do with it so far as can be seen. I cannot by willing cause a green patch to appear or to disappear. Nor will any act of thinking, inferring, conceiving, or abstracting influence the matter.

Some philosophers have asserted that the world of the not-I is in some way a *logical* consequent of mind. But mind is in that case usually thought of in a transcendental sense, as referring to a universal or cosmic mind. Discussions of such transcendental questions lie quite outside the scope and the spirit of our inquiries here. But I may hazard the remark—and it seems fair to say—that the logical dependence of presentations on mind has never been satisfactorily established.

Dependence may also mean the dependence of part on whole. To assert that presentations are dependent on minds in this sense would mean apparently that they are parts of minds. The application in a literal sense of the part-whole relation to minds seems inappropriate. But, if it is not taken in its literal sense, it seems to me that the assertion that a green patch is part of my mind can only be another way of alleging that it is 'mental'. And this view has already been discussed.

Hence I do not see any relevant sense in which it can be said that presentations are dependent on minds.

I shall only use the concept of independence in one reference. I shall call the public external world of objects 'independent', and I have already indeed made use of this language. I have spoken of the 'independent' external world. For that world is conceived as having existed before my mind, or any particular minds, came into existence, and in general as existing whether any minds are aware of it or not. This character I shall call its independence. That *this independence on mind is itself a construction of mind* is, of course, of the essence of our philosophy. But that need not deter us from the use of the word independence in the reference explained.

Finally, it has to be understood that *esse* and *percipi*, even when for the sophisticated mind they are not identical, are always correlative. It will be a part of our thesis that no existence can be conceived except in terms of actual or possible perception. The *esse* of the presentation while it is being perceived *is* its *percipi*. The *esse* of the office table in the dark night when no one is aware of it, though it is not perceived, yet has to be thought of *as if* it were perceived. If the reader is pleased to call this invariable correlation between existence and perception a dependence of one on the other I have no objection. It is a matter of words only. Personally, though I shall speak of the independent external world in the sense explained in the last paragraph, I shall not otherwise use the concepts of dependence and independence, having, in fact, no use for them.

CHAPTER VI
THE CONSTRUCTION OF THE EXTERNAL WORLD

OUR thesis is that belief in an independent external world is a mental construction. What is meant by a mental construction, what its logical characters are, will appear in due course. For the moment we must consider how our thesis can be justified. Its justification can only consist in the following two steps:

(1) It must be shown that our belief in an independent world is not given to us immediately in experience; that it is not an inference from anything which is immediately given in experience; and that to explain it as an instinctive or primitive belief is merely to admit defeat in our attempt to provide a rational explanation and justification of it. If these statements are admitted, it would seem to follow that only one other explanation is possible, namely that the belief is a mental construction. Or at least it will follow that such a suggestion is one which must be explored, and that if it is not accepted, the onus of suggesting some other explanation and justification will be upon those who dispute it.

(2) It must be shown how the mind could have set about constructing the belief, what steps it has taken in doing so, and why it has taken these steps. In other words, it is not enough merely to suggest that the belief must be a mental construction, but the details of the construction must be actually exhibited to the reader and shown to be plausible.

The propositions set forth under (1) have already been discussed, and I think proved, in the preceding chapter. We shall return to them again from time to time, and do what is possible to make them still clearer. But it is with (2) that we shall be chiefly engaged in this chapter. We shall attempt to exhibit the actual steps of the construction. But two remarks fall to be made by way of preface to this attempt.

Firstly, we must remind ourselves of a point which has already been made. The mental development which we are about to witness is primarily a logical development, but must nevertheless, according to our view, stand in some real relation to the actual history of mind. Our primary question will be, *how* can the solitary mind, shut up within its world of private phantasms, come to a knowledge of the solid permanent external world? How can it logically pass to that end? What is the logical justification of its belief? There never can be any logical passage, if by logical passage we mean inference. There is no evidence whatever to convince the solitary mind of the existence of the public world. Not only is there no demonstrative proof, but there is not even the faintest trace of probable reasoning. We shall conclude that the belief is a construction of the mind itself. And our main business will be to exhibit the logical order of the steps of this construction.

But it is also our view that the construction must actually have taken place in history, and indeed that it must take place anew in each individual mind. As to the first point, we surmise that somewhere in the history of life on the planet there must have been a time when the rudimentary minds of living organisms did not realize the existence of an external world, and that belief in it must have slowly evolved. Will it be asserted that the Cambrian trilobite possessed it? Or even that the present-day lobster does so? Must not the world of the trilobite have been something like that which we have described as the world of the solitary mind, only even more rudimentary in being less clearly realized than the picture we have drawn of it? Can it be supposed that rudimentary forms of animal life realize that the green patch which represents a tree to them to-day is the *same* as yesterday's green patch, and has gone on existing between whiles? Can we be sure that even the intelligent dog which is our companion can distinguish its dreams (i.e. its private world) from public reality? Be it far from me to dogmatize about obscure and perhaps insoluble problems of animal psychology. Yet it seems implausible to suppose that belief in an independent external world came ready-made into the world with the first breathings of life. And if it did not, it must have been evolved. (Will those, by the way, who think that this belief is a 'primitive belief' tell us whether it descended suddenly, like a bolt from the blue, upon humanity, or if not, how, when, and why, it evolved?)

Thus belief in an external world must have had a beginning in the dim past. It must have had stages of development. There is, of course, no direct evidence of these stages. Unfortunately we have, except in a metaphorical sense, no fossil minds. We have to reconstruct the development. *Why should the stages not have been the logical steps which, as we are about to show, would naturally lead the mind to that end?*

Not that it is meant, of course, that the minds of our human or pre-human ancestors consciously went over the steps of the construction. That would be absurd, and would be crediting them with the minds of modern abstract philosophers. But the philosopher only makes explicit what is already implicit in the mind. And the historical construction of the external world was, of course, implicit or subconscious. There is nothing unusual in such implicit processes. In practical life we act, not realizing our own motives. Other people, more acute than we are, detect those hidden motives. And it is not unreasonable to say that we actually acted from those motives, that it was through them that we were led to our actions. In theoretical matters we grope our way towards our conclusions, not realizing the logical reasons which are driving us on. Politically, peoples grope their way towards liberty, not understanding the rational end towards which they are moving, nor the ideals which are unconsciously shaping their minds. It did need a Freud to see these plain everyday facts.

We must hold, moreover, not only that the human mind has in the past implicitly gone through the stages of the mental construction which we are about to set forth, but that each present-day individual must do so somehow in his infancy. Has the mind of the three-days-old child any recognition of the independence and externality of the world? Does it know that the light which it sees is the *same* light as other minds see, that it is public, that it was there before it was seen and will be there after? Even to debate these questions seriously would be absurd. How then does each of us come by these beliefs?

It is quite possible, in the first place, that there is some kind of hereditary tendency to believe.[1] This tendency, which may have been transmitted to us along millions of years, this potential belief, will spring into actuality unnoticed as we develop, as a result of the faintest suggestions from other minds. This tendency must have originated in the minds of our ancestors through their implicit construction of the beliefs. Partly this. And partly in each one of us individually as we grow up, some such surmising, some such logical reaching out and groping, some such mental construction as will be described in the following pages, must be gone through deep down in the dim regions of our unconscious selves.[2] Here too there are many analogies to correct us if we are inclined to think this unlikely. Must it not be believed that in growing up each of us learns to use his vision? We have to learn to interpret the sensations which we receive through our eyes, and to recognize objects. It is well known that this process involves subtle and elaborate inferences, and these clearly must be carried on implicitly and unconsciously in very early childhood. It is no more unlikely that the infant implicitly goes through the process of constructing the external world than that it goes through the elaborate intellectual processes involved in the interpretation of visual stimuli. Both processes alike are no doubt enormously helped out by heredity and the facility gained thereby.

---

[1] Cf. R. F. Rattray's paper 'An Outline of Genetic Psychology' in the July 1931 issue of *Philosophy*. He writes: 'There is a considerable accumulation of evidence ... that the ovum and spermatozoon carry over an epitome of the ancestral memories of the whole of their ancestors.'

[2] R. F. Rattray, *op. cit.*: 'In the depth of subconsciousness are all the infinitely multifarious and yet unified experiences of the ancestry.'

THE CONSTRUCTION OF THE EXTERNAL WORLD

Our second prefatory remark is that the account which will be given of the construction of the external world does not profess to be anything more than diagrammatic. To give a precise and detailed account of the intellectual processes involved in vision would probably prove a task surpassing the subtlety of the human mind. And it is the same here. It will only be possible for us to mark out the essential, the most important, considerations which have led the mind to the construction of the independent world. I think we can still trace out the main steps of the ascent, but no more. Moreover these steps must necessarily be set out here in serial order, whereas it may be that the mind actually makes them either in a different order or possibly takes several steps simultaneously. We can do no more than pick out the main points in the progress and exhibit them in the order which seems to be the most logical.

Let us emphasize once more the nature of the starting-point. It is not the given in general, a given common to many minds. Such a common given is part of the very construction which still lies ahead of us. It is *my* given and no other from which I must start. Or to use impersonal terms it is the private given of the solitary mind. That mind is not aware of the existence of other minds, since the existence of other minds is not given. Much less, then, can it be aware of the givens of other minds, or of a common given, or of any kind of public world.

Before the solitary mind there passes, as in a dream, a shifting, unsolid, phantasmagoria of colours, sounds, smells, and other sense-data. It ebbs and flows. It changes continually like a kaleidoscope. When a sense-datum repeats itself, the mind can note the resemblance and apply its concepts of the given. It recognizes red, and distinguishes it from green. It also distinguishes its own acts of thinking, conceiving, comparing, attending, from the passivity of its sense-data, and can rise thereby to the distinction between the I and the not-I. It does not call this not-I either 'inside' or 'outside' the mind, either 'mental' or 'non-mental', either 'dependent' or 'independent' on itself, either 'real' or 'unreal'. All such distinctions lie in the future, and are the result of the construction of the external world which we are about to study.

Let us suppose that a green book is placed before the eyes, is removed for a short while, and is then placed before the eyes again. The solitary mind perceives this, not of course as a book, but as a series of appearing and disappearing flat green patches. On its second appearance it notes the resemblance of green to green, and applies its concept of the given, 'green'. But it has no reason for actually identifying the first green patch with the second. It will suppose that a green patch came into existence and then ceased to exist, and that after a while *another* green patch came into existence. And it will suppose that both green patches ceased to exist as soon as they respectively disappeared from its own vision.

Beyond this stage the solitary mind can never get. It is essential to realize that, *unless at this stage of development there come upon the scene the phenomena of communication with other minds, consciousness will remain at the low level just depicted for ever.* The solitary mind can never by its own unaided efforts come to believe that what it senses persists when it is not being sensed. The concept of the external world is a social product, and could not have existed but for communication with other minds. Without such communication any further progress of knowledge is absolutely blocked.

It would seem then that our next step should be to explain how we become aware of other minds. And that would really be the most logical procedure. But it will be more convenient to avoid interrupting the course of our argument at this point by a discussion on that topic, and to leave it over to be dealt with in a later chapter. For the rest of this chapter I shall therefore *assume* that the solitary mind has somehow (in a manner to be later explained) become aware of the existence of other selves, and has got into communication with them.

The justification of this procedure is simple convenience.

THE CONSTRUCTION OF THE EXTERNAL WORLD

In reality our knowledge of an external world and of other selves are interdependent, and must have grown up together *pari passu*. But we have to follow each interwoven thread separately. It does not much matter in which order we take them. But I think it will render the understanding of our argument easier if we do not break off here to consider the source of our knowledge of other minds. Assuming, then, that the solitary mind has now got into communication with other minds, we will proceed to trace out its further development in a series of mental constructions.

First Construction.

That the presentations of one mind bear to the corresponding presentations of other minds the relation of resemblance.

Suppose that a green book is placed before two minds A and B. They both see a green patch at once, and they are able by means of words, or signs of any kind, to communicate and compare notes of their experiences. The first construction set out above means that the green patch of A resembles the green patch of B in the same way as two green patches in the same mind may resemble each other and give rise to the concept of the given 'green'. It is ordinarily assumed, when two or more minds are surveying the same scene, that they all see, hear, and smell similar colours, sounds, and odours. When you and I look at a tree we assume that the tree which you see is like the tree which I see, and so on.

It will be carefully noted that it is not stated in this construction that the minds A and B see the *same* green patch, but only that they see two *similar* green patches. That these two green patches are numerically identical is a later idea which requires for its establishment a separate construction.

Now the fact that a common world has in fact been established, and that we are all able to talk to each other *as if* our several presentations resemble each other, does not prove that they in fact do so. All it proves is that between the series of presentations of one mind and that of another there is a correspondence of order or relation. In order to see this let us take a specific case. Suppose that minds A and B are both looking at the same green book at the same time. Suppose further that the book is then opened at a blank white page, is then closed again, and is finally removed altogether from the field of vision and replaced by a red book. This gives the series of presentations green, white, green, red. A and B now compare notes. The first presentation A calls 'green'. B notes the word and applies it to his first presentation, *whatever that presentation may have been and whether it resembled A's first presentation or not*. They then agree that whenever the presentation which appeared before them reappears they will call it 'green'. The same with the rest of the series, white, green, red. Provided that whenever A receives the presentation which *he* calls green B receives the presentation which *he* calls green, and similarly with all other presentations, they will then always agree in their descriptions of what they sense, whether the presentations of A actually resemble the presentations of B or not. Provided the order and relations of the two series of presentations agree in two minds, they will be able to communicate with one another, to discuss and compare experiences, and to build up a common world. That they do so, therefore, does not prove that the content of the presentations which they receive resemble each other in any way whatever.

Nor is there any other way of proving this fact. How can I possibly know that my red resembles your red, or that any sensation of mine resembles any sensation of yours? Obviously there is only one way in which it could be proved, and that would be by comparing our sensations, e.g. my red with your red. But who is to perform this act of comparison? I can never see your red and you can never see mine. And a third party who might be impartial can see neither. It is clearly the same with all our experiences. I cannot feel the pain in your leg, and whether what you call pain is in any way similar to what I call pain I have no means of knowing. There is therefore no possibility of proving the similarity of our presentations. It is not an inference which follows from any of the data with which we started. Not only is it not demonstrable. It is not even a probable conclusion. It is not an inference of any kind.

I have no positive assurance that my red is not your blue, or that what is colour to me does not make on your mind an impression similar to my impression of sound. I have no positive assurance even that our two sets of presentations are in any way commensurable. Your presentations may be wholly inconceivable to me, and such as do not exist in my universe at all. It is a common reflection that we cannot conceive a new colour, a colour unlike any colour in the spectrum. It is quite possible that the whole of your presentations are as inconceivable to me as is a new colour. Even if this is so, it would not be a bar to communication and to the establishment between us of a common world, so long as our presentations, though dissimilar in content, *correspond* in order and relations.

One way of interpreting these facts would be to argue that as the resemblance of the presentations of different minds is irrelevant to the establishment of a common world, we might leave it out of our construction altogether. We might dismiss it as not being part of the concept of a public world which we are endeavouring to build up. But this would be a mistake for two reasons.

In the first place, although it may be possible to conceive the common world without including the idea of the resemblance with which we are dealing, yet this is not the ordinary conception. It would be a highly unusual and sophisticated conception which would not occur to any one except a philosopher. Now we are not at present trying to exhibit the construction of philosophical ideas. That can be found in histories of philosophy. We are attempting to exhibit the construction, which has gone on perhaps for millions of years, of the ordinary human being's naïve realism, his belief in an independent world which goes on existing when he is not aware of it, and which exists for other people besides himself. And this naïve realism certainly does include the conception that the presentations of different minds resemble one another. The plain man takes it for granted that, when he sees a green object, another mind looking at the same object will receive a precisely similar green presentation. He will admit colour blindness as giving rise to exceptional cases, but this very exception, he will think, will prove the rule. (Colour blindness actually proves nothing, of course, except that, where it exists, there is a certain lack of full correspondence of relations between the presentations of the minds which differ.)

There is, moreover, a second reason why this first construction cannot be left out. Our second construction, it will be found, carries the mind a step farther. It will assert, not merely that the two presentations which A and B receive when they look together at the green book are similar, but that they are numerically identical. Now they cannot be identical if they are dissimilar. If we are later to identify them, we cannot now admit that they do not even resemble each other. And from this point of view it will be seen that our first construction is a necessary part of the general process of constructing an independent public world.

This conclusion too could be avoided by the expedient of asserting that when A and B look at the same book, they see *two* presentations of one object, i.e. that what we have to identify is, not the presentations, but the objects of which they are representative. And if so, of course, there is no necessity to hold that the presentations resemble each other. But the idea that there exists one 'object' behind the many presentations is itself a construction which will have to be made at a later stage. It will be found to depend upon the present construction and the series of constructions which follow. Therefore this present construction cannot be omitted.

We may proceed, then, with our construction. It is impossible to produce one tittle of evidence to show that your red resembles my red, or that in general the presentations of one mind resemble the presentations of any other mind. And yet the mind believes it to be true,

THE CONSTRUCTION OF THE EXTERNAL WORLD 105

and builds this belief into its conception of the public world. Since it is not given, and is not an inference from anything which is given, it must be a mental construction. And this means that the mind has simply *assumed* its truth, has invented it as a fiction which suits its purposes.

But this statement throws upon us the obligation of showing *what* the mind's purposes are. *Why* does the mind make this assumption? If we cannot show any natural probability that the mind would invent this idea, if we cannot show that it has good reason to do so, then it can hardly be said that we have rendered the construction plausible. But if we can prove that this assumption is exactly what we should expect the mind to make, that the mind has in fact good reason to make it, then we shall have done all that is possible towards rendering it probable that such has actually been the mind's course.

What reason, then, has the mind to take this step? The reason seems fairly obvious. As far as the evidence goes, the mind has before it two alternative beliefs, either of which it may adopt. When minds A and B are looking at the green book they may believe either (1) that their two presentations are similar, or (2) that they are dissimilar and even incommensurable. *Neither of these beliefs has any evidence whatever either for or against it.* The mind is entirely free to adopt whichever it pleases. Which will it adopt, and why? Will it not naturally adopt the *simpler*? And is it not clear that if the society of minds adopts the view that every mind has its own peculiar presentations unlike those of every other mind, this will lead to an enormously complicated universe? A perfectly unnecessary complication. To adopt the belief that the presentations of different minds resemble each other will be a great simplification of our picture of the universe. This view is chosen, then, because it is a simplification, and for no other reason.

This is our first example of what we shall later call *alternative truths*. A free choice between two equally unprovable assumptions frequently presents itself to the mind. We shall hold that in such cases both of the rival assumptions are equally 'true'. They are alternative truths. They are alternative paths each of which would have been equally legitimate for knowledge to have taken. But that one has actually been built into the fabric of human knowledge which presents the advantage of greater simplicity and economy of thought. Many examples will come before us. One of these may be mentioned briefly now, though its full significance must be left to be expounded on a later page. The choice between Euclidean and non-Euclidean geometries is on precisely the same footing as the choice between the beliefs that the corresponding presentations of different minds resemble each other, and that they do not resemble each other. But the mind has for most ordinary purposes chosen Euclidean geometry solely because for those purposes it is simpler. And when, as in relativity mechanics, non-Euclidean geometry is chosen, that choice also has been made purely because, for the particular purposes in view, that geometry is simpler. So it is here. And I have mentioned the example of geometry here in order to sow thus early in the reader's mind the seeds of the following thought. The principles which govern the mind's procedure in the most advanced science will be found even here too in the lowest and humblest kind of knowledge, viz. that which we receive through our senses in the perception of the ordinary objects of the external world. Knowledge is of a piece all through, and shows everywhere the same characters and processes. Just as the geometer may choose any geometry he pleases, so the mind *might* have chosen the path indicated by the assumption that the presentations of different minds bear no resemblance to each other. We might all have believed that. But knowledge has actually chosen the other path for the reason given.

It will repay us to consider at this point what *meaning* can be attached to the fiction which the mind has constructed for itself, and in what form of proposition that meaning will naturally express itself to the mind at the level of development which we have now reached. More precisely, what can it *mean* to assert that my red resembles your red? I understand at once what is meant by asserting that two reds, both of which are within my own experience, are similar. I compare them by looking from one to the other, and I then find this resemblance given. *And to say that any two things are similar seems to depend for its meaning on the possibility of their being compared.* But where any comparison between two things is impossible and inconceivable, has it any meaning to say that they are similar?

My red and your red exist in different universes which are absolutely cut off from one another. The consciousness of each of us is a separate world. Not only is a comparison of our experiences in fact impossible, but it is difficult even to find any self-consistent meaning which can be attached to the idea of such a comparison. It is not merely a physical impossibility for me to see your red. If that were all, the difficulty might conceivably be some day overcome by the advance of psychological science. But the difficulty is a logical one. If I could see your red, your red would have become mine and, in so far as I saw it, ceased to be yours, and therefore the conditions of the comparison would have vanished. Or to put it in another way. Suppose that I could annihilate the barriers of personality and get into your mind and see your red. Yet it is still *I* who see it. And how do I know then that the red which I see is the same as the red which you see? I cannot know this so long as I remain I. In order to know it I must cease to be I and become you. But if my personality and yours are thus fused into one, then there are no longer two experiences to compare, and no relation of resemblance can be asserted.

The difficulty of finding an intelligible meaning for our first construction is thus very great. And such a meaning *cannot* be found so long as we attempt to express it in the form of a categorical judgement. So far, the solitary mind has made only categorical judgements. It has asserted 'This is red', 'This red is like (or unlike) that red', 'Red is different from green', and so on. But as soon as the mind enters upon its career of mental constructions a new form of judgement becomes necessary to express its new insights. It has to *invent* the hypothetical judgement. Let us see how this is.

To say that any two things, even when they are both within my own experience, are similar, implies either that a comparison has been made or at least that it might be, and that *if* it were made the alleged resemblance would be seen. '*A* is like *B*' means either '*A* and *B* have been compared and found alike', or it means 'If we compared *A* and *B* we should find them alike'. An assertion of similarity is necessarily relative to a possible act of comparison. Hence 'My red is like your red' means '*If* we could compare our reds we should find them similar'.

The condition, as we have seen, is actually an impossibility. We could not conceivably compare our reds. But the mind does not boggle at this difficulty. It swallows it because it suits its purposes to do so, because unless it does so, it will never be able to build up a common world and a society of minds. We shall find that this is a characteristic, not only of this particular mental construction, but of all those mental constructions which have the character of creating or positing new existences.

We may bring this truth into relation with our previous conclusions by expressing it in another way. To the mind at its present stage, it must be remembered, the *esse* of the given is identical with its *percipi*. An *esse* apart from a *percipi* will be, up to date, inconceivable to it. Now resemblance is one of the concepts of the given, or in other words the resemblance of presentations to one another is, for the solitary mind, a *perceived* relation. Its *esse* will, of course, therefore be its *percipi*. But what has now been asserted by the mind, in this its first construction, is the existence of a relation of resemblance which is not, and cannot be, perceived. I *see* that the two red patches now opposite my eyes are alike. This is a direct act of perception. But if I affirm that my red patch resembles your red patch, this is to assert the existence of a resemblance which no mind in the universe can ever perceive. This assertion of an unperceived existence, even though it be of a relation and not of a presentation, is implied by our first construction, and is already a transcendence of our old point of view that *esse* and *percipi* are identical.

But how will the mind conceive this new *esse* which is not *percipi*? It cannot break with its past. No sudden and violent *volte face* is possible. For it, existence *is* being perceived. The new kind of existence cannot be out of all relation to the old. It may be an extension of the old, but it cannot contradict it. Now an existence which has no connexion with perception would completely contradict the fundamental notion of existence which the mind has already formed. It would not *be* existence, but something totally different. Hence the mind will express its new point of view in terms of the old. Its new *esse* must still be at least relative to *percipi*. And this means that its new *esse*, though not expressed in terms of an actual *percipi*, will be expressed in terms of a *possible* one. So that now and hereafter when the mind affirms that anything exists unperceived, what it affirms is that '*If* . . ., then such an existence would be perceived'.

This, of course, will be disputed by those who still cling to the preconceptions and prejudices of realism. They will assert that the affirmation of an unperceived existence is categorical, not hypothetical. And if the reasonings which I have adduced in the last chapter have not prevailed against those preconceptions, I am not aware that I can do anything further to prove my point. The essentials of our contention may, however, be shortly recapitulated. The initial state of the mind is necessarily solipsistic. The solipsistic or, as we have called it, the solitary mind has no reason whatever to believe in an unperceived existence. Until it gets into communication with other minds, it has no reason to think that its red patch exists when it is unperceived by itself, nor, of course, that any resemblance exists unperceived between its own presentation and that of another mind. Its *esse* is therefore identical with its *percipi*. Even when it gets into touch with other minds, it still never perceives an unperceived existence, nor can it ever infer such an existence from anything which it does perceive. But there are reasons, namely the necessity of developing its systematic communication with other minds, which force it to invent such an existence. This existence, e.g. the relation of resemblance which we are now considering, is not something that is *factual* or 'actually there'. It is merely supposed or hypothetical, and can be expressed only in the hypothetical form '*If* . . ., then it would be perceived'. This follows inevitably from the position that belief in an unperceived existence is a construction. For a construction *is* a supposal. Hence the only way in which our view that all existence is relative to an actual or possible perception can be escaped is by showing that unperceived existence is *not* a construction. And the only way of showing that would be to show that it is either an actual perception or an inference from an actual perception. That an unperceived existence could be perceived is an absurdity. And that it could be inferred from anything that is perceived will be admitted by every competent philosopher to be impossible. Hence our view seems the only feasible one.

In making the assumption of the similarity of the presentations of different minds, the primitive mind is performing a new kind of operation, something quite different from mere awareness of the given, from the concepts of the given, or from any possible inference therefrom. This new operation consists essentially in extending the given in imagination into a region in which nothing is given. It consists in imagining a given where there is none. It is essentially an act of imagination. I see two red patches within my own experience and I note the resemblance between them. This resemblance is itself something given. Taking this experience of a given resemblance as a model, the mind now *imagines* a similar experience where in fact no such experience either is or could be, namely between the presentations of two different minds.

The belief in the similarity of the experiences of different minds is the first of a long series of assumptions which the mind makes on its way to knowledge, the first of its mental constructions. And we shall find that the

THE CONSTRUCTION OF THE EXTERNAL WORLD

characters of this mental construction frequently repeat themselves. These characters are as follows:

(1) The belief which is constructed is such that it can never be either proved or disproved, nor can there ever be any the slightest evidence for or against it. It is pure assumption.

(2) The assumption cannot be given a categorical meaning. It has to be expressed in the form of a hypothetical proposition. If a categorical proposition is used to express it, such a proposition is merely elliptical.

(3) The antecedent clause of the hypothetical proposition expresses an impossible condition, that is, a condition which could not actually exist, but is only a supposal.

(4) The whole mental construction is a work of the imagination which supposes its experience extended into the void where there is in fact no experience. The construction is used to fill up gaps and voids in the given.

(5) The mind creates nothing new. Imagination uses always materials already supplied by the given.

Second Construction.

That the corresponding presentations of different minds are identical, and that there are not many universes, but only one.

Nothing, perhaps would appear so self-evident to the ordinary unphilosophic man as that there is but one universe, and that when he and his friend sit at the dinner table there is before them a single common table, not a separate table for each mind. And yet a little reflection reveals that it is rather the opposite principle which is really self-evident, namely that there exist as many universes as there exist minds. Your red presentation is not my red presentation. We have seen that there is no evidence that they even resemble one another. Much less, then, are they identical. When we both look at what we afterwards regard as one object, say a green book, a green patch is present to your mind, and another green patch is present to mine. There are two, not one. And when a thousand minds are observing the book, there will then exist a thousand green patches. Each mind has its own world which is separate and absolutely cut off from all others.

Now suppose that the minds *A* and *B* observe together the same series of events, say the appearance of the green book, its being opened at a white page, its being closed again, and finally its being replaced by a red book. The series of presentations then is (neglecting questions of size, shape, &c.) green, white, green, red. *A* and *B* compare notes, and they find that two precisely similar series of experiences have been presented to them. Whatever has happened in *A*'s world has had an exact counterpart in *B*'s world. There are still, of course, two separate worlds. But they run parallel courses, so that whatever happens in one happens in the other also.

A and *B* are like two people sitting in two cinema houses watching two cinema shows. The houses are quite separate from one another. It is impossible to see from one into the other. *A* cannot see *B*'s film, nor can *B* see *A*'s. But they discover that they can shout to each other through the thin walls which separate them and describe to each other the films which they are seeing. When they do so, they find that the films are similar. When a castle appears in one, a castle appears in the same situation in the other. When the heroine faints in one, the heroine faints in the other likewise.

As a matter of fact this description of affairs is not accurate. For there not only appear similarities between the two films but also divergencies. A penny which the hero is presenting to the heroine looks circular in one film but elliptical in the other. And not only this. Sometimes the films diverge altogether. *A* sees in front of him a landscape, while *B* is looking at a seascape. And so on.

These differences are at first ignored, to become later the bases of important modifications in the world which is being built up. *A* and *B*, it must be remembered, are primitive minds each of whom has only just made the discovery that another mind exists. What they seize upon, both as striking in itself and as useful to them, is the *agreement* which they find to exist between their two worlds.

This agreement forms the foundation stone of their future common world. Mere differences would lead them nowhere. If all the worlds of the various minds in existence were wholly different, with no features of agreement, why, then that would be an end of the matter; no common world could be built up; each mind would remain for ever in its private world. Hence it is the agreements on which A and B fasten as significant to them, ignoring the differences for the present.

A and B have discovered, by the first construction, the similarity, but not the identity, of their two worlds. But there are in truth not merely two minds in existence and in communication with one another. There are multitudes, $A, B, C, D, \ldots N$. And thus A and B and the other minds come to believe in the existence of multitudes of universes all alike and all running the same course.

But the multitudes of minds confronted by similar universes will inevitably come to talk, and later to think, *as if* there were only one. For this will present itself as an obvious labour-saving device, a simplification of thought and a convenience of conversation. When A and B both see a green patch, instead of talking about *my* green patch and *your* green patch, they will come to speak simply of *the* green patch. For there would appear to be no advantage in distinguishing them. And when it is remembered that there are not merely two, but millions of similar universes, this becomes more evident still. It will be excessively tiring to the mind to think of so many universes. To think of them all in terms of one universe, or *as if* there were only one, will be simpler and easier and will serve all purposes. So the belief in a single world becomes established, and the older view that there are many universes is forgotten. Like an organ which performs no function, it decays. The belief in one universe comes in the course of time to appear self-evident.

We have here, once more, an example of the principle of *alternative truths*. The mind is free to make its choice between belief in many universes or one. Both these beliefs would be 'true'. But one is simpler and more convenient for most of the mind's purposes than the other. And the simpler belief is chosen and embodied into the structure of human knowledge. But if there ever arises any purpose for which it is more desirable to adopt the hypothesis of a multiplicity of universes, that hypothesis will be adopted. The only purpose of this kind which, so far as I can see, is ever likely to arise, is in the writing of a philosophical treatise such as the present. For *our* purpose here—which I venture to say is as legitimately to be regarded as a normal human purpose as any other—it has proved essential to revert to the hypothesis of many universes. And the mind's procedure in all this is strictly analogous to its procedure in the higher regions of science, as for example in the matter of geometries.

The importance, appearing thus early in the history of knowledge, of the principles of simplification and economy of thought may appear to some to warrant a pragmatist theory of knowledge. It is too early as yet in the course of our inquiry to decide this issue. But I will, by way of anticipation, indicate the lines upon which I propose to proceed. The pragmatist would presumably hold that if two alternative hypotheses equally suit the facts, and if one is chosen solely because it is the simpler and more useful, that one alone is true and its rival false. This makes simplicity and utility constitutive of the truth. But I shall hold that the two alternatives are both equally true, though it may be that only one has been adopted into the system of human knowledge. The nature of truth is not determined by practical considerations, such considerations determining only which of two or more rival truths shall be selected for the practical or theoretical purposes we happen to have in view.

This second construction differs to some extent in logical characters from the first. There was no evidence either for or against the resemblance of corresponding presentations. The mind was absolutely unfettered by any kind of fact, and completely free in that sense. Here there is in a sense evidence *against* the view that is adopted, the view namely that there is only a single universe. For it is

THE CONSTRUCTION OF THE EXTERNAL WORLD

plain that *in fact* there are as many universes as there are minds. But the principle which is now adopted in justification of the second construction is that *facts or complexities of fact which can make no conceivable differences in the mind's outlook or in the accomplishment of its practical or theoretical purposes may be ignored and treated as if they were not facts.* When you and I look together at a green book, it may be a fact that there are two green presentations. But it will make no difference to anything in the universe (except perhaps to our epistemology, and for that we can make special provision as has been done here) if we talk and think *as if* there were only one common green patch. To do so will be much simpler and will facilitate the establishment of a common world and a society of minds. *Facts which have no conceivable bearing on anything are for the purposes of knowledge not facts.*

Nor is the second construction only expressible, like the first, in the form of a hypothetical proposition. We do not here suppose that something exists which is not and cannot be perceived. It is only in constructions which have that character that we are compelled to express them in the form 'If . . . , then we should perceive so and so'. In the present case we adopt a precisely opposite principle. We suppose that something which *is* perceived does *not* exist. The construction can therefore be expressed in the categorical form 'There *is* only one universe'.

Nor is there, of course, any question of the extension by the imagination of something given into a void in which in fact nothing is given. That too characterizes only those constructions which suppose something to exist which cannot be perceived.

Nevertheless the second construction is a true construction. For it is a belief which the mind does not find in experience or the given, and does not infer from anything that is experienced. It is a pure assumption.

Finally we must not omit to note the close resemblance which knowledge bears even here in its most rudimentary forms to the forms which we find in the most advanced science. What is called the hypothetical character (or, as J prefer to call it, the *constructional* character) of scientific knowledge is now well recognized among men of science themselves. Here is a quotation from a recent writer taken almost at random. 'Whether the man of science regards his atoms as having an ultimate reality or not, does not affect the validity of the theory; the theory is just as useful in introducing order and promoting discovery if they are merely polite fictions as if they are desperate realities'.[1] This writer has not envisaged the one further step which has to be taken if we are to make this idea fruitful in epistemology, namely to recognize that 'polite fictions' may enter into the constitution of reality, and form part of 'truth'.

Third Construction.

That the presentations of a mind may continue in existence unperceived by that mind, provided that some other mind perceives them.

The second construction was founded upon the agreement which minds found to exist between their separate private worlds. But it was noted in passing that between the various worlds there is not only a general background of agreement, but also a number of specific differences. And it was noted that these differences would in due course have to be reckoned with. The third construction is based upon such a difference, and is an attempt to meet the difficulties which that difference places in the way of a mind which seeks to carry out consistently the view that there is only one universe.

Suppose that the green book is placed before A for one second, is then withdrawn from his sight for one second, and is then finally returned to his field of vision for one second. And suppose that throughout this three seconds the book has been continuously visible to B. How do A and B, on comparing notes, account for what has happened? It is still true that for each of them the *esse* of the green patch is identical with its *percipi*. No doubt in the first construction the idea of an unperceived existence was implied. But it was scarcely explicit, and it applied, in any

[1] *The Mechanism of Nature*, by E. N. de C. Andrade, p. 6.

THE CONSTRUCTION OF THE EXTERNAL WORLD

case, not to presentations, but only to the relations between them. The mind so far has certainly not had this new notion pointedly brought to its notice. And it may be assumed that it continues in the old habit of thought, at any rate as regards presentations. It thinks that a colour patch exists only while it is being perceived. So that when the experiment mentioned above is made A will think that a green patch came into existence for one second, and then ceased to exist; that a second elapsed in which no green patch was in existence; and that then *another* green patch came into existence for one second. But B will give a different account of the matter. He will say that a single green patch existed continuously for three seconds. When A and B compare notes this discrepancy is discovered, and especially that B observed the green patch during the interval between the two appearances to A.

This, clearly, is a difference between the two worlds. A and B have just decided that their two worlds are one. They concentrated on the agreement and ignored the differences. Now the difficulties in their theory begin to break out. The elements of difference refuse to be ignored. Yet if they are admitted they will cause the break-up of the new theory of a single universe. For that theory depended essentially upon the supposed fact that the two, or the many, universes run parallel courses. The developing mind, then, finds itself in a dilemma. Either it must give up its newly found single universe which it has in common with other minds and go back to its world of private phantasms, or it must somehow explain the difference between its own world and that of its fellow mind consistently with its theory of a single universe. Just as in a scientific theory, when a new fact appears which seems to contradict that theory, either the theory must be abandoned, or the new fact must be explained consistently with it. The developing mind, to meet this difficulty, invents a new construction, namely the third construction which we are now to consider.

The facts to be explained would have caused no difficulty if A and B had not identified their two worlds as one.

So long as A's universe was regarded as different from B's, the fact that a colour patch appeared in one when it did not appear in the other would require no special explanation. There would be no reason why the two universes should agree. But now that they are supposed to be identical, any differences will have to be explained. An obvious case of this sort has now arisen. A and B were looking at the green patch. It disappeared from one of their universes, but not from the other. It remained continuously present to B's mind even during the interval when A was not seeing it. By the second construction the two universes are one, and it is supposed to be the *same* green patch which both have been observing. If this view is to be retained, there is only one conclusion which A can come to. He will be compelled to think 'Since the green patch which appeared to B is identical with the one which appeared to me, and since it went on existing in B's mind after it had disappeared from mine, it follows that *my* green patch went on existing in B's mind when it was absent from mine'. And the general conclusion will be drawn that presentations of one mind may continue to exist unperceived by that mind so long as they are perceived by some other mind. This is the third construction.

It will also follow for A, of course, that the green patch which he sees in the third second is identical with the green patch which he saw in the first second, and that it has persisted in existence (in B's mind) across the blank interval between the first and third seconds. The former belief of A that the first and second appearances of the green patch were two different green patches is superseded. It will be noted that this conclusion is itself a subsidiary construction, although I have not thought it of sufficient importance to erect into a separate construction. Whether you believe that two successive appearances of a green patch (whether separated by an interval or not) are two or one is really a matter of choice. The mind may choose either alternative, and which it chooses is determined by nothing except convenience. It is a matter of perfect indifference whether I regard this typewriter on which I am now writing as *one* typewriter throughout the hour in which I am using it, or as a succession of sixty typewriters each lasting a minute, or as a succession of three thousand six hundred typewriters each lasting a second. There is no *meaning* in either the assertion of multiplicity or that of unity. There is no meaningful difference between the two ways of looking at the matter. We invariably choose to think of one single continuing typewriter or other object, instead of a succession of momentary ones, simply because it is more convenient, because it is a simplification, not because it is 'truer' or more in accordance with the facts. Both points of view would be equally true, being in fact alternative truths. In the same way, then, when A comes to believe that the two green patches, separated by a blank second, are *one*, this is in reality a construction which A is under no obligation to make, but which suits his convenience.

But the main construction with which we are here concerned is the new belief that a presentation may go on existing unperceived by the mind to which it originally appeared so long as *some* mind is perceiving it. This will at first sight seem very revolutionary and subversive of A's and B's previous settled views. It may even be denounced by the bishops of the primitive world as contrary to religion. For up till now the fundamental truth of A's and B's universe was that the *esse* of presentations is their *percipi*. This was settled doctrine. It was pristine self-evident truth. It was a dogma which would have lasted for ever if only A and B had continued to regard their universes as separate. But now, because they have come to think of them as one, they are compelled to admit this new and revolutionary construction.

They will not, of course, admit as yet that a presentation may exist unperceived by any mind at all. They have had no reason to go so far as that. That will come later. But for the present the mind, while admitting that its presentations may continue unperceived by it, will still insist that they must be perceived by some other mind.

Esse is still in that way *percipi*, although that doctrine has received rather a strange twist.

For even this partial admission of an unperceived existence is plainly a paradox. The existence of *my* presentation obviously consists in the fact that it is presented to *me*, i.e. that *I* am aware of it. And to say that it goes on existing while I am not aware of it is like saying that it goes on existing after it has gone out of existence. But either *A* and *B* must swallow this paradox, or they must give up their common world. They cannot have it both ways. Faced with this dilemma they decide to swallow the paradox. They will not give up their common world. The convenience which it introduces into thought and action is too great to be sacrificed. And it is not unreasonable to suppose also that, having found companionship with each other, they fear the sense of loneliness and isolation which would result from their going back to their separate self-enclosed universes. So they accept the view that presentations go on existing when one is not aware of them so long as they exist in some one else's mind.

The first two constructions were adopted by the mind because they simplified its view of the world. The third construction is not made directly for this reason, but because it is forced upon the mind by the previous two. Having accepted the belief that there is only one universe, the mind cannot without self-contradiction hold out against the opinion that my green patch goes on existing in your mind even when I am not aware of it. Thus whereas the motive of the first two constructions was economy and simplicity, the motive of this third construction is consistency. This is frequently illustrated in the history of the development of knowledge. Having accepted one construction we are then compelled to create another in order to avoid a breach of the laws of logic. It is in this way that inference and logic in general perform their chief function in the world of thought, i.e. by ensuring that our various mental constructions do not contradict one another. This is also true in the history of science.

The logical characteristics of the third construction

THE CONSTRUCTION OF THE EXTERNAL WORLD 121

may now be noted. In the first place it is obvious that it cannot be proved. It is a pure assumption. The identity of the table which I see now with the table which you may see to-morrow when I am not here cannot be perceived, nor inferred from anything which is perceived. There is nothing to compel the mind to accept the third construction, except that it is necessitated by the previous construction which asserted the identity of the many private worlds. No doubt it may be regarded as an inference from that. But as that construction was itself an unprovable assumption, the same character descends upon its present logical consequent.

The third construction may be viewed as consisting of the following steps. Suppose we call A's green patch during the first second a, B's green patch during the first second b, and B's green patch during the following second (in which no green patch is present to A's consciousness) b'. Then by the second construction

$$a = b.$$

And by the subsidiary construction mentioned above (by which the successive momentary existences of a presentation are identified with one another)

$$b = b'$$

Therefore $\quad a = b',$

or in other words A's presentation during the first second is identified with B's presentation during the subsequent second when no green patch is present to A's consciousness. And this is the third construction.

It will be seen, then, that the third construction only advances beyond the second by adding to it the subsidiary construction. The logical characters of the second construction have already been described, and it remains only to consider those of the subsidiary construction. According to this the successive momentary existences of a presentation are identified with one another. And as already stated, the mind is perfectly free to accept this construction or not as it likes. It makes no difference *to the facts* whether you call a presentation which continues over two seconds one presentation or two or a thousand. It would be just as 'true' to regard it as a thousand as to regard it as one. The two or more ways of looking at the matter would constitute so many alternative truths. Each such alternative truth is merely a 'point of view' which the mind chooses to adopt. And it adopts the point of view set out in the subsidiary construction solely because it is the simplest and most convenient.

The subsidiary construction and the third construction do not, like the first construction, posit any new existence. By the first construction it was held that there exists a relation of resemblance between the presentations of different minds, which resemblance is not and cannot be either perceived or inferred. This was therefore the invention of a new existence which the mind assumed to suit its own purposes. And it had therefore the peculiarity that it was accurately expressible only in a hypothetical form. These peculiarities do not appear in the third construction because no new existence is there posited. All that is done by it is to identify two actually perceived presentations. This, of course, implies and stands upon the shoulders of the first construction. It implies an unperceived resemblance between the presentations which are identified, and the assertion of such a resemblance of course possesses the characters of the first construction. But these must obviously be credited to the first construction, not to the third. In so far as the third advances beyond the first it does not possess them. It possesses only characters similar to those of the second construction. It is expressible in a categorical judgement. But it is a true construction in that the content of that judgement is neither perceived nor inferred, but is invented by the mind.

Fourth Construction.

That presentations may exist when no mind is aware of them.

The next stage in the mind's creation of an external world is obviously that *A* should come to believe, not merely that his presentations may continue to exist unperceived by him, so long as *B* perceives them, but that they may continue to exist when no one at all perceives them. The human mind has *now* come to believe (I am speaking, not of philosophers, but of the naïve realism of the unreflecting) that green patches and the like exist in the world unperceived by any mind whatever. But there is a gap here which cannot be bridged by any evidence. How do I know that the desk in my office continued existing when I left it behind to-day and went out for a walk? I know it because during that period another member of my family stayed in the room and saw it there. This is precisely the case which is provided for by the third construction by which I believe that my presentation of the desk goes on existing in the mind of another person even when it is absent from my mind. But how do I know that the desk continued in existence when *no one* was in any way aware of it? The answer is that there cannot possibly, in the nature of things, be any evidence of this. There is evidence that things go on existing so long as *some one* perceives them, provided we assume that different people perceive the *same* things. But when *no one* is perceiving a thing, it is clear that no one can give evidence of its existence, and that there cannot be any such evidence. There is not, never has been, and never will be an iota of evidence that the universe or anything in it goes on existing when no mind perceives it or that it existed before there were any minds to perceive it. The belief must therefore be, according to our view, a mental construction.

What other view are we to take of it? That it is a 'primitive belief'? But that is merely to call it a prejudice. 'Belief in the existence of things outside my own biography', says Mr. Russell, 'must from the standpoint of theoretical logic be regarded as a prejudice, not as a well-grounded theory.'[1] When an eminent realist writer says this of his own views, what need have we of further witness?

And yet we must hold that we can do knowledge a better service than calling its foundations prejudices as

[1] *Analysis of Mind*, p. 133.

realists do. We can show that they are mental constructions, and that mental constructions *are* 'well-grounded theories', having their own logical structure and justification, which we shall study in due course.

One of the writers in that famous American manifesto *The New Realism* inveighed against the fallacy of arguing from the fact that it is impossible to find anything which is not known to the conclusion that all things are known. 'The falsity ... lies in its being a use of the method of agreement unsupported by the method of difference. It is impossible to argue from the fact that everything one finds is known to the conclusion that knowing is a universal condition of being, because it is impossible to find non-things which are not known.'[1] But the 'fallacy' of this is surely obvious. It consists in placing the onus of proof on the wrong side. Since we never find anything which is not perceived, we say that there is therefore no evidence that anything exists unperceived. And since there is no evidence there is no reason why I should believe it unless you prove it. It is up to the realist to prove that things exist unperceived if he asserts that they do so. The burden of proof is on him, and by the express admission of one of his own most eminent philosophers he cannot discharge it except by introducing a prejudice. The realist argument just quoted simply points out that the fact that no unperceived existence can ever be perceived does not prove that no unperceived existence exists. Of course it doesn't. But that is not the point. The point is that no one, realist or not, can prove that they *do* exist, and that therefore there is not the slightest reason to believe that they do. Therefore the belief that they exist must (unless we assert that it is a miraculous revelation, which, although it is inherently unphilosophical, unscientific, and absurd, is what the contentions of the realists in fact amount to) be a mental construction. You can take your choice between miraculous revelation and mental construction. As I have undertaken to follow reason to the end, and not to allow prejudices or miraculous revelations to be dragged

[1] *The New Realism*, p. 12.

THE CONSTRUCTION OF THE EXTERNAL WORLD 125

in when it happens to be convenient to our beliefs, I choose the second alternative. And I have no hesitation in claiming it as the only rational conclusion, and therefore as a certainty.

But a recent attempt to prove otherwise must be mentioned. Professor Lovejoy in his admirable book *The Revolt against Dualism* inquires what are the grounds on which can be rested our natural belief in realism. He thinks that it not mere 'animal faith'. He quite rightly traces back our belief in realism to our conviction that things go on existing during the intervals between our perceptions. And he proceeds: 'The starting-point of the argument for physical realism, I suggest, is the plain man's normal and reasonable belief that the processes of nature do not stop when he stops noticing them.'[1] And this belief is called a 'primary natural postulate'.[2] But it seems to me plain that 'the plain man's normal and reasonable belief'—the word 'reasonable' here is not justified and is clearly foisted in to bolster up the case—and 'primary natural postulate' are merely long and round-about phrases which really signify exactly the same thing as 'animal faith' or 'primitive belief'. It is plain that no *reason* is here given for our belief. Or what is given as the ground of our belief is simply the belief itself.

But Professor Lovejoy goes on more valiantly to an attempt to find reasons.

'The belief in the continuance of things or processes between perceptions', he says, 'is not a blank act of faith. . . . It may be said to be—not indeed rigorously verified—but strengthened by one of the most familiar of empirical facts—namely, that the same uniform causal sequences of natural events which may be observed within experience appear to go on in the same manner when not experienced. You build a fire in your grate of a certain quantity of coal, of a certain chemical composition. Whenever you remain in the room there occurs a typical succession of sensible phenomena according to an approximately regular schedule of clock-time; in, say, half an hour the coal is half consumed; at the end of the hour the grate contains only ashes. If you build a fire of the same quantity

---

[1] *The Revolt against Dualism*, pp. 267–8.   [2] Ibid., p. 268.

of the same material under the same conditions, leave the room, and return after any given time has elapsed, you get approximately the same sense-experiences as you would have had at the corresponding moment if you had remained in the room. You infer, therefore, that the fire has been burning as usual during your absence, and that being perceived is not a condition necessary for the occurrence of the process.'[1]

Our belief 'may be said to be—not indeed rigorously verified—but strengthened' by these considerations. These words indicate simply that the author feels the weakness of his case. He has to admit that his argument does not 'rigorously verify', i.e. in other words it does not prove its conclusion. But it is supposed somehow to strengthen it. We shall see that it does not.

The pith of the argument lies in the assertion that 'the same uniform causal sequences of natural events which may be observed within experience *appear*' (italics mine) 'to go on in the same manner when not experienced'. But the trouble is precisely that they do *not* appear. If they appeared they would be perceived. But that they are not perceived and do not appear is just why it is impossible to prove that they exist when not experienced. Thus if the word 'appear' is taken literally here the passage quoted merely makes an incorrect statement. But perhaps 'appear to go on' means simply 'seem to us to go on' or 'we think they go on'. In that case the argument gives no reason at all for our belief but merely states that belief over again. The argument then simply means 'we think, or it seems to us, that the same uniform causal sequences which may be observed within experience go on in the same manner when not experienced' which is certainly no argument at all.

It is plain that the whole of this reasoning is a *petitio principii*. You build a fire in your grate. If you stay in the room for an hour you get the series of experiences $a, b, c, d, e, f, g, h, i$. If you leave the room and return to it in half an hour you get the experience e. If you again leave the room and return to it in another quarter of an hour you get

[1] Ibid., p. 268.

the experience *g*. And so on. And you 'infer' that the terms *b, c, d*, &c., have occurred in your absence. But the only ground on which you can validly infer this is just your belief that things go on in your absence as if you were there. You cannot infer your conclusion from your belief in uniform causal sequences because your belief in uniform causal sequences plainly rests on belief in the general continuity of nature, i.e. the continued occurrence of events when you are not perceiving them. You must *first* come to believe in the continuance of the world when you are not perceiving it before you can come to believe in uniform sequences of causation when you are not perceiving them. Therefore the first of these beliefs cannot be inferred from the second.

We shall show, when we come to consider the category of causality, that it first originates within perceived experience. There are sufficient sequences *a—b* actually perceived to beget the conception of it. The existence of similar causal sequences *outside* actual perception is then assumed on exactly the same grounds as the existence of unperceived presentations is assumed, i.e. by a mental construction based upon the mind's necessity to simplify its world and economize its thought. The construction of the belief in causal sequences outside perception is in fact merely a particular case of the construction of the general belief in an independent external world.

The logical position is thus quite clear. You find causal sequences occurring while you are perceiving things. What right have you to believe that these sequences continue while you are not perceiving them? No argument exists to justify such an inference which would not *also* justify an inference from the general fact that you perceive objects to the conclusion that the objects exist while you are not perceiving them. And as there is admittedly no argument possible which would justify the latter conclusion, neither can any argument possibly justify the former. The truth is that you cannot by any logical acrobatics escape from the absolutely fundamental principle that no amount of perceiving things, whether they are objects, presentations, causal sequences, or anything else, can ever prove that anything exists unperceived. Professor Lovejoy's argument does not even 'strengthen'—much less 'rigorously verify'—the realist's conclusion. It is completely impotent. It is simply a fallacy. And we return, therefore, to the conclusion that all belief in unperceived existence must be, not an inference, but a mental construction.

It is true, of course, that Professor Lovejoy's argument, as well as that of the writer in *The New Realism*, is expressed in terms of objects, whereas the fourth construction which we are here considering is expressed in terms of presentations. But this clearly makes no difference. The philosopher has reflected that presentations such as green colour cannot, for various reasons, be regarded as belonging to the object when it is not being perceived. He therefore does not talk of presentations continuing in existence when no one is aware of them. He talks of objects. But the primitive mind, whose naïve realism we are here considering, has not got as far on the road of reflection as that. The savage presumably thinks that the trees are still green when no one is perceiving them, i.e. that all his presentations go on existing unperceived. But the philosopher's belief and the savage's belief are merely two different modes of expressing—each in a way suitable to his state of culture—the same fundamental conviction, namely, belief in the independence and continued existence of the external world when unperceived. The logic of the matter is unaltered either way. The principle is still the same, namely, that, as already stated, no amount of perceiving things, whether presentations, objects, or anything else, can ever prove that those things exist unperceived.

Taking it for granted without further argument, then, that belief in the existence of unperceived presentations *is* a construction, our next step must be, as in the cases of the previous constructions, to inquire *why* the mind creates this construction, and what leads it to do so. The general purport of the answer is clear. This construction is but a continuation of the mind's previous tendencies to simplification and economy of thought. The mind of A, we will suppose, has already gone so far as to construct the belief that its presentations continue to exist even when not perceived by itself, so long as some one else is perceiving them. This introduced a wholly new conception of existence. As a solitary mind, A was accustomed to think that the existence of everything was identical with appearance to itself. A left this point of view behind and came to think that his presentations might still exist in other minds though unperceived by himself. But if they can exist not only outside A's mind, but also outside B's, C's, D's ... N's minds, is it not possible to think of them as existing outside any mind at all? This thought will at first seem absurd and paradoxical. And there is, of course, no evidence to support it. But the paradox of believing that the presentation of a particular mind can go on existing when that mind is not perceiving it has already been accepted in the third construction. One may as well be hanged for a sheep as a lamb. And to extend this idea until it covers belief in presentations existing unperceived by *any* mind has obvious advantages. It results in great economy and simplification of thought-processes. Once it has flashed across the mind, it is seen that it is possible by means of it to explain the facts that forty green patches appear to forty different people at forty different times separated by time intervals by the simple theory of there being only one green patch in the outer world which goes on existing continuously even when unperceived.

This explanation would not be possible so long as the mind stuck to the view that presentations, to exist, must be perceived by some mind. For in that case there might be inconvenient breaks in the universe. A's green patch would continue to exist provided that B became aware of it before A closed his eyes. But if A closed his eyes first, before B became aware of the patch, then it would be impossible to hold that it was the *same* green patch which A and B saw. The green patch might be passed on like a ball from one mind to another, but there would always be the possibility of some one dropping the ball, in which case it would go ignominiously out of existence. A could pass on his green patch down the line $B, C, D \ldots N$. But suppose D happened to be asleep at the moment when C ceased to see it. D might perhaps wake up a few minutes later and see the green patch. But in that few minutes when *no one* was seeing it, it would be necessary to hold that it had gone out of existence, and therefore that D's green patch was not the same as C's, but a new one. And if by any chance all the minds in the universe happened to fall asleep at the same time it would be necessary for them to hold, when they woke up, that an entirely new universe had come into existence.

These results are inconvenient and make it plain to the mind that the view which it has adopted (the third construction) is only a half-way house, and that it must finish what it has begun. It has established with other minds a common world. It has abolished the multitude of universes in favour of one. This introduces a beautiful simplicity into its thought, which would otherwise be uselessly complicated, and it also renders society, the easy communication of mind with mind, possible. But this new simplicity and uniformity are incomplete. They depend on every one keeping awake and alert to see that things in the universe don't get lost and go out of existence. This is clearly unsatisfactory. It would be much better if the universe would go on of itself without some one having perpetually to watch it. From every point of view, therefore, the mind is impelled to adopt this fourth construction and to believe that the universe exists when no one is perceiving it. With this construction the independence of the external world is assured, though still further constructions are necessary before the ordinary naïve view of the world is complete. But we have before us already an independent external world, in that it is now existent whether any one is aware of it or not, and independently of any mind. Thus by a gradual and somewhat adventurous process, by means of dangerous and daring speculations, the self-enclosed solitary mind, for whom nothing existed except the fleeting phantasms of its own private

THE CONSTRUCTION OF THE EXTERNAL WORLD 131

world, has created for these phantasms an objectivity outside that world, thrust them forth into a strange, cold, mindless wilderness of an outer world, given them permanence and solidity, decreed that they shall have existed before mind itself was born and shall continue to exist after mind is dead. In this way that solid, permanent, everlasting universe was created by our minds.

The logical characteristics of the fourth construction are the same as those of the first. For, like the first construction, it creates in imagination a new existence, namely presentations during periods of time when no mind is aware of them, or, as we might say, unpresented presentations. These logical characters are the following:

(1) It is entirely unprovable, a pure assumption.

(2) It cannot be expressed in a categorical judgement, but only in a hypothetical judgement of which the antecedent clause is an impossible condition. For what categorical meaning can be attached to a statement that anything exists unperceived? We must remember that, for the solitary mind, *esse* is *percipi*. Even when the mind ceases to be solitary and has built up its common world, its conception of existence will not involve a complete break with the past. It must still think of existence as relative to perception. Existence is what is, or at least *might be*, perceived. Having regard to the fact that *esse* is originally *percipi*, the categorical assertion of an existence wholly out of relation to perception is equivalent to the assertion of an existence which does not exist. And this contradiction can only be avoided by the hypothetical form. To assert that anything exists unperceived can only mean that *if* the circumstances were suitable it would be perceived; it can only accurately be expressed in the form 'If . . . , it would be perceived'.

That the table exists when no one is aware of it means 'If some one were looking in the right direction, he would see the table'. That there exists a side of the moon which is turned away from the earth, and invisible to us, means that *if* one could travel out in space to beyond the moon, and *if* one could take up a suitable position for purposes of observation, one would see that side of the moon. That atoms exist means that *if* one could magnify sufficiently one would see atoms. This, of course, involves the view that it must be possible to imagine some kind of a model of anything which can reasonably be asserted to exist in the atomic world, a view which physicists are at the moment inclined to dispute. I shall discuss the issue in a later chapter. For the present I will only reiterate that it appears to me impossible to conceive any existence in a manner which does not involve the thought that in suitable circumstances that existence might be perceived. To assert that anything exists surely *means* that it can be perceived if one is in the proper position to perceive it.

(3) The 'if' clause in all these cases represents an impossible condition. It differs from such a proposition as 'If I look at the table, I *shall* see it'. This proposition refers to the future and it is possible that the condition may be carried out, i.e. I may look at the table in the future. And the future existence of the table, when I am looking at it, will be a perceived fact. But 'the table is *now* existing unperceived' means 'if some one were now looking at the table, he would see it'. But by hypothesis no one is now looking at the table, and therefore it is impossible that the condition 'if some one were *now* looking' should be fulfilled. Some one looking in the future will not be some one looking now, and no amount of looking in the future will ever satisfy the condition 'if some one were looking now'. Similarly if we suppose the physically impossible, namely that we shall some day have instruments of magnification sufficient to see atoms, that will show that atoms exist *then*, i.e. when they are seen. It cannot prove that they exist now. And this is the same as saying that the assertion 'atoms exist' is really a hypothetical proposition, the antecedent of which is an impossible condition, the proposition namely, 'if we were now looking through a sufficiently powerful microscope, we should see atoms'. The impossibility of the condition to which we are here referring is not, of course, the crude physical impossibility of making such a microscope, but the logical impossibility

of thinking at the same time both that we are looking and that we are not looking.

(4) The mental construction is a work of the imagination which extends actual experience into the void where no experience in fact exists. We merely imagine the green patch which we now see extended into the periods of time which are void of it in the sense that no one is perceiving the green patch during those periods.

(5) Clearly the mind creates nothing new. It uses the materials already supplied by sense. The table which we do not see is supposed to be exactly like the table which we do see. It is coloured, hard, square, &c. As we are so often reminded, atoms used to be thought of as being like tiny billiard balls. And even now, if we are right, they will have in the end to be thought of as in some way following sensuous patterns. But that is a disputed question which we must leave over to another chapter.

Fifth Construction.

That there exist 'things' or 'objects', which are not identical with presentations; and that the presentations are 'qualities' of the 'things'; and that the 'qualities' may change while the 'things' remain the same.

When a scientific theory is put forward, its function is to explain, or reduce to law and order, a set of facts. If it satisfactorily explains all the relevant facts known in connexion with the particular subject of the theory, it may be taken as a working hypothesis. If, later on, new facts become known which appear inconsistent with the theory, it must either be abandoned as false, or it must be modified in such a way as to bring it into conformity with the new facts.

Now one of the guiding insights of the present investigation is the conviction that knowledge must be all of one piece, that what characterizes the most advanced science will also often be found to characterize that elementary and everyday knowledge of common objects in the external world which even uneducated people possess. It has been the tacit practice both of philosophers and of men of science in the past to treat our everyday knowledge of the external world as something to be taken almost for granted, as something practically given to us *en bloc*, and as not having been subject to the same elaborate processes of inference, of the building, sifting, and testing of hypotheses, of criticism, of gradual development through continual adjustments to meet new facts, which have notoriously been the conditions of advance of scientific knowledge. *A priori* one might well have suspected that such a view of our everyday knowledge would be erroneous, and that there would be a continuity of method and epistemological character extending from the highest levels of knowledge throughout its lower strata right down to the bed-rock of our immediate sensations. And that this is true is one of the chief convictions which should emerge from our present investigations; in particular that what is known as the 'hypothetical', or, as I prefer to call it, the constructive, character of science extends also to our common perceptual knowledge of external things.

In the fifth construction, which we are about to examine, we have an example, precisely similar to those which are scattered broadcast throughout the fields of science, of a theory being modified to meet new facts which are inconsistent with it in its original form.

The primitive minds which met in communication with one another first noted the fact that their separate private worlds ran parallel to one another. We compared them to persons in separate rooms watching duplications of the same cinema film. This parallel character of the many private worlds was seized upon as a basis for the identification of the private worlds with one another, and their reduction to a single public world.

But there also appeared differences between the many private worlds. One kind of difference appeared when it was discovered that a presentation which existed both in your world and mine, and the two appearances of which we accordingly identified as *one* presentation, might persist in your world after it had vanished from mine. This discovery led to important modifications of the theory of

THE CONSTRUCTION OF THE EXTERNAL WORLD

the common world. It led to the belief that the common world is independent, that presentations can exist unperceived.

And now another set of differences forces itself upon the notice of the primitive minds and threatens once more to destroy their theory of the common world. It is discovered that when a number of minds are simultaneously looking at what they have decided to regard as the 'same' presentation, the private appearances to them of this presentation are in fact not exactly similar. There are slight differences which, in the enthusiasm of their discovery of the common world, had escaped notice. Suppose that they are all looking at the 'same' brown patch (which is what we afterwards come to describe as a penny). The sameness of its character as a brown patch to them all is what had first struck them. A more accurate comparison of notes reveals that it appears as a circle to A, as an ellipse to B, as a narrower ellipse to C, and as a thin band or rectangle to D. It is further discovered that to A it is so large that it occupies nearly the whole field of his vision, while to B it is much smaller, and to C and D it is so small as to appear a mere speck. (This we afterwards learn to explain by the fact that the various spectators are at varying distances from it. But that is a later story. What we have to concentrate on at the moment is the mere fact of difference.) Differences make their appearance not only in the visual world, but also in the worlds of touch, smell, taste, and hearing. The 'same' sound is very loud to A, but scarcely audible to B. And so on.

Now these facts are in flat contradiction to the theory of a common world which all the minds have accepted. For how can the 'same' brown patch be at the same time circular, elliptical in various degrees, and rectangular? How can it be several different sizes at once? How can the 'same' sound be both very loud and almost inaudible? A brown patch cannot be several inconsistent shapes at one and the same time. Contradictory characters cannot co-exist in the same presentations. And it looks therefore as if the whole theory of a common world will have to be abandoned unless it can be so modified as to meet the new facts. Can it be?

There is only one way in which it can be done. The same entity cannot be both the same and different. We must have one entity to bear the differences and another the identity. And this is the solution which the mind adopts. It invents the concept of the 'thing' which is supposed to support, or lie behind, the presentations. The presentations vary. They are different for each person. The 'thing' itself remains self-identical and without contradiction. The presentations become 'appearances' of the 'thing'. The circular, elliptical, and rectangular brown patches are regarded as so many appearances of one single 'object', the penny. This, as it seems, saves a nasty situation. The new conception is applied everywhere universally. The world is no longer made up of presentations, but is full of objects.

The conception is full of difficulties, but these are concealed from the primitive mind by the extreme vagueness with which it is held. *What* is the nature of the 'thing' which underlies the presentations of brownness, shininess, circularity, &c.? There is no reason for supposing it circular since some of its presentations are elliptical, nor elliptical since some of its presentations are circular. Moreover since circularity, ellipticity, and other shapes, are presentations, can any of them characterize what is by hypothesis different from any presentation? Can we attach any intelligible character to the 'thing' at all? Moreover, what is the relation of the 'thing' to the presentation? It is all very well to call the latter sometimes an 'aspect', sometimes an 'appearance', sometimes a 'quality'. But what do these words mean? What *is* an aspect, what an appearance, what a quality? And how are these conceptions related to the conception of the 'thing'?

These and many other difficulties there are, and the hopeless attempt to clarify and solve them has constituted no small part of the occupation in all ages of those philosophers who have failed to recognize that the conceptions which they are thus trying to make consistent do not represent real facts in the world at all, are not in their nature consistent and clear, but are no more than the makeshift devices of the primitive mind in its efforts to build up a common world. They are no more than essentially vague 'points of view' which that mind invented and adopted for its own ends.

But we are not here concerned with philosophers and their conceptions. We are concerned only with the primitive mind. And that mind cannot be expected to philosophize or think clearly. It holds the conception vaguely and confusedly without sense of its inherent difficulties. Or even if there are difficulties which are apparent to it, it will swallow them rather than adopt the only other alternative which is open to it, namely to give up its hardly found and newly cherished common world. For these reasons too *our* reconstruction of the concept cannot be too precise. It cannot rise to exact definitions, which are not only foreign to the primitive mind but impossible to supply in the nature of the case to a makeshift 'point of view'. We cannot say precisely how the presentation is to be conceived as related to the 'thing'. We cannot give a single clear answer to this question. Sometimes the presentation is conceived as an aspect, sometimes as an appearance, sometimes as a quality. Perhaps the view of it as a quality is the most characteristic of the primitive mind and the most generally employed. And for that reason only we have treated this construction as the construction of the 'thing' and its 'qualities'.

Just as the ether of space was invented without evidence of its existence because it was required to bear the undulations of light, so the 'object' is invented without evidence of its existence because it is required to bear the character of identity amid the changes among presentations.

As soon as this fifth construction has been created, it soon begins to appear that the theory of the 'object' possesses another advantage besides that which originally recommended it. The primary reason which led to its adoption was that when different minds were viewing simultaneously what they had decided to regard as the 'same' presentation, there were nevertheless differences between the appearances of it to different minds. Now not only is the same presentation thus different to different minds viewing it at the same time, but it is also different to the same mind viewing it at different times. The colour patches as we watch them change their colour, their shape, and their position. We watch a red patch turn gradually orange and then yellow. We watch a brown patch change before our eyes from circular to elliptical.

These changes seem to raise difficulties for the subsidiary construction by which it was decided to adopt the view that the successive momentary existences of a presentation are identical with one another and constitute 'one' presentation. There is no difficulty in this so long as the continuing presentation does not change its character. If the circular green patch remains circular and of the same shade of green, and does not move from its place, it is easy to regard its successive existences as existences of the 'same' presentation. But suppose the circular green patch gradually changes its colour, shape, and position. What warrant have we for regarding the whole series as 'one' presentation? If it is red and circular one instant, yellow and square the next instant, it obviously involves a contradiction to call the series the 'same' presentation. For how can a presentation, the essence of which is to be red, be the same as one the essence of which is to be yellow? And how can a square presentation be the same as a circular one?

The new concept of the 'thing' and its qualities has the advantage that it offers a ready solution of these difficulties. For now we can say that the 'thing' remains the same, while its qualities, which are the presentations, change. The leaf turns from green in the summer to yellow in the autumn. In spite of the change of colour we regard it as the 'same' leaf all through. But we could not do this if we had not invented the concept of 'thing' or 'object'. If presentations alone existed, then the green patch (which is the leaf in summer) is clearly *not* the same presentation as the yellow patch (which is the leaf in autumn). There would be two different leaves, not one. But by means of the concept of the 'thing' we circumvent this. It is true, we say, that the colour has changed. But the colour is not the thing itself. The colour is only a quality of the thing. Hence though the colour has changed, the thing itself has remained the same. Thus arises in general the important conception that *a thing may remain the same and self-identical while all its qualities change*. This is a construction which is convenient and simplifies our view of the world.

We will consider, lastly, the logical characters of the fifth construction.

(1) It possesses the essential character of all true mental constructions in that it cannot be proved true, is not derived from experience, but is simply invented by the mind to fill up a place in the mind's scheme of knowledge. It is obvious, in the first place, that the thing which lies behind the presentation cannot be sensed or directly experienced in any way. For if it could, it would itself be a presentation. Neither can it be inferred from the existence of presentations. Obviously any inference which would seek to pass from the perceptible world of presentations to an unseen and unknown world behind it must needs be a fallacy. It is idle to argue, for example, that presentations must have a cause outside themselves, and that this cause will be the 'thing'. For causation is a relation between things which we find in experience. In other words, it is a relation among presentations. When we say that a—b constitutes a causal series we mean that, granted the given conditions, this series is invariable in our actual perceptual experience. Experience warrants us in asserting that the causal relation subsists between our presentations among themselves. But this can give us not the slightest right to say that causes must exist *behind* presentations in a world which is never experienced at all.

It is clear, then, that the conception of the 'thing' is not inferred from anything which we experience, but is simply created by the mind as a fiction which gets it out of the logical difficulties into which it has fallen as a result of its belief in a common world. The object of the fiction is to give plausibility to the theory of the common world and to get rid of the contradictions which beset that theory when it is seen that it involves identifying a round with an elliptical coloured patch, or, in general terms, that it involves regarding mutually contradictory things as the 'same'.

(2) Constructions which assert the existence of anything take the hypothetical form. For such constructed existence is, of course, unperceived. And the mind's assertion therefore amounts to 'If . . . , we could perceive it'. Logically, this must also characterize the present construction. To affirm that an unperceived 'thing' exists behind our presentations can only mean, if we press it, that *if* we could get behind our presentations we should perceive it. It is true that such an idea is absurd and full of contradictions. If we could perceive the thing behind the presentations it would then itself become a presentation. It would therefore presumably require another 'thing' behind it. And this will lead to an infinite series. Moreover the conception of the possibility of perceiving things apart from their qualities is manifestly absurd, since the qualities of a thing are that by which alone it is possible to perceive it.

But, as already remarked, the whole conception of the 'thing' and its qualities leads to numerous logical difficulties, which have been a standing puzzle to philosophers who insisted on taking it seriously, but are lightly glossed over by the primitive mind which invented this makeshift idea. Nor need we trouble ourselves about this new contradiction. It is in the same boat with the old. The naïve mind holds the conception so vaguely that these difficulties simply do not appear to it. There are two different and inconsistent ways of looking at the matter. The primitive mind attempts to hold to *both* these ways, choosing whichever alternative happens to suit it at the moment. For we may, firstly, say that the thing is quite separate from its qualities, lying as it does behind them and supporting them. We adopt this point of view when we wish to explain how the same object can have contra-

THE CONSTRUCTION OF THE EXTERNAL WORLD

dictory qualities, e.g. how the penny can be both circular and elliptical at the same time. In order to explain this it is necessary to emphasize that the thing itself is something *different* from its presentations, so that it remains unaffected by the contradictory characters of the presentations. The difficulty about this point of view is that it leaves the thing itself absolutely without character and unknowable. It is a pure blank which we can never hope to reach, see, or understand. When this is pointed out, the primitive mind will veer round and adopt the following attitude. It will say that the presentations *are* the qualities of the thing itself, and that in knowing those qualities we are knowing the thing. The leaf is green, and soft, and shaped in such and such a way. When we know these characters, we know the leaf itself, for they are the characters *of* the leaf. When this point of view is adopted the difficulty which then arises is that it is no longer possible to explain the contradictory characters of things. For the separation between the thing and its presentations has been practically abolished, with the result that it is no longer possible to blame the presentations for the differences while preserving intact the sameness of the thing itself. If when we see the penny as circular we are getting knowledge of the real thing, the penny itself, then our neighbour who sees the penny as an ellipse must also be getting knowledge of it. It must therefore be both circular and elliptical at one and the same time. And this is precisely the contradiction which the whole idea of the 'thing' was supposed to avoid. Thus the primitive mind veers between these two contradictory points of view, adopting whichever is convenient at the moment, or confusing the two, and in any case failing to see the pitfalls and contradictions into which it is falling. This, I believe, is a fair description of the attitude of the average unreflecting man of to-day or of any period.

The logic of the matter cannot be pressed any further. The conception which the mind has invented to enable it to preserve its common world intact contains these contradictions immanent within itself. It is at bottom an inherently self-contradictory idea. Philosophers have spent their lives in writing volumes drawing out to their painful end all the aspects of these contradictions. But they can never be solved, because they are inherently there. They can never be solved except by understanding how they came there, by understanding that the concept of the thing and its qualities is a fiction invented by the mind for its own purposes, and invented without any great logical skill or philosophical insight. Because the mind which invented it was primitive, because the plain men's minds which still use it in their everyday thought to-day are primitive, for this reason these contradictions are there, and for no other reason. And to recognize this fact is the only possible solution of them.

Sixth Construction.

That with the different senses we may perceive the 'same' objects, and that the worlds of the different senses are, in general, identical with one another.

In front of me is a wall. I see it with my eyes, a yellow shiny surface, as it happens. I stretch out my hand and touch the wall. It feels hard and smooth. That the wall which I see and the wall which I feel are one and the same object is certainly part of the plain man's beliefs about the external world. And it is this belief which is asserted in the sixth construction. The construction refers, of course, to all the senses, not only to sight and touch. We think that the rose which we smell is identical with the rose which we see and touch. We suppose that the bell which we hear ringing is the same object as the bell which we see swinging from side to side. We may say, shortly, that we believe in the equivalence of the senses; and this equivalence is the essence of what is affirmed in the sixth construction.

This belief is very far from being self-evident. It is evident, on the contrary, that the facts, so far as they go, are against it. My visual percept of the wall is a shiny yellow patch. My tactile percept of it is a sense of resistence to my hand. Now a yellow patch cannot be identi-

THE CONSTRUCTION OF THE EXTERNAL WORLD 143

fied with a feel of resistance. The two do not bear even the faintest trace of resemblance to one another. When we identified my red with your red, we at least *supposed* that my red resembled yours and that, if any mind could perceive both, that mind would perceive the relation of resemblance between the two. But it is not possible to suppose that any mind could ever find a resemblance between a colour and a tactile percept. They have nothing in common except the formal fact of existence or being perceived. The scent of the rose, again, bears no resemblance to its visual appearance or its tactile character. The sound of the bell is totally unlike the look of the bell. The taste of a beaf-steak has nothing in common with its raw red colour.

The identity of the objects of the different senses with one another cannot therefore be perceived. And to suggest that it can be inferred would be idle. For if by the identity of the objects perceived we mean the identity of the actual percepts, e.g. the colour with the sound, the sound with the smell, and so forth, then clearly no inference from our percepts can establish what is plainly contrary to the percepts themselves. If, on the other hand, we mean by the identity of the objects the identity of the 'things' which underlie the presentations, then too no inference can be drawn. For, as we have already seen, no inference can pass from what we perceive to the supposed 'things' behind them. We cannot even infer the existence of the 'thing', much less its character of identity with some other thing. Hence it is plain that the belief in the equivalence of the senses, being neither perceived nor inferred, must be a mental construction. How then is this construction arrived at?

Suppose that we see an object having a sharp angle or point, say one of the prongs of a pair of scissors. We touch the point and we feel a pricking sensation. We move the pulp of the finger along one edge of the object, over the point, and down the other edge. This gives us a series of tactile and muscular sensations with a pricking sensation about the middle of the series. The acute angle which we see bears no resemblance whatever to the pricking sensation and the other tactile and muscular sensations which make up the tactile acute angle. The reader will remember that John Locke expressed the opinion that a man born blind, who knew by touch the difference between a cube and a sphere, could not, if he suddenly recovered his sight, tell by looking at them which was the cube and which the sphere. Since Locke's day this has frequently been verified experimentally in the cases of persons who have been born blind and were subsequently operated on for cataract.[1] This emphasizes the fact that the visual angle bears no resemblance to the tactile angle. The two have to become associated in experience before they can be identified.

Experience shows that these dissimilar percepts are correlated. It is found that *the one is invariably a sign of the possibility of the other*. Experience shows that whenever I see a sharp visual angle in an object I can, if I put out my hand, get the experience of the pricking sensation and the other tactile and muscular percepts which make up the tactile angle. Whenever I see a certain kind of red patch which I have come to interpret as a rose, I can, if I scent it with my nose, obtain the familiar odour. Whenever I see the kind of coloured surface which I have come to call a wall, I can, if I put out my hand, obtain the tactile sensation of resistance.

Thus the objects of one sense become associated with the corresponding objects of the other senses. This association goes no way towards proving their identity. But it leads the mind up to the point at which the construction of the identity occurs to it as a simplification.

This step would, however, never be taken if it were not for the previous construction of the 'thing' and its qualities. For it is clearly impossible to hold that a visual presentation is itself identical with a tactile presentation. The two, as we have seen, are wholly dissimilar and exist in different worlds. But when once the mind has come to believe that behind each presentation there exists an un-

[1] *The World of the Blind*, by Pierre Villey (English translation), p. 194.

THE CONSTRUCTION OF THE EXTERNAL WORLD

perceived 'thing', it then becomes possible to identify the 'thing' which lies behind the visual presentation with the 'thing' which lies behind the tactile presentation. There will then be no contradiction. It was seen to be contradictory to hold that the circular brown patch is identical with the elliptical brown patch. This contradiction was got rid of by attributing the identity to the 'thing' behind, while admitting the differences between the presentations. In just the same way it is now possible to identify the visual wall with the tactile wall by attributing the identity to the 'thing' behind them while still admitting that the visual percept is different from the tactile percept. If the same thing can, without contradiction, have two visual appearances, one circular and the other elliptical, why should not the same thing have two appearances, one visual and one tactile? Thus belief in the equivalence of the senses is made possible by the fifth construction, and is in fact no more than an extension of the same idea in a different field.

But it is not yet clear *why* the mind should adopt this construction. In reply to this question we must point once more to the general tendency of the mind to simplify its world and its thought by unifications wherever possible, and thus to reduce the number of objects with which it has to cope. We saw that the many private worlds of different minds were made to coalesce into one. So here, following the same tendency and the same motives of simplification and economy, the several separate worlds of the different senses are made to coalesce into one.

For without this construction we should each of us have to believe that he inhabits half a dozen different universes. There might be one visual world common to all minds, one tactile world common to all minds, and so forth. But the visual universe of us all would be different from the tactile and other universes. The universe of each sense would be wholly cut off from the others.

We could quite well do all our thinking and acting on this basis. It will make no difference whatever to either theory or practice whether we believe in the many worlds or in the one. If we retain the several worlds of the different senses, we shall still be able to correlate them. We shall still know that whenever we see a visual wall, we can at will feel a tactile wall by reaching out the hand. But just because it makes no difference which view the mind adopts, just because they may be regarded as alternative truths, the mind will adopt the simpler of the two beliefs. It has a passion for unification. It will unify wherever it sees an opportunity. It has already constructed a world common to many minds. It will obviously desire to proceed as far as possible with its simplification and to construct a single world common to all the senses. In the theory of the 'thing' and its qualities it sees a method of justifying this procedure logically to itself.

We need not spend long in describing the logical characters of the sixth construction, for they are similar in all respects to those of the second, third, and subsidiary constructions. Obviously it cannot be proved. You cannot by any conceivable means prove that the wall which you see is the same as the wall which you touch. Experience gives nothing more than that whenever you see a wall, there will also be a tactile wall present to your hand if you put it out. One experience is the *sign* of another. But nothing can prove that they are numerically identical. They are not. They are different. And it is merely a fiction of the mind to invent a common 'thing' behind the two experiences.

The logical principle on which the sixth construction depends is that existences which make no difference of any kind to our world, whether in the theoretical conception we form of it or in our practical reactions to it, may be ignored and treated as if non-existent. In the present construction we do not indeed treat the objects of any one of the senses as non-existent, but the difference between them is ignored. We do not treat as non-existent either the visual wall or the tactile wall, but we treat the relation of difference between them as if it were non-existent.

By means of the six constructions which we have con-

THE CONSTRUCTION OF THE EXTERNAL WORLD

sidered in this chapter there now rises before us something like the familiar world of our everyday experience. We started with a multiplicity of private worlds having no connexion with each other. There was in these worlds nothing permanent and nothing that existed independently of minds. There were no objects, but only presentations, and these presentations might with some show of reason have been accused of being—though I should not use the term myself owing to its very misleading character—mere 'subjective' phantasms or dreams. These presentations went out of existence as soon as one ceased to perceive them. Starting from such, we have arrived, by means of the six constructions, at a world which is not private but common to all minds, a world which is permanent and contains permanent objects, the existence of this world and of these objects being conceived as quite independent of minds. This world possesses, then, the essential characters of the public external world with which we are familiar.

It is true that certain aspects of the everyday world of experience, more particularly its location in a common continuous perhaps infinite three-dimensional space and a common continuous perhaps infinite time, have been left untouched. We shall consider them briefly in a later chapter.

I cannot hope that our reconstruction of the external world in this chapter will have been either complete or accurate. This, I must insist, has been no attempt at a pure *a priori* construction which *must* by an iron necessity have followed precisely these lines and no others. It has been no more than an attempt at a rough freehand sketch, in broad outlines, of the mind's development, emphasizing as much as possible its logical character. I have picked out only what seemed the salient points of the construction, and I have placed them in the order which seemed logically the most feasible. That the mind in its evolution has actually followed precisely the course here laid down would be too much to claim. And I shall be satisfied if the general method of the mind in its world-building activity has been rightly seized, if the logical character and justification of our beliefs has been correctly shown, and if it has been rendered plausible that at least in some such way as has been here described, and for some such motives and reasons as here given, our beliefs about that world must actually have arisen in the human or pre-human subconsciousness of our ancestors.

CHAPTER VII

FACT, CONSTRUCTION, AND HYPOTHESIS

IN our last chapter we took for granted that the solitary mind somehow attains to knowledge of the existence of other minds, and we undertook to explain later how this came about. To do so will be our next constructive task. But before attempting to carry it out, I wish to consider briefly some important corollaries of the conclusions which we reached in the last chapter. These corollaries refer to the part played in the development of knowledge by fact, construction, and hypothesis. It will be convenient to introduce the question of what place fact holds in our theory by considering a possible objection which might well be made at this stage to the argument of the last chapter.

I can imagine our critic wording his objection somewhat as follows: 'The building up by minds of a public external world', he might say, 'depends for its possibility upon the fact that the experiences of the different selves run parallel to one another in certain definite ways. There is between the courses of the various private worlds a parallelism which was pictorially brought out by comparing them to duplications of the same cinema film. It is this parallelism which renders the construction of the external world possible. If it did not exist, there could be no contact between the many minds, and each would remain for ever shut up within its world of private phantasms.

'Now this remarkable parallelism is simply taken for granted by the theory. It is wholly unexplained. As it stands in the theory it is simply a miracle. In order to explain it, shall we not be compelled to introduce either the disreputable and discredited theory of a pre-established harmony or some modern equivalent?

'For if we suppose that there is to start with no common world, but only a vast multitude of private worlds disconnected and independent of one another, is it not infinitely improbable that such a parallelism between them all should exist? Should we not rather expect each world to run its own course in its own sweet way, to be different from all the others, so that no common world could ever arise?

'This difficulty is created by the present theory, but does not exist for the theory of common sense realism. That view holds that the common world is not constructed by mind but is there already before mind comes upon the scene. The many minds come to it and find it. It is therefore natural on this theory that, as the many minds perceive the same world, their experiences should run parallel.'

Now it is quite true that our whole theory depends on the assertion of the parallelism, and that this parallelism is itself entirely unexplained by it. It is not, however, 'taken for granted' in the sense that it is assumed without proof. For the proof of its truth lies in experience. It is a *fact* that my world and yours agree in certain respects. It is found in experience that when A and B compare notes as to what they perceive, although they cannot prove the identity of the matter of their percepts, they can communicate with each other *as if* they were the same. This possibility of communication proves at least the similarity of the internal relations of A's world with those of B's world. It proves that, so far as the parallelism extends, there is a point to point correspondence of relations. This is the only parallelism on which our theory relies. No one disputes the existence of this parallelism, least of all the realist. For if he disputed it he would have to hold that the private experiences of the common world which arise in the many different minds are all different from one another, which would be equivalent to denying the existence of a common world altogether. This, it is evident, would destroy the possibility of realism or indeed of any theory whatever. It would reduce the universe to chaos. Hence the parallelism is a fact which is, and must be, admitted by all intelligible theories.

We cannot be criticized, then, simply on the ground

FACT, CONSTRUCTION, AND HYPOTHESIS 151

that we assert this fact. For all theories equally assert it. Nor can the charge against us be that we assert it without proof. For it is as certainly based upon empirical evidence as any other fact whatever. The gravamen of the accusation against us must be, I think, that we have not *explained* this fact. And it is assumed by our imaginary critic that common sense realism does explain it.

It is true that I have not explained it. I do not intend to do so. And I assert that there is not the slightest reason why I should. It is no part of the purpose of this book to explain ultimate facts. The purpose of this book may be roughly described as follows. We have sought, firstly, to ascertain what are the ultimate facts and certitudes which are presented to consciousness; and secondly, how the mind logically passes from these its ultimate premises to the rest of its knowledge. Prominent among these ultimate facts, for example, are our immediate sense-data.

It is no part of the business of our investigation to try to get behind the ultimate facts, or to explain them. I do not profess to be able to explain, for example, why a red patch is now appearing to me. I admit that I cannot explain it. And I think it probable that no one can explain it. It is an ultimate brute fact.

The spirit of our inquiry is entirely empirical. Our philosophy is an empirical philosophy. The astronomer observes the characters and the movements of the heavenly bodies. These are his facts, on which he builds his scheme of astronomical knowledge. He may seek to trace out the history of the stars, to show how they began in nebulae, and how they arrived at their present state. But he makes no metaphysical or ontological inquiries into *why* all these facts are what they are. For epistemology the colour patches, sounds, and odours, and the existence of myself perceiving them, are ultimate facts. We seek to show how knowledge has built these up into a common world. We seek to base upon them a theory of knowledge. To explain *why* the facts are what they are is no part of our undertaking.

Attempts to explain the ultimate facts of consciousness

have, of course, been made. Fichte accounted for our sense-data as being due to the self-limitation of the ego. Others have sought to explain the existence of the world (i.e. of the sum total of external facts) by transcendental theories of the Absolute, or by Platonic Ideas, or by theism, or by teleology. Whether these attempts could ever succeed, whether, for example, it could ever be shown that red is red because it is in accordance with the Idea of the Good that it should be so—on these questions I am not at present disposed to express any opinion. I shall say only that such attempts to reach beyond and behind experience into the metempirical reason of the universe are foreign to the empirical spirit of this inquiry and lie entirely outside its scope.

Now the parallelism which exists between the many private worlds is an ultimate fact. It is true that it is not one of the ultimate certitudes of the solitary mind. It is not an element of the given of any one mind. It cannot be, since it involves the comparison of the experiences of at least two minds. But it is nevertheless a *fact* as distinguished from a mental construction. It is a fact which, though not known directly and immediately by any one mind, is *inferred* by each mind from what it observes. As we shall see in the next chapter, the existence of other minds is an inference which each of us draws from his own private experiences. Having made this inference we find that intelligible communication is possible. And we then draw from this possibility of communication the further inference that there exists such a parallelism as has been described. Hence the only difference between the facts of our immediate sense-data and the fact of parallelism is that the former are directly known facts while the latter is inferred. This difference in no way invalidates our assertion that the parallelism is a brute fact. However we come to know it, whether directly or by inference, it is still an ultimate fact which has to be simply accepted and cannot be explained.

Nor is there any truth in the suggestion that, although our theory cannot explain parallelism, the theory of

FACT, CONSTRUCTION, AND HYPOTHESIS

realism can. When two minds A and B simultaneously look at a penny, the facts then are, according to our theory, that there exist two corresponding but not provably similar experiences which A and B agree (because they correspond) to call a brown patch, and that they together construct out of these experiences a common penny. According to the realist the facts are that there actually exists a single common penny, which is not constructed but is 'there'. But the realist can no more explain his alleged facts than we can explain ours. He can no more explain why there exists one common penny than I can explain why there exist two private but corresponding pennies. There is no reason for alleging that two parallel private pennies are any more mysterious, any more miraculous, or any more difficult to explain, than a single common penny.

Not only this. But the realist's account of the matter raises difficulties which are avoided by our theory. For the realist thinks that A and B both look at the *same* penny. But this is contradicted by the fact that what A sees is a round dull patch, while what B sees is an elliptical shiny one. To get out of this difficulty the realist is compelled to resort to all kinds of desperate shifts. He may assume that behind the presentations there exists a common 'thing' and that this 'thing' is not a construction but is 'really there'. If so, he soon finds that this conception is self-contradictory. It lands him in a quagmire of contradictions, some of which were noted in the last chapter, and all of which can be studied at length, if the reader is so disposed, in Professor Lovejoy's book *The Revolt against Dualism*. Our theory avoids all these difficulties by denying that the common penny is anything more than a mental construction, and by pointing out that contradictions may well exist in makeshift ideas which the mind invents for its own purposes. These contradictions were not apparent to it at the time when the constructions were made, i.e. at the dawn of the mind's history, and have only been brought to light by the investigations of philosophers. This seems a reasonable way of explaining these contradictions.

But the realist is committed either to attributing them to the facts themselves or to making various futile attempts to explain them away as not being really contradictions. Our view admits the contradictions, but simply attributes them to the fallibility of human ideas. In this our theory has the advantage over realism. Neither explains the facts. But realism, besides not explaining them, makes them self-contradictory.

We are all of us, realists and ourselves, in the same boat as regards explanation of facts. All facts are ultimately mysterious, inexplicable, even miraculous if you like. But they are all equally so. It is just as miraculous that there should be one brown patch as that there should be two or a million. If there is a parallelism between private worlds, this is no doubt inexplicable. But it would be equally inexplicable if all the worlds differed. Any brute fact, just because it is a brute fact, has simply to be accepted and cannot be explained. If it seems surprising to the mind that private worlds should correspond, this surprise is merely an emotional attitude which has no logical foundation.

For how is the fact that whenever I see a red disk you also see a red disk more wonderful or more surprising than the fact that whenever there is rain there are clouds, or than any other instance of causality, or of orderliness and harmonious working in nature? And if it is accounted sufficient to accept the uniformity and orderliness of nature as an ultimate fact which we cannot explain, why should it not be sufficient to accept the uniformity and harmony of the experiences of different minds as an ultimate fact which we cannot explain?

The parallelism of the private worlds is simply one instance of the ordered character of the universe. But because the thought of a multitude of independent worlds running parallel is an unfamiliar example of the general orderliness of nature, it perhaps appears more surprising to the reader than the familiar examples of causation and the common and well-known uniformities of nature. This attitude is understandable but not rational.

FACT, CONSTRUCTION, AND HYPOTHESIS 155

The universe is a cosmos, not a chaos. The cosmotic character of the universe has been explained by theories of theism, teleology, transcendental realms of rational forms, pre-established harmonies, and the like. With none of these theories are we concerned in this book. And the epistemologist who starts from the undoubted fact of parallel private worlds has just as much right to decline to attempt an explanation of this as the astronomer or the physicist has to decline to attempt an explanation of the law of causation on which the whole of his science rests.

We supposed our imaginary critic to inquire whether it was not infinitely improbable that, if the many private worlds are disconnected, they should yet run parallel. Perhaps it is, I reply, just as it appears infinitely improbable that a world ruled by blind chance should be an orderly and harmonious cosmos and not a chaos of colliding atoms. For all I know the fact that the world is harmonious and orderly may be a good argument for theism, teleology, or some similar theory. And for all I know the fact of the parallel worlds may constitute a new string in the theist's or teleologist's bow. For it is certainly part and parcel of the general orderliness of the world. It has made possible the construction of a common cosmos which may perhaps have been intended by the divine mind. But these are not the questions which I have undertaken to discuss. It is sufficient for my purposes that the parallelism is not more improbable than the law of causation or any other example of order in the world, and is in any case an undisputable fact on which I am entitled to build. I am asking for no further latitude than is granted to any science in the world, namely to build its theories on the facts, however surprising or unaccountable those facts may appear.

This discussion will have thrown some light, I think, both upon our conception of the nature of fact and upon its place in epistemological theory. But the nature of fact will be made clearer if it is contrasted with the nature of construction. And I will now proceed to some general remarks about the constructions which have already come before us in the last chapter.

The six constructions of the last chapter fall into two groups. I shall call these respectively (1) unificatory constructions, and (2) existential constructions.

(1) *Unificatory Constructions.*

The second, third, and sixth constructions of the last chapter fall into this group. Their common character is, not that they postulate any new existence, but that, on the contrary, they reduce the number of existences in the universe by identifying as the 'same' certain objects of consciousness which were originally 'different'. The second construction identifies my red with your red, my world with your world, and in general the private worlds of all minds with one another. It reduces the multitudes of *simultaneous* worlds to one. The third construction identifies my red at this moment with your red at a later moment. It begins the reduction of the many *successive* worlds to one. The sixth construction identifies and declares to be the 'same' the originally different objects of the different senses. It reduces the several worlds of sight, hearing, touch, &c., to one world.

Unificatory constructions rest upon the logical principle that superfluous existences, that is, existences which make no difference of any kind either to knowledge or to our practical activities, may be ignored and treated *as if* they were non-existent. As they are irrelevant to the mind's purposes, whether theoretical or practical, they may be cut out of the universe altogether.

The other chief logical character of unificatory constructions is that they cannot be proved, are not *facts*, but are simply serviceable fictions. They are not inferences from facts. One unificatory construction may indeed be an inference from another construction. Thus the third construction is an inference from the second. Or at least the second construction is *one* of its premises. The second construction declares that A's red is identical with B's red seen simultaneously. But B's red seen a second

FACT, CONSTRUCTION, AND HYPOTHESIS 157

later is identical with the red he saw during the first second. From these two premises it follows that the red which A sees during the first second is identical with the red which B sees during the following second (when A sees none). This gives us the third construction. In this way constructions may be connected *inter se* by the relation of implication. And when they do so they form systems of constructions. But they are never inferred from facts or perceptions. If they were they would cease to be constructions and become facts. If a system of two or more constructions is such that the particular constructions which are its members are mutually related to each other by implication, yet the whole system as a system is not inferred from anything, but is, on the contrary, assumed, created, or constructed by the mind.

(2) *Existential Constructions.*

The first, fourth, and fifth constructions belong to this group. Their common character is that in them the imagination invents the fiction of some new existence which is not given in, or inferred from, experience.

This new existence is conceived after the model of experienced existence, and is made in one way or another out of the materials of sense. Since it asserts an existence which is never actually experienced, it is always expressible only as an hypothetical proposition of the form 'If the circumstances were suitable, we should perceive the existence.' And the condition expressed in the antecedent clause is always an impossibility because by hypothesis we can never perceive, or be in a position to perceive, the new existence.

Since the mind is not compelled, either by the force of perceived fact or by the necessity of logical inference from perceived fact, to adopt constructed beliefs, the question why it does so must present itself. What makes the mind construct beliefs which are not implied or even suggested by the facts? What, in other words, are its motives? The answer to this question should be clear from the discussions of the last chapter, but may be summed up here as follows. The motive which has guided the mind to the constructions so far made, whether unificatory or existential, has been either (1) simplification, or (2) consistency. This may be briefly verified by reference to the six constructions.

The first, second, fourth, and sixth constructions were made for the sake of simplification. In the first it was found simpler and more convenient to regard the corresponding presentations of different minds as similar rather than as dissimilar. Either view would equally suit the facts and would be equally 'true' and workable both in intellectual thought and in practical action. The simpler of the two views was chosen. In the second construction it was found simpler to regard corresponding presentations as identical and to believe in one universe rather than in many. In the fourth construction it proved to be a simplification to suppose that things go on existing when unperceived, and that the world is continuous in time, rather than that it goes out of existence when perception ceases and that a new universe begins to exist when perception begins again. The sixth construction simplifies the universe by reducing the several worlds of the different senses to one world.

The third and fifth constructions, on the other hand, have been made for the sake of consistency. The mind having invented its theory of a common world was brought up hard against inconvenient facts which contradicted this theory. These facts were the *differences* which exist between the private worlds of the various minds. The motive of these constructions was to reconcile these differences with the theory of the common world and so get rid of the inconsistency. In the second construction A's red patch had been identified with B's. But the fact that B's patch goes on being perceived after A's has ceased to be perceived is inconsistent with this, unless it is held that A's patch may go on existing in B's mind after it has ceased to be perceived by A. In order to be consistent the mind was forced to take that view, and the third construction resulted.

FACT, CONSTRUCTION, AND HYPOTHESIS

Again the theory of the common world was threatened with disaster by the discovery of a multitude of differences between the private worlds. Of these differences, that between the round and the elliptical penny may be taken as typical. At first sight they appear to be fatal to the belief in the common world. But rather than go back on its tracks and renounce its common world the mind, by means of a bold speculation, or rather by a bold invention, finds a way out. It creates the idea that there exists a self-identical 'thing' behind the differences. It holds, without contradiction, both to the differences and to the identity by placing the differences in the presentations and assigning the identity to the 'thing'. This is just as if one were to avoid the contradiction of holding that the same object is both black and white at the same time and on the same part of its surface by saying that it is black on one side and white on the other. This invention of the 'thing' for the sake of consistency is the fifth construction.

We find again and again in the history of knowledge repetitions of this procedure. The mind, having invented a construction for the purposes of simplification and convenience, meets with new facts which do not square with the constructed belief. It is forced either to retrace its steps, abandon the ground which it has gained, and give up the construction or even the system of constructions (which may well constitute a large block of its scheme of knowledge), or, in order to avoid this, it is compelled to manufacture new constructions or systems of constructions which will reintroduce harmony and avoid contradictions. In this way human knowledge grows as well as by the accumulation of new facts and inferences.

It results from our epistemological analysis that two wholly different kinds of existence must be recognized. They are respectively (1) *factual* existence, and (2) *constructive* existence.

Factual existence is the existence of whatever is, has been, or will be actually perceived by any mind at any time or place.

The existence of my desk while it is being perceived by me or by any one else is a factual existence. Or rather, to be more accurate, the existence of the visual appearance of the desk while it is being seen, the existence of the tactile sense-data of it while it is being touched, and so on, are factual. But in the night when no one is perceiving the desk, when it is only supposed by the mind to be there, its existence is a constructive existence. Even while it is being perceived, only what is actually perceived is factual. Thus while I am looking at it, but not touching it, its visual sense-data have factual existence, but its tactile sense-data have only constructive existence. And at all times, whether the desk is being perceived or not, the supposed 'thing', behind the presentations and different from them, has only constructive existence.

The sun rising to-morrow has a factual existence. It *will* be actually perceived. The existence of Julius Caesar is also factual. For it *was* actually perceived.

For the purposes of epistemology it is essential to make this distinction between factual and constructive existence. *But for the purposes of all other knowledge it is essential to obliterate and forget it.* The whole point of the construction of the desk's existence when no one is aware of it is that we should *suppose* that it goes on existing when unperceived *in exactly the same way* as it does when perceived. To suppose this is obviously precisely what the construction consists in. It applies the concept of factual existence to all existence whether perceived or not.

Or we may put this in another way. There is a distinction between factual and constructive existence. But this distinction is one which makes no difference of any kind either to theory (except the theory of epistemology) or practice. I may suppose if I like that this typewriter either is not here when I do not perceive it or that its existence is then of a different kind. But what it is or is not during inter-perceptual periods makes no difference to me as a practical person wanting to use it for writing my book. So long as it is there whenever I turn to it, what else matters? Nor does it make any difference to my knowledge of it. The method of manufacture of typewriters, their mechanism, the metals of which they are made, the chemistry, metallurgy, and physics of these metals, any conceivable knowledge we might have of them, remains precisely the same whatever happens to them during inter-perceptual periods. It is, as we have seen, a logical rule of the mind that it ignores and treats as non-existent superfluous existences, existences which make no difference of any kind either to theory or practice. Therefore the existence of the distinction between factual and constructive existence is ignored. All existence is lumped together as factual, and this identification of the two kinds of existence may itself be regarded as a unificatory construction.

It is true that the distinction does make a difference to the theory of epistemology. But the human mind has not in the past regarded epistemology as of such paramount importance as to justify the distinction being retained as a part of ordinary knowledge. Epistemology may be left to look after itself. If and when its time comes, it can make the distinction for itself, as we have now done.

Moreover the attitude which the mind takes up in this matter must be regarded as 'true'. The greater part of our knowledge has been built up by mental constructions. If we are to admit this knowledge *as* knowledge, and not as falsehood, we must admit the constructed beliefs of which it is so largely composed as being truths. We must conceive that it is true that there is an independent external world, that things exist when no one is perceiving them, that the penny which you see is the same penny as the one I see, that the table which I touch is the very same table as the one I see. These propositions form a part of our admitted knowledge of the world. They are universally accepted as true. Unless we are to do extreme violence to all accepted standards of truth and to all acknowledged conceptions of knowledge, we must also admit them to be true, *and must frame our definition of truth so as to include them.*

These propositions belong to our common everyday

knowledge. If we consider what would generally be called scientific knowledge, as distinguished from common knowledge (though the distinction is, of course, a relative one) we shall reach a similar conclusion. Scientific knowledge, like common knowledge, is largely composed of mental constructions. This we shall see more clearly when we come to our chapter on scientific knowledge. For the present we shall only remind the reader that the so-called 'hypothetical' character of such knowledge is widely admitted at present even in scientific circles, and that, as has been pointed out, what is really meant by this 'hypothetical' character is that science is largely composed of constructions. If then we are to regard scientific knowledge as true, we must admit that truth includes constructions. The atomic theory of matter, not to mention the electronic theory, is a construction. But by saying this we do not mean that it is false. Its truth or falsity is not a matter on which the mere philosopher has any right to express an opinion. If its truth is guaranteed by competent scientific authority we shall accept that. And if it is true, then it will follow that a construction may be true. We have to take a broad view of knowledge, to regard it in something the same way as we regard the world of art. The world of art is a product of the immense labours of the human spirit. So is the world of knowledge. It has been constructed by countless minds working through countless centuries. And this great creation of thinking spirit is not to be dismissed as 'untrue' by philosophy, except at the peril of philosophy. And a philosophy which so concludes is not likely to live long.

Truth, therefore, must be held to include those constructions which have been once and for all built into the body of human knowledge and now form permanent parts of it. This, of course, will raise another problem. Constructions are fictions. And if *all* constructions are true, this will destroy the distinction between truth and falsehood altogether. For in that case any figment of a frenzied brain might claim to rank as truth. Evidently some constructions must be true, others false. And this

FACT, CONSTRUCTION, AND HYPOTHESIS

throws upon us the duty of distinguishing the nature of a true construction from the nature of a false one. We shall have to discover what are the conditions which render a construction valid and mark it off from invalid constructions. I shall attack this problem in due course, but I must beg leave to postpone it for the present. We have not advanced sufficiently far in our investigations to solve it. I shall return to it on a later page.[1]

We agree, then, that for all purposes both of practical action and theoretical knowledge it is true that objects exist unperceived, that unperceived existence is as much factual as perceived existence, and that there is no distinction between the natures of perceived and unperceived existence. To this statement there is only one exception, and that has to be made in the case of epistemology. As epistemologists we are bound to point out the distinction between factual and constructive existence. The growth of knowledge has long ago deliberately obliterated it. It was by turning the blind eye to this distinction that the great adventure of knowledge, the great creative work of the human spirit, began. And to forget and to deny this distinction must necessarily be a point of honour both with ordinary knowledge and with the sciences, for their being is bound up with such forgetting and denial. Only the philosopher, for his own eccentric purposes, which differ from those of other men, needs to remember here. Nor can it be said that there is any contradiction in this. For ordinary knowledge and for science there is no distinction. For philosophy there is a distinction. This may appear formally contradictory. But this after all means only that the distinction is of importance for the special purposes of philosophy, while it is of none for the purposes of science and ordinary knowledge, which may therefore ignore it and treat it as non-existent. And in this procedure there is no contradiction.

Hypotheses may assert either factual or constructive existences. Suppose I hear a scratching noise behind the

[1] In Chapter XV.

chest of drawers. I conjecture that this may be due to a rat. This is an hypothesis, the verification of which consists in seeing the rat when it is driven out with a stick from its hiding-place. The hypothesis asserts the factual existence of the rat. The rat, it is plain, is not a construction, but a fact.

It is true that the existence of the visual rat when it is not being seen is a construction, and it might be insisted, if we wish to be pedantically accurate, that when I say 'I believe that the noise is caused by a rat' this belief is not an hypothesis, but a construction. Most writers, however, would call it an hypothesis. And we can avoid a pedantic departure from common usage by means of the consideration that the belief really consists of two parts. Firstly, there is my general belief in an independent external world existing whether I perceive it or not. Secondly, there is my belief that among the objects in this independent world is a rat which is causing the noise. It is only the first of these two elements of my belief which is a construction, and that construction is no part of my present mental process in guessing at the rat, but was made long ago in the dawn of mind. If, granted the general belief in the independent external world, I now guess at a rat, this is certainly an hypothesis. I am not *now* constructing an unseen visual rat. The existence of unseen visual objects generally, including rats, has been constructed long ago. And my present act of supposing that the cause of the noise is a rat is not a new construction but an hypothesis.

On the other hand, the invention of the ether of space when it was required to be the carrier of light waves was not only hypothetical but was also a construction. For in this case there was posited not only the existence of the external world, but in addition the existence of a quite new kind of unperceived object.

Because hypotheses are thus concerned as much with factual existences and as with constructive existences, it seems to me that what is frequently called the 'hypothetical character of science' ought rather to be called its

FACT, CONSTRUCTION, AND HYPOTHESIS

constructional character, and that the use of the word hypothetical in this connexion rests on a confusion of thought. For what is meant by the so-called hypothetical character of science? Certainly not that all scientific knowledge consists in unverified hypotheses. An hypothesis, after all, ceases to be a mere hypothesis when it has been verified. It then becomes a theory or even a known fact. It was once an hypothesis that certain aberrations in the motions of the planets were caused by an unknown planet. When the existence of Neptune was verified with the telescope, our knowledge of this existence did not remain an hypothesis. It had become an observed fact. To assert that scientific knowledge is hypothetical in this sense would imply uncertainty and lack of proper verification of its conclusions. It would even imply that our knowledge of Neptune while astronomers were still calculating and searching was more 'scientific' than our knowledge of it after the telescope had been turned upon it. And this is certainly not what is meant by those who speak of the hypothetical character of science.

Do they mean, then, that science is concerned only with hypothetical propositions? This view is apparently sometimes intended, although it is plainly erroneous. It is, of course, true that science makes very wide use of hypothetical propositions, but only—it must be at once added—intending them as a means of advance towards categorical ones. Hypothesis is a *method* of seeking scientific truth. But the truth when found is in no wise hypothetical. Hypothesis is not the end at which science aims—as would seem to be almost implied by such a phrase as 'the hypothetical character of science'—but merely a means towards its ends. And its real ends are the attainment of categorical propositions.

One or two examples will make this clear. Einstein frames the hypothetical proposition 'If the geometry of space-time is such and such—which I suppose it to be—then the displacement of the orbit of Mercury will be so and so, and rays of starlight passing the limb of the sun will be bent in such and such an angle'. The displacement of the orbit of Mercury is known, and the bending of the light rays is measured. It is found that the facts regarding both agree with the deductions from the supposed geometry of space-time which are set forth in the above hypothetical proposition. The hypothesis is then, at least to some extent, verified, and Einstein hopes to be able to frame the categorical proposition 'The structure of space-time *is* such and such'.

The physicist, again, endeavours to arrive at the truth regarding the constitution of the atom by means of tentative hypotheses. He supposes the constitution of the atom to be such that it may be described by the characters, or by the mathematical formulae, x, y, z. Taking x, y, z, to be true, he attempts to deduce from them the known properties of matter as they are observed in ordinary life and in the laboratory. If his results agree with the observed facts, this does not indeed prove that his hypothesis is true. But it shows that the hypothesis explains all the relevant facts so far discovered, and that, if no further facts which contradict it come to light, there is at least a certain degree of probability that it may be true. What the physicist hopes is that in the end it may be actually proved true, so far as such proof is possible to his science. He hopes to be able definitely to propound the categorical proposition that the nature of the atom actually *is* given by the formulae x, y, z. Or if his hypothesis is proved wrong, he hopes to hit on the right one and then prove that the nature of the atom *is* expressed in the formulae p, q, r.

Hence it is not strictly true to say that scientific knowledge is in its nature hypothetical. It is, or aims at being, categorical. Yet those who speak of its hypothetical character clearly mean something important, and are seeking to express a genuine insight. And I believe that what they are really groping for and trying to express is the *constructional* character of science. This character is stressed in the writings of the famous French mathematician Poincaré, although he too uses what I hold to be the wrong term 'hypothetical'. It comes out clearly, again, in the passage which I have already quoted from Professor Andrade's book *The Mechanism of Nature*. Professor Andrade pointed out that even if the atoms are 'polite fictions', this will not affect the validity of the atomic theory, since it will be just as valuable in introducing order into our knowledge and promoting new discoveries.

Professor Eddington recently described certain features of the latest theory of the atom as 'a dodge, and a very good dodge too'. The only fault to be found with this statement is that the distinguished author of it seems to regard an unperceived existence or a character which is a 'dodge' as in some way different from and inferior to an unperceived existence or character which is 'really there'. He appears to think that other unperceived existences, such as the atom itself, are not dodges, but are 'really there'; whereas in truth even unperceived existences which are 'really there', including atoms and tables when no one is aware of them, are 'dodges, and very good dodges too'. And the belief that they are 'really there' is part of the dodge.

The suggestion which seems to be made by all these writers, however, is that many of the truths of science are 'polite fictions', ways of looking at the universe which enable us both to introduce order into our knowledge (the theoretical interest), and correctly to predict new experience (the practical interest), but yet that such polite fictions must not be denied the position of being genuine scientific truths. This is what is commonly referred to as the 'hypothetical character' of science. And it seems clear that this designation is inaccurate, and that we ought rather to speak of the constructional character of science. For 'polite fictions' are clearly constructions.

The essential distinction, then, between hypothesis and construction is that the construction is always a pure creation of the mind, and the existence posited by it, if any, is always a constructive existence; whereas an hypothesis need not possess this character. The existence posited by it may be factual, as is the case with the rat and the planet Neptune. It is true that an hypothesis may sometimes also be itself a construction. The present theory of the atom must, I think it will be admitted, be regarded as still an hypothesis, not a proved truth. And it is also, as I shall show more definitely later, a construction. So that some hypotheses are also constructions and posit constructive existences. But this is not essential to the character of hypothesis as hypothesis. The existence posited by a construction is always constructive. The existence posited by an hypothesis may be either factual or constructive.

We may sum up the results of this chapter as follows:
(1) A fact is something actually perceived.[1]
(2) The essential character of mental constructions is that they are pure creations of the mind to which no facts correspond.
(3) Existences which are posited by an hypothesis may be either factual or constructive.
(4) Though the method of science may be largely the method of hypothesis, yet the nature of scientific truth as such is not hypothetical. It is, however, constructional. And this is apparently what is meant by those writers who erroneously refer to the 'hypothetical character' of science.

[1] This is subject to the qualification that the mind which perceives or knows is itself also a fact. This will be brought out in the next chapter.

CHAPTER VIII
THE DISCOVERY OF OTHER MINDS

THE word discovery is used advisedly in the chapter heading. For other minds are *found* existing. They are not invented or constructed by my mind. Their existence is factual, not constructive. To this point, which is of fundamental importance in the theory, I shall return at the end of this chapter.

One point which emerged very clearly from our past discussion was that our belief in the existence of a public independent external world depends absolutely on our belief in the existence of other minds. The former belief would be impossible unless we had first acquired the latter. The external world is a social product. The solitary mind, unaware of the existence of minds other than itself, is a mind necessarily confined to a world of private phantasms. But it suited the convenience of exposition to take up first for investigation that belief which is really second in logical order, namely, belief in an external world. We had therefore to take the discovery of other minds for granted. We assumed that it somehow takes place, promising to explain *how* it takes place on a later page. The time to redeem our promise has now come. And the problem which we have to solve is this: how does the solitary mind become aware of the existence of other minds?

Let me say at once that, though I hope to exhibit this topic in something of a new light, I have no essentially novel theory to put forward. For the number of possible views is very limited, and they are well known. They reduce themselves in fact to two main types, both of which have been well represented in philosophical literature, though both admit, of course, of variations of detail in the manner of their presentment. The two possible types of theory are the following. It may be thought either (1) that we have direct and immediate knowledge of other minds, or (2) that our knowledge of them is indirect, being an inference based upon the bodily behaviour of the organisms to which we attribute minds. This latter view may be briefly put thus. I feel my own anger. I am directly aware of my own volitions. I am conscious of my own perceptions. But I cannot feel your anger, see your volitions, or perceive your percepts. I cannot see your red, or feel your anger, any more than I can feel the pain in your leg when it is cut off. I am thus not directly aware of your mind or its contents. I am only directly aware of the existence of your body and its behaviour. I perceive these with my senses, and I infer from them both the existence of your mind and the nature of its particular states. I see your face flush and your brows frown. I infer that this bodily behaviour is probably caused by the fact that you are a conscious being like myself, and that you are angry. I see you smile and conclude that you are pleased. I see you avoid a snake on the path. I explain this behaviour by the assumption that you perceived the snake. I infer generally that the actions of your body are due to your being a conscious mind, and that they are not the result of clockwork or other blind mechanism.

This second type of view is that which was almost universally held by philosophers until a comparatively recent date. The first theory, that of direct awareness, has grown up as a reaction against it, and is now held, in one form or another, by Professor Alexander, Professor C. C. J. Webb, Professor A. E. Taylor, and others.

Before discussing the details of the question at issue I must point out that it makes no essential difference to our theory of knowledge and existence which of the two views is adopted. All that is essential to our theory is to believe that other minds do actually exist, and that we do, in one way or another, come to attain a knowledge of them and enter into communication with them. Provided this is allowed, the construction of the external world as outlined in Chapter VI becomes possible. So long as the solitary mind *somehow* succeeds in getting into communication with other minds, it and they can then co-operate in building up the external world in the manner there described. Now it is admitted by the partisans of both the rival theories on this subject that other minds do exist, that we do come to have knowledge of them, and that we do communicate with them. Strictly speaking, that should be enough for us. However this knowledge is attained, whether directly or by inference, the fact that it *is* attained would be sufficient for our theory of the construction of the external world. We might therefore take this as granted by all philosophical schools and proceed with our investigations on that basis.

Nevertheless it does not seem right to leave the matter in that way. The problem is important for its own sake. Moreover it clearly lies directly in our path. We began with the solitary mind faced with its private world of colour patches, sounds, and the like, self-enclosed amid its private phantasms. We undertook to show how it passes out of that state, how it comes to have knowledge of external things and other minds. To explain by what means we come to acquire knowledge of foreign minds is clearly an integral part of that undertaking, and must not therefore be shirked. I am, however, anxious to make it clear that even if a different view be taken to that which I shall here adopt, this need not affect the rest of our theory of knowledge. That theory does not stand or fall by our solution of this particular problem.

It is true that the theory of inferential knowledge seems to fit in more easily with our philosophy than does that of direct knowledge. For the exponents of the latter view very often deny that our original state was solipsism. Some of them urge that our knowledge of other minds is actually prior to our self-consciousness, or at least prior to any full development of it. And this is out of keeping with a philosophy which, like ours, starts from the solipsism of the solitary mind. Nevertheless the theory of the direct perception of foreign minds is not in itself inconsistent with our philosophy, and could quite easily be combined with it. For the view that our consciousness of others is prior to our self-consciousness is not at all essential to the theory of direct knowledge. It might equally be held by the exponents of that theory that we are first aware of our own minds, and then reach a direct acquaintance with other minds just as we have a direct acquaintance with sense-data. And such a view would be quite consistent with our philosophy. From the point of view adopted in this book mind begins as solitary. It then becomes aware of other minds and of the parallelism which exists between its own world and theirs. Whether this awareness is direct or inferred, the mind will in either case proceed to enter into communication with other minds and to build up along with them a public external world. Our philosophy does not, therefore, commit us to the adoption of either of the rival views, and we may claim to be quite impartial as between them.

Turning now to the actual problem before us we must point out that the wording in which it is usually presented is ambiguous. How do I know that other minds exist? This may mean (1) what logical reasons have I for believing it, or in other words, how can I prove that it is true? Or it may mean (2) what psychological processes have led me to the belief? Writers on the subject do not as a rule distinguish between the logical and the psychological aspects of the problem, and I cannot help thinking that the recent reaction in favour of the theory of direct knowledge is largely due to confusion of the two points of view.

The theory which bases our knowledge of other minds on an inference by analogy from bodily behaviour is primarily an attempt to solve the logical problem. It tries to show the logical grounds of our belief. And it leaves the question open whether we actually, as a matter of psychology, reach our belief by way of logic, or by some other way such as that of instinct. Yet Professor Alexander criticizes it on the ground that 'it is flatly at variance with the history of our minds',[1] a criticism which is entirely wide of the mark, since it assumes that the argument criticized is concerned with the historical order and psychological origin of our belief. Professor C. C. J.

[1] *Space, Time, and Deity*, vol. ii, p. 31.

Webb, again, in his paper on 'Our Knowledge of One Another', falls into the same confusion. He 'cannot believe' that solipsism is a position 'that any one was really ever in'. And he makes much of the contention that we may be aware of other minds before we become fully aware of our own. It may very well be true that no one was ever a solipsist, and that we know other minds before we know our own (though personally I cannot accept the latter statement). But all this has no bearing at all on the question of the logical foundations of our belief.

If the question at issue is how as a matter of psychological fact we come to believe in the existence of other minds, then there may be many possible alternative replies. For there are many different ways by which differently constituted minds arrive at any given belief. Every one knows that some minds may reach a certain religious tenet by logic, other minds may reach the same belief by way of moral intuition, and yet others by means of some kind of mystic insight. Perhaps we come to believe in the existence of other minds, as Professor Alexander suggests, through the operation of 'social instinct'. Perhaps it is a matter of 'instinctive belief' or 'faith'; or perhaps it is a mystical revelation. A truth of any kind may come to be known in any number of ways. How do I become aware of the truth that the square on the hypotenuse of a right-angled triangle is equal to the sum of the squares on the other two sides? I may have come to believe this as a result of my practical experience in measuring land. I may have measured the sides of a great many right-angled triangles, then hit upon the relation of their squares by chance, and finally guessed that what I have found so often to hold true is a universal rule. Or I may, on the other hand, have arrived at a knowledge of this truth by way of authority. My teacher may have told me that the proposition is true, and I may have believed him without understanding any of the reasons. For all I know there may even be a 'geometrical instinct' which teaches some people such truths. We have certainly heard of mathematicians who seem to divine the solutions of their problems by intuition. But all this has no bearing at all upon the question of the *logical* foundations of the belief, and the problem of how to prove it true. The only answer to that question is the one discovered by Pythagoras. The logical foundation of this truth can only be found by going back to the axioms.

It could make no difference to this if it were shown that historically the truth of the theorem of Pythagoras was known first, and that the axioms on which it depends were discovered afterwards. The truth of the theorem would still logically depend on the axioms. Similarly, even if it be proved that knowledge of other minds is historically prior to consciousness of self, this can make no difference to the contention that our belief in other minds logically depends on analogical inferences from behaviour.

It is difficult to believe that we have any direct apprehension of other minds. If we see a man lying on his bed with glassy eyes, absolutely motionless and with expressionless face, we do not know whether he is alive or dead. We have to ascertain whether he is warm or cold, whether his heart beats, whether he breathes. It may be that he is fully conscious all the while and is pretending to be dead. If we have any power of directly apprehending other minds without regard to their bodily behaviour, how is it that we do not detect the presence of a man's mind in such a case? How is it that we may be deceived and believe that his consciousness has gone out of existence? How is it that we have to examine his body to find out the truth?

I will leave that question to be answered as best it may, and will pass on to other points of view. It is said that we possess direct knowledge of the existence of other minds. What is meant here by the 'existence of minds'? Or more briefly, what is meant by 'minds'?

The object of this question is to clear the ground by getting rid of at least one possible misconception. By the existence of minds in this context we do *not* mean the existence of a transcendental ego, of a spiritual unity, or of a 'thinking substance'. The man in the street believes that both he and his fellows possess minds. But he has no knowledge of transcendental unities or thinking substances. He has never heard of these matters. Now what we are engaged in trying to find out is not how philosophers arrive at their metaphysical conceptions of the nature of personality. What we are trying to ascertain is how ordinary men and women know that their fellows have minds. The belief in the existence of foreign minds which we are studying is the ordinary everyday belief of plain men. And this has nothing to do with metaphysical theories of personality.

When Smith says that he believes that Jones possesses a mind substantially similar to his own, what is it that he actually means? Not that Jones is a transcendental ego, but simply that Jones thinks, perceives, feels, and wills. The belief in the existence of other minds, which is the subject of our discussion, means then simply the belief that other men—and animals too—have thoughts, feelings, perceptions, and volitions. It is, in short, belief in the empirical content of minds.

It follows that the question whether we can have direct knowledge of other minds means: can we have direct knowledge that other people perceive, feel, will, and think? And I can see no difference between this and the further question: can we directly perceive the thoughts, feelings, volitions, and percepts of other people? And the answer to this question is axiomatic. We cannot. I cannot see your red, feel your pain, or perceive the thought in your mind. My consciousness is absolutely cut off from your consciousness, and there is no view from one to the other. I have already stressed this so much in previous chapters that I need surely not labour it again.

Direct knowledge of other minds must surely mean either knowledge of them as transcendental unities and metaphysical essences or knowledge of their empirical contents. These alternatives are, so far as I know, exhaustive. The former, as we have seen, is not in question; and if it were, no one surely, save a very bemuddled mystic, could possibly assert that we have a direct perception of other people's transcendental egos. The latter alternative is equally impossible, since no one can assert that we can directly perceive the contents of other minds.

Even telepathy, if it be a proven fact, shows nothing to the contrary. If A thinks of the number 5 and B thereupon sees the image of the figure 5 rise within his mind, he is still just as far as ever from having direct knowledge of the contents of A's mind. For it is within his own mind that B sees it rise, not within A's. And the image of 5 which B sees is his own image, not A's. Presumably the receiver of a telepathic message may even be unaware that the idea which he receives has emanated from another mind, and may think that it has arisen spontaneously in his own mind. And apart from all this, will any one allege that our ordinary knowledge that other people have minds is based on telepathy?

But all this, the supporters of the theory of direct knowledge will say, is not what they mean. We have not rightly understood them. They do not mean that we can directly perceive either the metaphysical egos or the empirical contents of other minds. What, then, do they mean?

I cannot be expected in the space at my disposal to ransack the whole literature of the subject in order to ascertain what every supporter of the theory has intended to convey. I shall content myself with a brief examination of the views of the most eminent present-day exponent of the theory, Professor Alexander.

Professor Alexander has carefully guarded himself against being supposed to contend that we have direct knowledge of the actual empirical contents of other minds. Such knowledge, he admits, must be gathered from bodily behaviour.

'I am not aware of B's mind as I am aware of his body, so that I should be able to inspect it and say what it is. Yet experience assures me that he has a mind. What sort of a mind it is, how the other mind feels in a given situation' [this means, I presume, what the empirical content of the mind is], 'I am left to divine sympathetically on the basis largely of analogy with my own. But that a mind is there, is assurance. It is not invented by inference or analogy, but is an act of faith forced on us by a peculiar sort of experience.'[1]

The appeal in a philosophical treatise to an 'act of faith' should be sufficient to bring us up with a jolt, and to arouse our suspicions of the whole argument. But of that later.

If I rightly understand the position taken up in this passage, it is this. We cannot be directly aware of the contents of other minds—that would be too absurd to be contended—but we can be directly aware of their bare existence. This implies that we might be aware of the bare existence of a mind while not being aware of any of its qualities, characters, or details.

Now suppose a philosopher were to put forward a parallel assertion regarding a material object. Suppose he said, 'There is present to my consciousness an object. I directly perceive the object. But I cannot perceive its colour, its shape, its size, its texture, its smell, its taste, or any single quality of it. All I can perceive is its bare existence.' Should we not reply that such a statement has no meaning? Bare contentless existence is an abstraction which may perhaps be conceived (although even that is very doubtful), but which certainly cannot be perceived. I am looking at a red pillar-box. I perceive that it is red, cylindrical, upright, hard, and so on. To perceive its existence is only possible by perceiving its qualities. Its existence *is* its qualities. And not to perceive any of the qualities is not to perceive the existence.

Will not exactly the same argument apply to minds? Just as the pillar-box exists only in its redness and other qualities, so the mind exists—apart from transcendental essences—only in its thoughts, feelings, perceptions, and volitions. The existence of the mind *is* the existence of this content. And it would be impossible to perceive the existence without perceiving the content. This is in itself obvious, and is also implied in the point already made by us, namely that the belief in the existence of other minds

[1] *Op. cit.*, vol. ii, p. 37.

with which we are concerned is the belief that other men think, feel, perceive, and will.

If any one doubts this, let him ask himself how he is aware of his own mind. By being aware of his own mind does he not mean simply being aware of his thoughts, feelings, and volitions? And supposing that he ceased to be aware of these, supposing that he ceased to be aware of any mental acts, could he be aware of himself? Would not his state be one of blank unconsciousness of anything, or at any rate a total absence of *self*-consciousness?

It may be alleged, however, that we can have a knowledge of the existence of things without a detailed knowledge of their characters. I know that there exists another side to the moon. But I do not know what colour it is, whether it possesses any mountains, or, if it does, what shape or height they are, or indeed anything in detail about it. I know that there exist many men in China of whose personal characteristics I am totally ignorant.

But this does not touch our point. Knowledge of the kind mentioned is always indirect or inferred. The point is that direct perception of an object must always consist in perception of at least some of its qualities, and that to speak of perceiving a bare existence is meaningless.

It is true, of course, that perception may be of only a few of the characters of the object. In fact this is always the case. I may perceive only the redness and shape of the pillar-box. It actually possesses innumerable qualities which I do not perceive. Perception of a few significant qualities is sufficient for recognition. And if Professor Alexander means that we perceive some very small minimum of the empirical contents of other minds and are thereby assured of their existence, then in that case he can be acquitted of the absurdity of supposing that we perceive the abstraction of a bare contentless existence.

But in the first place it is clear that this is not what he means. I need not argue the point at length. There is no trace of such a view in his pages, and it would, I think, be quite inconsistent with the passage already quoted. And in the second place, if he did mean this, he would only land himself in fresh difficulties. For then he would be back in the untenable position of arguing that we can directly perceive thoughts, feelings, and volitions in the minds of others. It clearly would not help his case to urge that only a small portion of such mental content is directly perceptible. On what principle could the distinction be made between what can be perceived and what cannot? Where could the line be drawn? And would not the adoption of such a position be similar to that of the lady who excused herself for having an illegitimate baby on the ground that it was only a small one?

Now in point of fact I do not think that Professor Alexander really means any of the untenable things which we have been discussing. It has been necessary to discuss them because it is necessary to eliminate all possible alternatives. We have to consider, not only what Professor Alexander means, but, so far as our space allows, the various possible meanings which might be attached to the doctrine of direct knowledge. And certainly that which interprets it as a species of perception is such a meaning.

But returning to Professor Alexander, let us ask ourselves again what it is that he does mean. The following seems to be a clue. I have so far assumed that his theory asserts the direct *perception* of one mind by another. But as far as I can remember, without too meticulously combing through his pages, he does not use the word 'perception' in this connexion. He always speaks of the direct 'knowledge' of one mind by another. Now knowledge is a very much wider term than perception.

To me it appears that direct knowledge of anything, as distinguished from inferred knowledge, *must* be some kind of perception, and cannot be anything else. Either the thing known is 'there', is immediately *present* to consciousness, in which case the thing is perceived; or it is absent from consciousness, and in that case my knowledge of it must be inferred. Immediate perception of a present object need not in all cases be held to be sensuous. It might be supersensuous, like the mystic's alleged intuition of God. I do not assert that such a thing as a supersensuous perception actually exists. It certainly is not a common experience, and it may be doubted whether it is not a subjective illusion. But what I do mean to assert is that if such a mystical intuition actually exists, and if it is—as it is usually alleged to be by those who claim to experience it—an actual immediate presence of the object to the mind, then it must be a species of perception. The object must either be present to the mind or absent from it. In the former case we have perception; in the latter case we have inference if we have any knowledge at all.

Perception, however, can only operate by the perceiving of the actual characters of the object. Direct knowledge of an object, therefore, can only consist in direct knowledge of such characters. Even if you refuse to use the word perception, will not the result be the same? How can there be any direct knowledge of an object which is not a direct knowledge of its qualities and characters? How can there be a direct knowledge of bare existence?

For my part I cannot admit or even conceive of any kind of direct knowledge of anything except some kind of sensuous or supersensuous perception. But I think it is possible that Professor Alexander is attempting to conceive of a direct knowledge which is not perception. Let us examine the means by which, according to him, we attain to direct knowledge of other minds. The experience on which that knowledge rests, he says, 'is a very simple and familiar one, the experience of sociality. . . . Our fellow human beings excite in us the social or gregarious instinct, and to feel socially towards another being is to be assured that it is something like ourselves.'[1]

Here then we have the solution of the riddle. Our direct knowledge does not rest upon a perception at all, but upon an *instinct*.

In order to attempt an appraisement of this contention we must go back once more to the distinction between the logical and the psychological aspects of the problem. In which sense is it that Professor Alexander purports to be solving the problem? If it is merely the psychological

[1] *Op. cit.*, vol. ii, p. 32.

aspect that he has in view, then there may be much to be said for his solution. To say that our belief in the existence of other minds is more or less instinctive and unreflective, and that the instinct is aroused as soon as we mix with our fellows, seems innocuous and may very likely be true. I do not think it could be accepted as a final analysis. For it is still possible to ask how the instinctive belief arose. And it is still possible to argue that it may arise from some subconscious inference similar to that which we employ when we judge the distance of a visual object. That judgement, be it noted, is in essence reasoned, but now appears in the upper levels of consciousness as instinctive.

Waiving that contention for the present, however, I must point out that a solution which relies on instincts is useless for the purposes of a theory of knowledge. Even if our knowledge originated historically in social instinct, this has nothing to do with its logical grounds. It is mere psychology. It throws no light on the logical foundation of our belief in other minds, nor upon the validity of our knowledge of them. For can it possibly be contended that an instinct is a good logical ground for a judgement of the intellect?

It is true that there is at the present day a large body of thought which tends to regard all logic and all reason as a mere cork tossed about on the vast ocean of instinct and desire. Our reasoned beliefs are represented as in reality the outcome of our desires, the rational element in them being merely our excuses for believing as we wish. Why the mind should, if reason has no regulative or compelling force, wish to have any excuses, why it should wish to appear reasonable to itself—that is a question which these thinkers never ask themselves and never answer. If they did, they would perceive the inconsistency of their position. But it is perhaps sufficient for us here to point out that as epistemologists we are concerned to study the validity of knowledge, and that the kind of view which we are discussing can only have as its logical culmination the denial of any validity to knowledge. But I cannot go further into that question here.

It is not clear whether Professor Alexander intends his teaching to be a solution of the logical as well as of the psychological problem. But it is not safe to assume that he does not. And we have therefore to inquire whether it can be said that in the social instinct we can find in any sense a good logical ground for believing in the existence of other minds.

Such a view may have, so far as I can see, two possible meanings. It may mean (1) that the existence of an instinct in an organism is usually proof that the means of satisfying the instinct exists; and that the existence of a social instinct is accordingly good reason for thinking that other minds exist to satisfy it. Or it may mean (2) that the instinct itself *is* knowledge of other minds, rudimentary knowledge perhaps, but real.

I do not think that the first of these two views can be what Professor Alexander intends to teach us. For it is clear that knowledge of other minds gained in this way would not be direct knowledge, but an inference. The major premiss would be the supposed empirical generalization that instincts in men and animals do not occur unless there also exist the means to satisfy them. The minor premiss would point out that we have a social instinct. And the conclusion that other minds exist to satisfy the instinct might be supposed to follow.

As this is clearly a mediate inference, it cannot be what Professor Alexander has in mind when he speaks of our 'direct knowledge' of other minds. And it is, in any case, an argument so weak-kneed and feeble that it would surely not be put forward by a philosopher of repute. The empirical generalization which is the major premiss has never received the detailed investigation and widespread observation which would be necessary to establish even its probability. It is the kind of reasoning put forward by theologians who are hard pressed to find an argument for immortality, and with whom the wish, being father to the thought, prompts empty generalizations of this kind. And even if it were true, would it follow that minds exist? The argument only purports to prove the

THE DISCOVERY OF OTHER MINDS 183

existence of whatever will satisfy the instinct, no more. But the social or gregarious instinct would be quite satisfied by warm, soft, moving, speaking, responding, but mindless automata. Hence it would be satisfied without the existence of minds. In any case it will not be seriously contended that our knowledge of the existence of other minds has either its psychological origin or its logical premisses in this weak argument.

I am driven to the conclusion that when Professor Alexander speaks of our direct knowledge arising through social instinct he must mean us to understand, not that we infer our knowledge from the instinct, but that the instinct itself *is* knowledge. It is always a dangerous proceeding to attempt to interpret the meaning of a philosopher in a form and in words which he has not authorized. And I may have misunderstood his contention. But this meaning seems to be the only one left after eliminating all possible alternatives.

It is not easy to criticize such a view logically, because it seems to be an attempt to transcend the confines of logic. But for that very reason it is to be profoundly distrusted. We used to be told that there is no knowledge in the mind which has not come to us by way of the senses. Now we are to be told that we can find knowledge in our instincts. Such a suggestion is a wholly new departure in philosophy, and appears to be an offshoot of that general irrationalism which is one of the most marked features of our age. And I think on every ground it is to be viewed with the utmost suspicion.

What is an instinct? It is at any rate, if I understand it rightly, some species of *feeling*. And it is understood to be specially marked by the absence of reflective thought. Most instincts, if not all, are concerned with practical activities, and have the production of such activities as their essential function. They are feelings which prompt the organism to some reaction, for example, the instinct of the bee to hive. Presumably such practical instincts exist psychically as blind impulses or desires to act in a given way without there being present to the mind any idea of the end at which the activity aims. How can such a blind impulse, feeling, or desire to act be described as knowledge? It seems not to be cognitive at all. And surely to describe it as knowledge is at least to use that word in a most unaccustomed sense, and—what is more important—in a sense quite different from that in which it is ordinarily said that we know that other minds exist.

Will it be said that in addition to instincts to act there are also instincts to believe this or that, cognitive instincts as we might call them? Such an assertion appears to me to involve a most questionable psychology. It seems rather to be true that no true instincts exist save those which are directed to action. But even if we granted the existence of such instincts directed towards knowledge, the application of that point of view to the present problem seems open to two criticisms. Firstly, the social instinct is *not* such a cognitive instinct, for it is definitely an instinct to act. Secondly, even if cognitive instincts exist, and even if the social instinct is one of them, yet to place any confidence in such feelings as grounds for our beliefs is in the highest degree dangerous; for such feelings cannot constitute a good logical ground for holding our beliefs.

As regards the first point, the social instinct clearly has behaviour for its end. It is an impulse to herd together, to act in co-operation, to enjoy the feelings of warmth and comfort which flow from the proximity and responsiveness of our fellows. Its function is to bring about that behaviour, not to bring knowledge into existence. Why should it bring knowledge into existence, seeing that the essential meaning of an instinct is an impulse which produces the necessary reactions of the organism *without* knowledge, without intellectual activity of any kind? Why should it bring knowledge into existence even as a by-product? And if that question seems unanswerable, how much more impossible is it to accept a doctrine which asserts, not that the instinct produces knowledge as a by-product, but that the instinct itself *is* knowledge?

Secondly, we cannot safely take our feelings and instincts as guides to truth, much less as themselves constituting a knowledge of the truth. To do so is to fall into a vicious mysticism which is the negation of philosophy. A theosophist once told me that his reason for believing in the doctrine of reincarnation was that 'he felt in his inmost being that it is true'. And it seemed to me that this was a very bad reason. Many religious persons of some other creed which does not happen to accept reincarnation would no doubt 'feel in their inmost beings that it is false'. They cannot both be right, and yet the 'inmost feelings' of one are as much entitled to respect and belief as the 'inmost feelings' of the other. And, as a social being desiring to herd with other organisms resembling myself and to rub my body against other bodies of the same general appearance and outline, I might possess very 'deep feelings' to the effect that other minds must exist. And yet this might well be false. How then does the mere existence of such a feeling, without any attempt at a rational justification of it, constitute knowledge?

An instinct is not good evidence of anything beyond itself. And if such irrational grounds are to be admitted as valid premisses for our beliefs about what is external to us, we may as well abandon logic, science, and philosophy. We may as well give up thinking, become mystics, and wallow in the mire of subjective feelings, visions, intuitions, ecstasies, and irrationalism generally.

I have previously commented on the weakness of giving as the grounds of our knowledge primitive beliefs and acts of animal faith. Such beliefs, as we saw, cannot be accounted more than mere prejudices. But they are a thousand times better than beliefs based on instincts. A prejudice is at least a cognitive act, and has a good chance of being the result of subconscious reasoning and so of being true and justifiable on logical grounds. It may have reason at its core. It may be one of the children of reason which has forgotten its parentage. But an instinct is nothing but a blind irrational urge. It is the negation of reason. Its *raison d'être* is to avoid and do without reason or thought or intelligence, to carry on the essential work and reactions of the organism without them. It has never at any time had any reason in it. And what are we to think of a philosophy which traces back our knowledge to such a source, which in fact goes farther and declares that such instincts not merely give rise to knowledge but *are* knowledge?

Whether social instinct is or is not knowledge is, after all, a question on which empirical evidence is relevant. Let me therefore place on record that the social instinct of at least one witness, namely myself, *is not knowledge*. I can distinguish clearly between my desire to associate with my fellows, which is a *feeling*, and my knowledge that they have minds, which is a *judgement*. No doubt the judgement and the feeling are intertwined, as are all elements of our mental states, will with feeling, feeling with thought. But they are nevertheless distinguishable and different. The feeling is not the judgement.

Thus the attempt to give 'direct knowledge' as the basis of our knowledge of one another breaks down. If by direct knowledge is meant any kind of sensuous or supersensuous perception, then it is clear that we have no such perception of the thoughts, feelings, and volitions of other people, and that only such perception of actual contents could constitute knowledge of other minds. If by direct knowledge perception is not meant, then the believer in such direct knowledge is forced to rely upon subjective feelings, and in general upon the irrational parts of our nature. This is likely to be true, I think, not only of the theory of Professor Alexander, but of all theories of this type. They cannot, without fairly obvious absurdities, rely on any kind of perception. And they are therefore forced to appeal either to instincts or to some kind of mystical assurance. We can accept neither.

We shall be forced back, therefore, upon some form of the theory of indirect or inferential knowledge. To see how it works out, we must go back to the beginning, to the solitary mind with which we started.

The solitary mind, then, is aware of itself, i.e. of its

activities in thinking, feeling, willing, and is also aware of the group of presentations which is afterwards identified as its body. As regards the first point, the mind's awareness of itself, it has been suggested by Mr. C. C. J. Webb in the paper already quoted that the consciousness of other minds may be actually prior to self-consciousness. He omits to explain, of course, whether he refers to logical or to psychological priority. Whether there is any sense in which his view may be true as a statement regarding the psychological or historical order of our ideas I shall not inquire. It certainly has no bearing upon their logical order. For if there is one indisputable fact about our knowledge of ourselves it is that such knowledge is direct and immediate. I have an immediate view, through introspection, of my own thoughts, feelings, and volitions. They are *given*. They therefore belong, just as much as do our sense-data, to the ultimate certitudes on the basis of which we build up our knowledge. It would be palpably absurd to suggest that I can only know the contents of my own consciousness indirectly by way of inference from my knowledge of yours. We are entitled, then, to take our knowledge of ourselves as a logical starting-point, as an ultimate given fact of which we are certain.

The solitary mind is also immediately aware of the presentations which make up its own body. It is not aware of its body *as* a body. For it has not yet arrived at the stage in which it knows objects or 'things'. What it has before it is not a continuously existing independent object which could be called a body, but only a series of fleeting presentations. Among these presentations, of course, are those which afterwards go to make up its own body. My present point is only that these presentations are as certainly and immediately known to the solitary mind as are its own acts of consciousness. So that the logical beginnings from which the solitary mind starts on its journey to its knowledge of other minds are twofold: (1) its knowledge of itself, i.e. of its own acts of thinking, feeling, willing, &c.; and (2) its perception of those presentations which it afterwards separates out from other presentations and builds up into the object which it knows as its own body.

The next necessary step is the gathering together of these latter presentations into a single group and the association of this group with the consciousness of the solitary mind. There are, strictly speaking, two steps here, but they may be taken together. For the gathering of the presentations into a group and the association of that group with the mind both arise out of one and the same experience.

It will be clear to the reader that the grouping together of the presentations and their association with a mind are not originally given. We do not start with them. We have somehow to arrive at them. For the association of my body with my mind, or in other words the discovery that my hands and feet belong to me, and are not mere indifferent parts of the landscape, is not originally given. In the logical beginning my hand is merely a pinkish colour patch among all the others. If there happens to lie adjacent to it among my presentations a green patch which is actually a tree, there is no more reason for supposing that the pinkish patch is part of me or has any special connexion with me, than for supposing that the green patch is part of, or has a special connexion with, me. Thus in the beginning I am not aware of the existence of my body at all. The presentations which compose it are merely a portion of the general world of phantasms with which I am surrounded.

I become aware of my body in the end chiefly because it insists on accompanying me wherever I go. There is a group of presentations which I can never get rid of. It accompanies me about as a group, and so becomes associated in my mind with myself, i.e. with my thinking, feeling, willing self. It is true that when the light is turned out I can no longer see my hand. But I can touch it. Or, if that language is too advanced for the stage of the solitary mind, we should rather say that when the light is extinguished I have a tactile sensation which I soon come to associate with the visual sensation which has disappeared. It is true again that a local anaesthetic will destroy the sense of touch in the part affected. But I can still see the part (or, I still have an associated visual sensation). So that in spite of temporary and partial obliterations of some of the presentations of the group, it is still true that on the whole this group of presentations accompanies me about wherever I go in a manner which is not characteristic of other groups. The group of presentations which composes yonder tree, even though it grows opposite my study window, is a comparatively rare visitor to my life. It visits me only for a few hours each day, and it has only done so for the last two years since I came to live in this house. I never saw it before that. It is the same with all groups of presentations except the group which is my body. They are all temporary and infrequent visitors. My body is simply that portion of my presentations which forces itself always upon me.

Taking my body as a whole, moreover, it does not change its size as I move about, whereas everything else does. As I walk forwards, what is in front of me increases in magnitude as it draws nearer; while at the same time everything behind me dwindles as it recedes. My body alone remains roughly constant. It is true that my hands and feet vary in size slightly according as I bring them nearer to my eyes or push them away. But this variation is small and is rigidly confined within certain narrow limits. My hand never vanishes altogether in the remote blue sky as does the dwindling speck of a sky-lark. It is still true to say, in spite of minor variations, that the size of my body remains roughly constant whatever movements take place relatively between it and surrounding objects. This fact also helps to pick out from among all others the group of presentations which make up my body.

There is also another set of facts which assists in the process of picking out the presentations which compose my body and setting them apart as unique. When a pin is pushed into my leg I feel pain. When my leg is stroked I feel a sensation which I may account pleasurable. But when a pin is pushed into a tree I do not feel any pain.

Nor do I receive any pleasurable sensation when the tree is stroked.

For these reasons, then, the various visual, tactile, and other presentations concerned first become thought of as a group instead of singly; and then this group becomes associated in my mind with *me* as a thinking, feeling being. It becomes 'my' body. I regularly associate the presence of the group of presentations with the presence of a mind, namely my own.

The next step is that I come to notice that there exist many groups of presentations which resemble the one which is my body. It is true that your body is unlike mine in the characteristics of which we have just been speaking. Your body does not accompany me about. It does not retain the same size whatever my movements relative to outside objects. I do not feel pain if a pin is stuck into it. But I can recognize it as like my body owing to its shape and colour, its general appearance and contour, its characteristic movements and postures, its special methods of behaviour, the sounds or cries which issue from it, and so on. These marks suffice to enable me to recognize the groups of presentations which are other people's bodies as similar to, and in the same class with, the group of presentations which is my own body.

It has been urged that primitive man, not having seen himself in a mirror, does not know the general appearance even of his own body, and therefore could not recognize other bodies as similar to it. It does not seem worth replying in detail to such a saltless argument, but I mention it since it has been put forward with apparent seriousness.[1] Apart from the existence of pools of water and other natural mirrors, it is surely obvious that we can see the whole of our bodies except our heads and back, and can explore our heads with our hands; and that in one way and another we should, even without mirrors, come to know our general appearance and its resemblance to the appearances of other persons. Will it be seriously con-

---

[1] For example, by Mr. C. C. J. Webb in the paper on 'Our Knowledge of One Another'.

tended that before the invention of mirrors every man went about quite unaware that his appearance resembled that of his fellows?

From this point the inference to the existence of other minds is quite simple, and proceeds much upon the well-known lines. The group of presentations which is my body is associated with my mind; and I come to think that its movements, gestures, and behaviour generally are caused by special kinds of mental content. When I am angry I hit out. In great pain I cry out. When I am frightened I sometimes run, sometimes turn pale and stand stock still. If I know a snake in my path to be poisonous, I make a detour to avoid it, or I pick up a stick and kill it. If I am amused I produce from my throat the peculiar kind of noise known as laughter. Now I also perceive around me other groups of presentations almost exactly like the one which I associate with my own mind. These groups behave in the same way as does mine. They laugh, cry out, run, smile, avoid snakes. Their general similarity of shape and colour, and their more remarkable similarities of behaviour suggest to me by analogy that with them are associated minds like mine, and that their behaviour is caused by fear, anger, amusement, knowledge—in general by a consciousness such as I myself possess. The inference to the existence of other minds is then complete.

The only way in which this differs from the usual form of the argument is that instead of bodies I have spoken of groups of presentations. For it must be remembered that we are still, when the argument begins, in the world of the solitary mind, and that in that world there are no permanent 'things', but only fleeting presentations. My body at that stage is no more than a group of such presentations. They go out of existence from time to time when I cease to be aware of them. But this will not prevent my recognizing the group as a group, and recognizing the similarities between groups on which the argument to the existence of other minds depends. For such recognition nothing more than the concepts of the given are required;

and the concepts of the given are all within the reach of the solitary mind.

The ordinary form of the argument which bases it, not on groups of presentations, but on bodies conceived presumably in the ordinary way as permanent and independent objects, is in this respect faulty. For the recognition of a body as a permanent independent thing, as existing for example when no one is aware of it, is itself dependent, as we have abundantly shown, upon our knowledge of the existence of other minds. And therefore our knowledge of other minds cannot be an inference from our knowledge of permanent bodies. But it can be, and is, an inference from groups of presentations such as can be recognized by the solitary mind. The knowledge of other minds is logically prior to the knowledge of 'things'. Therefore the knowledge of other minds cannot be deduced from 'things'. But knowledge of other minds is not logically prior to presentations, since the latter are logical ultimates or givens. Therefore presentations may be used as premisses of the argument.

Of course these subtleties are necessary only to preserve the strict logical sequence. The logical order is as we have laid it down. Even if we assume that the actual or psychological development of our ideas has been moulded by logic, by the very argument which we have just been examining, still it is not of course necessary to think that the mind has actually followed out the argument in all these refinements. Whatever is the logical order, knowledge of the external world of things and knowledge of the existence of other minds have no doubt actually grown up together. If these facts are remembered and understood, there will be no necessity for us to continue to speak, with clumsy pedantry, of 'groups of presentations' instead of 'bodies'. We may for shortness equate our argument with the usual argument based simply upon the body and its behaviour.

What is the relation between the psychological and the logical development of our knowledge of others? Are we

THE DISCOVERY OF OTHER MINDS

to think that they are entirely disconnected, that psychologically our belief has one origin, say, in the social or some other instinct, while logically it has another and totally different foundation, namely the argument based upon bodily behaviour? Or can we suppose that the movement of the mind in its history has been actually directed by logic, or in other words that the argument by analogy from bodily behaviour has been what has led it to its belief; so that the logical and the psychological developments will have been coincident?

These are difficult questions to answer, and possibly the truth lies somewhere between the extremes. If logic has played its part in actual historical development, it must have been, of course, a subconscious logic similar to that which we found reason to think must have operated to produce belief in the existence of a public independent world. In Chapter VI we attempted to lay bare, and to make explicit, the logical foundations of the belief in an independent external world. Those foundations consisted in a series of constructions. But although this development was primarily logical and ideal, we were led to think that the actual historical development must have been in some way dictated by it. The evolving human mind must have somehow felt the logic of the situation and built its world accordingly. But the logical steps, i.e. the constructions, were only implicitly or subconsciously taken, with the result that they appeared in the upper levels of consciousness in the form of an instinctive belief or animal faith.

I do not think the case for a subconscious logical development of the belief in other minds is quite so strong as was the case for such a development of the belief in an independent external world. There is an important difference between the two. There exists no specific instinct which could reasonably be said to offer an explanation of how our belief in an independent external world arose. So there seems no course open save that of attributing it to unconscious logic. But for our belief in other minds there exists a specific instinct, namely the social instinct, on which the belief can with at least a show of reason be fathered. I cannot see how our instinctive belief in an external world could possibly have arisen except by way of subconscious mental constructions such as we outlined in Chapter VI. I do not think that any psychologist would admit into his list of the instincts a separate instinct whose function it was to produce such a belief. For all the instincts seem, after all, to be directed to practical ends. And it makes no difference to any practical action whether or not we believe that things go on existing when they are unperceived. Nature is not likely, therefore, to have endowed us with any special instinct in the matter. An instinctive belief in such a case can scarcely mean anything except a belief which is unreflecting because its grounds are unconscious.

But with the belief in other minds the case is different. There undoubtedly *is* such a thing as a special social instinct. It is directed to various practical activities of co-operation. Animals hunt in packs. Fishes move in shoals. It would probably be absurd to say that this social instinct is the result of unconscious logic. For, in the first place, it is not an opinion or an idea, or a thought of the intellect such as would be the conclusion to an unconscious train of reasoning; it is not a cognition at all, but a mere impulse to a practical activity. And in the second place it is an impulse which is strongly developed in such low forms of organism that they can scarcely be suspected even of the glimmerings of unconscious thought.

But although the social instinct may be something quite different from any unconscious reasoning, it does not follow that the social instinct is actually the origin out of which our knowledge of one another has grown. So far as I can see, Professor Alexander merely asserts this, or at least suggests it, but produces no evidence at all to support it. And not only is no evidence produced, but the thing itself appears to be not a little unlikely. How can an instinct grow into an intellectual opinion or thought? How can an impulse to act turn into a judgement?

I do not say that the thing is impossible, or that the questions just asked are unanswerable. But it is clear that

THE DISCOVERY OF OTHER MINDS

they involve most obscure and difficult problems of psychology. And it is also clear that we are under no necessity to answer them in this book. Our concern as epistemologists is with the structure and validity of knowledge, not with its history. The validity of knowledge depends upon its logical justification, not upon its psychological genesis. Hence both as regards belief in the external world and belief in other minds, our primary and indeed our sole essential concern is with this logical basis. Wherever possible it seems useful and interesting to show that logical and psychological development are not indifferent to one another, that logic has often been at the heart of history, and that many human beliefs, even when they may appear instinctive, are not wholly abandoned of reason, but are rather guided by an implicit logical sense. The belief in an external world appeared to be such a belief. There exists no instinct on which it can plausibly be fathered. It makes no difference to any practical activity. It does not seem likely that any blind impulses to act can have given rise to it, seeing that such impulses could perform their function and produce their correlated activities without the arising of any such belief. How then could it have arisen? The most probable answer is that it arose, not from instinct, but from thought, from the world-constructing activity of the thinking mind, the operations of which have been, however, quite unconscious.

But the case does not seem so clear as regards our belief in other minds. This may have arisen as an unconscious inference from the movements and behaviour of other bodies. Or it may have some more irrational and instinctive origin such as that suggested by Professor Alexander. For there is at least in this case a suitable instinct lying close at hand which can be suspected of having something to do with the origin of the belief. The issue seems to me to be doubtful. And I would therefore prefer to express no decided opinion, but to leave the question open for the decision of those whose proper business, after all, it is, namely the psychologists.

Our conclusions may be summed up as follows. The

logical justification of our belief in other minds can only be by way of the argument by analogy from bodily behaviour (modified in the manner shown in this chapter). It is useless to appeal to the social instinct, or to any other kind of irrational feeling, for this justification. This is really all that the strict limits of our inquiry require us to decide. The psychological origin of our belief is a totally different question. Whether the belief historically arose out of the social instinct, or whether it arose from subconscious reasoning by analogy from bodily behaviour, or whether both sources contributed a share to the belief, is a question for psychology, to settle which is no part of my task, and which I prefer to leave undecided.

To this summary of results, however, I must add my conviction that recent philosophy has failed to keep the two questions separate, has in fact confused them together; and that the attack made by so many recent writers on the older theory, which based our belief in other minds on the analogy of bodily behaviour, has been a grave error due to this confusion.

It has to be admitted, of course, that the argument from bodily behaviour—the only genuinely logical argument which exists—does not yield certainty, but gives only a probable conclusion. This, as is well known, is true of all analogical reasoning. There is no means by which I can be absolutely *certain* that any mind exists except my own. It is *possible* that in addressing this book to my readers I am the victim of a complete delusion in supposing that they exist as conscious minds. It is possible that the whole universe is a dream of mine, and that all the other people in it are dream people. The contrary of this cannot be proved with absolute certainty. The argument by analogy from bodily behaviour goes as far as is possible towards proving the real existence of other minds. But it is a probable conclusion only.

But what of it? On the probable evidence before me I am prepared to believe. I am prepared to build up my universe on this basis. And one must remember that not only analogical, but all inductive reasoning, leads only to probability. After all, it is only probable that the sun will rise to-morrow. Yet no one ever lost a night's sleep over the uncertainty.

Whatever be the degree of probability which attaches to the reasoning by which we justify our belief in the existence of other minds, it is at any rate a genuine *inference*. The procedure of the mind which it involves is not a mental construction, but an inference. This is of the utmost importance because it is consistent with the view that the existence of other minds is factual, and not merely constructive. Other minds are facts, not inventions of mine.

The truth of this is not altered, of course, by the point that the inference is only probable, not certain. The word 'fact' in this context has reference to the nature of the existence, not to the truth or untruth of the statement that the fact exists. *If* other minds exist, the nature of that existence is factual, not constructive. The question whether our knowledge of their existence is probable or certain has no bearing at all upon this.

Other minds, then, are not a mental construction of mine. If they were, this would mean that my mind alone has factual existence, while all other minds have only constructive existence. This would be equivalent to a final and crushing solipsism from which there would be no escape. Admittedly our philosophy began in solipsism, but we do not intend it to end there. When I assert the existence of other minds I do not mean that I have invented them to explain phenomena. I mean that they actually and factually think, feel, and will. My assertion that your mind exists and thinks is not an hypothetical proposition like the existential mental construction. It does not mean 'If . . . then your mind would be perceived'. It is a categorical proposition which asserts that your mind actually thinks, feels, &c. This is not a constructive, but a factual existence.

The only kind of factual existence which we have so

far studied is that which is actually perceived. It is that whose *esse* is (or was originally for the solitary mind) *percipi*. The factual existence of the external world consists in its being known. But the factual existence of the internal world of mind consists in the fact that it is the knower. Its *esse* is not *percipi*. To say that its *esse* is *percipere* would be to use too narrow a term. We may say that its *esse* consists in the fact that it is conscious. That which neither knows nor is known, for example the unperceived table, can only have a constructive existence. But whatever either knows, e.g. the self, or is known, e.g. the table while I am looking at it, has factual existence. Constructive existence is that existence which is thought as independent of consciousness. But other minds are themselves consciousnesses. Therefore their existence is factual, and they are not mental constructions.

CHAPTER IX
SPACE AND TIME

WE will now return from the consideration of the mind's knowledge of itself and of other minds to its knowledge of the universe outside. We have traced the development of that knowledge from the private and intermittent phantasms of the solitary mind to the establishment of a public external world which is solid and independent, and which exists continuously even when no mind is aware of it. Fleeting private presentations have been replaced by permanent public objects. We had before us, at the close of Chapter VI, something like the ordinary world of everyday knowledge.

But to one important feature of that world we have given no consideration at all. Space and time, even as they appear in common knowledge—and taking no account of scientific concepts of them—do not belong to the world of the solitary mind. We have therefore to consider from what given elements in perception they have been developed, and what course that development has taken.

It must not, of course, be supposed that, because we have first dealt with the development of a public independent world, and only now come to the question of space and time,—it must not be supposed that such is the true order. A public external world is not first established and then afterwards space and time. Neither the logical nor the psychological order could be so represented without absurdity. Actually, no doubt, the two grow up together. Even logically the two developments are so closely interdependent that the separate consideration of them is only possible by means of an abstraction. But in matters so complicated we are compelled, for convenience of exposition, to consider first one branch of the development and then the other. And the order we have chosen to adopt is merely one of convenience.

The problems connected with the philosophy of space and time are so many and so difficult that anything like a complete review of them is out of the question here. Such a review would require at least a separate volume to itself. I shall therefore confine my investigations to only one aspect of the question, that aspect which falls directly in the natural path of our inquiries. My object will be to show that our knowledge of space and time is riddled through and through with mental constructions; or, to put the same thing in a different way, that space and time as we know them are themselves mental constructions. And éven my treatment of this one aspect of the problem can be no more than sketchy and diagrammatic, confining itself to the consideration of key positions. I shall detail some of what appear to be the main constructions involved. But I do not deny that there may be many more constructions in our knowledge of space and time besides those here to be laid down.

At once I shall be asked, 'what kind of space and time are you talking about?' It is now recognized that many kinds of space and space-time are possible, and that more than one kind may be actual in different parts of the universe. Is it Euclidean or non-Euclidean space or space-time that is to be the subject of the discussion? Is it the infinite space which was believed in by the older scientists? Or is it the finite space of Einstein or de Sitter?

I reply that the purpose of this chapter is not to consider advanced scientific ideas, whether of one school or another, whether those fashionable to-day or those which the fathers of our present scientists promulgated. Its purpose is to consider space and time as they appear in the common everyday knowledge of mankind. We have not as yet advanced far enough with our inquiries to begin thinking about science. We are at the very beginning. We have not yet justified even the commonest conceptions of space and time, conceptions such as the existence of empty space, the existence of three dimensions (not to speak of four as yet), the continuity and simultaneity of space, the identity of tactile with visual space, the existence of a common or public space and time. None of these ideas exist in the beginning for the solitary mind. We have to begin at the beginning and develop them. That is the object of this chapter. Something will be said in later chapters of such questions as the Euclidean or non-Euclidean character of space, and the space-time of relativity mechanics. I will, however, say here in anticipation—since it will assist the reader to understand the general point of view adopted—that in my view all kinds of space and time, and of space-time *continua*, are mental constructions. They are alternative truths, of which the mind may incorporate into knowledge one or other according to its needs, and provided only that it neither contradicts the facts of perception nor the laws of logic.

For our starting-point we must go back again to the beginning, to the world of the solitary mind. Space and time as we now know them will not be found there. But something must be found there out of which space and time must have developed. This something will, of course, be an element of the given. To arrive at the starting-point for our present inquiry, therefore, we have to ask ourselves the question, out of what elements of the given have space and time been developed? What kind of rudimentary or embryonic space and time exist for the solitary mind? What is given to it as immediate and ultimate certitude? The answer to these questions has already been made fairly clear in a previous chapter. The solitary mind begins, not with any kind of space or time, but with extension-spread and duration-spread.

Our extension-spreads and duration-spreads are private to each of us. The red patch which I see has extension-spread. You see what we afterwards agree to believe is the 'same' red patch. But they are not given as the same. The sameness is, as we have abundantly shown, a later construction. And as the two red patches are not originally the same, so of course the extension-spreads which they carry are not the same. In the beginning therefore my red patch has one extension-spread and your red patch another. They are quite distinct from one another, and they exist in different private universes. It is, of course, the same with duration-spreads. We start, then, not, as is sometimes said, with a multiplicity of private spaces and times, but with a multiplicity of private extension-spreads and duration-spreads.

The next point to note is that even within the private world of each solitary mind there is not a single continuous extension-spread and duration-spread, but a multitude of quite disconnected spreads. The red patch (which may be a pillar-box) disappears from my vision when I look away from it and reappears as a second and distinct red patch when I look again. Since the first red patch is not the same as the second red patch, therefore the extension-spread of the first is not the same as the extension-spread of the second. Nor are the two even continuous with one another. Other presentations with their spreads intervene. Or a period of unconsciousness may intervene. During intervals of sleep or unconsciousness of any sort the spreads disappear along with the presentations, and entirely new ones are created when consciousness again becomes active.

Further, we must not forget that the extension-spread which the solitary mind gets through sight is different from that which it gets through touch and muscular sense. The worlds of touch and sight are separate universes, and the spreads within them are numerically distinct and totally different in kind from one another.

Moreover, though the extension-spread of touch probably has three dimensions, the extension-spread of sight has only two. The visual world as given is flat and without depth. The third visual dimension is, as I shall endeavour to show in detail, a construction. This, of course, is a controversial question, and many philosophers will not agree with me. I shall give my reasons for my opinion later in this chapter.

Empty space, again, does not exist for the solitary mind at the beginning of knowledge. We cannot directly perceive emptiness, pure nothingness. Empty space, or at any rate empty visual space, is a construction. The given extension-spread does not continue beyond the edge of the presentation to which it pertains; or, if it does, it continues only into another presentation. It does not continue into nothingness. Therefore empty space is not given.

For the same reason visual extension-spread does not continue outside the actual present visual field. It is bounded by the limits of the visual field. When I move my eyes round to a new set of objects, the first visual field not only disappears from view, but also, since its *esse* is *percipi*, ceases to exist. And its extension-spread ceases to exist along with it, and a new extension-spread comes into existence. For the solitary mind space does not spread out indefinitely into distance beyond what is actually seen. And certainly there is no room in such a mind for infinite space.

These, then, are some of the main characters of our starting-point. From this starting-point space and time as we now know them (whether Euclidean or non-Euclidean, whether finite or infinite) are developed by means of a series of constructions. And I shall now endeavour to set down a few of the main constructions in such order as may appear both logical and convenient. And in this endeavour I must once more guard against misconception. Not only are the following constructions probably not the only ones, but further it is not to be thought that the order in which I have placed them is a cast-iron order which is unalterable. Euclid adopted a certain order for his theorems, and it was a logical order in the sense that theorems which appeared earlier in his book are used as premisses for theorems which appear later. But it is well known that both the proofs and the order might have been different from what they are without detriment to the science. And if this is true of a complete and systematic development of the rigorous science of geometry, how much more will it be true of a series of theorems which profess to be no more than samples of the general procedure of the mind in the development of its knowledge of space and time.

First Construction.

That there exists for each mind a single continuous private visual space and a single continuous private tactile space.

For the solitary mind the extension-spread of a presentation ceases to exist along with the presentation as soon as the latter ceases to be perceived. That alone has extension-spread which is *now* present to the sight or touch. What lies outside the immediate visual and tactile fields has no existence, and therefore, of course, no extension-spread. Now let us, for the moment, use the word 'space' to mean the whole extension of whatever is comprised within a particular visual or tactile field. The single red patch has extension-spread. But the whole visual field which includes at one and the same time the red patch and a large number of other extended presentations we will call a visual space. Thus my space at this moment includes the extension-spreads of the presentations which represent the white piece of paper I am writing on, the brown patch of the table, a small piece of yellow wall, a row of books, &c. But the presentations which I perceived in the adjoining room before I came in here, and which I cannot perceive now, are in a different space which has now ceased to exist. Each mind, therefore, experiences a large number of spaces *which are not simultaneous but which follow each other successively in time.*

When a period of sleep or other interruption of awareness intervenes between the perceptions of two spaces, then those spaces are entirely cut off from one another. They do not in any way continue into one another. But when different spaces succeed each other continuously in time, as happens when I turn my head slowly round or when I pass from one room to another, then these successive spaces flow into one another. As I turn my head away from what I am now looking at, a new space begins to come into view which joins on to the old space. Suppose the first space is called a,b,c,d, and the second space e,f,g,h. While I am perceiving a—d, e—h is non-existent. For its *esse* is *percipi*, so that as it is not yet perceived it follows that it has not yet come into existence. When on the other hand I have turned my head right round and am perceiving e—h, then a—d is non-existent; for it has ceased to be perceived and has therefore gone out of existence. But when my head is turned only partly round, then I shall

SPACE AND TIME

perceive the intermediate space c,d,e,f, which comprises parts of both the previous spaces. It is in this way that successive spaces flow into one another.

But by the fourth construction of Chapter VI 'presentations may exist when no mind is aware of them'.

It follows that the extension-spreads of presentations —and, in general, that spaces—may continue to exist when no mind is aware of them.

By means of the fourth construction of Chapter VI the mind realizes the idea that presentations, instead of dropping out of existence when the mind ceases to perceive them, continue in permanent existence independently of the mind. As soon as the mind realizes this, the successive spaces of its experience become welded into one simultaneous space. For as the head is turned round, and as e—h comes into view, it is no longer necessary to hold that a—d has ceased to exist. It continues its existence unseen. So also before the head is turned it is not necessary to suppose that e—h has not yet come into existence. It too has existed unseen. So that a,b,c,d,e,f,g,h now constitute a single simultaneous space the parts of which are perceived at successive times. For the solitary mind at its starting-point there existed many successive spaces. Now these are being replaced by one space the parts of which exist simultaneously but are perceived successively.

This process of unification need not stop anywhere short of completion. The successive spaces which I perceive during a continuous period of consciousness will obviously coalesce into one, since they flow directly into one another. But even the spaces which are separated by intervals of sleep or other forms of unawareness will follow the same rule. For general experience will teach us that unperceived spaces join on to perceived spaces. For example, I perceive to-day the space a,b,c,d while I am travelling in a railway train and looking out of the window. Then I doze for a moment, and on awaking I perceive the space i,j,k,l. These two spaces do not join on to one another, but as a result of the fourth construction of Chapter VI they are conceived as simultaneous and as permanently existing. But the next day I pass the same way again and I perceive the space a,b,c,d and immediately adjoining it and continuous with it the space e,f,g,h. This is the space which I missed during my doze yesterday. By combining the two days' experience and holding fast to the view that all the spaces which I perceive continue existing even when they are not being perceived, I easily conclude that the space a,b,c,d,e,f,g,h,i,j,k,l is one continuous and simultaneous space. In this way periods of unconsciousness are bridged over and all perceived and unperceived spaces coalesce into one.

Similar considerations hold of tactile spaces. Their continuity is learned by such elementary experiences as the passing of a finger along a surface. But these experiences are successive, and will give rise to a number of successive spaces. The permanent existence and simultaneity of these tactile spaces is a deduction from the fourth construction of Chapter VI, similar in all ways to the deduction just made in the case of visual space.

The curious opinion of Platner and others that men born blind could not obtain from touch alone any idea of space, but that for them time must serve instead of space, is now known to be erroneous.[1] But it is worth noting that it was apparently based upon a failure to observe that the perceptions of visual and of tactile space *as given* are precisely on a par as regards successiveness. It was pointed out by those who held this opinion that the sensations which arise from such experiences as passing one's finger along an edge or a surface are all successive. They would easily give rise, therefore, to the idea of time, but could not originate the notion of the simultaneously co-existing parts external to one another which is of very essence of space. It was evidently thought that sight has some advantage over touch in this respect. It was thought that though we only touch things successively we see them simultaneously. It was thought that the panorama of visual space lies before us and that the parts of it are *seen*

[1] See *The World of the Blind*, by Pierre Villey, p. 197 (English translation).

as simultaneous. But this is manifestly a mistake. The visual field is exceedingly small. What lies within one and the same visual field is no doubt seen as simultaneous. But the spaces (and their contents) which are so large that they cannot be got within one visual field can only be seen by successive acts of vision. The sweeping of the eye round the four walls of the room, or the action of the person in a moving train who looks out of the window on the passing scenery, is precisely analogous to the passing of the finger along a surface. No doubt vision gives a *small* simultaneous space, namely that which can be got into one visual field. But touch also gives as simultaneous the space which can be felt by one stretch of the hand or other part of the bodily surface. The hand's breadth or other such tactile unit corresponds to the visual field. No doubt it is true that vision has certain advantages over touch. But our point is that neither gives a single space. Both give a series of successive spaces. And the one single space, whether tactile or visual, is built up by the mind out of these. In spite of certain obvious advantages which sight has over touch, there is no difference of principle between the construction of visual space and the construction of tactile space. Both begin with a series of small successive spaces. And both convert these by means of a mental construction into a single simultaneous space.

Thus there comes to exist for each of us a single private visual space and a single private tactile space. That is as far as the present construction professes to take us. And we will now examine the characters of the construction.

The essential features of space with which we are concerned are (1) continuity, and (2) simultaneity. Continuity as here understood does not refer to the well-known mathematical conception which goes by that name, but has reference only to the common fact that every part of space flows without a break into the next part. Space and time are both continuous, but space alone is simultaneous, i.e. its parts are all simultaneously existent. This simultaneity is what distinguishes space from time.

Now the character of continuity is *given*. The immediate visual field consists of parts which are continuous, and the space within the visual field is therefore given as continuous. Moreover its continuity with the next adjoining visual field, which arises when one turns one's head or walks into the next room, is also given. It is true that there exist breaks in the given continuity at points where sleep or unconsciousness of the external world supervene. These gaps are filled up by the mental construction.

Simultaneity, except within the very narrow limits of the visual or tactile field, is not given. The simultaneity of the paper and the table on which I am writing is given, since both are actually perceived in the same visual field at the same time. But the simultaneity of the space I now see with the space which I see a second later when I turn my head round is not given, since the two spaces are seen successively. In this case their continuity is given, but not their simultaneity. Nor is the simultaneity of two spaces outside the limits of the perceptual field an inference from anything which is given. While I am now perceiving the space a—d, I have no reason whatever for believing that the space e—h is in existence. It cannot be inferred from anything which I am now seeing. The simultaneity of the two spaces, therefore, cannot be perceived, since they are perceived successively. And it cannot be inferred, since no inference can possibly pass to an unperceived existence. The unperceived space here is in exactly the same position as the red patch or other presentation which is unperceived. We saw in Chapter VI that the mind can have absolutely no reason for believing in the existence of an unperceived presentation, i.e. its existence cannot be inferred from anything that is perceived. And it was for this reason that we concluded that the belief is a construction. In exactly the same way the mind cannot have any reason for believing in the existence of an unperceived space, i.e. of a space now lying outside the visual or tactile field. The existence of such a space can neither be perceived nor inferred. Therefore it must be a construction.

Without any construction we might indeed have a continuous series of successive spaces—so long at least as we do not fall asleep. But the idea of a single space, all parts of which are simultaneous, cannot be reached without construction.

We have held this idea to be a construction because it can neither be perceived nor inferred. It may be pointed out, of course, that it is an inference from the fourth construction of Chapter VI. That construction established that presentations may exist outside the present perceptual field. That of course implied that the space or extension-spread of the presentations must similarly exist unperceived. And the present construction of a single simultaneous space merely consists in drawing that deduction and combining it with the given experience of continuity.

This is quite true. But the fact that our belief in such a space is in this way an inference from a previous construction does not nullify the view that this belief is itself a genuine construction. The essential character of a construction is that it is a belief in something which is not given and cannot be inferred *from what is given*. It may, however, be inferred from another construction. Constructions are in fact frequently connected to one another by links of logical implication; so that we get chains or systems of constructions. Scientific knowledge consists largely, not of isolated constructions, but of networks of them, each construction being logically implied by all the others. It is in this way that knowledge becomes systematic. But so long as none of the constructions which are members of the system can be deduced logically from any perceived fact the whole system will be constructional, not factual. So it is in the present case. The present construction regarding space is practically an inference from the previous constructions regarding presentations. But it does not for that reason cease to be a genuine construction.

This construction is existential in type. One might be at first disposed to class it as unificatory. For it seems to reduce the many spaces to one. But this would be a mistake. In the true unificatory construction two or more different things are declared to be the 'same', i.e. to be numerically identical. For example your red patch is declared to be the same as my red patch, although there are palpably two, not one, in factual existence. But in the construction which we have just described as regards space no such process of declaring two different things to be numerically identical takes place. The many private spaces which are welded into one are not declared to be identical but merely to adjoin each other and to flow into each other. The space a—d is conceived as running into the adjoining space e—h. They are also conceived as simultaneous. But no one supposes that they are identical. Their identity would, however, be implied if the construction were unificatory.

The essence of the present construction is that it posits the existence of unperceived spaces simultaneously with perceived spaces. It constructs, therefore, an unperceived existence, and is accordingly an existential construction.

It possesses accordingly the characters of all existential constructions as laid down in Chapter VI. It can only be accurately expressed in the form of an hypothetical judgement having an impossible antecedent clause. It means 'If I were now somewhere else as well as where I actually am, I should perceive another space simultaneously with the space I am now perceiving, and continuous with it'. The condition is impossible because I cannot be in two places at the same time.

Second Construction.

That there exists for each mind a single continuous private time.

This construction does for time what the last construction did for space. The two constructions are parallel, and the present one may be very shortly treated. The many spaces were welded into one space of which all the parts were (1) continuous, and (2) simultaneous. Of these two characters only the first applies to time. Simultaneity is absent from it. Hence all that the present construction has to do is to weld the many times into one continuous

SPACE AND TIME

time. While I am awake and aware, I perceive a continuous stream of presentations in a continuous time. The continuity is here given in immediate perception. But suppose I go to sleep for half an hour. When I wake up a new time begins which is not continuous with the last. It is only in this way that there exist for each mind at the starting-point of its knowledge a number of disconnected times.

The construction which unites these is very simple and obvious. Like the last construction this one also is involved in the fourth construction of Chapter VI. Presentations exist when I am not aware of them. I learn from other minds that while I was asleep the red patch which I saw before I fell asleep continued in existence until I saw it again on awakening. It follows that the two disconnected times of which I was aware were joined by a stretch of time which was unperceived by me.

The construction is existential, since it invents an unperceived time. It means 'If I were awake while I am asleep, I should perceive the flow of time'.

Third Construction.

That visual space and tactile space (and any other perceptual spaces which may exist) are identical with one another.

The words contained within brackets are not important. It might be asserted that in addition to visual and tactile spaces there exist auditory, olfactory, or even gustatory spaces. If any such spaces exist—regarding which I express no opinion—they will at any rate come to coalesce with the visual and tactile spaces by means of constructions essentially similar in principle to that by which the visual and tactile spaces coalesce. The words within brackets are inserted merely for the sake of completeness and to cover that possible point. And I shall not refer to the question again, but shall confine my inquiries to the spaces which are admittedly the only really important ones, namely visual and tactile spaces.

The present construction is merely a corollary of the sixth construction of Chapter VI, which asserted 'that with the different senses we perceive the "same" objects, and that the worlds of the different senses are in general identical with one another'.

We saw the difficulty of identifying the visual table with the tactile table. They bear no resemblance to one another at all. Yet the mind identifies them. It must clearly be the same with the spaces which they occupy. Visual extension-spread does not bear any resemblance to tactile or muscular extension-spread. They are totally incomparable, incommensurable. But the two are associated in experience in such a way that the one is always a sign of the other. When the construction of the 'thing' underlying appearances or presentations comes before us, as it has already in Chapter VI, then those characters of the 'thing' which are in different sense-worlds, but are signs of one another, become identified. The solid appearance to the eye is identified with the sense of resistance to touch. And similarly the visual extension-spread is identified with the tactile extension-spread. They are but the two appearances in the two sense-worlds of the 'same' space which is occupied by the 'same' object or 'thing'.

The present construction can be exhibited as a direct deduction from the sixth construction of Chapter VI. For if the tactile table is identical with the visual table, then the spaces which they occupy must be the same.

This construction, like the last, is an inference from a previous construction. But it is not an inference from any perceived fact. It is possible to prove it in the sense that it can be deduced from a previous judgement. But that previous judgement is itself a construction, an assumption which cannot be proved. Therefore the present construction cannot be proved, and is in the last resort merely an assumption which fits in with other assumptions. It is therefore a genuine construction.

Its character follows that of the sixth construction of Chapter VI. It is unificatory.

Fourth Construction.

That there is but one space common and public to all minds, and one time common and public to all minds.

SPACE AND TIME

By this construction private spaces and times disappear and cease to exist. They are all swallowed up in a common space and a common time. So far we have of course been dealing only with private spaces and times. The many successive spaces of each mind fused into one. Then the private tactile and the private visual space of each mind fused into one space. Now the final step in the same process is taken when the many private spaces coalesce into a single public space, and the many private times into a single public time.

It seems hardly necessary to labour the derivation of the construction after the detailed description we have given of previous similar constructions. As with the last two constructions, the present one follows closely the development of the public external world given in Chapter VI. The many private worlds having coalesced into one public world, it is obvious that the many private spaces and times will coalesce into one public space and one public time. The present conclusion is thus simply a corollary to the second construction of Chapter VI, which laid it down that 'the corresponding presentations of different minds are identical, and that there are not many universes, but only one'. If the red patch which I see is identical with the red patch which you see, then it follows that the spaces and times which they occupy must be identical. This at once yields the present construction.

The construction is of the unificatory type. And it is a genuine construction as being incapable of proof, except by deduction from a previous construction.

The order of the constructions of this chapter up to date is no doubt open to comment. By the third construction my visual space was identified with my tactile space, so that the various private spaces of each separate mind are reduced to a single all-embracing space, which is, however, still private to that mind. By the present construction my private space is declared identical with yours and with the private spaces of all other minds, so that the many private spaces are reduced to one common space. It is possible that this order of constructions might have been different.

For example, we might have exhibited the mind as first identifying the various private visual spaces with one another to make a public visual space; next as having done the same thing with the many private tactile spaces; and finally as having identified the public visual space with the public tactile space so as to produce the single space, common to all the senses and to all minds, which is the space of our ordinary present-day knowledge.

There would be much to be said for such an order. And this illustrates how, as I have already pointed out at the beginning of this chapter, different orders among the various constructions of the mind on all subjects may be possible. Thus the order adopted in the present chapter does not profess to be rigidly exclusive of all other orders, and has been chosen largely from considerations of convenience.

Fifth Construction.

That visual space possesses a third dimension.

Opinions differ as to the origin of the third or depth dimension in visual space. It may be held to be either (1) given, or (2) inferred from what is given, or (3) constructed.

The view (1) that it is given, is apparently that taken by William James and by more recent writers such as Dr. C. D. Broad. The view (2) that it is inferred, is that of Berkeley. The view (3) that it is a construction, is the opinion which will be adopted in this book. For the existence of the third visual dimension cannot be proved by an inference as Berkeley thought.

It will be observed that our statement of the construction in the heading refers to visual space and leaves out all reference to tactile space. That is because, in my view, tactile space stands on a wholly different footing from visual space in this respect. I believe that the third dimension of tactile space is given in perception, is there from the start; but that in visual space only two dimensions are given, so that the third has to be constructed.

If we take touch and muscular sense together, the space

which they yield appears to be three-dimensional from the outset. The three dimensions are immediately given. They are not, however, given by pure touch alone without the aid of muscular sense. If I stand in the garden by the outside corner of my house, I can pass my finger-tips along the wall which faces me, and when they reach the corner I can then pass them along the wall which lies at right angles to this, i.e. the wall which goes away from me into the depth dimension. But as far as pure touch is concerned there will be no change of sensation after passing the corner. I shall receive three successive sensations, namely (1) the feel of my fingers passing along the wall which faces me—which may reasonably be supposed to give rise to the idea of a surface, (2) the sharp feel of the corner, and (3) the return of the feeling of my fingers moving along a surface. The third sensation will be identical with the first, though it will be divided from it in time by the second. But the interruption of the corner will make no difference. And the third sensation being identical with the first, there is nothing in the experience which could give rise to the idea of a change of direction or dimension.

The two surfaces at right angles thus give rise to identical tactile sensations. The muscular sensations, however, will differ. While I am passing my hand along the wall which faces me, my arm is being moved from side to side. After it passes the corner my arm must be stretched out away from me to follow the wall. The muscular sensations of the two movements will be quite different from one another, and this difference will be sufficient to give rise to the idea of a dimension different from the two surface dimensions, i.e. to the third dimension.

And it would seem that by feeling the angle of a cube I should be able to receive a direct impression of three dimensions. I pass my finger from the point along the three converging edges. The pure touch sensations in the pulp of the finger will not give dimensions. They will only give line or surface. But the muscular sensations of hand and arm will differ for each of the three edges and will constitute rudimentary perceptions of the three dimensions.

It is for this reason that I hold that in tactile-muscular space (which is what is ordinarily called tactile space) the three dimensions are *given*.

But visual space is totally different. It is flat. To the extent of holding that the depth dimension is not given, i.e. not directly perceived, I agree with Berkeley. He long ago propounded the view that 'distance, of itself and immediately, cannot be seen. For, distance being a line directed endwise to the eye, it projects only one point in the fund of the eye, which point remains invariably the same, whether the distance be longer or shorter.'[1] Our estimates of the distances of objects, he explained, are inferences. In the case of objects close at hand there are the muscular sensations involved in the convergence of the two eyes and the accommodation of the eye muscles. In the case of far away objects we judge by the apparent size of the object, by our estimate of the sizes of the objects which intervene, by the colour (' blue hills far away'), and a number of other factors.

Berkeley's opinion held the field, and was almost universally regarded as established, until quite recently. It is now widely disputed. William James considered that the depth dimension is as much sensationally original as the two superficial dimensions. He thought that what we primarily experience is a sensation of *volume*, and in proof of this he appeals to many experienced feelings, such as that glowing bodies appear 'roomy', look luminous 'through and through', and so forth.[2] But these experiences prove nothing, except what is already admitted, namely that *now*, after our sight has been developed and educated, we *feel* that we have perceptions of distance and depth. The question is whether, when we feel that we can immediately sense distances and depths, we have before us real cases of pure perception, or whether they are not rather cases in which cognitive processes of construction or inference have been involved, but have sunk, through use and wont, down to the perceptual level and become

---

[1] Berkeley, *A New Theory of Vision*, paragraph 2.
[2] James, *Principles of Psychology*, Chapter XX.

embedded there. Suppose I judge that an object is at a certain distance from me because I see certain other things intervening which I know by experience to be of such and such a size. A great deal of thinking is involved here. Yet such judgements become automatic by frequent practice. They become unconscious, and thereby sink to the level of the immediate. They are then mistaken for perceptions. Now all that James does is to quote numerous examples of experiences of what *appear* to us to be direct perceptions of the voluminousness of objects. But this procedure simply begs the question. It does not prove that the supposed perceptions are really such, it does not prove that they are aboriginal or known to the solitary mind. My view is that they are a product, not an original element. They are the result of deep unconscious constructions, of cognitions the separate discursive steps of which have sunk into the subconscious, or perhaps have never risen out of it. Such unconscious thought-processes appear in the upper levels of consciousness in the guise of immediate feeling or 'intuition'. These feelings are then seized upon by writers like William James to prove that depth and distance are aboriginal perceptions!

Dr. C. D. Broad is one of the more recent writers who appear to hold views essentially similar to those of James. Dr. Broad says, 'it is perfectly obvious to me that I do sense different patches of colour at different visual distances'.[1] This makes it clear how each of us is, after all, enclosed in his own private world. For Dr. Broad can see distance. I, unfortunately, cannot. It is 'perfectly obvious' to me that I do *not* sense patches of colour at different visual distances. In the garden in front of my window in this tropical country in which I am writing is a coco-nut palm, and at some distance behind it another coco-nut palm. I can see that the trunk of the former appears larger than that of the latter, and that the details of the fronds and the lines of the bark are on a larger scale. I see various other differences between the appearances of the two trees. And I see the grassy ground which intervenes

[1] C. D. Broad, *Scientific Thought*, p. 295.

between them. Experience has taught me to judge from all these facts that one lies at a distance behind the other. But I am absolutely unable on analysis to detect in myself any direct perception of visual depth.

If there is such a direct perception of visual distance, how is it that all the stars appear to be at the same distance from us? We know that enormous differences of distance exist, that one star is a hundred times further from us than another. How is it that we have not even the faintest trace of a perception of this? That we could not measure the exact relative distances by eye might be understandable. But surely there ought to exist *some* difference between the perception of the star which is three light-years away and the perception of the one which is three hundred light-years away. There is in fact no difference at all, and the reasonable way of explaining this is to think that we have no perception of distance. Will it be replied that we have the sense of depth for objects which are close to us on the earth, but that it fails us when we come to deal with interstellar distances? But this is purely arbitrary, an *ad hoc* assumption invented to explain away the difficulty.

Again, if there is a direct sense of visual distance, how is it that we are often deceived about such matters? Flat pictures can be made which in suitable circumstances will actually be taken by an unsophisticated observer to be a group of objects having depth and three dimensions. A flat light-coloured disk can be painted and shaded in such a way that it will be mistaken for a sphere. And such a flat disk and a real sphere placed side by side may be indistinguishable from one another. This shows that the sensations received from a three-dimensional world are identical with those received from a two-dimensional world, and that there is no special sensation of distance peculiar to the former. It shows that there is no difference between the *perceptions* of three-dimensional and two-dimensional objects, but that the difference lies in the *interpretations* which our intellects place on them. And it surely follows from this that no perception of distance exists. And if we are deceived by a flat picture which looks as if it had depth, this impression of depth must be a part of our interpretation, since sensation as such never deceives us.

I therefore think that Berkeley was right, and that all that is given in sight is a flat, coloured, two-dimensional surface.

The third dimension not being given, we have next to ask whether it is inferred from anything that is given. Now it is true that, the general idea of visual distance having once obtained an entrance into the mind, the judgement of particular distances may be a matter of inference. I know that certain peculiarities of sensation (such as the larger or smaller appearance of an object, the appearance of intervening objects, the muscular sensation caused by the convergence of the eyes on a very near object) are signs of greater or lesser distance from the eye. But all these inferences presuppose that visual space has three dimensions and that the mind is aware of this. They presuppose that the idea is already in the mind. The fact that one coco-nut palm looks twice as big as another does not prove that the first is nearer to us. From this difference in size you could not infer the existence of a depth dimension. For the same appearance, the same difference, exists in the painted picture of the coco-nut trees, and in that case there is no depth dimension. But, when once it is known and admitted that three dimensions exist, then various phenomena of visual sensation become signs from which the greater or less distance of objects may be inferred. So that, although particular distances may be inferred in the various ways well known since the time of Berkeley, the existence of visual depth is not itself an inference from anything given in vision. There is clearly nothing in the fleeting colour patches which we see (and we see nothing else) from which the idea of depth could be deduced.

Since the third visual dimension is neither given nor inferred from what is given, we are left with the alternative that it must be a mental construction. The only question which we have to face is how and why the mind made this construction. Let us turn to that issue.

Suppose that we perform the experiment, beloved by all philosophers, of rotating a penny in such a way that, having first appeared circular, it becomes an ellipse of increasing eccentricity, until it at last (when placed edgewise on) shows only as a very narrow rectangle or band. Now, if we had only the sense of sight and no sense of touch, we should probably explain this series of appearances as mere *change of state*. I need hardly remind the reader that change is, as far as outward appearances go, of two kinds. Change of spatial position is called motion. But there are many changes which are not motions, as when the leaf changes its colour from green to yellow. This is change of state. Now my point is that although *we* explain the changes in the appearance of the penny as due to motion (rotation), this explanation would not occur to a being possessed of no sense except that of sight. He would not have attained the idea of a third dimension through touch, and he could not attain it through sight. He would therefore be without it. Nor would the idea dawn upon him as a result of watching the rotating penny. For he would explain that quite simply to himself, not as due to motion at all, but to change of state. He would say that the circular brown patch had contracted to an ellipse and then to a narrow rectangle. This only involves change of colour. For suppose the background on which the penny appears is white. Then the change from circle to ellipse and ellipse to rectangle is nothing more than the fact that a part of the flat surface of the visual field which was brown becomes white. Such a being, then, will not explain the phenomena of the rotating penny by means of the third dimension.

But now suppose that I have the sense of touch, and that the rotation of the penny has been caused in the usual way by my turning it round in my fingers. While it appeared circular I could pass my finger across the flat disk. From this I received certain tactile sensations. Now it is part of the constructed concept of external existence—the construction of which the mind has already completed—that the object of touch is identical with the object of sight.

SPACE AND TIME

I have therefore identified the tactile extension-spread given in the act of passing my finger across the penny with the visual extension-spread of the penny. Although they bear no resemblance to one another at all, and although they exist in quite separate universes, I have yet for my own purposes constructed the view which consists in ignoring these differences and asserting that they are the 'same'.

I now turn the penny edgewise on. The circular visual extension-spread has *disappeared*. But I can still pass my finger across the surface of the penny even though I cannot see that surface. The tactile extension-spread therefore is still perceived and still exists. Here is a contradiction. The visual and the tactile extension-spreads are supposed to be identical, yet one has gone out of existence while the other still exists. In this dilemma I must do one of two things. I must either abandon the belief that the tactile and visual extension-spreads are identical; or I must assume that the visual extension-spread still goes on existing when it is unperceived. If I adopt the former alternative, my entire world of public external existence, so elaborately built up, comes tumbling down, cracks to pieces. So I am compelled, in order to be consistent, to assume that the visual extension-spread goes on existing when it is not seen. This idea fits in very well with my general scheme of things, in which I have assumed the continued existence of things when they are not being perceived. So I adopt it without hesitation.

But the idea of a flat surface which is out of sight is precisely the concept of the third visual dimension. This is not, of course, a definition of the third dimension which would satisfy a geometer. But geometry with its straight lines and right angles is a later construction which does not exist at the primitive stage of the development of knowledge which we are discussing. The conception at which we have arrived is the only possible definition of the third visual dimension in terms of pure perception. Depth or distance is simply a line or surface in space which is so placed that we cannot see it.

In this way, then, the third visual dimension is constructed. That it is a genuine construction is shown by the fact that it can neither be perceived nor can its existence be proved. That it cannot be perceived is the discovery which we owe to Berkeley. That it cannot be proved follows from first principles. For it is by hypothesis a visual appearance which is unseen. It is the old story of the impossibility of proving the existence of a percept when no one is perceiving it. We can no more prove the existence of the third visual dimension than we can prove that the table continues existing in the night when no one is there to perceive it.

It may, of course, be represented as an inference from previous constructions. It follows, in fact, from the view that tactile and visual space are identical. For we know by perception that tactile space has three dimensions. And therefore, if visual space is identical with it, visual space too must have three dimensions. That is really the pith of the present construction. But the view that tactile space is identical with visual space is itself a construction, an unprovable assumption. Therefore in the end the existence of a third dimension in visual space is also a construction, an unprovable assumption.

It is a construction of the existential type. It is therefore correctly expressed only in the form of a hypothetical proposition with an impossible antecedent. The assertion that there is a visual extension of the penny along an invisible line can only mean 'If I were in a position which I am not in (i.e. rotated through a quarter of a circle) I should see the extension-spread of the penny'. This is an impossible condition since I cannot both be in my present position and in another position at one and the same time.

Sixth Construction.

That empty visual space exists.

That empty tactile space exists is apparently given. Resistance to the pressure of one's hands gives the material object or filled space. The absence of resistance with consequent free muscular movement would seem to give the rudiments of an empty tactile space. I pass my hand along a surface. I receive (1) tactile sensations in the pulp of the fingers, and (2) muscular sensations in the arms and hands. The combination of these two gives filled space, i.e. the existence of objects (presentations) with their extension-spread. The occurrence of the muscular sensations without the corresponding tactile sensations, as when we make the same movements as if we were passing the hands along a surface without actually touching a surface, would seem to give the necessary foundation for the idea of empty tactile space.

But since visual space is as perceived wholly different from, and having nothing in common with, tactile space, we cannot therefore conclude that what is true of the latter is also true of the former. And when we examine visual space it is clear to us that empty visual space is not given. You cannot *see* empty space. What you see is always a coloured surface, and the coloured surface has a flat extension-spread. The whole of the visual field is full. It is a full space of two dimensions. The idea of a visible emptiness or a visible nothingness is something which the mind is unable to picture. It is unthinkable.

Full space is thus given. It is just as much a sensed quality of the visual field as colour. It is, in the form of extension-spread, primarily simply a quality of objects. And it would appear to be a somewhat extraordinary circumstance that the mind should suppose that the quality of an object can extend beyond the object itself and exist on its own account without the object. Yet this abstraction is exactly what we mean by empty space. We *now* think of space and matter as distinct from one another. We speak of matter as 'occupying' space, and of space as something existing in its own right and 'containing' objects. But originally we must surely believe that matter and space were inseparable, and that the hypostatization of space as itself a sort of 'thing' which can exist without matter (empty space) is a construction of the mind.

How and why has this construction come into being? One common explanation is that we are compelled to assume empty space in order to allow for motion. But a very little reflection will show that this is not the case. We must remember that we are speaking here both of visual space and visual motion. Tactile motion is, of course, a totally different thing from visual motion, until the two are artificially identified as part of the general construction which identifies the visual object with the tactile object. Now there is no justification for the view that we are compelled to assume the existence of empty visual space in order to explain the existence of visual motion. For visual motion is much more naturally and simply explained as mere change of state, in fact as change of colour.

This will perhaps be obvious from what we said regarding the rotating penny under the head of the last construction. But let us take also another example. Suppose that I am looking vertically downwards from the ceiling on to a billiard table below me, and that a white ball is rolled across it. What I actually see at any moment, i.e. what is given, is a green surface with a small white disk on it. The white disk is seen to pass from one side to the other. The solitary mind, aware of nothing but the flat colour patches, not aware of either the existence of solid objects or of the third visual dimension, certainly would not explain the appearance of the green surface with the moving white disk as due to the motion of anything through empty space. It could quite easily explain the phenomena by supposing that successive portions of the green cloth (or green surface presentation) *turn* white, and that the portion where the white patch was a moment ago *turns* green again. This way of regarding the matter will satisfactorily explain all lateral motion across the field of vision. As to motion which we are now accustomed to explain as motion along the line of vision, this only *appears* as an increase in size (if the object is approaching) or a decrease in size (if the object is receding). The white disk on the green background grows larger or smaller, takes up more or less of the visual field. The white swallowing up the green, or vice versa, can obviously be far more simply explained as change of colour than by elaborate constructions of third dimensions and empty spaces.

To have explained all visual motion as mere change of colour in the visual field would be just as legitimate and just as 'true' as to explain it by the hypothesis of free movement in empty space. The mind might just as well have adopted the former explanation, built it into the system of knowledge, and constructed the rest of its world in accordance therewith. This would have been an alternative truth, and would no doubt have so altered the whole of our outlook on the external world that a whole system of constructions, a whole system of knowledge different from that which we now possess, would have grown up. We should have had an example, not only of a single alternative truth, but of a complete alternative system of knowledge.

Why, then, has the mind not done this? Why has it adopted the more complicated method of explaining the experienced facts by the hypothesis of free movements in empty space? The ultimate answer is that to have adopted the view that the facts are due to mere change of colour would have come into conflict with the already constructed concepts of external existence and the equivalence of the senses. Those concepts had already been constructed by the mind before it came to deal with the problem of visual motion. And the mind could not be expected to go back on its tracks, to throw overboard its public external world, and to begin its world-building over again on another plan. Of the two alternative explanations it will choose that which is consistent with its previous constructions. Let us see how this is.

By the fifth construction of this chapter the mind constructed the third visual dimension. When once this has been done, the concept of empty visual space follows as a necessity. Two green boxes stand against the white wall of my room. I can see the wall between them. If there were no third dimension, I should say that what I see is a flat continuous coloured surface with a white patch in the middle and green patches on each side. But now, through the concept of the depth dimension, I learn that the white wall is not really between the two boxes, as it appears, but behind them in a different plane. I believe this because, by passing my hand along the sides of the boxes which lie out of sight along the depth dimension, I feel that they possess a third tactile dimension, and my constructed belief in the equivalence of sight and touch compels me to think that there must also be an invisible visual dimension. Thus I am forced to the conclusion that the white patch (the wall) is *not* between the two green patches, but behind them. What, then, *is* between the green patches? If it is not the white wall which I *see* between them, then it must be nothing. There is clearly an extension-spread between them, a distance, which I had supposed to be white. I had supposed that colour and extension-spread always went together; that a colour must always be extended, and that extension must always be coloured. I am now compelled to believe that there must exist an extension-spread between the two boxes which has no colour and no other quality of any sort, or in other words that extension-spread must exist on its own account by itself. When I arrive at this conclusion I have constructed the concept of empty visual space.

Thus we see that in the last resort empty visual space is a concept which is forced upon us by our original construction of a public external world. In order to arrive at that world we had to identify the world of touch and the world of sight. That was part of the construction. We now find that that identification compels us to construct empty visual space. Hence it is now clear that to explain the visual phenomena of movement as mere change of colour, and to deny the existence of empty visual space, would have been inconsistent with our previous construction of a public external world. Therefore we adopt the belief in the existence of empty visual space.

Empty visual space is therefore itself a construction which is inferred from previous constructions. It is not given. And it is not inferred from anything that is given. It is constructed for the purpose of squaring with conceptions already constructed. We could certainly have built

SPACE AND TIME

up our world without it. But if so we should have to have built it up on some totally different plan. And it is possible that we should have had to give up any active world-building at all and to remain content with our separate worlds of private phantasms.

Seventh Construction.

That there exist relations of equality between distances, areas, and volumes in space; and that exact measurement becomes thereby possible.

This is the construction which makes geometry and the application of mathematics to space possible.

The special point which it is necessary to make clear here is this: that when we say that any spatial magnitudes, say two straight lines AB and CD, are equal, we are stating something which is not given and cannot be proved. *It is impossible, in spite of Euclid or any other geometry, to prove by any valid reasoning that two straight lines, or two areas, or two volumes, are equal to one another.* And when we speak of them as equal, we are making use of a conception of space which is a pure construction, a fiction invented to suit the mind's purposes.

All measurements of space, it will be obvious, are based upon the concept of equality, and would be impossible without it. When I say that a rod is six feet long, the meaning of this assertion is that if it is divided into six *equal* parts, each of these parts will be *equal* in length to the standard foot. Measurement is only the application of the concept of equality to particular lengths, areas, or volumes in space.

The fundamental character of measurement in modern science will also be obvious. It is even said that exact physical science is concerned with measurement and with nothing else. Such science, Professor Eddington has impressed upon us, is purely a matter of pointer readings. But the pointer readings on a dial, whether they measure electrical charges, temperature, the pressure of light, the frequency of vibrations, or whatever else, are dependent upon the supposed fact that the dial is divided into *equal* spatial segments. Thus if physics is based upon measurement, and measurement is based upon the concept of equality, then if equality is a mental construction, it will not be too much to say that practically the whole of physics is a system of mental constructions. The far-reaching character of the present section will therefore be clear.

Let us see, in the first place, what immediate perception gives us in the way of material for the concept of equality. It is clear that the relations of larger and smaller, and of rough similarity in size, are given. When a man stands beside his house, the fact that the house is bigger than the man is immediately perceived by the eye. When two walking sticks are placed upright on end we immediately perceive the fact that their tops are level, and that they are therefore similar in length. And it might well be supposed that these facts are sufficient to give us the perceptual basis of exact measurement, and that they disprove our statement that the concepts of equality and measurement are constructions.

But this is not so. Let us compare spatial magnitude with intensive magnitude. It is given in perception, for example, that some pains are more intense than others, and that some are roughly similar in intensity. But it is nevertheless not possible to measure the intensity of a pain, or to say that one pain is twice as great as another. The same is notoriously true of all psychic elements. I know that I was more angry when you slapped me in the face than when you merely turned your back on me. But I cannot measure the intensity of my anger in either case. It is true that attempts are made, with some success apparently, to measure the strength of the bodily commotions which accompany the emotion. But that is not the same thing as measuring the intensity of the psychic experience. It is well known that the difficulty of exact measurement in psychology is one of the principal reasons why psychology falls short of being an exact science like physics.

This shows that the mere fact that the relations of greater and smaller, and of similarity in size, are given in perception, is not in itself a sufficient basis for measurements of space. It shows that the fact is not inconsistent with the view that spatial measurement depends upon mental constructions.

I would go farther and suggest that the supposed intrinsic difference between the nature of spatial magnitudes and the nature of what I will call psychic magnitudes is illusory. It is commonly believed that space is in itself of such a nature that it can be precisely measured, while psychic elements are in themselves of such a nature that exact measurement is not applicable to them. And the marked difference between physics as an exact quantitative science and psychology as a merely qualitative science is thought to be due to the essential difference of subject-matter.

I believe that this is incorrect, and that as regards their original perceptual elements physics and psychology are on exactly the same footing. Perceived differences of size such as are involved in the comparison of the house and the man are in themselves, I suggest, differences of *degree* which are incapable of precise estimation, and are in all respects similar to perceived differences in the intensity of a felt pain or anger. The difference between physics and psychology does not reside in their subject-matter, but in the fact that in the former case the human mind has successfully invented fictitious concepts of equality and measurement which it *imposes* upon space but does not find there; while in the latter case the mind has failed to discover a suitable construction. Mathematics is no more applicable to the raw material of perceptual space than it is to pleasures and pains. It has been made applicable by the cunning devices of the human mind.

Or we may put the same thing in another way. You may say, if you like, that the nature of space itself is such that it lends itself to exact measurement, and that this is not true of psychic magnitudes. But if so, we must add that this essential nature of space is itself a mental construction.

The truth of these suggestions, which are, I suppose, rather novel, and therefore not likely at once to find a ready entrance into the reader's mind, can only be proved in one way, namely by showing that space as perceived is *not* capable of exact measurement. This again can only be proved by showing that the equality of two spatial quantities can neither be perceived nor inferred from anything that is perceived, or in other words that it must be a mental construction. When once this is proved, it will follow that, though greater and less exist in perceptual space, this greater and less cannot be measured, without the use of fictions, any more than psychic elements can be. With this the essential difference between extensive and intensive magnitudes disappears. Let us proceed, then, to the proof that equality and measurement are constructions.

Suppose that the rigid rod AB is considered equal in length to the rigid rod CD. What is *meant* by the concept of equality here, and how is it arrived at? It appears to mean that if I pick up AB and superimpose it upon CD, I shall perceive that the two ends coincide, A with C, and B with D. If this happens the rods are called equal. This is the only meaning which can be assigned to the concept of equality.

Now the actual coincidence of two or more lengths may be given in perception. I mean that we may actually see two rods lying along each other with ends coinciding. If we choose to name this *perceived* relation 'equality', then such equality would be simply a concept of the given. It would be a perceived fact, and as such would have of course no element of construction about it.

I pass over the difficulty that, if two lines actually coincide, they become one single line, so that the relation of equality cannot with any degree of accuracy be said to hold between them. When two rods are seen to lie together in the manner described, they are actually at a very small distance from one another. So that even this concept of perceived equality cannot be given any precise meaning. But it is more pertinent to our inquiry to waive this, and to point out that this concept of perceived or given equality is not what is meant by the geometer when he speaks of equal lines or volumes, and that it is useless for any purpose of measurement, and therefore for any scientific purpose. The only concept which is valuable for purposes of measurement is that which conceives of two quantities as equal *when they are apart from each other*, i.e. at a distance from one another.

When we measure a rod and say that it is six feet long, the six equal divisions of the rod do not coincide but lie apart from one another in different, though continuous, parts of space. When I say that anything is a yard long in the room in which I am writing, I mean that it is equal in length to the standard measure which may be deposited in a place several thousands of miles away. Thus the only concept of equality which is of any real service either in science or in the common measuring operations of life involves the belief that spatial magnitudes may be equal to one another when they are separated in space. Now it is this kind of equality which can neither be perceived nor proved.

That it cannot be perceived will, I think, be readily granted. I obviously cannot perceive the equality of two straight lines which are so far apart as not to lie in the same field of vision. And it is equally true that I cannot perceive their equality when they lie close together in the same field of vision. By glancing from one to the other I can perceive that they are roughly similar. But in the first place such a judgement is obviously very rough and ready. In the second place, it is merely a crude example of the method of proving equality by superimposition. For it consists in so disposing the eye that the images of AB and CD fall successively upon the same portion of the retina. Thus it is constituted by the superimposition of one retinal image upon the place just occupied by the last. But proof of equality by superimposition is entirely fallacious.

Suppose we wish to prove that $AB = CD$. They are some inches distant from one another. We pick up AB, move it a few inches, and place it upon CD. Finding that the ends coincide we pronounce the two straight lines equal. Now this process no doubt proves that when the two lines are together they are equal, if by equality we mean actual perceived coincidence. It proves the identical proposition that when they coincide they coincide. But this is all it proves. It entirely fails to prove that the two lines are equal when they are at a distance from one another, which is the only thing that we want proved.

If the reader supposes that we are making the point that the proof is incomplete because the length of the lines might have changed during the process of superimposition, he has only gathered half the real issue. It is true that it may be urged that proof by superimposition assumes without any justification that the length of the lines remains 'the same' throughout the operation. And this assumption vitiates the proof. But the real difficulty goes much deeper than this and relates to the question what is *meant* by 'the same', or by equality, in these conditions. To say that AB remains the 'same' length for one minute means that AB *now* is equal to AB *a minute ago*. Here we get the concept of the equality of quantities separated by periods of *time*. To say that $AB = CD$ *now*, is to assert the concept of the equalities of quantities separated by distances of *space*. What do these concepts mean?

They clearly have to be interpreted in terms of actual coincidence, in terms of that kind of 'equality' which is perceived when we see that two rods are lying one on the other and that their ends coincide. To say that the two rods AB and CD, which are six inches apart, are equal, can only mean that *if* they were now lying together they would coincide. But we recognize this 'if' at once as an old friend. It imports here the impossible condition in the antecedent of the hypothetical proposition which expresses the existential construction. It is impossible that while AB and CD are six inches apart they should at the same time be coincident. Yet this is the meaning involved in the idea of equality. For the proposition $AB = CD$ does not assert a relation between them *in the future* (when they are brought together), but *now* (when they are apart). The *present* equality of AB and CD, when they are apart, can never be proved, because when they are brought together the present is gone, and their coincidence a minute hence does not prove anything about their relations *now*. Hence the equality of quantities separated in space can never be proved.

It does not help to reply that in order to prove that $AB = CD$ we can take a third rod EF, place it along AB till the ends coincide, carry it across the intervening distance to CD, make it coincide with CD, and thus prove the equality of AB to CD. For this proves nothing of the kind. It proves that $AB = EF$ *at the moment when they coincide*, and that $EF = CD$ at some later moment when *they* coincide. But in order to prove that $AB = CD$ it has to be shown that EF, during the moment when it is coinciding with CD, is equal to AB, or in other words that $AB = EF$ when they are separated by a distance of space. Our proof assumes that this is true. But this is itself the very principle we set out to prove, namely that two rods may be equal when separated by a distance. The argument is a *petitio principii*. Thus it is impossible to prove by any method whatever, that two lengths of space are equal to one another. And the same considerations of course apply to areas and volumes.

It is hardly sufficient to say that the concept of equality at a distance is an assumption. For to say that the proposition $AB = CD$ is assumed to be true implies that although we cannot prove it to be true we can at least give it a clear meaning. But our real difficulty with the concept of equality is that we cannot attach to it a clear and consistent meaning. We understand what is meant by the proposition $AB = CD$ when the two are actually coinciding. The equality is then merely another name for the perceived fact of coincidence. But when they are not coinciding, what does it mean? It can only mean that *if* they were brought together they *would* be equal, i.e. coincide. It thus asserts something about a possible future. But it does not assert any intelligible relation between the two straight lines *now*. The concept of equality purports to express a relation which actually now exists between two things, but it actually expresses only a relation which they would have if . . . In other words it does not express any *existent fact* at all.

It will be recognized, I think, that all this is merely another way of saying that equality is an existential construction. It possesses all the special marks of such a construction. For (1) it asserts the existence of a relation which is incapable of proof or verification. (2) It can only be expressed in an hypothetical proposition with an antecedent which states an impossible condition. (3) It is an extension of a concept of the given into the void where nothing is or can be given. The concept of equality, meaning actual coincidence, is applied by the mind to cases where there is no coincidence, just as the mind applied the concept of *percipi*, i.e. existence, where nothing is perceived. And finally (4) the mind's construction is composed of materials taken from the given. The material in this case is actual coincidence which is given in perception.

This result should serve as a useful commentary on the theory of the external world as a mental construction which was set forth in Chapter VI. If the reader is 'toughminded' he will very likely have thought that theory fantastic. That the solid world is created by individual minds out of their private phantasms; that the table is not factually there when no one is looking, but is a construction of the imagination; these views, it may be thought, are merely intellectual curiosities. For it is obvious in spite of all sophistries that the table does exist when no one is looking at it.

But I would have the 'tough-minded' reader reflect upon the parallel case of the concept of spatial equality. Our views upon external existence will no doubt be disputed by some competent philosophers. But that it is impossible to prove equality of lengths or other magnitudes, or even to attach a clear and direct meaning to the conception, will be admitted, I think, by every competent physicist and mathematician. This leads direct to the view that the concept of equality, and therefore the concept of measurement, are mental constructions having exactly the same characters as those which we have attributed to the construct of external existence. But toughmindedness and common sense, if left to themselves, would unhesitatingly condemn such views as far-fetched and fantastic nonsense. Which shows that we cannot trust common sense and tough-mindedness. It is better to trust in reason carried to its final conclusions. Common sense is ever ready to follow reason so long as its conclusions are familiar and expected. But as soon as a strange and unusual conclusion, calculated to shock the average unintelligent mind, is reached, common sense deserts reason and turns against it. Common sense would certainly have dismissed as fantastic the physical theories of Einstein and Niels Bohr. But science has become too strong for its views to be ridiculed out of existence by common sense. Philosophy unfortunately is not in this strong position. Yet the tough-minded reader who feels inclined to dismiss as nonsense the theory of independent external existence as a mental construction might do well to reflect on these considerations.

It will have to be admitted by every competent judge that in such matters as the measurement of spatial magnitudes the mind constructs its concepts, and that they cannot be found in the given. Is it not antecedently probable that if we dig back into the obscure beginnings of the mind's fundamental ideas of existence, independent externality, and the like, we shall find similar constructional operations being carried out? Is it not probable that knowledge is all of a piece, in its underground foundations as in its superstructure?

Eighth Construction.

That there exist relations of equality between periods of time; and that the measurement of time becomes thereby possible.

Here the constructive character of our concepts is more obvious than it was in the case of space. For it was pointed out long ago, by John Locke in fact, that whereas we can superimpose spatial lengths upon one another, it is impossible to perform a similar operation for time periods.

We can take the rod *AB* and place it upon the rod *CD*. But we cannot take the present period of sixty seconds and place it upon a preceding or succeeding period of sixty seconds, and so 'prove' the two periods equal.

Superimposition as a proof of spatial equality is fallacious for the reasons discussed. But even this fallacious proof fails us in the case of time. It cannot be applied. Time periods are measured by clocks, whether these clocks consist of pendula, atoms, the earth moving in its orbit, or other such. But nothing can prove that two swings of a pendulum, two complete orbital movements of an electron, or of the earth, occupy *equal* times.

Spatial equality defined as actual coincidence is *given*. But there is no kind of temporal equality which is given. Therefore to find a meaning for temporal equality we have to go back to the given kind of spatial equality, and interpret it in terms of that. In other words equality of time is thought of on the analogy of equality of space, and is based upon an artificial application of spatial concepts to time.

To assert the equality of two periods of time can only mean 'If it were possible to superimpose one period on the other, in the same way in which it is possible to superimpose one spatial length on another, they would coincide'. One could not find a case in which it is more obvious that the antecedent of the proposition which expresses the construction states an impossible condition.

It is also obvious that the concept of temporal equality is a further extension of the idea of coincidence (which is a concept of the given) into a void where that idea has no existence and no real applicability. There is a double extension involved. The concept of actual space-coincidence is first extended to spaces which are not coincident. This gives us the construction of the equality of spaces at a distance from one another. This idea is then further extended to time.

It is obvious finally that the concept of temporal equality is constructed ultimately out of the material of the given, i.e. out of the actual coincidence of objects in space.

Thus it possesses all the characteristics of the existential construction. The existence constructed is, of course, a relation, not a 'thing'.

We began with the many private extension-spreads and duration-spreads of the many solitary minds. By means of the eight constructions detailed in this chapter we have advanced to a single continuous public space and a single continuous public time. Visual space which began with two dimensions has been seen to develop three. Empty space has made its appearance. Tactile space has been identified with visual space. Space and time have both become measurable. In a word we have advanced from the rudimentary position of the solitary mind, with its many private perceptual spreads, to the space and time of common everyday knowledge. We have advanced to the space and time which ordinary men conceive as surrounding and containing the universe in which they live.

But the conceptions of equality and measurement which came last in the process of development bring us to the threshold of the more advanced questions of geometry and physics. It is through the seventh and eighth constructions alone that these sciences become possible. These constructions are their foundations. These more advanced questions belong, however, not to common everyday pre-scientific knowledge, but to science itself. And since the aim of this chapter is to proceed only as far as the position of common knowledge, I shall stop here. Questions of Euclidean and non-Euclidean spaces and space-times will be treated under the head of advanced knowledge in Chapters XI and XIV. And I shall have some few observations to offer on the subject of the space-time of relativity mechanics under the head of scientific knowledge in Chapter XIV.

There are, however, two other topics to which I will here briefly refer before closing this chapter. They are (1) the question of the infinity or finitude of space, and (2) the question of fourth, fifth, and further dimensions of space. It is true that neither of these topics belongs to the realm of common knowledge. Both are advanced and, in their scientific aspect, abstruse. But their epistemological aspect, which is all that concerns us, can be quite simply treated. And it will be convenient to make here what brief remarks I have to offer on these subjects.

The infinity of space has been accepted in the scientific world until very recently. Now, under the influence chiefly of relativity mechanics, astronomers and physicists have begun to posit various kinds of finite space. Epistemology is not concerned to decide which view is true. That is a question for the special sciences. Our only interest in the matter is to note that both views alike are constructions. The present issue in the scientific world may be defined as the question which of the two (or more) constructions is true.

The way in which the construction of infinite space has developed is fairly obvious. It depends on the prior construction of empty space. When once empty space has been invented, when once space is believed to extend beyond the edges of objects, there appears to be no reason for supposing that it stops anywhere. Infinite space is thus an inference, not from any perceived fact (in which case it would not be a construction, but a fact) but from previous constructions, especially from that of empty space. Its own existence is therefore constructive.

That the concept of finite space is also a construction will be evident for the same reasons. For a finite space, too, unless it is confined to actual perceived spaces, involves the idea of empty space. Moreover it depends upon other constructions as well. These constructions, which belong to the current body of scientific thought, are more or less abstruse in their nature. But it will suffice for our purpose to point out that finite space is a deduction from certain geometrical 'axioms'. I shall show in the chapter on mathematical knowledge that those axioms which are not analytical propositions are mental constructions. And since finite space is a deduction from those axioms which are constructions, it must be itself a construction.

Which of the rival constructions is 'true' is, as already stated, a question for the scientists. What in general dis-

SPACE AND TIME

tinguishes a valid or true construction from an invalid one (i.e. from a mere figment of the imagination) is a question for epistemology. But it is a question which cannot be answered until our investigations into the nature of knowledge are concluded. We shall have to face it in a later chapter.

A word, finally, about modern speculations regarding possible four-dimensional, five-dimensional, and n-dimensional spaces. The question is *not*, it must be carefully noted, anything to do with the four-dimensional *space-time* of relativity physics. For the fourth dimension in that case is time. It is not a fourth dimension of space. To confuse these two ideas is a common mistake in the popular mind, and one which we must, of course, avoid. The question which we are here considering is that of the possibility of genuine *spatial* dimensions beyond the third.

The attitude of epistemology to the problem is quite simply stated. It is this. The human mind has already constructed the third visual dimension, and has consolidated its position around it. It has become embodied in the everyday knowledge of the mind. It is no longer strange, but is taken as a matter of course. This construction was made necessary in order that the mind might explain its experiences (chiefly the experience of change) consistently with the concept of an independent public external existence. There is not the slightest reason why the mind should not construct any number of further dimensions if they too are found necessary to bring consistency into its knowledge, as that knowledge advances. It is true, of course, that such further dimensions will be inventions. But so is the third visual dimension. And so are the greater number of 'truths' which constitute knowledge. The fourth and further dimensions will be just as 'true' and as 'real' as the third dimension, or indeed as the independent existence of the external world, which is surely the most firmly established of 'truths'.

Such a necessity for constructing further dimensions is now, apparently, beginning to be felt in the physics and astronomy of to-day. And there is nothing impossible in the prediction that the men of some far future date may come to take these further dimensions for granted in exactly the same way as we now take the third dimension. And then a further strange development may take place. The human mind, having long ago constructed the third dimension, *forgot* the processes of construction. They sank into the unconscious. Hence we now *read* the third dimension into perception. We imagine that we *see* distance and depth. Just in the same way the men of the far future, having constructed an n-dimension, may forget the constructions. All the intellectual processes connected with them may become buried in the unconscious. Then those men will imagine that they actually perceive the n-dimension, see it with their eyes, feel it with their hands. And if so, we may expect that the realist philosophers of that time will be misled. They will argue that, because the fourth and fifth dimensions are actually experienced as seen, they are therefore part of the visual given, and that belief in their existence as independent of mind is a 'primitive belief'. And any one who says that they were once constructed, and are not 'there' independently of such construction, will be derided in the name of common sense.

There is one consideration, however, which may give pause to these pleasant prophecies. The construction of the third visual dimension took place in the remote past, presumably when man was emerging from the brute, or perhaps earlier than that. It was therefore always unconscious, whereas the present constructions of science are being consciously carried out and recorded. Perhaps for this reason they will not be forgotten.

CHAPTER X

CONCEPTS OF THINGS

THE solitary mind was not aware of 'things', but only of presentations and the relations which subsist between them. The only conceptual thought of which it was capable consisted in what we called the 'concepts of the given', i.e. concepts such as 'red', 'sound', 'quality', 'between', &c. But we have now reached a far more developed stage of the mind's evolution. This stage may be briefly characterized by saying that in place of presentations we now have 'things'. Conceptual thought will therefore be enormously enriched. And its general level may be indicated by the phrase 'concepts of things'. It is not, of course, meant by this title to exclude from this stage the concepts of the relations and actions which things have between one another.

There is a certain incorrectness in the initial statement that the mind has now arrived at the awareness of 'things'. For what was constructed in Chapter VI was no more than the general conditions of thinghood, not the details of particular things. Though the sense-world now presents itself to the mind as public, as independent of perception, and as generally consisting of the two strata of 'thing' and 'quality', yet it is still a continuous undivided sense-manifold not yet carved up into discrete things.

The final step towards the familiar and common-sense world of tables and chairs, men and women, horses and stars, is this carving up of the sense-manifold into separate objects. Before my eyes is a many-coloured world. The medley of colours appears to be continuous in all directions both within the visual field and outside it. It is true that the patches of colour have edges, that the green ends here and the red begins there. But though the boundaries of 'things' may often coincide with the boundaries of these colours, this is by no means always so. And we must remember that the sense-manifold is not only visual, but extends to all the senses. What principles, then, govern the division of the manifold into separate things?

It will be obvious that the carving out of things, and their further subdivision into smaller things, or sub-things as we might call them, is to a large extent arbitrary, and that it varies on different occasions and with different people. The desk on which I am writing may be regarded as a single thing. Or the various pieces of wood of which it is composed may each be regarded as a separate thing, and the whole desk as a collection of many things. Or again we may view each atom or electron in the desk as a complete thing. How we carve up the continuum is thus largely a matter of convenience.

It is, however, subject to certain regulative principles. In the first place, the corresponding presentations of different senses must be grouped together and not separated. The visual sharp angle and the tactile sharp angle (the prick of the skin) must both be assigned to the same thing. If they are separated and assigned to different things, the results will be inconsistent with the fundamental constructions which the mind has set up regarding the external world. In the second place, the spatial and temporal grouping of presentations will be reflected in the grouping of things. This rule is not absolute. But it would not be usual to include in one thing presentations which are far apart in space or time and are separated by a number of intervening presentations. The solar system may no doubt be regarded as one thing, although Neptune is separated from the sun by thousands of millions of miles. But then the members of that system do form, in relation to the fixed stars, a single compact spatial group. In the third place, if any group of presentations are found habitually to move about together relatively to other presentations, i.e. if they always 'hang together', they will usually be regarded as constituting one thing. We pick up a stone and throw it. The whity-brown colour, the shape, the mass, &c., all hang together. So we usually think of them as constituting one thing.

Apart from these general guiding principles the division

CONCEPTS OF THINGS

of the world into things seems to follow the purpose which the particular thinker has in view. We speak of the whole earth as a single thing for the purposes of astronomy, and as millions of separate things for the more general purposes of life.

This free discretion of the mind as to what constitutes a thing, a discretion the exercise of which appears to depend upon convenience and purpose, may well serve as a simple example of the relations which subsist between knowledge and action. It may be urged that the division of the sense-continuum into things at all is only undertaken for the purposes of easy manipulation, and that how it is divided up in a particular case depends wholly upon the particular purpose in view. And the conclusion may be drawn that the test of the truth of any such division is only its success in handling experience. But the conclusion does not follow. For it may equally be held that all conceivable divisions of the sense-continuum into discrete things are equally true, even the quite useless ones, but that the mind selects from among these truths those which suit its purpose.

Leaving this point, we may now assume that the mind whose progress we have been studying has before it the common world of 'things' as we now know it, the world of tables and chairs and houses and stars.

The next necessary step is that the mind should *recognize* objects of different kinds as what they are. It must be able to say 'This is a tree', 'This is a man', 'This is a star'. It must classify the things which its carving up of the sense-continuum has produced. In other words the formation of the concepts of things becomes necessary.

As to how such concepts are formed it is not either possible or necessary to say very much. They depend in all cases upon the recognition of resemblances and differences. We class together a group of things which resemble each other in definite ways, and the idea of the class is the concept. The mind's power of recognizing resemblances and differences and of founding general ideas upon them must be accepted as an ultimate fact of which no further account can be given.

It is no doubt important to remember that the concepts which we habitually use are not always concepts of what would ordinarily be called 'things'. We also continually use concepts of relations, actions, &c. But in the epistemological inquiries in which we are now concerned I do not think that any harm will be done by our discussion being mostly confined to the concepts of things. Most of what we have here to say of them may be understood to apply equally to the concepts of relations and actions.

The number of resemblances which it is possible to notice among the different members of any random collection of things is indefinitely large. And things may be grouped, or classified, according to any of these resemblances. Therefore the things in any given area of the world, however small that area may be, can be classified in an indefinitely large number of different ways. It follows that the mind has to *select* from among possible concepts those which it wishes to use. How is this choice determined?

There cannot be any doubt that the choice is determined by the purpose we have in view. For some of the purposes of gardening we may classify plants as weeds, flowers, flowering trees, fruit, &c. The botanist, because his purpose is different, classifies them quite otherwise. The chemist will classify metals according to their chemical characters; the engineer according to their hardness and durability under wear and tear; the jeweller according to their preciousness and beauty; the minter of coins according to their preciousness and malleability; the poisoner according to their capacity for forming poisonous salts; the aeronaut according to their lightness combined with their strength. The librarian classifies books as fiction, poetry, biography, science, &c. The bookseller classifies them as best-sellers and 'the rest'. In all these cases different points of resemblance among the same set of things are selected and made the basis of concepts.

It is sometimes argued from this that the function of the

concept is the manipulation of things in action, and therefore that the criterion of the validity of concepts is their success as instruments of action.

It is really saying the same thing when it is argued that the concept is essentially interpretative and *predictive*. The concept contains a great deal more than what is given in perception. To what is perceived it adds an interpretative element. This element of interpretation enables us to predict future possible experiences, and so to regulate our actions. Suppose I see before me a round yellowy-red object. I recognize this on sight as an apple, i.e. I apply the concept 'apple'. All I *see* is the colour and the shape. But the concept 'apple' means much more than this. It implies, for example, that the object will taste sweet, will have a white, juicy interior when cut open, &c. Now when I see the round yellowy-red appearance, and when I apply to it the concept 'apple', I am thereby *interpreting* the visual appearance. And the concept enables me to predict future possible experience in various ways. I can predict, for example, that if I bite the apple it will taste sweet. Thus the reddish-yellow colour and the shape become signs to me that the visual experiences which I have of them will be followed in certain circumstances by another quite different experience, namely, the sweet taste in the mouth. So it is with all such concepts. In front of me is an extended dull greyish surface. To apply to this appearance the concept 'wall' is to predict the future possible experience of hardness and resistance if I stretch out my hand and touch it; and of pain if I run my head against it. To recognize a small buzzing black and yellow object as a 'wasp' predicts the future possible experience of being stung if I irritate it.

All this is really implied in what was said in the previous paragraph about our choice of concepts being determined by the purpose we have in view. The jeweller classifies metals by their rarity and beauty. The concept 'gold' implies for him that the qualities by which he recognizes gold are signs of the possible future experience of selling it at a high price. The same concept 'gold' means for the engineer that the qualities by which he recognizes it are signs that he will never be able to use the substance as an engineering material. Thus the application of a concept means that the perceived characters A, B, C, D are taken as signs of the unperceived characters M, N. It may be that M is relevant to my purpose, while N is relevant to yours. In this way the concept guides the actions of both of us in the carrying out of our special purposes.

From considerations such as these the inference is drawn that the concept is nothing but a device of the mind for enabling the organism to attain success in action. And since the *function* of the concept is only to help forward successful action, it would seem to follow that the only validity the concept can have must reside in its successful fulfilment of this function. To say that a judgement or a concept is 'true', therefore, can mean nothing but that it 'works' in practice.

These conclusions do not follow from the premisses on which they are supposed to be based. As far as the premisses are concerned there is nothing seriously wrong. Not only will we admit that concepts are now used by the mind as guides to action in the manner described. We will lay it down, further, that in all probability *conceptual thinking would never have come into existence on the planet but for the pressure of biological necessity.*

Let us dwell a little upon this question. We must first make clear the distinction between free and submerged concepts. When we see an apple, recognize it, and eat it, we do not necessarily place before our minds the abstract idea or concept of 'apple'. There does not pass through our minds the explicit judgement 'This is an apple'. Without any such judgement or abstract thinking the fruit is *recognized* as what it is, and the reaction of eating follows. The act of recognition, however, implies some kind of unrealized conceptual operation of consciousness. But it is a part of the act of perception, not a free thought in the mind. In such a case we say that the concept is implicit or submerged in sense-perception, and that it has not risen to the level of a free concept. When, on the other hand, we think abstractly about the concept 'apple' it is then a free concept.

If any one objects to our description of the act of ordinary recognition as involving an unrealized, implicit, or submerged concept; if it is said that a concept is in essence an abstraction, and cannot be said to exist except as an abstraction; I shall not argue the question. It will be sufficient for our argument here if it is admitted that in all probability the genuine or free concept has evolved; that it took its starting-point from the act of recognition; and that the process of comparison involved in the act of recognition may therefore be legitimately regarded as in some sense potentially conceptual—since it actually developed into the concept. I shall continue to use the distinction between free and submerged concepts meaning no more than this.

All abstract thinking and reasoning depends upon the presence of free concepts. A performing dog can probably be trained to recognize the difference between a wooden triangle and a wooden circle, and to react differently to each. We should say, then, that the concepts of triangle and circle must be implicit or submerged in the canine consciousness. But the dog would be incapable of geometry. Geometry only becomes possible to a mind in which the concepts of triangle, circle, &c., have freed themselves from their immersion in the concrete and have become abstract.

We assume that animals are not capable of any high degree of free abstraction. Professor Julian Huxley says: 'There is no evidence at present that even the highest animals possess ideas or even images.'[1] And again, to quote the same author, 'the further we push our analysis . . . the more we have cause to deny to animals the possession of anything deserving the name of reason, ideals, or abstract thought'.[2] The mere philosopher might perhaps have hesitated to make such positive and unqualified statements. The doctrine of evolution has made us suspicious of sharp lines between the animal and the human. Human powers of abstraction must have evolved out of

[1] *The Essays of a Biologist*, p. 97.   [2] *Op. cit.*, p. 106.

potentialities latent in the minds of our animal ancestors. And it would therefore seem unsafe to deny that there may be in some animal minds some faint glimmerings of the abstract. But even so, these glimmerings cannot amount to much. And I think it will be both safe and relevant to our inquiry to say at the lowest that, roughly speaking, the power of using free concepts is a special and noticeable characteristic of man which appears to be more or less absent from the animal mind.

Now when we say that conceptual thought could never have come into existence but for the pressure of biological necessities, we are, of course, thinking primarily of free concepts. But it will strengthen the case for an evolutionary view of knowledge if we can trace free thought back to its origin in submerged concepts. Before men attained high powers of abstract thinking, their human and prehuman ancestors must first have *acted* by the light of submerged concepts. Not only men, but animals also, *recognize* objects. Men and animals alike recognize their food, their enemies, their mates, and so on. In the act of recognition what we have called submerged concepts are involved. And it is surely a reasonable supposition that the free concepts of the human intellect must have been developed out of the submerged concepts of our ancestors. Such an evolution would be no more than the making explicit of what was implicit. But the use of submerged concepts takes place only in the act of recognition. Therefore it is a reasonable hypothesis that all concepts, that is to say all abstract thoughts, have developed out of the germ of them which exists in the psychological act of recognition.

Now recognition is obviously a mental power which was developed under pressure of biological necessity for the purpose of fulfilling definite functions in the life of the organism. From the very dawn of life there must have been something which dimly corresponded to the act of recognition. The lowest organisms must in some faint and instinctive way have selected from, or concentrated upon, certain parts of their environment. And when we come to the higher forms of animal life, the acts of recognition which we find seem essentially similar to our own. The mammal clearly recognizes its food, its mates, and other objects which are of practical concern in its life. And it is obvious that it has developed this mental power for practical ends, and not from any thirst for 'knowledge' or 'truth'!

When we rise to the consideration of the power of using free concepts, two propositions present themselves which would appear to be fairly certainly true. The first is that this power of abstract thought must have been developed for exactly the same practical reasons as caused the development of the act of recognition. The practical functions of free concepts are the same as the functions of the act of recognition. The second proposition is that the power of free concepts came into existence in the evolution of the race because it possesses marked *advantages* over the bare power of recognition. Individuals which showed any tendency to possess the power of free thought therefore survived and propagated their kind.

These points will both become clearer if we ask ourselves the questions, why we think in concepts at all, and what advantage the method of free concepts has over the method of bare recognition with its submerged concepts. The answer to the first question is that the function of free concepts in practical life is the same as the function of bare acts of recognition, namely to enable the organism to distinguish the various helpful and harmful elements of its environment and to react to them in the most appropriate manner. The next point is that in carrying out this function the method of the free concept is in every way superior to the primitive method of bare recognition. The method of recognition is very limited in its scope and is liable to mistake. The organism must be able to distinguish its enemies from its friends. Any stratagem which its enemies develop may deceive it. And in the long run the only method of being sure is to develop and use the power of abstract thought. The majority of stratagems by means of which primitive man entraps either animals or his human enemies rely precisely on the hope that his victim will not *think*, i.e. will not use the free concept, but will act blindly on the method of recognition. A poison is substituted for good food, and is made to *look like* good food. The whole intention is that the victim shall be misled by an erroneous act of recognition. The victim recognizes as good food by its mere appearance what is in fact poison. The only way in which such error can be avoided is by developing a more powerful method of distinguishing that which will advantage us from that which will harm us. And that more powerful method is the free concept.

Leaving savages behind, we may illustrate this point more easily by turning to our own more advanced mental life. The method of bare recognition is often good enough for us. I recognize my brother on sight. I recognize an apple placed on the table for dessert. But if it happens that any doubt arises as to *what* an object is, it has to be settled by the method of the concept. This method depends upon the fact that the concept of a class of objects attributes to that class a number of qualities other than those which, in any particular case, are being perceived. We see a red round object and call it an apple. The redness and roundness is all that at the moment we perceive. But our concept of apple attributes to it numerous other qualities which at the moment we are not perceiving, such as its taste, its aroma, its juiciness, its interior softness or hardness, &c. Our actual perception of an object may be confined to experiencing the two characters of the object A and B. But the concept of the object attributes to it other qualities, and may be represented by the expression $ABCD \ldots N$. If then we perceive only AB the method of bare recognition jumps to the conclusion that the object is an $ABCD \ldots N$. This conclusion may well be a fatal mistake which may cost the organism its life. For there may be another class of objects which is represented by the expression $ABPQ \ldots X$. The organism perceives only AB and jumps to the conclusion that the object is an $ABCD \ldots N$, whereas it is in fact an $ABPQ \ldots X$. This is what happens when the rat mistakes poison for good food.

CONCEPTS OF THINGS

The method of the free concept on experiencing AB proceeds to test the hypothesis that the object is an $ABCD \ldots N$ by finding out whether the qualities $CD \ldots N$ are present, or at least whether some of them are present. To distinguish between an $ABCD \ldots N$ and an $ABPQ \ldots X$, it will be sufficient, after experiencing AB, to investigate whether the object possesses the quality C. If not, it is not an $ABCD \ldots N$. Something red and round is presented to me. I cannot distinguish its appearance from that of an apple. But I suspect that it may be one of those india-rubber imitations of apples which one buys for the purpose of playing a joke on one's friends. I therefore try to cut it open with a knife to see whether it is easily cut and whether its inside is white, juicy, &c. I may further taste it to see whether it is sweet. If it satisfies the necessary tests, I subsume it confidently under the concept 'apple'. The chemical analysis of substances proceeds on exactly the same principle, except that the qualities used as crucial tests are as a rule more remote from popular knowledge.

If we are not sure how to distinguish between a number of things, the only sure method is to get hold of good definitions, i.e. concepts, of the classes to which they might belong, and ascertain which definition each object satisfies. But this is only possible if we have before our minds the abstract idea of the classes, i.e. free concepts. This is the method of the free concept.

The power of abstract thinking must surely have been evolved out of the act of bare recognition. And it must have resulted from experience of the fatal mistakes which may arise from a blind reliance on the method of bare recognition. That method consists in taking account only of the immediately perceived characters of the object. When the danger of this is brought home to the organism by bitter experience, there will be a tendency to attempt to associate with the perceived characters of the object a number of unperceived characters. 'Apple' comes to mean to the mind not only the round and red appearance which is the perceived character sufficient for bare recognition, but also a white juicy interior, a sweet taste, and a number of other characters which are usually unperceived when the object is first seen. As soon as the meaning of 'apple' comes to include unperceived characters, it is clear that the meaning is being lifted out of the plane of perception into that of thought. The freeing of the concept from its submergence in the concrete has begun. And with the evolution of the free concept we have passed above the level of mere consciousness and reached that of mind or spirit.

These considerations seem to establish beyond doubt the contention that conceptual thought has been developed as an instrument for executing the practical purposes of life. And when one comes to think of it, one could scarcely hold any other view. For not only has the history of thought in the past been largely dependent on practical purposes, but even now nearly all thought is directed to practical ends. Even those who are eminent for their powers of abstract thinking, scientists, mathematicians, and philosophers, yet spend a very great part of the twenty-four hours using their minds as instruments towards the practical activities of food-getting, travelling to and from their places of avocation, arranging for shelter, clothing, and the rest. And the average plain man uses his power of conceptual thinking almost exclusively in the service of practical ends. No one, except the stage caricature of the professor unable to see beyond the windows of his classroom, would suppose that mind exists only for the purpose of doing higher mathematics and learning Greek. The amount of conceptual thought which is, on the planet, directed towards 'knowledge for its own sake' must be extremely small, almost negligible in comparison with the amount expended on practical activities.

In favour of the pragmatic view of knowledge we have, then, three facts. (1) Concepts have been evolved by the organism for practical purposes. (2) They are still mainly used for practical purposes. (3) Their inner structure proclaims their practical import. For they are *predictive*. And their predictivity has for its function the guidance of actions.

CONCEPTS OF THINGS

I have put these facts as strongly and fully as possible in order to do justice to a view with which I disagree. Is the inference justified which some philosophers draw from these facts, the inference, namely, that the concept has no validity except that which it derives from its usefulness in practical action? I do not think so.

If, in the first place, we cast our minds back to what was said on an earlier page regarding a similar topic, we shall remember that the mind, faced by practical problems, *selects* those resemblances among its experiences which seem likely to help it, and erects them into concepts. It leaves alone those resemblances which do not appear to be helpful. This explains why nearly all commonly used concepts have the mark of practicality. Things in a given area of experience may be classified in an indefinitely large number of ways according to what resemblances are used as the basis of the classification. From the possible classifications the mind selects those which are useful for its own particular purposes. And the classification which is useful for one purpose may be unsuitable for another. That is why the jeweller, the engineer, and the mint-master classify metals in quite different ways.

From this it appears that the usefulness of a concept is not the same thing as its truth. A concept is true if it is based upon a resemblance which actually exists in the field of experience. And the resemblance may be entirely useless for any human purpose.

All that was said on this matter when we were considering the concepts of the given is equally true of the concepts of 'things'. The principles are exactly the same. As a rule we collect things into classes which are useful to us. But the validity or truth of the classification depends in no way upon this utility but upon whether the resemblances on which it is based are real and have been correctly noted. All concepts correctly based upon real resemblances are true. But some such concepts might well be useless for any ordinary human purpose. Others, the majority, are useful relatively to some purposes and useless relatively to others. The jeweller's classification of metals is useless to the engineer, and the engineer's classification is useless to the jeweller. But they are both true.

When we considered the concepts of the given we saw that those concepts are constructed by the mind in no arbitrary fashion. They are tied to the given. The given is the irreducible stubborn kernel of knowledge which the mind can neither make, alter, nor destroy. The concept 'red' is determined by the relation of likeness between two red patches. The mind does not create, but discovers, this likeness. The concept could not be otherwise than it is, whether useful or useless. Its validity does not depend upon whether it advances any human purpose, but only upon whether the resemblance has been correctly noted.

It is exactly the same with the concepts of 'things'. There is only one difference between the concepts of the given and the concepts of things which is of importance in the present connexion. That difference consists in the fact that concepts of things possess the character of predictivity, while concepts of the given do not. This was pointed out in Chapter IV, and it is only necessary now to remind the reader of the point. To classify an appearance as 'red' predicts nothing. To classify it as 'apple' predicts a sweet taste. (No doubt it might be said that to classify it as red predicts that a certain frequency of vibration will be shown on an indicator, or that it will come out black in a photograph. But this is not knowledge contained in the bare concept itself. Any one might know what 'red' means without knowing either of these facts.)

Possibly this indicates that the pragmatic element finds itself more at home among the concepts of things than among the concepts of the given. But it makes no essential difference. The concepts of things are predictive and are used as guides to action. But this does not constitute their validity. Their validity consists in the reality of the relations of resemblance which they assert.

Our general conclusion is that the concepts of things, like the concepts of the given, are tied to the given, and determined by it, and that the mind only selects from among all possible true concepts those which are useful to it.

CONCEPTS OF THINGS

It may be thought that this will commit us uncomfortably to the 'correspondence' theory of truth, or the 'copy' theory as it is sometimes called. I must answer, firstly, that it is far too early for us to draw any conclusions as to the general nature of truth. Many further aspects of the problem must be investigated before we can formulate a solution. But secondly, if we must, tentatively and provisionally, give at this point some rough indication of our bearings in regard to the correspondence theory, I would say that there is an element of truth in it. The truth of a judgement is in some way determined by the given. There must be in some way a correspondence between the given and the thought. But I would remind the reader that the externality of the world, its independence of mind, is itself a creation of the mind. The usual embarrassments of the correspondence theory, therefore, can scarcely touch us. That theory is impossible and untenable if it is supposed that thought is a copy of something absolutely independent of and outside thought in the ordinary realist sense. But we do not adopt the absurdity of supposing that our perceptions are images of something unseen and unknown beyond or behind them. There can be for us no talk of a correspondence between something inside the mind and something outside it. If there is any kind of correspondence involved in the notion of truth, it will not be between our percepts and an unperceived 'thing' behind them. It will be a correspondence *between the percept and the concept.* And the correspondence between percept and concept is not the relation of copy to original. Percept and concept are, in that sense, incommensurable and wholly unlike each other, since the percept is individual and the concept universal. A concept corresponds to a percept when it is a concept which correctly applies to that percept. The proposition 'This is red' is true if the concept 'red' agrees with the percept, i.e. if the percept is red. But if the concept 'red' is misapplied to a green percept, then the resulting proposition is false. These remarks are to be taken as merely preliminary and tentative, and I shall leave the question at that for the present.

The course of our inquiry so far lends no countenance to the view that the validity of a concept resides wholly in its success as an instrument of practical activity. This is not true either of the concepts of the given or of the concepts of things, the two logical stages of the concept so far examined. And we begin to suspect that such a view rests upon an elementary confusion. It is true that the concept must have been evolved, under pressure of biological needs, for practical ends. It is true that the function of thought in the world to-day appears to be rather that of an instrument of action than that of a means to 'pure' knowledge. Most men, that is to say, use their powers of abstract thought in practical rather than in theoretical interests. But because truth is useful it does not follow that its truth consists in its utility. Did not Bacon long ago sum up in three words all that can legitimately be said as to the relation of knowledge to action? 'Knowledge is power.' Knowledge enables us to *do* things. Bacon did not need either the doctrine of evolution or the teachings of the pragmatists to convince him that the concept is a valuable instrument of successful activity. But it never occurred to Bacon to suggest that, because it is often useful to know a true proposition, therefore this usefulness is what constitutes its truth.

CHAPTER XI
MATHEMATICAL KNOWLEDGE

WE have now completed a definite stage in our journey. We began with the given of the solitary mind. We have advanced to a point at which all the details of the everyday world of common knowledge stand out before us. I now know that other minds exist as well as my own. I know that what I see, hear, and touch is not merely my private and evanescent percept, but consists of 'things' which are public in the sense that other people as well as myself are aware of them; that these things exist when no one is aware of them; and that they have their being in a single continuous three-dimensional public space and in a single continuous public time. In reaching these results we have analysed in principle the logical evolution of the whole of what I call 'common knowledge', by which I mean that knowledge of the world which has been attained by the whole human race, by all normal human beings without any special training or education, by uneducated people, and even by savages.

We have thus finished our examination of 'common knowledge'. We must now pass on to the epistemological analysis of the more advanced kinds of knowledge, of the knowledge which has been evolved by specially civilized and cultured peoples. This will include, for example, science, mathematics, and philosophy. And I will call it in general 'advanced knowledge' to distinguish it from 'common knowledge'.

I need hardly say that between these two kinds of knowledge there is no hard and fast line. Much less is there any difference in essential epistemological character. Indeed one of the main lessons which I am attempting to drive home is that all knowledge is of a piece, and that the epistemological features of the highest truths of science are one with those of the humblest perceptual knowledge. The distinction between common and advanced knowledge is not one which is intended to have the slightest scientific basis. It is merely made for the purpose of having before our minds some rough idea of how far we have travelled and how far we have still to go. Moreover, as I am about to explain, the point we have reached is one at which some change of method is necessary.

Our method so far has been to proceed logically step by step from the elementary certitudes of the given right up to the establishment of all the main features of the common world. We hoped to establish a connected and rigorous chain of logical propositions stretching from the first point of the development to the last. We hoped to leave out nothing essential, but to examine in detail the whole field of 'common knowledge'.

It is obvious that we cannot hope to carry out this comprehensive procedure when it comes to the consideration of 'advanced knowledge'. To do so would require, for example, a complete and encyclopaedic elaboration of all the knowledge contained in all the sciences, of all mathematics, of all history, &c. Theoretically speaking, we hold that the entire fabric of human knowledge might be logically developed in this way from its most primitive beginnings. Its development has been continuous. We should be able to advance logically step by step from the elementary certitudes of the given up to the highest pinnacles of the most advanced science. We should be able to show how and why every brick in the vast structure of knowledge has been laid where it is by the creative mind. But to do this would obviously be an impossible task in practice. It would necessitate not only an examination of the whole field of human knowledge, but its articulation in the form of a logical evolution.

All we can actually do is to examine very briefly a few selected but typical pieces of scientific, logical, mathematical, and other knowledge. And the objectives which we shall keep before us will be the following: (1) We shall attempt to show that advanced knowledge possesses in the main the same epistemological characters as we have already found to be possessed by common knowledge, especially the feature of advancing by means of mental constructions. This will bear out our view that knowledge is all of a piece and governed by the same principles throughout. (2) We shall endeavour to ascertain whether, consistently with the above, any *new* epistemological principles emerge. And this means in particular the investigation of the doctrine of so-called 'necessary truth', with which we have not so far met. (This will no doubt emphasize the essentially arbitrary nature of our distinction between common and advanced knowledge. For the mathematical proposition $2+2 = 4$ has been supposed to possess 'necessary truth', and because it is mathematical, we include it in the category of advanced knowledge. Yet I suppose it is known to most savages.) We shall finally (3) attempt to incorporate all such principles, both those already discovered in our analysis of common knowledge and those which may yet emerge, into a single comprehensive theory of knowledge.

For reasons of convenience I shall begin with the study of mathematical knowledge, with special reference to geometry.

Our inquiries have shown us that knowledge is not entirely free. In spite of the 'will to believe' we cannot believe whatever we please. Knowledge is tied down at its lower end. It is tied to the given. And we have now to inquire whether it is tied at its upper end also. The given compels me to think thus and thus. I cannot think 'This is red' if the greenness of the 'this' stares me in the face. Is there any similar compulsion in the conceptual sphere? Does the concept itself ever compel me to think thus and thus? The assertion that it does is the essence of the theory of 'necessary truth'.

When we say 'This is red' we are stating a mere fact. No doubt we are under compulsion to think this fact. But the compulsion comes from the fact itself, not from the mind. It is thought of as a compulsion which comes from *without*, from the external world. Consequently there appears to be nothing within thought which is necessary. That the object before me is red is considered a mere contingency. It might well have been otherwise. It might have been blue. It would not have been possible to predict, without looking at it, that it would be red because it *must* be.

But the thought that $2+2=4$ is supposed to be *necessary*. It is not a mere fact like the redness of the object before me. Two plus two not only *is* four. It *must* be. It could not be anything else. It is conceivable that the object before me might have been blue. But it is inconceivable and impossible that two and two should ever be five. In the same way geometrical truths, such as the axioms of Euclid, were at one time supposed to be necessary truths.

The doctrine of necessary truth has exercised a profound influence in philosophy, and every epistemology must needs examine it. It goes back at least to the time of Plato. In the *Meno* Socrates is represented as showing geometrical figures to a slave and, by means of skilful questions, eliciting from the slave various propositions of geometry. The point is that Socrates *tells* the slave nothing. He only asks questions. It is assumed too that the slave is wholly ignorant of geometry. Yet being shown the figures, and being asked the right questions about them, he enunciates geometrical truths. Since he was neither told them by Socrates nor knew them before, where did he learn them? It appears from this that the mind can somehow produce geometrical knowledge out of itself. And Socrates concludes that this knowledge must have been remembered from a previous life in another body, and bases thereon his belief in the doctrine of reincarnation.

No doubt it would appear strange to us nowadays to base an argument for immortality or reincarnation on geometry. But that is not the point. What I wish to emphasize here is that we have, in this passage of the *Meno*, a clear anticipation of the doctrine of necessary truth. Plato has seen that there appears to be a kind of knowledge which is not derived from experience, which is, in some way, prior to experience. This is, so far as I know, the earliest hint of the doctrine of *a priori* knowledge which has played so large a part in some modern philosophical theories. Plato based upon it the doctrine of reincarnation. Modern theorists have built upon it a species of transcendentalism, a belief in the existence of another world beyond experience, which, if true, would be no less profoundly important.

It was Kant who, in modern times, was responsible for this. Hume had shown that necessity cannot be derived from experience. Experience can only prove that a thing *is*, never that it *must* be. We see that something is green. No amount of staring, no amount of examination by a microscope, can ever reveal any 'must be' in the experience. Nor will the multiplication of facts or experiments alter the case. You may pile facts upon facts for ever, but they still only 'are'.

But in geometry, Kant thought, we know not merely that a proposition is true, but that it is necessarily so. Since this knowledge cannot be derived from experience, it must be imposed upon experience by the mind. And since Kant believed that geometry gives us knowledge of space, he argued that space is ideal, a form of our perception which is not in things themselves, but which our minds create as a framework into which things have to fit themselves before they can enter into our knowledge.

Since he believed that necessity also attaches to the categories, he drew the same conclusion as regards them. They too constitute a framework which the mind imposes upon nature. Through this gateway there entered into modern philosophy the doctrine of a universal cosmic mind. And upon this depended the whole of that kind of transcendental idealism which dominated European philosophy from the time of Kant till about thirty years ago. So great has been the influence of the doctrine of necessary truth.

Necessary truth has been attributed to
(1) The propositions of geometry and mathematics generally.
(2) Categorial knowledge.
(3) Logical knowledge.

I shall in this chapter investigate the first of these heads, leaving the others for later examination.

Geometry is a system of truths which follows by logical necessity from a set of axioms, postulates, and definitions. Definitions are admittedly merely analytical propositions, i.e. propositions in which the predicate is an analysis or partial analysis of the subject, so that what they state is merely the meanings of terms. With the postulates we need not concern ourselves. It is of the axioms mostly that we shall have to speak. According to the older views, they were regarded as necessary or self-evident truths. They were incapable of proof and did not need it. The guarantee of this truth was their intuitively perceived necessity. It *must* be true, so it was thought, that two straight lines cannot enclose a space. This self-evident character of the axioms rendered them fit to be the ultimate foundations, the ultimate premisses, of geometry. It was upon this basis chiefly that Kant reared his doctrine that space is not an ultimate reality.

Kant of course had other arguments by which he sought to prove the ideality of space, but with these we are not concerned. And as for this argument, the whole basis of it has been completely undermined by two discoveries: (1) that certain of the axioms of Euclid are not self-evident, nor necessarily true, but are pure assumptions for the truth of which there is no guarantee; and (2) that those axioms which are not pure assumptions are disguised definitions, or analytic propositions.

The first of these discoveries is the result of non-Euclidean geometry. There seems to be an idea in some quarters that it is a consequence of Einstein's theory of relativity. This is a mistake. The theory of relativity has no direct bearing upon the views of space and of necessary truth which we are discussing. Indirectly it has had an influence by bringing non-Euclidean geometry into the limelight of popular discussion. But non-Euclidean geometries had been known to mathematicians for nearly a century before Einstein's theory was propounded. The layman might, however, have continued to regard them as mathematical curiosities, mere puzzles remote from reality, had it not been for the fact that Einstein has insisted that the space in the neighbourhood of the sun and other gravitating masses actually *is* non-Euclidean, and that this has to be taken account of in explaining such concrete matters as gravitation and the orbits of the planets. All this has forced non-Euclidean geometry upon the popular imagination. But apart from this Einstein's physics has absolutely nothing to do with the questions we are discussing.

The discovery of non-Euclidean geometry arose chiefly from reflection upon Euclid's axiom of parallels. That axiom may be stated in the following form: *If l be any straight line and p any point outside l, then there is one and only one straight line through p, and in the plane which contains p and l, such that it does not intersect l.*[1] Most of the axioms, it was thought, might be self-evident. But this axiom of parallels certainly is not. Generations of mathematicians, therefore, tortured their brains to madness in the effort to find a proof of this proposition. All attempts failed. And it was therefore suspected that the axiom is neither self-evident nor capable of proof by deduction from any simpler or more fundamental axiom, but that it is logically independent of the other axioms. This led Lobachevsky and Bolyai, working independently of each other, to proceed on the assumption that perhaps it might be legitimate to regard the axiom of parallels as untrue, and to suppose that some other hypothesis about non-intersecting straight lines might be true instead of it.

The geometry of Lobachevsky if founded on the assumption that through the point *p more than one straight line may be drawn such that it will not intersect l.* At the same time Lobachevsky adopts all the other axioms of Euclid. From these foundations he proceeds to deduce as logical consequences a number of theorems which constitute the body of his geometry. In this geometry, of course, many

[1] I am indebted to the kindness of Dr. C. D. Broad for this way of expressing the axiom.

of the theorems differ from those of Euclid. For example, in Euclid's geometry the sum of the three angles of a triangle is equal to two right angles. But in Lobachevsky's geometry the sum of these angles is always *less* than two right angles. And many other consequences follow which from a Euclidean point of view we should regard as very strange.

On this question of pairs of non-intersecting straight lines there are three logical possibilities and only three. (1) Through the point p there is *one and only one* straight line which does not intersect l. This is the assumption made by Euclid. (2) Through the point p there is *more than one* straight line which does not intersect l. This is the assumption adopted by Lobachevsky. The third logically possible alternative is that (3) through the point p there are *no* straight lines which do not intersect l. This third assumption is that upon which Riemann built his geometry.[1] This geometry is different from both Euclid's and Lobachevsky's. In Riemannian geometry, for example, two straight lines can enclose a space, and the sum of the three angles of a triangle is greater than two right angles.

The geometries of Lobachevsky and Riemann are just as internally self-consistent as that of Euclid. And their foundations are just as sure. For if the new axioms on which they are built are neither self-evident nor capable of proof, exactly the same can be said of Euclid's axiom. Between the three geometries there is, so far as *internal* evidence goes, nothing to choose.

Whether one or other can be established by *external* empirical evidence, for example by measuring the angles of some huge triangle in stellar space and seeing whether they are more than, equal to, or less than two right angles, is another question, to which I shall revert. But the present point is that it is proved that the axiom of parallels is not a self-evident or necessary truth at all, but a pure assumption.

Whoever is biased in favour of Euclid may perhaps

[1] I am also indebted to Dr. C. D. Broad for this way of exhibiting the logical relations of the three geometries to one another.

attempt to retain one hope. The axiom of parallels is not self-evident and has not been proved in the past. But is it not perhaps still possible that mathematicians may yet find a proof? Perhaps it may be one of those mathematical problems which may be believed to be soluble though not yet solved. Vain hope! For Beltrami has proved that to prove the doubtful axioms is logically impossible.

If one or the other set of axioms can be established by astronomical measurements or other empirical evidence, then they are propositions founded on experience. In that case they possess no more necessity than any other statement of observed fact. If no such experimental proof is possible, then the axioms under discussion, to whichever geometry they belong, are pure assumptions. It is then entirely a matter of convenience which geometry we choose to adopt. In that case too they clearly cannot be regarded as necessary truths.

But what about the *other* axioms of Euclid, those which no one has ever doubted, those which are common to all the different geometries? Are not they at least universal and necessary truths? The Kantian might still attempt to found his argument for the ideality of space on that ground. But unfortunately for him this position too is untenable. For those axioms of Euclid which are not unprovable assumptions like the axiom of parallels are disguised definitions. They are no doubt universally and necessarily true, but only because they are analytic propositions which state nothing more than the meanings of terms.

As an example of an axiom which is merely a disguised definition take the following: 'Magnitudes which can be made to coincide with one another are equal.' It is easy to see that this is nothing but a definition of what we mean by the term 'equality of magnitudes'. A rod AB is called equal to a rod CD when we can pick them up, put them together, and find that the ends coincide. This is what we *mean* by calling them equal. And this meaning of the term equality is all that is stated in the axiom.

The axiom 'The whole is greater than its part' is a partial and incomplete definition of the part-whole relation. Whatever the complete definition of that relation may be, it will certainly imply and include the fact that the whole is greater than its part.

Definitions are analytic propositions. They merely state the meanings of words. 'All horses are animals' is an analytic proposition. 'Animal' is, of course, part of the meaning of the word 'horse'. Analytic propositions are eternally true. They are universally and necessarily true because they make no statement about outward facts, but only express our decisions as to how we intend to use our terms. A horse must always necessarily be an animal for the simple reason that animal is part of the meaning of the word horse, and if any object placed before us were not an animal we should not admit that it could properly be called a horse. The universality and necessity of those Euclidean axioms which are not pure assumptions is of exactly the same character. If two rods will not coincide we shall refuse to admit that the word 'equal' can be used of them. It must be eternally true that if P is a whole and p a part of it, then P must be greater than p, because, if not, we should not call P a whole and p a part of it.

But the whole point of Kant's argument was that the axioms are synthetic propositions. He thought that they stated real truths about space, truths which no mere analysis of concepts or knowledge of the meanings of terms could yield. 'This horse is lame' is a synthetic proposition. You cannot discover its truth by analysing the meaning of the word 'horse'. Lameness is not a part of the definition of a horse. You can only discover that this horse is lame by examining it.

If it were really the case that we could, as Kant thought, assert synthetic propositions about space which yet had the property of necessity, this would certainly be a most remarkable fact. We can understand why an analytic proposition is universal and necessary, namely because it is tautologous. But how can universality and necessity attach to synthetic propositions? They cannot be gathered from experience, and since synthetic propositions are not tautologous their necessity is not lent to them by logic. Kant found no way of explaining this except by assuming that space itself, regarding which he supposed that we have such necessary synthetic knowledge, is a product of our own minds. If the axioms were synthetic propositions, we might have to explain their necessity by some such far-reaching metaphysical hypothesis. But they are not. Those which are not pure assumptions are definitions or analytic propositions, and their universality and necessity are quite simply explained without having recourse to the speculation that space is unreal.

Our present aim, however, is not to discuss the nature of space or Kant's views thereon, but to decide whether knowledge, as well as being tied at its lower end by the given, is also tied at its higher end by the necessity of its own concepts. We wanted to sift the doctrine of necessary truth as it is alleged to appear in mathematics, in categorical knowledge, and in logic. The result so far attained is that geometry does indeed contain necessary truths, but that they are purely analytic. This means that their necessity is not peculiar to mathematics or to geometry. It is exactly on the same footing as the necessary truth of the propositions 'All horses are animals' and 'All unicorns have one horn'. In other words it is not a mathematical necessity at all but a purely logical necessity.

You cannot admit the truth of a proposition the predicate of which contradicts the subject. 'This unicorn has two horns' *must* be false because the word unicorn *means* a particular kind of animal with one horn. You *must* admit the truth of a proposition the predicate of which is included in its subject-concept such as 'horses are animals'. Why *must* you? Obviously because to do otherwise would be self-contradictory. And the necessity not to contradict onself is a law of logic, not a law of mathematics.

This is a very important result. It does not mean that there is no necessary truth in geometry. But it does mean that the source of this necessity is pushed back, out of the sphere of mathematics, into that of pure logic.[1] The truths of geometry are not *in themselves* necessary. They are deductions from logical laws. We shall therefore be compelled, in attempting to solve the problem whether knowledge is tied at its conceptual end, to carry our study into the sphere of pure logic. We shall do so in the chapter on logical knowledge.

What has been proved in detail of geometry is equally true of arithmetic and other branches of mathematics. The proposition $2+2=4$ is necessarily true only because it is analytic. The necessity of mathematics generally, then, will have to be studied under the head of logic.

It may be asked whether there is any universal and necessary knowledge of time, and the irreversibility of time may be given as an example. But the opposite of this, namely the reversibility of time, is inconceivable. Suppose that all natural processes were reversed; that grey-haired old men grew younger and returned to the cradle; that oak trees retreated slowly into acorns. This, it is surely obvious, would not be the reversal of the time-order. The acorn would then come *after* the oak instead of before it. Its date would be later instead of earlier. The reversibility of time itself would mean that a later moment of time must become an earlier moment. But this is merely a contradiction in terms. To speak of the reversibility of time is precisely like speaking of the blackness of white. The truth that time is irreversible is thus no doubt universal and necessary. But the proposition is analytic. Irreversibility is part of the concept of time. 'Black is not white' is a necessary truth. So is the denial of any other self-contradiction. But all such denials are implied by the law of contradiction, and their necessity is lent to them by logic.

[1] It is true that mathematical philosophers now tend to disregard the boundary, and regard the two spheres as indistinguishable. Even if this is admitted, it does not traverse my point, which is that the necessity of mathematics is simply a general logical necessity. Indeed it strengthens that point.

We have investigated the supposed necessity of mathematical truth up to the point at which it disappears out of the territory of mathematics into that of logic. We have decided to pursue it over the boundary in a later chapter. But in the meanwhile we must face another problem. Apart from the question whether mathematical propositions are necessarily true, what is the meaning of saying that they are true at all? What is the nature of mathematical truth? And has the answer to this question any bearing upon the general problem of truth which confronts epistemology?

Let us begin with the simplest kind of arithmetic. What is the meaning of saying that the proposition $2+2=4$ is true, and that the proposition $2+2=5$ is false? I cannot doubt that this knowledge, like all the knowledge we have so far studied, is tied by the given. In other words these propositions refer to concrete facts. To say that $2+2=4$ is true because, if you take two things and place them in a group with two other things, then the whole group will be four things. The proposition is true because it agrees with the empirical facts. The proposition $2+2=5$ is false because it is contradicted by the facts. It is of course true, as so often stated, that mathematics is about numbers, and not about pigs and horses or any other particular things. In the same way the law of gravitation is about masses in general, not about the earth, the moon, or any other particular mass. But the truth of the law of gravitation resides in its applicability to the earth, the moon, &c. Arithmetical laws are similarly general and apply to all numerable things. But their truth must reside in their applicability to particular things. No doubt the mathematician is only interested in the concept of pure number. But, unless that concept had application to the real world, mathematical propositions could not be described as either true or false.

Exactly the same must, in my opinion, be said of geometry. But there are several difficult questions involved here, which it will be necessary for us to discuss. Physicists are busy discussing whether space is Euclidean or non-Euclidean, or whether it is Euclidean in some places and non-Euclidean in others. What we are here concerned to ascertain is, not which of these statements is true, but what is meant by saying that any of them is true. To say that space is or is not Euclidean seems clearly to imply that Euclidean geometry applies or does not apply to space. It implies that *some* geometry applies to space, and therefore that some geometry—whether that of Euclid, Riemann, or Lobachevsky—is true. What is meant by the statement that a geometry is true?

There appears to be a tendency in some quarters to identify its truth with its internal self-consistency, and to assert that the ascription of truth to it in any other sense is unmeaning. Mathematicians are fond of picturing themselves as existing in a world of their own, a world of abstract symbols, completely aloof and cut off from all concrete reality. They are superior to mere 'things' and haughtily decline to know anything about them. Mr. Bertrand Russell tells us that 'mathematics may be defined as the subject in which we never know what we are talking about, nor whether what we are saying is true'. And I once knew a mathematician whose hobby was gardening, and who, throughout an entire hour's lecture on the irregular polyhedron, referred to it absent-mindedly as the 'irregular rhododendron'.

That pleasant soul the mathematician in the dialogue at the beginning of Professor Eddington's *Space, Time, and Gravitation*, expresses himself as completely unconcerned whether the axioms of geometry are true or not. For him they are simply propositions from which he will deduce the logical consequences. He is equally prepared to deduce the consequences of any other set of propositions. *Which* set of propositions he works with, and whether they are true or false, is to him a matter of indifference.

This rather tall talk of the mathematicians fulfils its function in the world by expressing a pleasant and amusing pose. But it will mislead us if we take it too seriously. It is regrettable to have to point out to the mathematician that arithmetic does in the end apply to pigs and tons of coal, and that the theorem of Pythagoras is concerned with the measurement of solid bodies. But such is the truth.

No branch of knowledge exists cut off and alone in a universe of its own. It is surely a platitude that knowledge is one, and that every part of it stands in some definite relation to every other part. And mathematics cannot be an exception. It must stand in relation to the real world of concretes. A system of geometry must be either true or false. And its truth cannot consist in the mere fact of its being internally self-consistent.

It is pointed out by those who wish to keep geometry free from contamination of the world that it is not necessarily—as Kant supposed—the science of space, and that it has not even any essential connexion with lines, angles, and points. It can be so generalized by the use of symbols that the symbol may stand for a line or it may stand for *anything*. So that the truth of the system is independent of whether there are such things as lines, points, &c., or not. Geometry then becomes an exercise in pure logic. A reader of it might understand completely the whole of such a system of geometry without even knowing what a line or a point is.

But this argument is irrelevant. No doubt geometry can be generalized till it ceases to be geometry and becomes some kind of mathematical logic. In the same way arithmetic can be generalized till it becomes algebra. But it is still true in spite of this that the proposition $2+2=4$ is a law which applies to pigs, horses, and cabbages. Nor is this truth embarrassed by the mathematician's irrational and imaginary numbers. And it is still true, in spite of the generalization of geometry into something more abstract, that the theorem of Pythagoras (whether in its ordinary or in some more remote and abstract form) can be applied to, and is true or false, in some sense yet to be defined, of plots of land and other material things. The generalization of geometry may be important, both practically as the development of a more powerful mathematical instrument, and theoretically as showing the dependence of mathematics on logic. But it has no bearing on the problem with which we are at present concerned, the problem of the truth of geometry.

Neither need we be alarmed when we are told that geometry can be made, so to speak, to stand on its head. We can begin, it appears, with the proposition p (which may be one of Euclid's axioms) and deduce from it the theorem q. The order of propositions 'p therefore q' is the order adopted by Euclid. But we can reverse this order without in any way injuring the validity of the mathematical structure. We can begin with the proposition q, treat it as our initial assumption or axiom, and deduce p from it as a theorem. This possibility may appear to favour the complete independence and self-sufficiency of geometry. But it does not. The two ends of the system, p and q, must both *mean* something. They must have some application to the real world, and they must make some true or false statement regarding it. Whether we begin with p and end with q, or vice versa, is a matter of complete indifference. The fact that two propositions are mutually deducible from one another has no bearing upon the question of what is meant by the truth of the propositions.

The discussion whether space is Euclidean or non-Euclidean implies that some geometry applies to, and is true of, space. This again implies that geometries have a reference to a reality outside themselves, and are not wholly self-enclosed. It does not necessarily imply, however, that if one geometry is true the others must be false. And I shall in fact argue that *all* the admittedly self-consistent geometries are true; and that which one we choose to adopt in any case is a question, not of truth, but of convenience. I shall return to this point later.

If then a geometry, whether Euclidean or non-Euclidean, must claim to be in some sense true of the real world, we must now go on to inquire how this truth is to be understood. *What* is meant by saying that a geometry is true? The question presents difficulties at the outset because, as has often been pointed out, geometry deals with apparently non-existent objects. There is no such thing in the world as a line, i.e. an object which has length but no breadth. Neither do such things as circles, planes, and points exist. What corresponds to a line in nature is the edge of the leaf of the plantain-tree which stands opposite my window. What corresponds to the straight line is the edge of my desk. What corresponds to a circle is the wheel of my motor-car. But none of these things are the perfect objects imagined by geometry. The edge of the plantain-tree is vague and indefinite, and must be regarded as having at least *some* width. The edge of my desk is not perfectly straight, as the microscope or even the naked eye will show. The wheel of my car is not perfectly circular, and in any case is not a mathematical line with no breadth.

Perhaps for this reason there arose the idea, favoured by Kant and others, that geometry is the science, not of rigid solids, but of pure empty space. There are no material things which can be said to be circles, lines, or points. But these objects, it may be thought, exist in pure space. Geometry in speaking of a straight line refers, not to the edge of my desk, but to a line between two points in empty space.

For my part, however, I am unable to discover any lines, circles, or points in space. When I look out into space I see either a material object or absolutely nothing. Possibly this is due to the fact that my sight is poor and that I have to wear spectacles. But I think it more likely that it is the same with all of us, and that we cannot see lines and circles in space because they are not there to see. Lines and circles are not *given*. Nor are they valid inferences from anything that is given. They are abstractions. They arise by the mind abstracting from the characters of real things and their relations. So that in the last resort geometry must apply, not to space, but to material things.

Now let us in the light of this supposition endeavour to interpret in terms of actual things some simple proposition of geometry. We will take for this purpose the fourth proposition of the first book of Euclid. This theorem states that if two triangles have two sides and the contained angle equal, then the triangles are equal. The proof depends upon the axiom that 'magnitudes which can be made to coincide with one another are equal'.

It is obvious that if this proposition is intended to apply to triangles in pure space it can have no meaning. You cannot move one part of empty space from where it is and superimpose it upon another. And if there were such things as lines and triangles in empty space they likewise could not be moved. In order to give the theorem any meaning we have to think of actual things. If, for example, we cut out two triangular pieces of metal which approximately satisfy the conditions laid down by Euclid about the angles and sides, then if we put one on top of the other we shall find that these objects roughly coincide with one another. That is the meaning of Euclid's fourth proposition. And the truth of the proposition consists in its correspondence with the empirical facts.

But it may be objected that statements about pieces of metal and the like are not what is found in books of geometry. They speak of perfect pure triangles, circles, &c. If material things were perfectly circular, triangular, and so on, then we might say that geometry applied to them. But they are not. What exists or does not exist is, of course, entirely a matter of empirical evidence. And observation easily decides that there are nowhere in the world any pieces of metal having three sides which are straight lines and such that their angles and sides absolutely coincide.

Geometry is, so far as we see at present, in exactly the same position as a science which should take as its fundamental axiom or assumption the proposition 'Unicorns are one-horned horses'. From this we might deduce the theorems 'Unicorns have four legs', 'unicorns are mammals', 'unicorns have two eyes', and the like. Such a science, if called true at all, must be called universally and necessarily true. For the axiom on which it depends is a definition or analytic proposition, and all the theorems deduced from that axiom are equally analytic propositions.

MATHEMATICAL KNOWLEDGE

But what such a science could not from its own resources tell us would be whether there are in the actual world any unicorns. To answer that question we must have recourse to empirical observation.

Geometry seems to be just such a science, and observation tells us that there are in the world no such things as pure lines and triangles, and no such things as perfectly triangular or circular pieces of matter. What then is the application of geometry to things, and wherein does the truth of the science lie?

Clearly, though there are no exact triangles and circles, there do exist objects which can, for practical purposes, be regarded as roughly triangular, circular, &c. And the truth of geometry must have something to do with this. My desk-top is roughly a rectangle. I could superimpose on it another desk-top such that the edges and corners would roughly coincide, and I should then call them equal in size. And the diagonal of my desk-top if measured will be found to be such that the square on it is roughly equal to the sum of the squares on the two unequal edges. What the theorem of Pythagoras seems to assert is that this will always be true in all similar cases.

But there is still a gap between the ideal truth of geometry and the empirical truths about the measurements of real things which correspond to them. How is this to be bridged?

It does not appear to be a problem difficult of solution how the mind constructs the concepts of ideal figures. The mind having begun a certain process finds nothing to stop it in its continuation of the same process to the ideal limit. We have, for example, empirical knowledge of elastic bodies. We can arrange them in a series of increasing elasticity. The mind can then continue the series beyond what is actually given in experience. It arrives ultimately at the concept of perfect elasticity, although no perfectly elastic body is ever found in experience. In the same way the mind creates the ideas of infinite space and of the mathematical continuum. Bodies are extended. There is no logical contradiction in mentally carrying the extension beyond the bodies outwards indefinitely. Hence the concept of infinite space. Again, the mind finds that between the members of a series it can always insert intermediate members. There is no reason why this process should ever stop. Hence the idea of the mathematical continuum. The method of constructing geometrical figures is no different. We find in experience strips or bands of material which we can arrange in a series of decreasing width, while the length remains the same. We have only to continue this process in thought to its ideal limit to arrive at the concept of the geometrical line.

Consider the formula $v = gt$ for the acceleration of bodies falling in an absolute vacuum. We have no experience of an absolute vacuum. Experiments can be made in the normal atmosphere or in any partial vacuum which our physical apparatus can produce. And it is found that the nearer we approach to an absolute vacuum the more nearly it is true that $v = gt$. This formula is therefore set up as an ideal limit.

Now in all cases where it is possible to construct an ideal limit towards which empirical facts may approximate, there result two consequences. (1) The statement of the ideal limit being taken as fundamental premiss or axiom, there may be deduced from it a series of propositions which will have the characters of a deductive science. Provided we admit the truth of the fundamental axiom (i.e. provided we ignore its ideality or variation from the real) the propositions of the science will be universally and necessarily true. (2) This science will be actually true of reality in the same degree as its original premiss is true of reality. That is to say, the nearer real things approximate to the ideal limit imagined in the original axiom, the more nearly will all the propositions of the science be true of real things.

We can deduce from the concept of ideal elasticity propositions which are true of real elastic bodies in the degree in which they approach to ideal elasticity. From the formula $v = gt$ we can deduce results which become progressively truer as real conditions approach a perfect vacuum.

Geometry is a science of this kind. The ideal limits which we set up are straight lines, circles, triangles, &c. We deduce from these assumptions a set of propositions which are rigorously and necessarily true *if* the assumptions are true, i.e. if we ignore their ideal and abstract character. And the more nearly my desk-top approaches to an ideal rectangle, the more nearly will the theorem of Pythagoras be true of it. This explains (1) why geometry, if taken in abstraction from reality, is an exact deductive science possessed of rigorous certainty, and (2) in what sense it is nevertheless true of empirical reality.

Jurisprudence offers not unhelpful parallels. For example, the definition of contract is likely to include the conception of the agreement of two minds. And the law lays it down that if there is an agreement between two minds of the specified kind, then certain rights and duties will arise. Given this assumption the law becomes in some degree a deductive science. In point of fact, however, there is no such thing as a perfect agreement, since two minds, however well attuned, always misunderstand each other in some measure. But observation of the moral and business customs of men shows that where there is a rough agreement of minds, rights and duties come into existence. Where the divergence of minds is so great as to amount to what is called mistake, no obligations arise. Between the two extremes there may be many intermediate possibilities. And common sense would conclude that the nearer the agreement is to perfection the more decidedly ought the rights and duties to be enforced. An ideal limit—perfect agreement—is thus conceived and expressed in the form of a definition, from which rigorous deductions can be made. The definition here corresponds to the axioms of geometry which are, as we have seen, disguised definitions.

One might without difficulty construct a science of the ideal man. Man would be *defined* as perfectly rational, wise, just, humane, moral, artistic, and so on. From this one would conclude that men in given circumstances would do thus and thus. Such a science would be in the same position as regards reality as geometry. Just as we argue that, because in perfect geometrical circles the relation of the circumference to the radius is $2\pi r$, therefore this relation in the case of the wheel of my motor-car will be somewhere round about that; so we might argue that since a perfectly just man would do thus and thus, therefore Smith, who is well known to be just as men go, will actually do so and so.

Our conclusion is that the truth of geometry consists in its empirical application to real things. But it may well seem that difficulties are raised for such an opinion by the existence of the non-Euclidean geometries. For it might be argued as follows. If the truth of a geometry is thus its application to the real, then it is clear that we must decide *which* of the rival geometries is true and which false by seeing which applies to the facts of the real world. This could only be done by measurement. We should have to measure the angles of some vast interstellar triangle, and see which geometry they fit. But there is good reason to believe that such a course is fundamentally fallacious, and that no such measurement could possibly decide between the geometries. Therefore the question of which geometry is true cannot depend on which fits the empirical facts. And in that case it is difficult to believe that truth in geometry means what we have stated it to mean.

Let us first get clear as to why astronomical measurements cannot decide between the different geometries. Suppose we measure an astronomical triangle, and find that the sum of its angles is equal to two right angles. We draw a conclusion in favour of Euclid. If we find the sum of the angles less or more than two right angles we conclude in favour of Lobachevsky or Riemann. What is wrong with this argument?

We may ignore the practical difficulties of measurement and the inaccuracies of human methods and instruments.

We may assume that a perfectly accurate measurement has been taken. If then we find that the sum of the angles exceeds two right angles, cannot we deduce that the geometry of Riemann is the true one? We can if we like, but this conclusion will be based on the assumption that *light travels in straight lines*. We can also explain the measurement of the angles which we have made on the opposite assumption, namely that light travels in curves and that the geometry of Euclid is true. There is no good reason whatever for supposing that light follows a straight path, except that this is a convenient basis for optics. But the laws of optics could equally well be worked out on the assumption that light travels in curves, except that the expression of these laws would be more cumbrous. Thus, if we make the astronomical measurement imagined above, it is a pure matter of convenience whether we keep the ordinary laws of optics and alter our geometry to that of Riemann, or whether we keep to Euclidean geometry and alter the laws of optics. We can choose whichever course we like, and the one which we shall actually choose will of course be the one which is simplest to work.

What then is meant in the theory of relativity when it is stated that space in the neighbourhood of gravitating masses *is* non-Euclidean, and that the famous observations of stellar displacements made at eclipses of the sun definitely support this view? What is meant is simply that the easiest and most convenient way of explaining the displacement of the star is to assume that light travels in straight lines and that a non-Euclidean geometry is true. By altering various other laws and conventions of science we can explain all the facts on which the theory of relativity and Einstein's law of gravitation is based on the Euclidean hypothesis. The whole theory of relativity can be expressed in terms of Euclidean geometry. But to explain the facts in this way would be vastly more complicated.

Thus we see that no measurements can prove that one geometry is truer than another. Such experiments only show which is the most convenient. And it was for such reasons that Poincaré expressed the opinion that to ask whether a geometry is true is meaningless. Geometries, he said, are not true at all, but only convenient; and some are more convenient than others. And this may well appear to be in contradiction to our view that geometry has truth and that this truth consists in its applicability to concrete things.

The contradiction, however, is only apparent. We can admit the truth of Poincaré's contention that the choice between geometries is decided by nothing more than convenience, but stick to our own opinion that geometries have truth in that they apply to the real world. In other words, *all the three geometries are true*, since they can all be applied to concrete reality. But the choice between them does not depend on any difference in their truth but on differences in their relative convenience in use. It is certainly nonsense to speak of one geometry as *truer* than another. From this Poincaré seems to have concluded that no geometries are true. I would conclude, on the contrary, that all geometries are equally true.

We can see this if we will consider some of the illustrations of his views with which Poincaré is so lavish. He compared the different geometries to different languages. Just as it is purely a matter of convenience whether you say what you have to say in English, in French, or in German, so it is equally a matter of convenience whether you use Euclidean or non-Euclidean geometry. Or again, to ask whether the geometry of Euclid or that of Lobachevsky is true is like inquiring whether the truth about the temperature is given by the Centigrade or the Fahrenheit thermometer; or whether a distance is more correctly measured in yards or in metres. It is entirely conventional on which scale we measure temperatures or by what units we measure distance. It is equally conventional which of the geometries we use.

This is all quite true. But these very illustrations of Poincaré's imply, not that no geometry is true, but on the contrary that all geometries are true, that they all express the same truth in different ways. You can express the same truth in English, French, or German. It is a mere matter of convenience which language we use. But this fact does not imply that none of the languages can tell the truth. Fahrenheit and Centigrade thermometers both give truth about the temperature. Measurements of a distance in yards and in metres may both be accurate.

Thus we come back to the conclusion that mathematical knowledge is about 'things', and is tied to the given in the same way as other knowledge already investigated on earlier pages. This does not, of course, enable us as yet to establish a general theory of the nature either of mathematical or any other truth. It establishes only one preliminary point in the theory. It shows that mathematical knowledge does not differ from other varieties of knowledge, except in the fact that it is more abstract. All knowledge, whether it is comparatively concrete or comparatively abstract, refers in the end to sensible reality, and takes its meaning and its truth from that reference. No knowledge can, like a balloon, cut its moorings to the earth and rise into empty space.

It has long been recognized by mathematicians and logicians that the three axioms regarding non-intersecting pairs of straight lines which lie at the basis respectively of the three geometries are not self-evident and necessary truths, but pure assumptions. But how and why the mind can make such assumptions, what its justification for doing so is, and what is the general position of such assumptions in the scheme of human knowledge—on these questions, so far as I know, mathematicians and logicians have had nothing helpful to say. These geometrical assumptions, proved by nothing, founded on nothing, not self-evident, hanging in the air, and yet the foundations of the rest of geometry, have appeared as mere mysteries. Mathematics is a mysterious science, ruled over by magicians. They, of course, can do anything. It is quite right that they should place at the base of their science unprovable assumptions which have descended to them apparently straight out of the empyrean. And this wand-waving mystery business has been skilfully cultivated so as to impress the simple-minded. It was supposed that it was *only* mathematics which could behave in this queer way. No other science or branch of knowledge could take as its fundamental premisses unproved assumptions. Biology, chemistry, geography, history, could not do it. Certainly common sense could not do it. These geometrical axioms, therefore, were thought of as unique in knowledge.

But now it would seem that we can at last bring these axioms into line with other knowledge. For our investigations throughout this book have shown that they are not unique, that, in fact all knowledge is based upon just such unprovable assumptions. And in this way we can bring geometry with its axioms into general epistemological theory, and not leave it standing outside, a mysterious exception to all rules. For there is no essential difference between the logical position of such a proposition as that which asserts that the table exists when no one is looking at it and the logical position of the three axioms regarding non-intersecting straight lines. These axioms are just as much mental constructions as the proposition about the table. For they possess the essential character of all mental constructions, namely that they cannot be proved by any conceivable means. They are not given. They cannot be inferred from anything that is given. They are creations of the mind.

To what type of construction do these geometrical axioms belong? Are they unificatory or existential? They certainly are not unificatory, for there is no sense in which it could be said that they abolish superfluous existences or reduce many existences to one. And at first sight it may appear difficult to recognize them as existential constructions. For the existential construction to which we have so far been accustomed always creates in imagination a new sense-object, or at least a new relation between sense-objects. The table when no one is aware of it is a sense-object conceived as existing outside actual perception. The resemblance between your red and my red, which was the first construction of Chapter VI, was the creation of an unperceived relation between two sense-data. The geometrical axioms do not appear in this way to assume the existence of sense-data or their relations outside the sphere of perception. But a closer examination reveals that the apparent difference is merely due to the more abstract character of geometry. The geometrical axioms create, not sense-objects outside perception, but geometrical objects. For the existences with which they are concerned are the intersections or non-intersections of straight lines in an unperceived extension of space.

Any space which we actually perceive (or imagine) must be a limited space. For the sake of simplicity we will think in terms only of visual space. Any actually perceived visual space is of course limited by the boundaries of the field of vision. We perceive (1) that many straight lines within this space intersect, and (2) that many pairs of straight lines reach the boundaries of the space without intersecting. Our previous constructions have taught us that space continues indefinitely beyond the limits of our perception. And therefore as regards the pairs of straight lines which are not seen to intersect within the visible space the question arises whether they will intersect if they are extended beyond it. Some of them undoubtedly will. But will they all? Will there be any pairs which, however far they are produced, will never intersect?

It is to this question that Euclid, Lobachevsky, and Riemann give different answers. Riemann's assumption is that *all* the straight lines will intersect, that there are no pairs of non-intersecting straight lines. Euclid's assumption is that if you take a given straight line *l* there is, through a given point outside it, one and only one straight line in the same plane which will not intersect *l*. Lobachevsky's assumption is that there is more than one such straight line.

The constructions are therefore existential because they deal with the question of the existence or non-existence of points of intersection outside the field of perception. Riemann asserts that in all cases such points of intersection exist. Euclid makes one exception, Lobachevsky more than one. Clearly then what these assertions mean is 'If you could perceive the continuation of straight lines outside the limits of perception, you would perceive the existence of points of intersection in all cases, in all cases except one, in all cases except more than one'. The existence constructed is the point of intersection outside experience. And we have, as usual, the 'if' clause expressing an impossible condition.

Since, as we have seen, all the three geometries are true, they constitute, therefore, an interesting example of the possibility in knowledge generally of *alternative truths*. We have previously had instances of such alternatives. We saw that certain changes in the visual field, for example the appearance of a white billiard ball moving across the green cloth of a billiard table, might be explained in two ways. We might believe either (1) that visual space is two-dimensional and that the observed change is no more than a change of state, to wit, a change of colour. Or we might believe, on the other hand, (2) that that visual space has three dimensions, that empty space exists, and that the motion of solid bodies such as billiard balls takes place in this empty space. The mind might have adopted either of these explanations. There is nothing to prove one as against the other. Even to-day if any mind wishes to adopt the first alternative there is nothing to prevent him doing so, nor anything to prove him wrong. But he would have to face the difficulties which the human mind in general faced when it came in the course of its evolution to this particular parting of the ways. The mind actually chose the second alternative because the first would have been inconsistent with the other constructions regarding the external world which the mind had already made and to which it had committed itself. The first alternative would not for that reason have been 'false'. For the beliefs regarding the external world with which it conflicts were themselves not 'facts' but simply constructions, which the mind was under no compulsion to adopt, and which it could drop, if it wished, in order to embrace the first alternative regarding the motion of the billiard ball. But the first alternative could not be incorporated into the body of knowledge already developed. If the mind had adopted it, it would have had to undo practically the whole of its previous work. It would have involved a reconstruction of practically the whole of our knowledge of the external world on lines totally different from those along which that knowledge had actually developed. Therefore, although the two explanations must both be regarded as 'true' in themselves, yet the mind has had, in the interests of consistency, definitely to accept one and reject the other.

The three geometrical axioms are in the same way alternative truths. But they differ from the example considered in the last paragraph in one interesting and important respect. In that case the mind had definitely to choose one alternative and reject the other. But it is not necessary for the mind to accept one of the geometries and reject the other two. Mathematicians are not divided into three hostile armies flying the banners of Euclid, Riemann, and Lobachevsky. They accept all the geometries and use on each occasion the one which suits that occasion. We could only incorporate into human knowledge one out of the two alternative explanations of motion. But all three geometries are incorporated into knowledge. What is the reason for this difference?

The reason appears to be quite simple. In the case of the two hypotheses regarding motion, whichever we adopt has logical consequences of the most far-reaching character. If we adopt the hypothesis that motion is mere change of state, this would necessitate radical alterations in the whole field of human knowledge. But the adoption of one or other of the geometrical axioms only involves minor adjustments within the restricted field of geometry itself. It makes no difference to anything outside geometry. Whichever geometry we adopt we shall not have to alter our beliefs that there is a common external world existing independently of perception, that tactile and visual space are identical, that 'things' exist and have qualities. Much

286 MATHEMATICAL KNOWLEDGE

less shall we have to alter our botanical, zoological, or historical knowledge.

We may represent the position diagrammatically as follows:

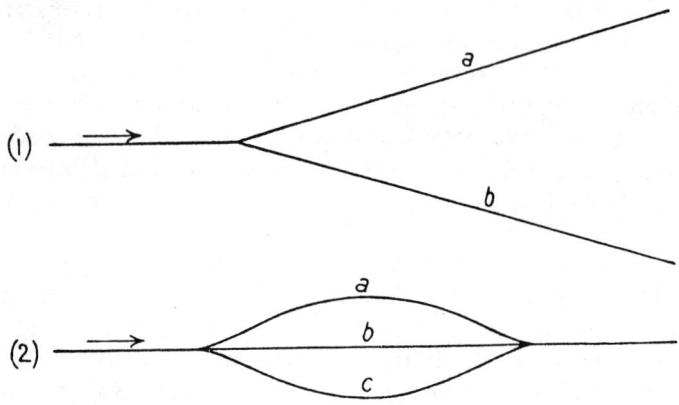

Diagram (1) represents the conditions of choice between the two hypotheses regarding motion. The mind in its evolution may be supposed to move in the direction of the arrow. It reaches at a certain point a parting of the ways. It may either take the road *a* or the road *b*. But the two paths never meet again. Therefore it cannot take both paths. It has to choose one and reject the other.

Diagram (2) shows the conditions of choice between the three geometries which are represented by *a*, *b*, and *c*. They diverge, but meet again. The mind can take whichever path it pleases, and yet afterwards proceed exactly as it would have done if it had taken one of the other paths. You can explain the facts of astronomy, say, either by Euclidean or by non-Euclidean geometry. Whichever course you take you come back to the same point. The rest of science and knowledge remains unaltered. The divergence is only within the restricted field of geometry which is represented by the bulge in diagram (2). The rest of human knowledge is represented by the line before and after the bulge.

But although the mind may select either of the three

alternative geometrical truths, it cannot select more than one at a time. It cannot mix up the three, or two of the three, together. Having chosen the path *a* it must proceed along that path until it arrives at the point at which the three paths meet again. It cannot skip across from *a* to *b* or *c* in the middle of the passage. In other words if you begin with the Euclidean axiom you must continue along Euclidean lines. You cannot assume in one and the same astronomical or geometrical problem both that the Euclidean axiom of parallels is true and that the three angles of a triangle are in sum greater than two right angles. Such a procedure would involve a self-contradiction. Hence what compels the mind to take in each case either one or the other of the alternatives, but not more than one, is the laws of logic.

In order to meet the above, the traditional presentation of the laws of logic, and in particular the law of contradiction, may have to be altered. For we see now that three mutually incompatible propositions may all be true. They may be alternative truths. And the law of contradiction as traditionally worded would hardly allow this. Nevertheless the law that we must be self-consistent is preserved in the condition that, if we accept one of the three alternatives, we must accept all the theorems which flow from it, and that we cannot mix up the three systems inconsistently. It does not therefore appear that the law of contradiction is false or that it will have to be radically altered. The spirit of it, namely the necessity that the various propositions which we hold *together* must be mutually compatible and that our thinking must be internally self-consistent, is retained. Probably no more than a rewording of it to suit modern discoveries regarding alternative truths is necessary. To pursue this topic further and to attempt such a restatement belongs to the science of logic, and not to epistemology. And I shall therefore not do so here.

We may now summarize those of our conclusions which are important for the general problems of epistemology.

(1) Mathematical propositions are necessary. But this necessity is due to their being analytical propositions. In other words their necessity is derived from logic.

(2) Hence, our problem being to ascertain whether there is anywhere any such thing as necessary truth which is not derivative, but possesses its necessity in itself, or in other words whether knowledge is tied at its conceptual end as it is at its origin in the given, we must answer that our search of mathematics has not disclosed any such necessary truth or any such tie. For the necessity of mathematics is not in itself. It is merely a case of the necessity of logical laws. There is no such thing as geometrical or mathematical necessity. There may be logical necessity, which applies to mathematics as to everything else. To understand this logical necessity—whether it is real or illusory—and what it implies, we must await our study of logical knowledge in a later chapter.

(3) Mathematical propositions, like other propositions, are either true or false. Mathematical truth is not the same as internal self-consistency, as has sometimes been supposed. It refers to reality outside mathematics.

(4) This outside reality consists in sense-data and concrete things generally. Mathematics is exactly like all other knowledge in this respect. The view that it exists in a world of its own, cut off from concrete things, is false. Geometrical and other mathematical propositions are true when what they assert about concrete realities is true. Mathematics, like all other kinds of knowledge, is tied by the given.

(5) The three geometries of Euclid, Lobachevsky, and Riemann are all true, and equally true. They are alternative truths. Poincaré was mistaken in supposing that to attribute truth to geometry is meaningless.

(6) The three axioms which lie at the bases of the three geometries are existential constructions of the ordinary type, and are similar in all ways to the existential constructions which are involved in our everyday knowledge of things in the external world.

CHAPTER XII
CATEGORIAL KNOWLEDGE[1]

IT must be admitted that, in sandwiching the consideration of the categories between mathematical and scientific knowledge, we are perhaps dealing with them outside their natural place. For the categories are not part of advanced knowledge. They are concepts which come into play in the most elementary thinking in everyday life. And perhaps therefore they might have more naturally been classed with common knowledge. But my excuse must be that we have to examine the question of the supposed necessary character of the categories, and that it is more convenient, therefore, to treat of them in conjunction with mathematical and logical knowledge, which have also been supposed to exhibit the character of necessity.

In the tradition of modern philosophy the categories have been regarded as concepts of a special kind, clearly marked off from ordinary concepts, and possessing a sort of privileged position among them. The categories were a kind of aristocracy in the world of concepts. Such ordinary concepts as 'white', 'sweet', 'house' were treated by many philosophers with scant respect, and by some with positive discourtesy. Croce, for example, dismisses them contemptuously as 'pseudo-concepts'. But every well brought up philosopher in the past has always taken off his hat in the presence of 'quality', 'quantity', 'causality', 'substance', and the like.

The questions which we have to examine are roughly the following. Are the concepts which have usually been classed as categories different in any important way from other concepts? Do they occupy any special position or perform any special function in the world of knowledge? What is the difference, if any, between them and ordinary concepts? And in particular are they, as some philosophers

[1] I use the word categorial—for which there is, I am afraid, no precedent—to characterize knowledge through categories; the adjective categorical having been appropriated by common usage to another meaning.

have supposed, repositories of 'necessary truth'? What light does the study of them throw on the general problem of the nature of knowledge, i.e. upon the wider questions of epistemology?

If we examine the history of the categories in modern philosophy, we shall find that accounts vary as to the supposed points of difference between them and ordinary concepts. In fact it is far from being precisely clear what a category is, or how it is to be defined. Sometimes it is said that categories are more fundamental to thought than other concepts, sometimes that they are more abstract. Professor Alexander calls them 'pervasive' concepts, by which he appears to mean that the characters of which they are the concepts pervade the whole of existence and not merely a part of it. For example 'white' is a concept. But it only applies to *some* objects in the world, not to all. Only some things are white, while others are green or blue or without any colour. 'White', therefore, is not a category. 'Existence' and 'quality' are also concepts, but they are concepts which are all-pervasive. They apply, not to some things only, but to all. Everything in the universe is an existence, and everything must necessarily possess some kind of quality. Existence and quality are therefore categories. Other commonly mentioned categories are quantity, causality, substantiality, identity, diversity, relation.

The all-pervasiveness of the categories is what Kant called their *universality*. In general, Kant's doctrine of the categories is the most striking and distinctive in modern times. Kant regarded the categories as possessing both universality and necessity, and as being non-sensuous or 'pure'. These were the characteristics by which categories were distinguished from ordinary concepts. And it will be agreed that, if they had all these remarkable characters, they would certainly stand out from among other concepts as quite distinct from them. Most modern thinkers have, however, abandoned belief in the 'pure' non-sensuous character of the categories. This leaves us with universality and necessity. Universality, or pervasiveness, would generally be admitted of them. Indeed, if it were not, the last vestige of difference between categories and other concepts would disappear. Necessity is a more difficult matter to decide on. It is, however, a question of the utmost importance. Kant asserted that the categories were necessary in the sense that they are sources of 'necessary truth'. We cannot possibly afford to pass over such an assertion unexamined. It is a part of our special purpose to ascertain whether knowledge, besides being tied at its lower end by the given, is also tied at its upper or conceptual end. The assertion of necessary truth anywhere is the assertion that knowledge is tied at that point. We are bound to examine any such alleged examples of necessary truth with the utmost care.

Indeed, it seems to me that the only real importance which the categories can claim to possess is bound up with the assertion of their necessity. If they have not this necessity, it does not appear that there is much real justification for distinguishing them from other concepts as a special class by themselves. They may still be pervasive, while other concepts are not. But is this a very important distinction? All existents, we shall be told, possess *quality* of some kind. And as quality is thus universal or pervasive, it is called a category. But if there is no *necessity* in this, then it is a mere contingency that everything has quality. It merely happens to be so. It might be the case, although it is not, that everything in the universe might happen to be white. In that case 'white' would be a category. Thus unless there is necessity, it appears to be a matter of mere chance, and nothing essential, whether a concept is placed in the class of categories or not. The distinction between categories and other concepts might in that case have a certain factual interest for the science of psychology—a category being regarded as a sort of psychological curiosity—but it is difficult to see that it could have any philosophical bearings of first-class importance.

If we give up necessity, what other distinctive marks of the category have we? To distinguish categories from other concepts by their greater abstractness or their more 'fundamental' character seems to lead nowhere. All concepts are abstract, some more, some less. Or perhaps it is more correct to say that the generality of the abstraction is greater in some cases than in others. Quality is clearly more general or more abstract than colour. But at what point of abstraction is the line to be drawn between categories and other concepts? And when it is drawn, of what use is it? As to the 'fundamental' character of categories, the meaning of the word fundamental in this connexion is far from clear. I suspect that when philosophers say that categories are those concepts which are most 'fundamental' to human thought, what they actually have in their minds is a confused notion of universality and necessity.

The Kantian definition of categories as universal and necessary concepts seems to be the only definition which (1) clearly and precisely marks them off from other concepts, and (2) invests them with real importance in philosophy. Their universality is generally admitted in all accounts of them with which I am acquainted. Hence their necessity is what we have to concentrate our attention on. We need not consider here the validity of the idealistic conclusions which Kant sought to draw from the universality and necessity of the categories. He concluded that they are, like space and time, forms which the mind imposes upon reality as a pre-condition of reality entering into knowledge. We are not concerned with this argument. But if it is established that the categories are a source of 'necessary truth', this will obviously be of the utmost importance for epistemology. It will establish the existence of a new tie in knowledge at this point. If, on the other hand, we do not find that the claim of the categories to necessity is justified, it will then become doubtful whether philosophy need retain the distinction between categories and other concepts. In that case the philosophy of the future might well allow the whole doctrine of the categories to die out. Its sole importance has been derived from Kant's ascription of necessity to the categories. If this is omitted or denied, we have nothing left except 'pervasiveness'. And pervasiveness, without necessity, becomes no more than a curious and interesting fact.[1]

Our study of the categories will make no pretence of being complete, if only because no authoritative list of them has ever been given. We may ignore, from our point of view, Aristotle's list. It is not very clear from what point of view he drew it up, and it cannot in any case withstand modern criticism. The list given by Kant—the famous Kantian twelve—has had the most influence in modern philosophy, but has nevertheless not been universally accepted. Some of Kant's immediate successors and admirers reduced his list below twelve, while Hegel increased it inordinately to over a hundred. Professor Alexander has his own list. The majority of modern writers somewhat vaguely describe as categories such concepts as quality, causality, substance, relation, without attempting to make a complete list and without precisely delimiting the boundaries between categories and those other concepts on which they do not confer the honour of categoriality.

In these circumstances it would be difficult for us to attempt a complete study of *all* categories. Fortunately it is not necessary. For the conclusion to which, as we shall see, our investigations will lead us, is that the Kantian doctrine of necessity is false in regard to the categories as it was in regard to geometry. We shall find that any necessity they possess is derived, like the necessity of geometry, from the laws of logic, and has to be pushed back over the boundaries of categorial knowledge into the realm of logic. Categories will therefore cease, in our theory, to play any role of first-class importance. They will take their place in the theory of knowledge along with other concepts, among which they will be accorded no special seat of honour. All that is necessary for us, therefore, is to investigate a fairly representative list of those

[1] This remark applies, of course, only to concepts. It must not be interpreted as meaning, for example, that the universality of laws is unimportant!

concepts which appear to have been regarded by common consent as having the best claim to be considered categorial. If these prove not to possess the character of necessity as conceived by Kant, it does not appear likely, in the absence of proof to the contrary, that that character will attach to any of the more obscure and doubtful claimants to the position of category which might be raked up from the limbo of philosophical literature. At any rate, the onus of proof will lie upon those who disagree with us.

Nor shall I study the categories in any special order. The order of our investigation will be determined purely by convenience of exposition.

The object of our inquiries will be threefold, (1) to ascertain whether there is or is not in the categories any such necessity as Kant supposed, (2) to determine whether the categories fulfil any special function in knowledge which would distinguish them from other concepts, and (3) to throw upon the theory of knowledge and the problem of truth any further light which it seems possible to obtain.

The categories which I shall select for our study will be the following: being, existence, quality, unity and plurality, identity and diversity, substance and accident, possibility, causality, reality, relation. This appears to be a fairly representative list, and to contain typical and important categories. They have all of them been treated as categories by the majority of philosophers who have written on the subject.

1. BEING

1. *The meaning of the category.* I shall distinguish being from existence, and existence again from reality.

The connotations which we attach to these terms are bound to be to some extent arbitrary. Different writers have used them in different senses, and there is no universally accepted 'right' sense. How this could be the case if these categories are in any significant sense necessary I leave it to those who defend their necessity to determine.

Being cannot be defined because it is an ultimate simple notion incapable of further analysis. Whatever is has being. It follows that whatever exists has being, and that whatever is real has being. But the term being is wider than the terms existence and reality. Reality and existence are both more specific determinations of being. Hence although all existences and realities have being, it does not follow that all being is existent or real. There may be beings which are neither.

The distinctions between being, existence, and reality may be made clearer by the following. The term existence as I shall use it here applies to all beings which are apprehended as belonging to the public independent world of things. By existence, in short, I mean public independent existence. Thus a red patch appearing to the solitary mind and apprehended merely as a red patch has being. It certainly 'is'. But it has not attained the level of 'existence'. When, however, this same red patch is apprehended as a pillar-box, when it is believed to be visible to other minds and to exist when no one is aware of it, then it is credited with 'existence'.

By reality I mean what is apprehended in veridical perception as distinguished from what is apprehended in dreams, hallucinations, and delusions. What is apprehended in these latter states is unreality.

The reader may be tempted to think that existence as here defined is the same as reality as here defined. This would be an error, however. I shall not discuss the point now. It will become clear when we investigate existence and reality specifically. At the moment we are investigating the category of being.

2. *The question of necessity*. If it is now clear what is meant by being as distinguished both from existence and reality, we may proceed to consider the question whether it possesses necessity in the sense in which Kant attributed necessity to all the categories. Now clearly it does in some sense possess necessity. The proposition 'Whatever is is' is necessarily true. Not all things are white. But all things have being. Not only do they all have it as a matter of fact, but they all *must* have it. The white object merely happens to be white as a fact. It might as well have been blue or

any other colour. But every object must *be*. It is impossible to conceive of anything to which the character of being does not attach, since that anything should *be* without *being* is a contradiction in terms. This category therefore does possess necessity.

But this necessity is merely that of the identical proposition 'Whatever is is'. That proposition is necessary because it is merely analytic, or rather identical. It is necessary in precisely the same sense as 'All horses are animals' is necessary. In other words its necessity is not in itself. It is derived from logic. The position is the same as that which we find in mathematics. The proposition $2+2=4$ is necessary only because to contradict it would involve a breach of the laws of logic. We found that there is no such thing as mathematical necessity in the sense of a necessity peculiar to, and having its foundation in, mathematics. The necessity of mathematics is derived from logic. And as far as the category of being is concerned we may say similarly that there is no such thing as a special categorial necessity. There is nothing but the logical necessity which applies to the category of being as to all else in the world. Hence once more the 'necessary truth' of which we are in search eludes us, escapes over the boundaries of categorial knowledge into the territory of logic, where we shall, in due course, pursue and study it.

3. *Epistemological type*. Categories will be found to be of two types, factual and constructive. Factual categories are concepts of what is actually perceived. Constructive categories are concepts of what has been engendered by mental construction. Such categories are themselves mental constructions. This distinction corresponds, it will be seen, to the distinction between factual and constructive existence which we discussed in Chapter VII.

Since factual categories are concepts of what is actually perceived, it follows that they are simply *concepts of the given*.

Being as a category does not show any traces of mental construction. Being, of course, includes existence, in the sense that whatever has existence also has being. Existence, however, includes the existence of sense-objects when they are not being perceived. That existence is constructed. And it might therefore be argued that being possesses to that extent a constructive character. But that is not the correct way of regarding the question. The concept of being might have been formed by the solitary mind contemplating its colour patches, its sounds, and its other sense-data. Therefore the concept of being is possible without any constructive element, and does not rest upon any construction. It is simply a concept of the given. That it is afterwards extended to unperceived objects does not make it a mental construction. For the same might be said of such a concept as 'red'. 'Red' is a concept of the given, and no one would suggest that it is a construction. Yet we extend it to unperceived objects. We conceive that the pillar-box is red when no one is looking at it. It is the same with being. Being is, therefore, a factual category.

2. EXISTENCE

1. *The meaning of the category.* To say that anything 'exists' means that it is a public object, whose being is not dependent on its being perceived, and which does, or may, continue to exist when no mind is aware of it. This statement of connotation appears to be in accord with common usage. For when the plain man speaks of what exists, he is thinking of tables and chairs, of stars and comets, of horses and dandelions. He is not thinking of the fleeting colour patches of the solitary mind, the existence of which, as distinct from the tables and chairs and other things which they afterwards become, he hardly recognizes.

Some philosophers have distinguished existence from being by defining existence as that which fits into the systematic network of relations which we call the world-order. We have reserved this connotation, however, for the term 'reality'. So for us existence means public independent existence.

2. *The question of necessity.* A category is necessary if it is impossible to think the universe without it. Thus 'being' possesses necessity (though this necessity is not original,

but derived from logic) because it is impossible to conceive a universe of which it would not be true to say that 'it is' and that the things of which it is composed 'are'. The concept 'white' is not necessary because it would be quite possible to think of a universe with no white objects in it. In the same way it is quite possible to think of the universe without using the category 'existence'. It is quite possible to hold that things do not exist when I am not perceiving them, that they are not in an external world common to all minds, and indeed that there are no other minds to whom they could appear. It is quite possible for me to hold that there is nothing whatever except *my* given. We are not, of course, speaking of what is *practically* possible or impossible, but of what is possible to thought. The question of necessity which we are investigating is a purely theoretical question. However much practical exigencies may compel us to think this or that, such compulsion is not what is meant by necessary truth. My present contention is that it is *logically* possible to thought to refuse to accept the category of existence and to remain at the level of the solitary mind. No doubt this is a practical impossibility, but it is not impossible, or even difficult, for thought.

The difference between thinking the world without the category of existence and thinking the world with it seems to be similar to the difference between the Ptolemaic and Copernican astronomical systems. You can, if you like, work out the motions of the planets, stars, moon, &c., with the cycles and epicycles of the Ptolemaic system. The disadvantage of doing so is not that any one can prove it to be 'untrue', nor even that any instructed person will suggest that it is untrue, but solely that it is complicated and inconvenient. But think in terms of the Copernican system, and the motions of the heavenly bodies are reduced to simplicity.

It is just the same with the idea of existence. The mind began, we saw, with a crowd of fleeting phantasms which we called the given. Each mind had its own world and its own given. But these many worlds coalesced into one. This one world was assumed, not because there was or could be any 'evidence' for it, not because it was 'truer' than the theory of the many worlds, but because it enormously simplified thought. There is therefore nothing to prevent any one who pleases from thinking of the universe in terms of the many minds, each with his own separate world, in which phantasms come and go, but in which there is no permanence and no solidity. It is, in other words, quite possible to think the universe without the use of the category of existence.

We are not here speaking, of course, of questions of *practical* necessity or convenience. And yet it is perhaps worth while to point out that, even from a purely practical point of view, it is not impossible for a mind to do without the category of existence. No doubt for us *now* to do so would be highly inconvenient and indeed quite absurd. But the human race *might* have chosen to adopt that course. And it is not clear that animal minds do not actually do so. The organism can feed itself and avoid danger (its two chief necessities) without any belief in existence. Bread satisfies hunger just as well whether you believe that it goes on existing when it disappears into your stomach or whether you suppose that it ceases to exist when you no longer see it. It also makes no difference to its practical effect whether you believe that other minds exist and see it or whether you regard it as your privately existing bread in your private world. All you have to do if you wish to do without the category of existence is to think that a certain kind of white patch, if caused to disappear in a certain direction (i.e. down your throat) is followed—though it no doubt itself ceases to exist—by the sensations which we associate with satisfaction of hunger. But of course, as already noted, this question of practical possibilities is not really relevant to the problem of necessity which we are discussing. The point is that there is no impossibility of thought in doing without the category of existence, and hence that the category does not possess the character of necessity in the sense in which we are employing that term.

3. *Epistemological type.* The notion of existence in the

sense in which we have defined the term is an existential construction; or rather it is a complex of such constructions. The category, therefore, is to be classed as a constructive category.

3. QUALITY

1. *The meaning of the category.* The term quality may be used in two quite different senses. It may be used to refer, firstly, to the qualities of a *thing*, and the quality may be conceived specifically as not standing alone but as appertaining to something *of* which it is the quality. Taken in this sense quality belongs to the same group of concepts as 'property' in the conception of the 'thing and its properties' and 'accident' in the conception of 'substance and accident'. This meaning of the term quality will receive consideration under the heading of the category substance and accident. And we need say nothing further of it here.

The other possible meaning of the term quality is its connotation as one of the simple concepts of the given. Before ever mind came to be aware of 'things', it was aware of the given and noted those simple relations of resemblance which the given presents. Not only does red resemble red. Red also resembles blue, and the common character of the two is called colour. If we rise a step yet higher in degree of generality, we find that there is a resemblance between the characters of being coloured, sweet, hard, scented, loud-sounding, smooth, rough, &c. All these are said to be *qualities*. Quality as here conceived is thus a very elementary concept which comes into being, or which at any rate might logically come into being, at a stage of mind so early that the conceptions of existence and of 'things' have not yet been constructed. This is the category of quality. It is a 'concept of the given'.

2. *The question of necessity.* Quality is essentially bound up with being, and we cannot conceive any being without some quality. For that which had no quality, no character, no distinguishing feature of any kind, would *eo ipso* be nothing and void. It could have no being. It was by

means of this reasoning that Hegel identified quality with being in one of his famous logical deductions. The quality of anything, he argued, *is* its being. The greenness, softness, shape, &c., of the grass *is* the grass. If we try and imagine the grass with these and all other qualities removed, what would be left standing before the mind after such removal of all the qualities would be absolutely nothing. The being of the grass thus disappears with the quality. Being and quality are, he urged, identical.

We need not, of course, follow Hegel's actual identification of quality and being. It is no part of our plan to do so. For us, being and quality are essentially different concepts. But the argument brings out very clearly the fact that, since it is impossible to conceive of any being without quality, quality is a *necessary* concept. Things not only do possess qualities as a matter of fact. They *must* possess qualities, since a thing without qualities is inconceivable.

But on examination it soon appears that this necessity is not anything which has its source in the category itself. It is derived, like the necessity of the category of being or of those geometrical axioms which are not constructions, from the laws of logic. For if we fix our minds on the idea of the given, we shall find that being and quality are merely two aspects of the given. Consider a red patch. Its redness and its being are the same thing viewed from different angles. The being of a red patch is its redness. The being of a blue patch is its blueness. Therefore blueness and redness are different *kinds* of being. The quality of a thing, then, is the particular kind of being it has. Therefore quality might be defined as 'kind of being' or as 'specific being' or as 'determined being'. And the proposition that 'all being must have quality' is equivalent to the proposition that 'every being must be some particular kind of being'. It seems clear that this is necessary, but that its necessity is derived from logic. It is in reality analytic. This will become clearer if we consider the proposition 'every animal must be some particular kind of animal', i.e. must be either a lion or a tiger or a giraffe, or . . ., &c.

It may be argued that this is not analytic because the concept 'animal' does not contain the ideas of the specific characters either of the lion or of the tiger or of any other particular beast. It is true that it does not. But I maintain that the concept 'animal', though it does not contain a reference to the specific characters of the tiger or the lion, does contain the thought that every particular animal must have *some* specific character. Otherwise the concept 'animal' would be completely contentless and empty. This would be the case even if there existed in fact only one kind of animal, i.e. if the genus animal contained only one species. Thus the proposition 'every animal must be some particular kind of animal' is a necessary truth, and it is necessary because it is analytic.

It appears that the proposition 'every being must have quality' is on all fours with this. Quality means nothing but the specific character of any being. And the concept 'being' must contain the thought that all being has *some* specific character, although it does not contain the thought that it has this or that particular character. For if not, being would be completely without content and equivalent, as Hegel thought, to nothing. Hence to assert that there could be being without any quality would involve a breach of the logical law of contradiction. For it would involve that there could be a being which is not a being. Hence the proposition that 'All being has quality' is a necessary proposition because it is analytic. And we conclude that the category of quality is in the same boat as the category of being. It possesses necessity, but this necessity is merely derived from logic.

3. *Epistemological type*. In the category of quality there are none of the constructive elements which we found, for example, in the category of existence. It contains nothing whatever which is not *found* in the given, except of course its abstract character as a concept. It is of precisely the same character as the more sensuous concepts such as 'red', 'blue', 'loud', &c. Its 'truth' consists in the correspondence of the thought with the percept, i.e. with the given. Quality is given in sensation, and when we think

CATEGORIAL KNOWLEDGE 303

it conceptually we have the category. It is clear therefore that it is a category of the factual type.

4. UNITY AND PLURALITY

1. *The meaning of the categories.* There does not appear to be any likelihood of misunderstanding or ambiguity in regard to these categories. There may be *one* sovereign in my pocket, or there may be *many*. The categories of unity and plurality are simply the 'one' and the 'many' of such a statement.

2. *The question of necessity.* We cannot conceive a universe of things to which the categories of unity and plurality do not apply. A thing must necessarily be one thing. And there must necessarily be many things in existence. For even if we try to imagine a universe consisting of only one object, we can only conceive it as containing a multiplicity of parts. Hegel was apparently right in thinking that the one and the many imply each other, so that the idea of one is impossible without the idea of the other. The 'one' is only intelligible against a background of multiplicity; it is the *not*-many. Likewise the 'many' is only intelligible as the *not*-one. Hence if it is admitted that the idea 'one' is implied in the thought of any possible being or any possible universe, it follows that the idea 'many' is also implied therein.

But this is because unity and plurality are parts of the concepts of whatever we think of. The idea of 'a house' contains within itself the thought that it is one object. So of course does the idea of 'a flower', or 'an atom', or 'a planet' or 'a red patch', or any other object. It would clearly be self-contradictory to try to think of a house which is not one house. And if we take any other single thing it would be self-contradictory to think of it as not being 'one'. If, on the other hand, we take any collection of things, whether the whole universe or some smaller collection, it would be self-contradictory to think of it as not 'many'. That is to say, the proposition 'this thing is one thing' is an analytic proposition. And the proposition 'these things are many' is likewise analytic. They are therefore necessary. They differ from such a proposition as 'this thing is white' which is synthetic, and which does not possess necessity.

Hence it is plain that the necessity of the categories of unity and plurality is not in themselves, but is derived from the laws of logic.

3. *Epistemological type.* Unity and plurality are not constructed, but given. They make their appearance in the earliest conceivable experiences of the mind, before any constructive world-building begins. They are concepts of the given, and belong to the factual type of category.

5. IDENTITY AND DIVERSITY

1. *The meaning of the categories.* If the given experience which confronts us at any moment consists, shall we say, of a green patch and a red patch side by side in the same visual field; and if we symbolize these by A and B respectively; then it is at once evident that 'A is not B', or in other words that these are two *diverse* experiences. If both the patches are green, and even if they are exactly the same shade of green, yet if they are spatially separated it will still be true that 'A is not B', i.e. that they are diverse. Diversity is thus an ultimate notion, a concept of the given, which, as such, cannot be defined, although its application is quite clear.

The meaning of *identity* is not so clear. If it entirely excludes diversity, it appears to be practically meaningless. In order to have any real significance the concept of identity must assert the identity of two things which are, or originally were, thought to be diverse. The assertion that *one* thing is identical with itself does not appear to contain much meaning or value. It is what we may call *pure* identity, and is symbolized by the formal proposition 'A is A'. It is true that this appears in the logic books. But even if it has any meaning (which I doubt) it is a wholly trivial meaning.

In order to give any real significance to an assertion of identity, it must assert the identity of two diverse things. It is then of the form 'A is B'. This is the case if I say that the piece of paper now before me is *the same* piece of paper which I had before me thirty seconds ago when I began writing this sentence. It is often carelessly assumed that this is an assertion of empty self-identity of the form '*A* is *A*'. It is forgotten that the white patch *now* and the white patch *then*, even though they continue into one another, are *two* experiences, not one. And their identification is the assertion of the identity of two diverse presentations. It is possibly because this is forgotten that significance is attached to the empty self-identical '*A* is *A*'. It is supposed that the propositions 'This house is the same house as I was living in yesterday', and 'I am the same man as I was a year ago', are propositions of that form. And as they are certainly both significant and important it comes to be thought that empty self-identity is significant and important. But this is a mistake. The propositions just quoted clearly assert the identity of diverse things, and are therefore of the form '*A* is *B*'.

Suppose now that I assert that the green tree which I am now seeing is identical with the green tree which you are seeing at the same instant. This is the ordinary assertion involved in the coalescence of our many private worlds into one public world. This again is clearly an affirmation of the identity of two diverse things, and is of the form '*A* is *B*'.

For the purposes of our discussion here I shall take the category of identity to mean the significant and important '*A* is *B*', not the futile and barren '*A* is *A*'.

2. *The question of necessity.* Diversity is given and is a feature of all experience. It is closely bound up with the category of plurality. For whatever is many is diverse, and whatever is diverse is many. Diversity certainly possesses the character of necessity, since we cannot conceive any universe without diverse elements. But this necessity stands on the same footing as the necessity of the category of plurality. What was said of the necessity of plurality applies *mutatis mutandis* to the necessity of diversity. That necessity is, therefore, not in the category itself, but borrowed from the laws of logic.

Identity, however, is by no means on the same footing. If by identity we mean pure identity, the barren 'A is A', then it may be the case that this kind of identity (if any meaning can be attached to it) is a feature of the given, and no doubt possesses the same kind of necessity as the other pervasive concepts of the given which we have already studied. But if by identity is meant the identification of two diverse experiences, then it is clear that it is not given. It is clear that it is the mind which declares to be one what is given in experience as two.

It is also clear that the category does not possess any necessity. It is on a par in this respect with the category of existence. In fact it is involved in, and is a part of, the category of existence. The most important step which the mind took in its establishment of a public external world was the identification of the many private worlds as one world. But this was not a necessary step in any sense which is relevant to the search for 'necessary truth'. The mind could have remained, if it had chosen, in its private world of phantasms. It might have continued to think in terms of many worlds instead of one. Nothing would have been different except that all thinking would have been more difficult, complicated, and inconvenient. Its choice was similar to the choice between Ptolemaic and Copernican astronomy. The concept of identity is a device of the mind for simplifying the universe. But there is no compulsion of thought to use it.

3. *Epistemological type.* Diversity is a factual concept. So is identity in the barren sense of $A = A$, if identity in that sense has any real significance. Both diversity and identity in this sense merely repeat in *thought* what is given in the *thing*. They are merely the universals of certain particulars. This is the same as saying that they are factual.

But identity in the more advanced sense, in which what is asserted is the identity of two diverse givens, is an interesting example of the constructive type of category. Let us consider a very simple example of its application. I am looking at a green book now lying on my table. I say it was also there a minute ago, that it has been there during the intervening sixty seconds, and that what has been there during all that period is the 'same' book. Here, in this idea of the 'sameness' of the book, is the category of identity. Now this identity, this sameness, is certainly not given. What is given is a series of experiences bearing to each other the relation of resemblance; a series of green patches occupying a series of 'specious presents'. They follow each other continuously in time. There is no break between them. But, in spite of this continuity, any two in the series are just as much diverse or numerically different from one another as if they were two patches of colour separated by an interval of empty space. Nowhere can we find the identity among the elements of the given. A 'thing' which persists in time is a series of *different* appearances strung together like beads on a string. But the string is invisible. It is not given in sight or in any other sense. It is *thought*. It is a fiction, an invention which the mind makes for its own purposes.[1]

In order to support the fiction of identity the mind invents further concepts, such as *substance*, to help it out. The identity is made plausible by supposing that there is one substance beneath the many diverse appearances. This phase of thought will be studied in the next section.

People frequently raise what appear to be most puzzling questions of identity. If only it were realized that identity is a convenient fiction, and that consequently it can be used when it is found useful but dropped when it is not, these questions would all cease to be puzzling. It will be worth while to give one or two examples. The identity of the series of appearances of the 'same' book is not usually called in question by common sense. It is considered obvious. But trouble begins when more or less rapid changes are observed to be taking place within what is supposed to be the 'same' thing. A wave travels across the face of the water. We know that the particles of water do

[1] Since writing this I find the following at p. 164 of Dr. F. C. S. Schiller's *Logic for Use*: 'All identification involves fiction, because it feigns the non-existence of the differences which always exist between two cases of "the same".'

not move horizontally forward with the wave. They only move vertically up and down. All that moves forward is the *shape*, and even this, of course, changes as it goes along. Is it, then, the *same* wave which travels across the water? Or is it a series of *different* waves? The supposed identity of our bodies throughout a period of years raises a similar problem. It may be that not one of the molecules which constituted my body ten years ago is still included in it. Wherever change is in progress within the boundaries of what is supposed to be one and the same persisting object, the same problem arises in more or less acute form. The leaf which changes slowly in the autumn from green to red is really just as much an example of the problem as the rapidly changing wave.

These enigmas all arise because we persist in thinking that identity is something which is 'there' in exactly the same way as the appearances themselves—the red patches or whatever they may be—are 'there'. It is supposed that to assert that anything remains the 'same' throughout a period of time is to assert an objective fact about it. Consequently the identity must be either really 'there' or not 'there'. It cannot be partly there and partly not there. Nor can it be there for one person and not for another. Hence the wave puzzles us since it seems to be partly self-identical and partly not, and since it seems to depend to some extent upon the way of looking at it which each person has whether he regards it as identical or not; so that in a sense it seems to vary from person to person. Then we ask ourselves 'Is the identity really there or not? How are we to decide whether it is the same or different?' And these questions appear very difficult to answer.

All these difficulties disappear as soon as we realize that identity is not given, is not factually 'there', but is simply a convenient fiction. Hence if the mind *thinks* identity, then there *is* identity, while if the mind does not think identity, then there is none. For as with all constructions, the only reality which identity has consists in its *being thought*, not in its factual thereness. It may be said to be there if you like, but its thereness is a mental construction.

Whether the mind thinks identity into any particular subject-matter or not is purely a matter of convenience. Is it simpler to think of the moving wave, the growing body, as one rather than as many? If so, then the wave or the body will be thought of as one, and will *be* one for all purposes of theory and practice. But if it is more convenient to think of the successive appearances as many, then they *are* many. These are alternative truths, and the mind can take its choice.

There is, of course, nothing which is not changing. But some things change very slowly, others very fast. Those which change very slowly, such as the mountains or even the pyramids, we consider relatively permanent. And with regard to these the troublesome questions about identity do not seem to arise. The wave appears to give rise to a problem, but the mountain does not. No one ever dreams of doubting that the mountain is the 'same' to-day as it was yesterday. This shows how entirely arbitrary is the question whether we are to regard a series of appearances as one or many.

Is the picture which is thrown on the screen by a cinematograph many or one? We know that the film itself consists of a series of pictures which are spatially separate, so that no one would think of identifying them. But the series of pictures thrown on the screen all appear in the same spatial situation, but one after another in time. The series of appearances of the pictures thus exactly resembles the series of appearances of the green book. Is the picture, then, as we see it on the screen, one or many? I am watching, say, a man's face on the film, the features of which are quite motionless. I watch it for half a minute without perceiving any change. Is it the same face all the time, or is it a series of different faces?

When the matter is put in this way it becomes obvious that the question is without substance, that it is, as we are wont to say, 'merely a matter of words'. You can think of it as one picture or you can think of it as a series of many pictures. It does not matter in the least which you do. The concepts of identity and diversity will both be 'true' of it. You have your choice between alternative truths. It is the same with all these questions of identity.

The alternative truths regarding identity and diversity differ from most other sets of alternative truths, however, in the following respect. In most cases all normal human minds choose one and not the other of the alternatives. For example, it is theoretically a matter of choice whether we think of one common world or of many private worlds. But the human mind in general long ago decided on the first alternative. No one ever adopts the latter. This is because it is *always* more convenient to think in terms of a common world. But this is not so with identity and diversity. One mind may choose to regard the wave as one. Another may prefer to think of it as many. But there is no difference in principle between the two sets of alternatives.

It may still be asked of the supposed self-identical green book which lies before me on the table: is its identity 'real'? Is the identity 'really there'? The answer to these questions clearly depends on what you mean by 'reality' and 'there'. Taking the latter first, we might interpret 'there' to mean 'actually given in perception'. In that sense identity is certainly not there. For it is not given and it cannot be perceived. But then in that sense the table which no one happens at this moment to be perceiving is not there. If, on the other hand, we admit, as I think it is reasonable to do, that the unperceived table is nevertheless there, then its thereness is a construction, and we shall also admit that the identity is there. Similarly with reality. If you insist that reality only includes what is there in the first sense, i.e. what is actually perceived, then the identity is not real. But for our part we shall not take such a narrow view of reality. We have included in 'existence' both factual and constructive existence. We have made it clear that valid constructions are a part of 'truth'. Constructive existences must also, therefore, be admitted to be a part of reality. Consequently to the questions whether the identity of the book is real and is there we reply in the affirmative.

CATEGORIAL KNOWLEDGE 311

Certain mystical philosophies, not content with using the category of identity in its usual limited application, attempt to force the whole world into its groove, and to make the entire universe one huge identity. 'All is One', they say. Certainly this One is not given, at least not to most of us, although the true mystic is apt to assert that it is given to him in a vision or in some kind of supersensuous 'intuition'. But if it is not given, it is a construction of thought. It is not my purpose here to consider the validity of this kind of transcendental philosophy. But in view of our recent investigations it is impossible not to reflect that, even if it be held that such a philosophy is true, its truth must still be considered a mental construction. It is no more than a 'way of looking at' the universe which may be true, i.e. legitimate, but which will not for that reason exclude from truth other equally legitimate ways of looking at the universe—alternative truths. It is quite possible that there may be several true philosophies, just in the same way as there are several true geometries.

6. SUBSTANCE

1. *The meaning of the category.* It is not clear that the terms substance and accident have always meant exactly the same thing throughout the history of thought, or that they have even now any one determinate connotation which is universally accepted. Can it be said that the word substance has and had the same meaning to Aristotle, to Spinoza, to Descartes (when he spoke of 'thinking substance'), and to the modern chemist? It is obvious that Spinoza and the chemist *apply* the word differently. Spinoza applied it to that ultimate reality out of which he considered that the whole world arises. The chemist, on the other hand, applies it to lumps of clay or metal. But in spite of this wide difference in application, it does not follow that there is not a single connotation in both cases, since the chemist may attribute to lumps of matter the very same characters which Spinoza attributed to ultimate reality. And this is, in fact, roughly the position. Absolute sameness of connotation there cannot be. It is quite true,

as Dr. Schiller and others have pointed out, that no word is ever really used twice in the same sense. There will always be small variations. But it may be said that, allowing for such variations of meaning, the various senses in which the word substance has been used in the history of thought seem all to go back to a common root-idea. If we can state this root-idea we shall have at least the main features of the meaning of the category.

The conception of substance and accident seems to be an attempt to define more precisely and scientifically the vague and popular concept of the 'thing' and its qualities. It has, at any rate, grown out of that popular concept. Here is the thing before me, the physical table. It is square, brown, shiny, and hard. These adjectives express its *qualities*. They do not appear to stand for *things*. Brownness and shininess are not things for the reason that they are not conceived as existing on their own account apart from the table. You can have a brown table, a brown pair of trousers, a brown piece of paper, a brown anything. But there must be, it is supposed, something which *is* brown. Brownness cannot exist by itself. Thus the 'thing' comes to be regarded as *that which has its being in itself, that which exists independently of anything else*. This gives us the definition of substance. The 'quality' comes to be regarded as *that which cannot exist by itself, but depends for its being on the substance*. This gives us the definition of accident.

This is the ordinary meaning of the category of substance as applied both by the plain man and by the chemist to material things—although it is probable that neither of them makes that meaning explicit before their minds. It is also the meaning of Spinoza's Substance. His Substance was equivalent to God, or the ultimate reality. It was not material or physical. But it was defined as 'that the conception of which does not depend on the conception of another thing from which it must be formed'.[1]

Strictly speaking, no doubt, the idea of permanence is not necessarily involved in the concept of substance. We

[1] Spinoza, *Ethics*, Definition 3.

CATEGORIAL KNOWLEDGE

might, logically, think of a quite momentary existence in which the relation of substance and accident held good. But in practice the idea of permanence is invariably super-added to that of substance. It is then conceived that the substance remains the same, self-identical, while the accidents or attributes undergo change. The leaf changes from green to yellow or red. It is supposed to be the same leaf all through its many changes. It is thought that the substance remains immutable, but that the colour changes. Hydrogen and oxygen combine to form water. The atoms before and after the metamorphosis are supposed to be the same. The substance is unaltered. But the qualities have become different.

2. *The question of necessity.* In no sense can the category of substance and accident be regarded as a necessity of thought. It was invented by the Greeks. But men thought quite reasonably about the world before the Greeks began to philosophize, and they managed to conceive it, to think and to reason, and to control experience, without this category. It may be urged that it was implicit in their thought, that it was actually used by them without its being realized, and that all Aristotle did was to make it explicit. But this is clearly not correct. Substance and accident is plainly a philosophical refinement of the popular concept of 'the thing and its qualities'. That is the category which is used by the plain man, and was so used before Aristotle. And its use was not implicit but explicit. Substance and accident was the result of an effort on the part of the philosophers to analyse and clarify this popular concept, and to give precision to its vagueness. Substance and accident, therefore, in so far as it differs from thing and quality, is nothing but a philosophical theory, an invention of the philosophers. How is it possible to maintain that an idea which no one but a few philosophers understands is a necessity for all human thinking?

The absence of necessity also follows in another way from the fact that substance and accident is the philosophical version of thing and quality. The concept of 'thing' implies 'existence'. It is bound up with that whole circle of ideas. But 'existence' itself has been shown not to be necessary. If you choose to think of the table, not as a substance having qualities or attributes, but as a bundle of qualities, without substratum, which happen to accompany each other about the world in a regular kind of way, you can get along perfectly well. You can even control and predict experience. You have found that the experiences 'brown' and 'shiny' and 'square', in certain conditions which you know with fair accuracy, go about in company with the experience 'hard'. Hence when you get the fórmer experiences in those conditions you can predict that if you thrust your finger out towards the brown patch you will get the experience 'hard'. There is no necessity to think either of 'things' or of 'substances' at all.

3. *Epistemological type*. The concept substance is closely akin to the concepts thing, existence, and identity, and like them is a constructive category.

We say of the table ,'It is brown, shiny, &c.' 'It' is thus conceived as something existing apart from its qualities. But what sort of a thing is 'It' apart from its qualities? Abstract from the table its brownness, its shape, and *all* its qualities, and what is left? Absolutely nothing. The supposed substance, lying beneath the qualities as a support or substratum, can never be perceived and cannot even be imagined. To think a substance without any qualities is the same impossibility as to think of being without quality. Hence the thought of substance is not given in perception. Nor is it inferred. It is therefore constructed.

The construction is of the existential type. A substance is supposed to exist in order to support the accidents. The assertion of its existence can only mean 'If we could strip off the accidents, we should then perceive the substance'. In reality no such 'stripping off' is possible, nor is such an act of perception. It is surely clear that it is absurd solemnly to invent philosophical subtilties to explain away the difficulties in the conception, for the reason that the whole conception is nothing but a makeshift device of the mind, a 'way of looking at things', which it happens to find convenient, but which was never intended to withstand precise and searching philosophical analysis and criticism. The category of substance and accident, properly understood, should not take itself so seriously as that.

Hydrogen and oxygen are supposed to combine to form water. The substance remains the same throughout the change of qualities. That is the mind's *way of putting* the facts. But what are the facts? I am not concerned here with the meaning of the scientific theory of atoms. I shall have something to say about that in a later chapter. I am only here concerned with the implications of the concept of substance, whether its structure is conceived as atomic or not. The facts, then, i.e. the givens, are as follows. Firstly, we have a group of experiences, a group of sensations, which we conceptualize as due to the presence of hydrogen and oxygen in a retort, the presence of a flame inserted into the retort, &c. This whole group of presentations suddenly disappears and is replaced by a totally different group. There is the loud sound of the explosion, and a set of presentations comes into existence which we conceptualize as due to a number of drops of water in the retort. That is *all* that is given. These are the only 'facts'.

We may 'explain' these facts how we like. We may say simply that the oxygen and the hydrogen have ceased to exist, and that water has been created or has begun to exist. Or we may adopt the more elaborate and complicated hypothesis that there are certain 'substances' which have remained the same, while the 'qualities' have changed. There is absolutely no evidence for this view, nor is it possible that there ever should be any. There cannot in the nature of the case be any evidence for the existence of a substance which is by hypothesis without sense qualities and which it is therefore impossible to perceive and entirely outside any possible experience. Thus the view that hydrogen and oxygen atoms remain unchanged while their qualities change, and that the two gases 'combine' to form water, is a dodge of the mind.

We have here a clear case of alternative truths. The view usually adopted is that just referred to as a dodge.

But the view that the oxygen and hydrogen cease to exist and that water suddenly begins to exist is certainly quite as 'true'. It is indeed simpler and nearer to the facts. But the reason why the more complicated alternative is adopted in this case is that it fits in better with the mind's previous constructions of the external world. The idea of permanence has been definitely adopted into those constructions. The world of 'things' becomes the world of substances. It is part of this whole scheme of ideas that the substance or the 'thing' persists unchanged while it hides shyly beneath the veil of its changing qualities. The mind which has once taken this line will prefer to explain the phenomena of the water by the hypothesis of a 'combination' of atoms which in themselves persist unchanged, the change being somehow mysteriously attributed to the influence of the fact of 'combination'.

In general, of course, the mind adopts the *simpler* of two alternatives. But the simpler of two general world-views may involve taking the more complicated of two possible views of some smaller problem or of some particular patch of the world. That is what has happened here. It is simpler to believe in a single public world of 'things' than in millions of private worlds of fleeting presentations. But belief in the single public world inevitably led on to the idea of things which persist unchanged under a change of qualities. And so, though this is not in itself a simplification, but rather a complication, it is yet implied in what is in general a simplification of the whole world-view.

7. POSSIBILITY

1. *The meaning of the category.* Possibility is one of the group or cluster of categories—identity, substance, and now possibility—which centre round and are closely bound up with the category of existence. This will appear as we proceed.

Possibility as a category, i.e. as a character of the external world, must clearly apply to that world and not merely to our knowledge of it. It must not be merely a characterization of our state of knowledge or ignorance.

CATEGORIAL KNOWLEDGE

A possibility must be something which, in some sense, is part of the real world. For example, it may rain to-morrow or it may not. We commonly say that either is a possibility. But the possible in this sense is a concept which does not qualify the outer world at all, but only qualifies our knowledge of it. What is meant is simply that we do not know whether it will rain to-morrow or not. To-morrow's weather, when it comes, will be *actual*. This notion of our uncertainty about the world, which is often expressed by means of the word possibility, is *not* the meaning of the category which we are to examine. I mention it only in order to exclude it and to avoid ambiguity.

Genuine possibility is opposed to actuality. The possible is in some way a part of the world which is never actual. The possible, therefore, is something which has no existence. How the real world can be regarded as somehow including a part which has no existence is at present a mystery which we shall have to clear up. But nothing is easier than to give examples. 'If the Germans had sunk the British fleet, they would have invaded England.' 'If the horse I backed had won the Derby, I should have won a hundred pounds.' But the Germans did not sink the British fleet and they did not invade England. The horse I backed did not win the Derby, and I am still without my hundred pounds. It is clear that these propositions do not express any facts which ever did or ever will exist in the world. They are supposed to express possibilities which might have happened, but did not. Things and events in the world are considered as frequently coming to points at which their roads fork in several directions. Of the several possible roads events can only take one. The one they do take is called *actual*. All the others are, or were, *possibilities*.

The propositions quoted above as examples refer to the past. I chose past possibilities to illustrate my point designedly. For possibility cannot in that case be confused with our ignorance of the future. But examples of present and future possibilities are just as easy to find. 'If I stretch out my hand, the wall will feel hard.' 'If I bite the apple, it will taste sweet.' 'If I look at Mars through a large enough telescope, I shall see the polar ice caps.' Propositions of this kind express possible, as distinguished from actual, experience. I am now looking at the wall. The present visual experience is actual. The feel of the wall is a *possible* tactile experience which I might have *if* I stretched out my hand. It is essential to the notion of possibility that the antecedent of the hypothetical proposition which expresses it shall *not* be fulfilled, that I shall *not* touch the wall, bite the apple, &c. For if I do these things, the experience then ceases to be possible and becomes actual (assuming that my prediction has been correct). The proposition 'If I stretch out my hand I shall feel the wall' expresses a possible experience, which is not actual, only so long as I do *not* reach out my hand.

Possibility is only expressible by means of an hypothetical proposition. We may no doubt say '*x* is a possibility'. But this nominally categorical proposition is in reality hypothetical. It means that *if* certain conditions were fulfilled, then *x* would actually exist.

2. *The question of necessity*. There can be no kind of necessity in this category. It is, of course, essential to any rational prediction and control of experience. Our thinking would, without it, be confined to an almost inconceivably rudimentary stage. It is, therefore, a practical necessity. But it is in no sense a necessity of thought. We could theoretically confine our attention to what is actually given or actually existent to the exclusion of all mere possibility. There would be nothing illogical or self-contradictory in such a course.

3. *Epistemological type*. Possibility is a constructive category. The construction is existential, for it creates in imagination an existence which is not actual. It sets up an hypothesis which cannot conceivably be proved, and which, in fact, posits an existence which is not a part of the actual world. That it cannot conceivably be proved will be evident if we consider the following case. Suppose we are in a totally dark room. I say 'If I had switched on the electric lights, we should now see the walls of the

room.' This is alleged to be *now* a possible experience. It is not a prediction of future experience. It cannot be that, since it does not assert that I *shall* turn on the light, or that we *shall* see the walls. It does not assert anything whatever as to what *will* happen in the future. It purports to make an assertion about the present. It asserts that if the room were now light, instead of being dark, we should see the walls. But it is obvious that this can never be proved. If I turn on the light, the resulting visual experience of the wall will in the first place exist at a time future to, or later than, the moment in which the assertion was made. And in the second place the experience will have ceased to be possible and will have become actual, so that it cannot prove the existence of a possibility.

Not only can possibility never be proved. It is even contrary to the facts, which makes its character as a construction or fiction even clearer. Consider the proposition 'If I put out my hand, I shall feel the wall hard.' This does not assert that anything *is*, but only that something *might be*. But what does this 'might be' mean? A fact, an existence, a reality, either is or is not. There is no half-way house in the universe for any 'might be'. A 'might be' is simply an 'is not'. Hence possibility is no part of the actually existing universe. There is no such thing as a possible experience. This makes its character as a fiction quite apparent.

The importance of the category of possibility is, however, very great. It is involved in every existential construction. It is involved in every scientific hypothesis which asserts the existence of something which cannot be perceived, e.g. atoms, ether, electrons, &c. These all depend on the concept of possible experience. That concept lies at the root of, and renders possible, the construction of the external world.

For the notion of possible experience is simply the assumption that things exist when no one is aware of them, the wall when the light is out, the hardness of the wall when no one is touching it. We must remember that in the early stages of knowledge, when the mind was aware of presentations and nothing else, *esse* was identical with *percipi*. Even now all existence has to be conceived in terms of perception. Even an unperceived existence is thought of, and can only be thought of, *as if* it were a perceived existence. To exist does not now mean simply to be perceived, because the mind has determined otherwise, has projected existence out beyond its own perceptions, has invented an unperceived world. But all thought, all knowledge, has its roots in perception. The unperceived world which the mind has invented also has its roots in perception, and is made in the image of what is actually perceived. The mind could not invent anything really new. It merely takes the materials of the given, i.e. of what it actually perceives, and builds them up into its fictitious worlds. The table which exists when no one is aware of it is supposed to be brown, shiny, hard, square, and in all other ways just like the table we see. In the last resort everything that the mind invents or constructs has its roots in perception, goes back to perception, and has to be understood in terms of perception. Thus if we say that a thing exists when no one is aware of it, what do we mean? We mean, simply and solely, that although no one is now looking at, or perceiving, the thing, yet *if* any one looked he *would* see it. This, however, is the formula by means of which the category of possibility is expressed. So we see that the category of possibility and the notion of unperceived existence which we discussed at such length in Chapter VI are really one and the same construction.

A few examples may serve to make the point clearer. What do I mean by saying that Melbourne exists on the other side of the planet? This existence must be ultimately explained in terms of perception. My statement means probably that some minds (the inhabitants) are actually perceiving Melbourne. But if by any chance there are no minds there to perceive it, then my statement can only mean that *if* I travelled round the globe I should perceive Melbourne—or in general, of course, that if any mind were suitably situated it would perceive Melbourne. What is the meaning of the assertion that the moon has a side turned permanently away from the earth, so that it has

CATEGORIAL KNOWLEDGE 321

never been seen? It means that *if* any one could look round the back of the moon, he *would* see the other side.

Thus the mind's invention of the notion of possibility was perhaps the most important step it ever took in its advance to knowledge. By inventing an imaginary realm of possible, as distinguished from actual, experiences, it opened up the way to all future existential constructions. It rendered possible the notions of permanence, existence, and of a public independent world.

8. CAUSALITY

1. *The meaning of the category.* I shall make no attempt to analyse or define the concept of causality, for the simple reason that it is too difficult. It is so complicated and controversial a matter that it would require an elaborate and extended treatment which it cannot be given here. It has proved a stumbling block to a long series of philosophers and logicians, and many varying views have been expressed.

Here is Mill's definition:

'We may define, therefore, the cause of a phenomenon to be the antecedent or concurrence of antecedents, on which it is invariably and *unconditionally* consequent.'[1]

The following is Professor Alexander's view of the meaning of the concept:

'Space-time or the system of motion is a continuous system, and any motion within it is continuous with some other motion. This relation of continuity between two different motions is causality, the motion which precedes that into which it is continued in order of time being the cause and the other the effect.'[2]

Mr. Bertrand Russell is for ousting the words cause and causation altogether from the philosophical vocabulary. The notion of cause, he considers, is useless and is not actually used in the sciences. He would substitute for causality the notions of law and functional dependence.

Miss L. S. Stebbing, commenting on this, points out

[1] Mill's *Logic*, Book III, Chapter V.
[2] *Space, Time, and Deity*, vol. i, p. 279.

that though Mr. Russell's observations apply well enough to sciences such as astronomy and mathematical physics, they are inapplicable to such sciences as biology, where the notion of cause is still freely used. Causality is in general a concept which is useful in the less advanced stages of knowledge. Miss Stebbing concludes that there is no reason for rejecting the notion of cause, that 'there are causal uniformities', and that 'scientists continue to investigate causes'. She considers that 'the main reasons for the attempt on the part of philosophers to reject the notion of cause are to be found in the difficulty of stating precisely what exactly the concept involves, and in the close connexion between the traditional treatment of causation and the general problem of the validity of inductive inference'.[1]

With these essentially sane remarks we may agree. We shall believe that the word causality does represent a reality in the universe. Its definition is, however, a matter of great complexity and difficulty. There is no reason to think that the problem of defining it is not completely soluble by the human mind. But it may be admitted that a satisfactory solution has not yet been found. The task of finding one obviously cannot be undertaken here. And we must rest content with the belief that causation is a reality, and that though we may not be able accurately to define it we nevertheless know in a general (if vague) way what it means.

2. *The question of necessity.* Necessity has been asserted of causality in two quite different senses. It has been thought (1) that between a cause A and its effect B there is a necessary bond, and (2) that causality is necessary in the sense that it is impossible to conceive a universe without it.

It is difficult to understand how the first of these two views can now be put forward. The anthropomorphic attribution of compulsion to the cause, the idea that the cause *compels* the effect, has long been given up, and need not be discussed, since it is not likely to find any advo-

[1] *A Modern Introduction to Logic*, pp. 289–90.

cates. The only other sense in which it might be supposed that an effect *necessarily* follows its cause would be exemplified if it could be alleged that the relation between cause and effect is similar to that between premiss and conclusion in an inference. This would be a case of logical necessity. But that no such relation holds has been clear ever since the days of Hume. Given the premisses on which Euclid builds, we can deduce his conclusions without waiting on experience. But no one could predict that the explosion of oxygen and hydrogen in a retort would give rise to water until experience had shown that it is so. It cannot be said, therefore, that cause A is necessarily followed by effect B. The utmost that we can assert is that A is *always* followed by B. The relation is believed to be invariable and universal, but not necessary.

The second sense in which necessity has been asserted of causality is similar to that in which it has been asserted of other categories. Just as it is said that there could not possibly exist a universe without quality, or without being, or without unity and plurality, so it said that there could not exist a universe without causality. But this assertion is clearly without foundation. Kant and his followers seem to have mistaken the great importance of the category, the fact that it underlies all knowledge and is the main pillar of science, for necessity. But this, as has been repeatedly pointed out, is a confusion. Practical necessity, practical importance, are not the same thing as necessity of thought. The fact that causation is not a necessity of thought is shown by the fact that it is quite possible to conceive a universe in which it has no place. It is quite easy to imagine a world in which changes occurred without regularity, rhyme, or reason; in which a boy sometimes grew up into a man and sometimes turned into a melon; in which sugar sometimes tasted sweet and sometimes bitter; in which nothing could ever be predicted for the reason that nothing ever turned out twice alike; in which there were no uniformities. That such a world is conceivable is proved by the fact that we have already a recognized name and concept for it, namely 'chaos' as distinguished from 'cosmos'. And we have before us nightly in our dreams a world which is partially of this chaotic kind.

Thus causality does not possess the same kind of necessity as do quality, being, unity, and plurality. A universe without quality or being cannot even be brought before thought. But a universe without causality can.

3. *Epistemological type.* Causality is a category of the factual type. It is a generalization from what is actually given in experience, not a constructive positing of some entity which is not given. It is based ultimately on elementary repetitions or patterns of sensation. We notice that a certain kind of green patch is followed by a certain kind of sound. This pattern repeats itself incessantly. But it is observed that not all green patches of the same kind are followed by the sound. It is only so when the green patch is accompanied by certain other kinds of sensation. By observation of the various conditions which are present, and by eliminating those which seem irrelevant, it gradually becomes possible to frame laws of succession in such a way that they shall be invariable. The illustration of the green patch and the sound is, of course, purely diagrammatic, and is not intended to represent any real case of causation. For the only point with which we are here concerned is to show the factual character of the category, the fact that it is based upon what is actually given in sensation, and not, like existence or possibility, upon fictions of the mind.

It is true that the law of causation as usually stated assumes that the future will be like the present and the past. But this does not render the conception a construction. What the justification of the assumption is need not be discussed here. It is a question for logic. But the assumption is not, in any case, a construction. For it neither abolishes a superfluous existence (unificatory construction) nor invents any new existence (existential construction). When we say that the sun will rise tomorrow we are not inventing any new existence. The rising of the sun to-morrow is, or will be, factual. It will be actually perceived.

Moreover the assumption that the future will resemble the past is not confined to the concept of causation. It applies equally to all other factual concepts. We assume that the concepts 'red', 'loud', 'colour', 'unity and plurality', will apply to the world in the future as in the past. The assumption is not peculiar to causation, but is applicable to all concepts, factual and constructive alike. Hence it clearly does not show that causality is a constructive category.

Another possible source of confusion on this point must be briefly eliminated. The concept of causality no doubt covers causes and effects which are not experienced but constructed. It is extended by the mind from the area of actual experience in which it originated over the whole of existence, factual and constructive. The cause of a noise in the room is believed to be a rat behind the chest of drawers. In so far as the visual rat is unseen, it is a constructive existence. But this, again, does not make causality a constructive category. For the element of construction lies in the concept of 'existence' as applied to the rat. It does not lie in the category of causality. And we must not credit it twice over in our accounts. The factual character of causality is proved by the consideration that it *could* have been formed by simple observation of what is actually perceived. It could theoretically have been formed by the solitary mind before it created any constructions at all. The fact that we apply the concept 'brown' to the table which no one is perceiving does not make 'brown' a construction. As we know, it is a factual concept of the given. Exactly the same argument applies to causality.

9. REALITY AND UNREALITY

1. *The meaning of the category.* By this category I do not mean Reality, with a capital R, as opposed to appearance —some ultimate transcendental metaphysical Reality which may be supposed to lie behind and beyond the ordinary world of things. Such a use of the word reality

may be perfectly legitimate, and such a conception of reality may, for all I know, contain truth. But reality in that sense is a highly sophisticated concept of philosophers. It is understood only by a few people, and is certainly not one of the underlying primary categories of common thought. By reality I mean here *what is apprehended in veridical perception*. By unreality I mean what is apprehended in dreams, hallucinations, and delusions. The house in which I am now writing this book is, I believe, a real house. The house of which I dreamed last night was unreal.

But we must probe farther into the meaning of the category. How do we distinguish between the real and the unreal? Why do we say that the house seen in a dream is not real? What is the principle of differentiation?

Perhaps the most obvious reply, the one which we should be inclined to give off-hand when first faced with this question, would consist in suggesting that there is, in real presentations, some intrinsic superiority of quality by which they can be distinguished from unrealities. Their images, it may be thought, are more vivid, strike with greater force, are clearer, steadier, and so on. But the suggestion that the distinction between what is real and what is unreal can be based on such supposed intrinsic qualities is wholly untenable. Images in hallucination may be just as vivid, may strike with just as much force, as images of reality. The fact that they completely deceive the subjects of them shows that there cannot be any intrinsic quality in the presentations which distinguishes them from realities.

If we pass from the consideration of hallucinations to that of ordinary dreams, it may be supposed that here at least we have some intrinsic inferiority in the dream-image. It may be alleged that dreams are usually *fainter* than reality. But is this not a mistake? Is it not our waking *memory* of the dream that is faint? The dream itself, I suspect, is as vivid as reality. But we usually carry back only a faint and obscure memory of it into the waking world.

CATEGORIAL KNOWLEDGE

It must at any rate be clear that so doubtful and variable a point of difference cannot be made a satisfactory criterion of the distinction between the real and the unreal. Vividness, clearness, and the like, are qualities which vary in degree. Therefore, if we had no means of distinguishing reality from unreality except by means of such qualities, we should expect the real and the unreal to shade off into one another. No sharp line could be drawn, but there would be between the two a kind of doubtful region of the half real. We should be in constant doubt as to how to classify our images, and as to whether we were, at any particular moment, dreaming, suffering from delusions, or awake and sane. There would be constant disputes as to whether a thing which appeared to a number of people was real or not. Some would take one view, some another. Evidently clearness and vividness are not the criteria by which we distinguish.

If we go back for a moment to our primitive solitary mind, with its elementary colour patches and other phantasms, it would seem that such a mind would be confronted with a procession of presentations none of which could be distinguished either as realities or as unrealities. Assuming that there were no distinctions of vividness and clearness, or at least that such distinctions were irrelevant, all the images would stand on the same footing. All would be alike. It must be *afterwards*, therefore, as a result of its own constructive operations, that the mind somehow sorts out its presentations into two heaps which it calls respectively real and unreal.

It may be suggested that those presentations are real which the mind projects out of itself into the public external world, those to which it attributes 'existence'; while the rest remain subjective, internal, and so unreal. This is quite true. But it merely repeats, without solving, our problem. For we are still left asking *why* the mind projects outwards *some* of its presentations into the world of reality and leaves others as mere presentations. How does it differentiate between those which it will project outwards and those which it will not?

If it be said that a presentation is classed as real if it is that of an object which is external to us, while a dream-image is not so, we are once more merely repeating the problem without solving it. For an external object means merely an image which the mind has decided to objectify, to thrust out of itself into 'existence'. And the question is why the mind treats some images in this way and some not.

The next suggestion is likely to be that in cases of reality the sensation is caused by certain definite kinds of external stimulus. When I see the table, light waves are travelling through space to my eyes; they stimulate the retina, and vision results. Parallel remarks apply to the other senses. The stimulation of the nerve-endings by external agencies is not found in dreams and hallucinations, or if found at all—as in the case of the man who, when the door bangs, dreams of an assassination—only in an incomplete, partial, or mutilated form. This is the type of explanation of our difficulty which is likely to be put forward by unphilosophical men of science.

But it is clear that men distinguished between realities and dreams before they had any knowledge of nerve-endings and their stimulation by waves or other agencies. Therefore the normal human method of distinguishing realities from unrealities cannot depend on such considerations.

This 'scientific' solution is, as we might expect, a part of the truth. It is true so far as it goes, but it is not sufficiently radical, does not get to the root of the matter. We shall find in it a valuable clue, but we must observe that the reference to 'external' stimuli begs the question at issue. The very question which we are trying to solve is: how do we know the difference between things which are 'really there', i.e. things which belong to the 'external' world, and things (or images) which do not? It is, of course, circular to make 'external' stimuli the criteria of differentiation. If we start, as we must, by taking all images as on an equal footing, none more real than others, then none of them will be more 'external' than others. We cannot, therefore, differentiate between them by asserting that those are real which are caused by 'external' stimuli, since to do so would assume that we already knew which are external and which are not. This 'scientific' explanation amounts to no more than defining real things as those among our perceptions or images which are caused by, or interrelated with, real things (stimuli)—an obviously circular definition.

But this explanation, though inadequate, affords us the clue of which we are in search. To say that reality is what is connected, by causation or other systematic relationships, to other real things, does not define reality, since it is circular. But it suggests the truth that realities constitute an ordered system, while unrealities do not.

Originally, before the primitive mind in its solitude, there drifts a procession of colours, sounds, odours, &c., all equal in status, not differentiated into the real and the unreal. This procession is little more than a chaos. But the mind both *finds* order in it and *brings*, by means of its concepts and constructions, order to it. The presentations are sorted out and placed in pigeon-holes with proper labels attached. The relations which subsist among them are noted and classified. Groups of associated presentations in the course of time become 'things'. The categories come into operation, and above all the category of causality. Laws of co-existence and succession are discovered. There results what we call in general the 'world-order'. Things in the world are found to be systematically connected by means of a network of relations and categories. The vast majority, *but not quite all*, of the mind's presentations can be fitted into this world-order. And here we reach the solution of our problem. *Those presentations which fit into the world-order are classed by us as real. Those which are 'wild', in the sense that we cannot fit them into the world-order, we class as unreal and dismiss as dreams, delusions, and hallucinations.*[1]

Suppose that I see a baby turn into a water-melon. I

[1] The differences between dreams, delusions, and hallucinations are important to psychology, but not to epistemology. All alike are, for us, unrealities.

at once conclude that I was in a dream or suffering from hallucination. The event which I saw take place before my eyes is disapproved and condemned as unreal. This is because it cannot be fitted into the network of causal and other relations. Babies usually grow gradually into adult human beings. This represents a regular systematic sequence among our presentations. When a regular sequence has been overwhelmingly established it becomes a causal law. If anything conflicts with it, then either we must modify our law, or we must condemn that which conflicts with it as an unreality.

Real fires, it has been said, leave burns on our flesh if we are so foolish as to place our bodies in them. Real knives cut and leave wounds. But fires in a dream do not burn us, nor do dream-knives wound us. But this only means that these dream entities cannot be fitted into the world-order, i.e. into the order of knives and fires which behave in a normal and well-brought-up manner. These disorderly fires and knives cannot be fitted into the jig-saw puzzle of existence. And they, and all other bits of experience which will not fit in, are lumped together and classed as unreal.

It may appear that this is mere majority rule. Because in the majority of cases our presentations follow the pattern AB, the minority of cases in which the sequence is AX or AY is condemned as unreality. This is to some extent true. I prefer to regard babies turning into grown men and women as real largely because this is so frequent, whereas babies turning into water-melons is comparatively rare. But we *might* have to revise our estimate. If I, with great frequency and regularity, noticed babies turning into water-melons, so that such cases became a majority, and babies turning into adults became rare; and if this experience of mine was confirmed by the experience of other people; we should then all certainly begin to wonder. We might come to consider the water-melon experience real and the other unreal.

It is not, however, fundamentally a question of majorities. It is a question of order as against disorder.

CATEGORIAL KNOWLEDGE

It happens that the orderly part of experience is by far the larger for most of us. But it is not on this account that we class it as real.

We are not usually confronted, of course, with two rival world-orders, but rather with a world-order on the one hand which we call the real, and with patches of orderless lawless chaos on the other which we call the unreal. But if dreams took on a systematic form and continued each night where they broke off the previous night, we might have something like two rival world-orders. And it is conceivable that we might then have difficulty in making up our minds which of the two was real. Or we might be forced to the conclusion that we inhabited two independent real worlds. But this is not the normal position. And it is usually easy, as things are, to distinguish the little patches of lawless chaos which appear here and there in our experience from the general fabric of ordered experience which is reality.

We can now see where the 'scientific' theory takes its place, a real but subordinate place, in the true view. The correlation of sensations with nervous stimuli is not the root of the matter. It is itself merely a particular instance of that general correlation of all parts of veridical experience with all other parts which constitutes the world-order.

It will be noted that the correlation of my sensations with my nervous processes does not exist *for me* as a direct experience, but only as hearsay. It exists primarily as part of the experience of some outside observer, which I take up indirectly into my world in accordance with the principle of the coalescence of the many private worlds into one common world. This correlation exists for the outside observer as follows. He observes the existence of the table and the existence of my eye in some position in space related to the table. He infers, from other observations made in the laboratory, the existence of changes in my retina, optic nerve, &c. He cannot observe my sensation of the table, i.e. the presentation in my mind, but he can infer the existence of this from my own statement that

I see a table. These experiences of his, his vision of the table, his belief in the existence of nervous changes in my body, and his hearing me say that I see the table, are correlated according to regular laws and form part of *his* world-order. His world-order, by further comparison and correlation of numerous private worlds, becomes part of the common world-order, and so exists for me too. My experience of the table is then pronounced by him, by me, and by all others in agreement, real.

Thus the point is that the nerve-stimuli which are regarded as the cause of my presentations are themselves only presentations in some one else's experience, or, if they are themselves invisible, are inferred from other presentations (pointer-readings in the laboratory, perhaps), and are conceived as presentations which *could* be seen or otherwise perceived *if* the circumstances were suitable. In the end, therefore, the correlation of nerve-stimuli with presentations is simply a particular case of the correlation of presentations with one another. To explain presentations by external causes does not get to the root of things because external things are themselves presentations. Hence the source of the distinction between the real and the unreal has to be sought, in general, in the relations of presentations, not to those particular presentations which we call nerve-stimuli, but to all other presentations in the world, i.e. to the world-order.

This truth also absorbs into itself the partial view that the real is what every one perceives (or would perceive if suitably situated), whereas the unreal is what exists only in an individual's private world. The real table exists in the public world. The dream table exists only in my dream, and no one else can perceive it. Thus, according to this view, *shareability* of perception is what distinguishes the real from the unreal.

This is no doubt quite true in a general way, although it is not certain that crowd-hallucinations might not exist. But however that may be, the fact that my presentation exists only in my mind, and is invisible to other people, simply means that it is a presentation which I cannot fit

CATEGORIAL KNOWLEDGE 333

into the general world-order, which is, of course, a public world-order.

Thus the true concept of reality is that which defines it as whatever fits into the world-order. And the error of the two other explanations which we have just considered, i.e. (1) shareability, and (2) correlation with nerve-stimuli, consists in the fact that they seize on particular instances of this general principle and give them as the explanation instead of giving the general principle itself. Thus these explanations, though true up to a point, are incomplete, partial, and one-sided.

2. *The question of necessity.* Reality represents part of the mind's deliberate decision to conceptualize the world and to build a cosmos out of its presentations. This procedure is no doubt forced upon the mind by the facts, i.e. presentations actually order themselves in such a way as to make their conceptualization and their ordering by the mind possible. But this might not have been so. There is no necessity of thought in it. Just as we can easily conceive a lawless chaotic world destitute of those regularities and sequences which we call causal, so we can easily conceive a world so chaotic that we could not reduce it to any intelligible world-order. From which it follows that the category of reality is not a necessity of thought.

3. *Epistemological type.* The category of reality is in a sense the concept of concepts. For it includes in itself all the mind's previously developed concepts, and is itself the concept of their applicability to the world. To say that anything is real is to say that the categories of existence, causality, identity and diversity, relation, and so forth, apply to it. For to say that the categories and concepts of the mind generally apply to it is to say that it can be fitted into its place in the world-order. Thus it includes the concept of existence and other constructive categories. But since it does not itself add any new construction to knowledge, it is to be classed as a factual category. This is on the principle, previously laid down, that we must not credit constructions twice over in our accounts. Moreover it is an observable *fact* that a real object is part of a

CATEGORIAL KNOWLEDGE

systematically ordered world of images. It is an observable fact that the objects in dreams and hallucinations are 'wild' and constitute part of a chaotic world.

10. RELATION

1. *The meaning of the category.* Relation appears to be an indefinable ultimate. It is true that certain particular kinds of relation may be defined in terms of simpler relations. For example, if succession is necessarily implied in causation, then the definition of causation will include the relation of 'before and after'. But relation as such cannot be defined. The term, however, denotes a vast multitude of different kinds of relations. There are spatial and temporal relations, relations of resemblance and unlikeness, the relation of cause to effect, of mind to its object, of logical antecedent to consequent, of ratio in numbers, of person to person in society or in any organization, and a whole host more. It is not to our purpose here to enter upon any detailed classification of the different kinds of relations.

2. *The question of necessity.* If things exist, even if no more than presentations exist, then relations between them must exist. The attempt to conceive a universe without relations is equivalent to the attempt to conceive a universe without things or even presentations. Even if the universe consisted of nothing but one patch of red colour, the relation of resemblance would hold between the parts of it. There would also exist the relations of diversity, whole and part, &c. As it is thus impossible to conceive anything whatever existing without relations, it follows that relation as a category possesses necessity.

But it is not necessary to labour over again the explanation of this necessity. As with being, quality, and other similar categories, the necessity of relation is derived from logic.

3. *Epistemological type.* Relation is a factual category. Relations exist in the simplest conceivable experiences, the colour patches, sounds, &c., of the solitary mind. Relation is thus a concept of the given, and therefore it is

factual. As always in such cases, of course, the concept gets extended to constructive subject-matter. Thus we speak of the relation of substance and accident. But this extension, as we have already seen in similar cases, does not alter the factual character of the concept.

CONCLUSIONS

(1) The following, out of the categorial concepts which we have examined, possess a necessity which is derived from logic: being, quality, unity and plurality, identity (of the empty kind, $A = A$), diversity, and relation.

The following possess no necessity of any kind: existence, identity (of the meaningful kind, $A = B$), substance, possibility, causality, and reality.

As we should expect, we find when we survey this list that the following propositions hold: (*a*) *No constructive concepts are ever necessary.* Constructions by their very nature are not forced upon us by any logic, i.e. they are not inferences. They are optional. This is true of existence, identity (of the meaningful variety), substance, possibility, and reality. (*b*) *Necessary concepts are always concepts of the given, i.e. factual concepts.* (*c*) *Some factual concepts are necessary, some not necessary.* Examples of necessary factual concepts are all those given above as necessary. Causality and reality are factual concepts which are not necessary.

These relations may be summed up in the following table:

	Factual.	*Constructive.*
Necessary	Being Quality Unity and Plurality Identity ($A=A$) Diversity Relation	
Not necessary	Causality Reality	Existence Identity ($A=B$) Substance Possibility

It must be remembered, of course, that this table does

not profess to be complete. It contains only those concepts whose claims to categorial honours we happen to have examined.

(2) Up to the present we have followed the usage common among philosophers in calling all the ten concepts investigated in this chapter 'categories'. But the results of our discussion show that this usage of the word is ill-conceived. For there does not seem to be any point in continuing to regard the non-necessary concepts as categories at all. In fact the term, as applied to them, would appear to be a misnomer. It seems reasonable to lay it down in the first place that *no constructive concepts ought to be called categories*. The very fact that a notion is a mental construction implies that it is *not* primordial and original, that it is *not* fundamental to thinking, but is a product of sophistication. The case in which this is most obviously true is that of substance. Existence, meaningful identity, and possibility are at least very ancient concepts the origin of which is probably lost in the beginnings of the development of mind from the pre-human to the human stage. All our everyday common knowledge, even the most elementary kind, involves them, and must have done so since the beginning of human thought. Although theoretically they are not necessary, in practice they are indispensable to all our thinking. But substance is an invention of yesterday. It is not much above two thousand years old. It does not belong to common thought at all, but to the sphere of philosophical speculation. It is surprising that it has ever been allowed to figure in lists of the categories.

What is true of substance is also true, though less obviously, of existence, identity, and possibility. Although their invention by the human mind is buried more remotely in the past, yet they too are the products of creative human thinking. They belong to the superstructure, not to the foundation. And we must conclude that they have been wrongly classed as categories.

It seems reasonable to lay it down in the second place that *even factual concepts, if they do not possess the character*

CATEGORIAL KNOWLEDGE

of necessity, should not be classed as categories. The examples on our list are causality and reality. Causality is no doubt primordial and fundamental in the sense that it is not a construction but a concept of the given, a concept which the solitary mind might theoretically have framed from bare observation of its data before it began any world-building at all. But then the same might be said of such concepts as 'red', 'loud', 'colour', which no one would dream of classing as categories. Hence in order that a concept may be included among the categories (whether it is supposed to be pervasive, like causality and reality, or non-pervasive like 'loud' and 'colour'), it is not enough that it is a concept of the given, or a factual concept. And it seems reasonable to suggest that, if we are to retain the doctrine of the categories at all, only those concepts of the given which are *necessary* should be included. For only thus will there be any important difference between categories and other concepts. The mere difference between pervasive and non-pervasive does not seem to be of much importance. Some concepts apply to only a few things, some to many, some perhaps to all. But because a concept happens to apply to everything, this does not by itself constitute it as a different kind of concept. For its pervasiveness appears to be purely contingent and a matter of chance. But if a concept *necessarily* applies to everything, this may reasonably be regarded as setting it in a class apart by itself.

If we follow this rule causality and reality will be ruled out. The reasons why causality has been wrongly called a category appear to be twofold. (1) Its enormous importance in knowledge has been mistaken for necessity. (2) It has been regarded as of vital importance to the logical theory of induction, and philosophers have supposed that unless causality were considered a necessary concept the validity of inductive argument would be in danger. As to this second reason, we must leave logicians, now deprived of the necessity of causality, to make up their accounts as best they can. I shall have something to say on this score in the next chapter. But what is relevant for us at present to notice is that *both* these reasons imply that causality was classed as a category because of its supposed necessity; and that, now we have stripped it of necessity, there is no longer any reason to regard it as such.

Similar remarks, with minor modifications which the reader can work out for himself if he desires, apply to reality.

(3) Assuming that we are going to retain the doctrine of the categories as a part of philosophy, and that we are going to apply the principles just explained, then, of the ten concepts examined by us the only ones which are genuine categories are being, quality, unity and plurality, identity ($A = A$), diversity, and relation. The rest are excluded.

(4) The genuine categories possess necessity, but not in their own right. Their necessity is on a level with that of mathematics. It is derived from logic. In our search for necessity, then, we do not really find it either in mathematics or in the categories. We find only the shadow of it here. Or, to change the metaphor, the source of it is elsewhere. We must follow it over the boundaries of mathematical and categorial knowledge into the realm of logic, and study it there. This we shall do in the next chapter.

(5) This robs the categories of much of their old-time epistemological dignity. They are deprived of the right of posing as in some sense mysterious beings, very superior to mere 'empirical' concepts, constitutive of the world, ultimate realities, independent of experience, which existed in godlike beatitude 'before all the worlds'. They can no longer claim to be, as they were in the Hegelian system, identical with God himself. We need no longer burn incense to them. They are simply ordinary concepts, formed by the human mind in exactly the same way as other concepts. They are based, like the humblest sensuous concepts, 'red', 'loud', and the rest, upon observation of resemblances.

(6) It becomes a question, therefore, whether it is worth while to retain in philosophy any doctrine of the categories at all, or any distinction between them and other concepts.

CATEGORIAL KNOWLEDGE

It does not seem to be a matter of any great importance how we decide this issue. It is really no more than a question of words. The issue is whether the word 'category', thus robbed of the greater part of its connotation, can still perform any useful function, or express any valuable meaning. If not, we might erase it from the philosophical dictionary. But perhaps it will be more consonant with that moderation and tolerance which should characterize all philosophers if we decide to be mild and lenient with it. We will allow it to be retained as a name for those factual concepts which derive from logic the character of necessity, if and when there is any cause to distinguish them from other concepts. Categories may be allowed to exist, *very much humbled*.

(7) In some of those concepts which have been miscalled categories—existence, identity ($A = B$), substance possibility—we find once more the character of mental construction. Both unificatory and existential constructions made their appearance. This needs no further labouring. It is repeated here only to emphasize the wide range of construction in all knowledge.

CHAPTER XIII
LOGICAL KNOWLEDGE

LOGIC concerns epistemology from two points of view. Epistemology must determine (1) what is the *function* which reasoning performs in the building up of knowledge, and (2) whether logical knowledge possesses the character of *necessary* truth. We will discuss first the question of function, and afterwards that of necessity.

This is not a treatise on logic, and it is neither possible nor necessary that we should discuss at length the internal affairs and problems of the science. Great advances have been made in modern times, especially by the exponents of mathematical logic. The syllogism can no longer claim to be the sole valid form of mediate inference. But it is generally admitted by modern formal logicians that the syllogism is *one* of the valid forms. And as it is still the best known, I shall take it for the purposes of our study as the type of deductive reasoning. It will be found, as we proceed, that what can be said of the syllogism regarding our two problems of (1) function, and (2) necessity, can be generalized so as to apply to all forms of deductive reasoning.

To discover the single ultimate law of reason which validates all forms of inference, whether syllogistic or not —if there exists such a law—is obviously not a task which can be undertaken here. It is the job of the pure logician. But it would appear at least that all forms of inference agree in that they are modes of ensuring *consistency*. In the last resort what logic does ensure is that the body of knowledge to which it is applied, whether mathematics, mechanics, morality, politics, or any other, shall be internally self-consistent. *If* you assert Euclid's axiom of parallels, then you must, in order to be self-consistent, admit that the three angles of a triangle are together equal to two right angles. Or *if* you adopt any other and rival axiom, then you must admit whatever other propositions follow from it. If you admit that selfishness in general is wrong, then you must admit that any particular act of selfishness (of which you have yourself perhaps been convicted) is wrong. To admit the premisses of a valid deduction, whether it is syllogistic or not, and to deny the conclusion, is inconsistent. That is the lesson of every logic.

Hence the ultimate principle of logic may perhaps be called *the law of consistency*. How it should be formulated, or whether it is possible to formulate it in a single statement, are questions which we must leave to the logicians to answer. But it applies at any rate to all forms of inference. Suppose our argument is symbolized by

$$P$$
$$Q$$
$$\text{Therefore } R.$$

This may stand for the syllogism:

$$\text{All } S \text{ is } M.$$
$$\text{All } M \text{ is } P.$$
$$\text{Therefore all } S \text{ is } P.$$

Or it may stand for the argument:

$$A > B$$
$$B > C$$
$$\text{Therefore } A > C$$

(where $>$ stands for 'is bigger than') which is *not* a syllogism at all. Or it may stand for *any other kind* of valid deduction of a conclusion from two premisses. But whatever it stands for, its principle is consistency. If you assert the truth of P and Q, then you cannot consistently deny the truth of R. The same principle would clearly apply to any argument in which the number of premisses is not two, but one, or three, or any other number. It therefore applies to all deductive reasoning.

It is admitted that the form of the syllogism, though it ensures consistency, does not guarantee material *truth*. For if the premisses are false, the conclusion, though validly drawn, may also be false. Therefore, if the syllogism is to be of any use as an instrument of proof, all will depend upon obtaining true premisses. How are we to obtain these?

The premisses may perhaps have been obtained as the conclusions of prior syllogisms. But in that case the problem is only pushed back a step. For how can we be assured of the truth of the premisses of the prior syllogism? If we go back to still earlier syllogisms it is obvious that we cannot stop at any point, and that we are led on to an infinite regress. And that means, of course, that we can never *prove* our conclusion. How, then, is the infinite regress to be avoided?

Now it is true, of course, that sometimes a premiss may be given to us by direct perception. But we can only perceive particular cases, never a general principle. The premiss which asserts that Socrates is a man (in the famous syllogism about the mortality of Socrates) is known to be true because it was perceived at the time by numerous persons. But from two particular premisses nothing follows. In every syllogism there must be at least one general principle. And general principles cannot be perceived. Hence we are still left with our question so far unanswered, namely, how we are to avoid the infinite regress, and where we are to obtain the general principles which have to serve as premisses?

As against the argument of the last paragraph it might be pointed out that it is possible to produce valid deductive reasonings which have no general principle stated in the premisses. These are never syllogisms, of course, but such reasoning as that since $A > B$, and $B > C$, therefore $A > C$. But I think it will be admitted by logicians that in all such cases a general principle is involved, though not explicitly stated, and that the validity of the argument depends upon this principle.

To the question how the infinite regress is to be avoided two answers are possible. Firstly, we may get back to 'axioms', truths which are known as truths by immediate intuition, and which therefore do not require to be proved by earlier syllogisms. Secondly, our premisses may have been supplied by inductive reasoning.

LOGICAL KNOWLEDGE

The first of these proposed solutions, however, is entirely vain. There are no such things as axioms in the sense desired. The logical laws of thought may perhaps be quoted as exceptions. But they are purely formal and give us no information regarding facts. The law of contradiction can tell us that an object cannot be both white and not-white, but it cannot tell us whether it is in fact white or not. Now we require for our premisses general principles regarding actual matters of fact, such as the mortality of man, the nature of gravitation, or the laws governing the distribution of flora and fauna. Therefore the laws of thought, even if we admit that they are self-evident and necessary, will not do as axioms on which the syllogism can fall back. And apart from the laws of thought no axioms have ever been produced which will stand critical examination. The onus of proof is obviously upon those who assert the existence of axioms. And if they have never been able to produce a single indisputable example of an axiom, if the supposed axiomatic character of their examples has always evaporated upon examination, we are entitled to conclude, till they can prove the contrary, that none exist. And that is the actual position of affairs.

The only supposed axioms which can claim to have been at any time generally accepted as axioms by all instructed persons are those of mathematics. But it is now known that all the axioms of mathematics are either (1) analytic propositions, or (2) propositions which are not self-evident and which can be disputed. The analytic axioms are certainly self-evident. But they do not yield any material truth. They only explain the meanings which their authors propose to attach to words. It will always be true, and it is a self-evident and necessary truth, that the whole is greater than the part. But this is because the part is by definition less than its whole. On the other hand, those axioms of geometry which are not analytic—such as the axiom of parallels—are also not self-evident. Hence the solution of the problem of the infinite regress by means of axioms fails.

The other suggested solution of the problem, namely,

that the truth of our premisses may be assured by inductive reasoning, takes us outside the sphere of deductive logic. I shall postpone dealing with it to a later section in the present chapter. For we may at once draw a valuable conclusion from the considerations already adduced, namely that, unless we have recourse to induction, *the syllogism by itself can never prove any truth*.

This conclusion can be generalized. It is true, not only of the syllogism, but of all deductive reasoning, including those non-syllogistic forms which modern logicians have discovered. For in all deduction the conclusion follows from premisses, and the question arises how the truth of these premisses is to be assured. Either we must rely on axioms or on induction. Therefore it follows that *deductive reasoning by itself, i.e. without the aid of induction, is never a sufficient instrument for proving the truth of any conclusion*.

It is well known that the syllogism, if it is regarded as a method of proof, is a *petitio principii*. Consider the following syllogism:

    All Etonians wear top hats.
    Smith is an Etonian.
Therefore, Smith wears a top hat.

If we do not already know that Smith wears a top hat, then we cannot possibly know that all Etonians do so. Since Smith is a Etonian, it can only be true that all Etonians wear top hats, if it is true that Smith wears one. Therefore the major premiss 'All Etonians wear top hats' *assumes* the truth of the conclusion that Smith wears one. The syllogism, therefore, does not prove its conclusion at all. It assumes the truth of the conclusion in the major premiss. If it is regarded as a proof, it commits the fallacy of begging the question.

This does not mean that the syllogism is worthless as an instrument of thought. What it means is that the assumption that the function of the syllogism is to *prove* the truth of propositions is false. What the function of the syllogism is will be discussed in a moment. But it is clear at any rate that its function is not proof.

LOGICAL KNOWLEDGE

Exactly the same argument will apply to *any* deductive reasoning. No argument of the form

$$P, \text{ therefore } Q,$$

can be valid unless the proposition P assumes the truth of the conclusion Q. Hence we reach, by a different route, the same result as we reached at the end of the last section, namely *that deductive reasoning by itself is not a sufficient instrument for proving any truth. Its function, in fact, is something other than proof.*

For generations the enigma of the infinite regress and the enigma of the *petitio principii* have baffled logicians. They have attempted to pick little holes. They have tried to show that the syllogism is not 'really' a *petitio*, or that axioms really do exist. These attempts have all failed. But the solution of both difficulties is perfectly simple. It stares one in the face. The difficulties have arisen because *logicians have erroneously assumed that deductive reasoning is a method of proof, and that the function of reasoning is to prove truths.*

By means of reasoning we understand, no doubt, the full implications of our beliefs. But we do not arrive at those beliefs by means of reasoning. We reach them by means of constructions and assumptions together with an application of these to observations of fact. The function of reasoning is solely to ensure that these beliefs are consistent with one another. The syllogism

$$P.$$
$$Q.$$
$$\text{Therefore } R.$$

does not prove the truth of R. What it proves is that *if* you hold the beliefs P and Q, you cannot deny the truth of the belief R. It shows that you cannot hold the beliefs $(P+Q)$ and not-R together. This will be true of all deductive reasoning. If we symbolize the premisses (whether one or more) by P and the conclusion by R, then the result of deductive reasoning is to show that if you hold P, you cannot deny R, i.e. that P and not-R is an inconsistent and therefore impossible combination of beliefs.

From this it is clear that reasoning never tells us what we *shall* believe, but always what we shall *not* believe. It forbids us to believe P and not-R together. We have, as a result of reasoning, no *positive* knowledge of any kind. We do not know whether P is true, or whether R is true. All we have is the negative knowledge that $P+$not-R is not true. Thus the necessity which logic imposes upon us—if we are going to believe in such a necessity—is purely negative and prohibitive. Its commands are never 'Thou shalt', but always merely 'Thou shalt not'.

Logic places alternatives before us, but never tells us which alternative we are to choose. You can believe not-R, but if so you cannot believe P. Or you can believe P, but if so you cannot believe not-R. You can believe either P or not-R, but not both. You have your choice between the alternatives $(P+R)$ and $($not-$P+$not-$R)$. But no logic and no reasoning can ever tell you which of these two you ought to believe. This is really saying no more than that the function of deductive reasoning is to guarantee, not truth, but consistency—an old enough doctrine, to be sure.

The conclusion that the function of the syllogism is not proof solves both the problem of the *petitio principii* and the problem of the infinite regress. We need not trouble about the syllogism being a *petitio*, because that only invalidates it if we persist in regarding it as a *proof* of the conclusion. It does not invalidate it if we regard it as merely pointing out that we cannot consistently hold both to the assertion of the premisses and the denial of the conclusion.

As to the infinite regress (apart from premisses inductively supplied, the question of which we shall study in a moment) similar considerations apply. The infinite regress is an objection to the syllogism if it is viewed as a means of proof, but not if we assign to it the more modest function of merely ensuring consistency. For there is not the slightest objection to the process of combing through our beliefs and weeding out inconsistent combinations going on for ever. We find by this means that the combination of *P* and not-*R* is inconsistent. Going back, we find that the combination of *O* and not-*P* is inconsistent; then that the combination of *N* and not-*O* is inconsistent. We may comb through the entire field of knowledge in this way. The process will naturally go on for ever, and indeed ought to do so. Thus the infinite regress is a fatal objection to the view of the syllogism as an instrument of proof, but accords admirably with the view of it as an instrument for eliminating inconsistencies.

But if deductive reasoning proves nothing, if it does not yield us any positive beliefs, where are we to get these beliefs? The logician will probably reply to this question that we are to get them by means of inductive reasoning. Formal logic, he will say, only guarantees consistency, but induction gives material truth. It is not necessary for the syllogism to go back either to axioms or to an infinite regress. It can go back to premisses the truth of which has been proved by induction. Thus we may prove the mortality of Smith by deducing it from the proposition that 'all men are mortal'. This latter proposition is known to be true, not because it has been proved by any prior syllogism, much less because it is supposed to be self-evident, but because it is proved true by induction.

This leads direct, however, to what Dr. Broad has called 'the skeleton in the cupboard of inductive logic' and the 'scandal of philosophy'.[1] For all induction involves the fallacious argument from the particular to the general, the illicit jump from 'some' to 'all'. *Some* samples of water (extremely few) have been observed in the laboratory or elsewhere to freeze at 0° Centigrade and to boil at 100° at sea-level. We conclude inductively that *all* water, including those samples which never have been and never will be observed, freeze at 0° and boil at 100°. Of the animals and vegetables in the world an almost infinitesimal fraction has been examined, and these have been found to consist of cells. It is concluded inductively that *all* organic matter is composed of cells. It is assumed not only that

[1] *The Philosophy of Francis Bacon,* pp. 66 and 67.

these inductive conclusions will be found true in all cases in the present and the past, but that they will be true in the future too. Not only is it believed, on the strength of a few particular cases of observations on water, that water in the unexplored parts of the earth at the present boils at 100°. It is also believed that the law will hold true tomorrow and a hundred years hence. We assume that the future will resemble the past, and that the same laws and uniformities will operate in the future as operate now.

It is obvious that it is illicit thus to argue from particular to general. It involves basing upon experience conclusions which experience does not justify. For undoubtedly when we thus argue, for example, about water, our conclusion is supposed to be based upon experience. But how can experience justify any conclusion which goes *beyond* experience? However many times we observe that particular S's are P's, how can this possibly prove that the next S we meet will be a P, or that all the unobserved S's in the world now, or to be in the world in the future, will be P's?

Unless there is some other logical principle on which we can fall back here, it is clear that this argument from particular to universal, which all induction involves, is totally fallacious. So logicians have tried to find or invent some other logical principle on which induction can fall back. This principle has been called the principle of 'the uniformity of nature'. The precise definition which ought to be given to this phrase is not very clear. But it may be said in a general way to mean that there is complete regularity in nature, and that the behaviour of nature may be analysed into 'uniformities' or laws. It is clear that 'the uniformity of nature' is merely a collective name for all the particular uniformities or laws the validity of which is in question. Hence it stands itself in exactly the same need of justification as do the particular uniformities which are subsumed under it. To hold that because some S is P therefore all S's will be P's, is an unjustified assumption. But the uniformity of nature is merely the assumption that all these minor assumptions are true. How is it possible to justify the proposition that all water behaves uniformly

LOGICAL KNOWLEDGE

by means of the supposed principle that all nature behaves uniformly? How can we justify an assumption merely by making a bigger assumption which includes it?

Thus we are brought back once more to the question what logical grounds we can possibly have for believing that nature, *outside* the limits of our observations, obeys the same laws which we have found to operate in observed cases. How can an observed fact, or any multitude of observed facts, ever prove an unobserved fact? Is there the slightest logical ground for believing that the universe will obey the same laws to-morrow as it obeys to-day? Is there the slightest logical ground for believing that the sun will rise to-morrow? Have we a right even to the view that the same laws of nature as those to which we are accustomed hold good in portions of the earth which are still unexplored?

Since the time of Hume logicians and philosophers have tortured their brains over this problem. It is assumed that there must be some valid way of *proving* the uniformity of nature. All inductive reasoning depends upon this principle as its ultimate premiss, just as geometry depends upon its axioms. There is not the least reason to assert—although philosophers have been found to assert—that it is a 'necessary truth', or that it is self-evident. But if not, it follows that this ultimate principle of induction itself stands in need of proof. Now it cannot be proved *deductively*, because there is no higher or more general principle under which it can be brought and from which it can be deduced. It is itself the most general of all generalizations. It cannot be proved *inductively* because it is itself the principle which all induction assumes as valid. Therefore it cannot be proved at all.

In spite of this, logicians continue to believe that there must be *some* solution, that it must be possible in some way to *prove* the uniformity of nature, or to show that it is logically valid. But although generations of logicians have racked their brains over it, no one has ever suggested a rational solution, and the problem remains the 'scandal of philosophy'.

The history of this problem thus bears a suspicious resemblance to that of another which we have already had occasion to mention, the problem of the axiom of parallels. Generations of mathematicians racked their brains trying to prove Euclid's axiom. There must be a solution of the problem, they thought, if only they could find it. But as no valid proof ever presented itself, mathematicians in the end came to the conclusion (which Beltrami afterwards proved mathematically!) that there *is* no proof of the axiom of parallels, or in other words that it is a pure assumption.

The whole history of the logical problem which we have been considering surely points to the likelihood of a similar ending. The obvious reason why logicians have laboured fruitlessly to find a logically valid basis for the principle of uniformity is simply that it has not got any logically valid basis, or in other words that it is a pure assumption. How long it will take logicians to come to this conclusion, it is difficult to predict. Perhaps another fifty years. They are at present still hunting for a proof of uniformity just as the mathematicians kept on hunting for a proof of the axiom of parallels. Human hopes in these matters die hard, and logicians are no more logical than other people.

For our part we shall adopt the view which is plainly dictated by reason. The belief in the uniformity of nature is a pure assumption for which no valid reasons whatever can be given. There is nothing in this conclusion which need surprise any one who has followed the argument of this book. We have seen that from its earliest stages knowledge constantly uses assumptions which are incapable of proof, and that it could never have advanced a single step from its starting-point if it had not done so. The whole fabric of human knowledge is built upon an elaborate foundation of assumptions, some of which we have studied in the earlier chapters of this book.

It will naturally be asked whether the principle of the uniformity of nature, being now recognized as an unprovable assumption, is for that reason to be classed as a *mental construction* similar to those which we have studied in earlier pages. It has in common with all constructions the fundamental character that it is assumed without proof. But there are important differences. In order to see these, we will break up the uniformity of nature into particular uniformities. It is, after all, only a general name which covers all particular uniformities, so that instead of considering the general principle we may consider instead some particular cases. Take first the proposition 'Water freezes under normal conditions at 0° Centigrade'. We have observed this to happen in a few cases. We assume that it happens, and will continue to happen, in all unobserved cases. That an unobserved sample x freezes at 0° means: 'If we had perceived the freezing of x, and had applied a thermometer, we should have perceived the mercury in the thermometer standing at 0°'. It is of course an impossibility that we should have perceived what is by hypothesis an unobserved case, and the hypothetical proposition with the impossible antecedent no doubt points to the presence of an existential construction. But it seems clear that the element of construction here belongs, not to the particular assumption about freezing, but to the underlying conception of 'existence'. What is constructed is the fact that the unobserved water exists at all. When once this unobserved existence is constructed, the further ascription to it, rightly or wrongly, of this or that particular quality, whether it be freezing at 0° or being colourless or white or any other, is not a new construction, though it may be an assumption.

Now consider a belief which results from applying the principle of uniformity to the future. 'The sun will rise to-morrow.' This is a pure assumption, of the truth of which there is and can be no proof. But the rising of the sun to-morrow, when it happens, will be a *fact* and will be actually perceived. Hence my belief that the sun will rise to-morrow cannot be regarded as a construction. It stands in clear contrast, for example, to the construction of 'the table when no one is perceiving it'. This table is a pure invention or fiction. It never factually exists at all. Its existence can never be perceived or verified. For that any one should ever perceive a table when it is not being perceived is a flat self-contradiction. But the rising of the sun to-morrow is not a pure invention which no one will ever perceive. It will, on the contrary, be perceived when it happens. The existence which is assumed is, or at least will be, *factual* in character, and it therefore cannot be regarded as a construction.

We could, of course, define the meaning which we propose to attach to the word construction in such a way as to include assumptions such as that of the uniformity of nature. But it seems better to exclude them. The word construction clearly implies something that is *made* by us, something that is invented, created, or fabricated. This meaning applies very well to the unperceived table and to all the constructions which we have so far examined. But it does not apply to the principle of uniformity, which is not a fiction, but is an assumption regarding *facts*. Hence it will be better to call it simply an assumption, and not a construction.

In another way, too, the principle of uniformity differs from any construction. This is in regard to its *justification*. A construction is always such that it can neither be proved nor disproved, nor in any way tested or verified in experience, so that we are at liberty to assume it or not assume it as we please. If we do assume it, we do so, not because the facts prove it, but because it is more convenient or simple to do so than not to do so. For example, no one can prove or verify that there exists an unperceived table. It makes no difference at all to the facts whether we believe in one or not. It does, however, make a difference to our convenience of thinking in the manner shown in Chapter VI. We therefore adopt the assumption. The justification of a construction is always convenience, simplicity, economy, or consistency.

But what justifies the assumption of the uniformity of nature is the *event*. My assumption, which I make to-day, that the sun will rise to-morrow, cannot be proved now. There is *now* no logical basis for it at all. And it is,

LOGICAL KNOWLEDGE

therefore, quite right to insist that it is an unprovable assumption. But it will be *justified* in the particular case, though not of course as a general principle, when to-morrow the sun actually rises. Subsequent justification, of course, is not in any sense proof. For proof consists in logical grounds which are *prior* to the proposition proved. Thus a construction makes no difference to the facts, and is not justified by them, but by convenience. And because it makes no difference to the facts, it is a matter of choice whether we assume it or not. The opposite assumption would always be just as *true*. It would be just as true to think that no table exists when no one is perceiving it as to think that it does exist. It would be just as true to believe in many private worlds as in one public world. But these conditions do not hold of the assumption of the uniformity of nature. It *does* make a difference to the facts, and it is not a mere matter of convenience, whether I assume that the sun will rise to-morrow or whether I assume that it will not. The whole question is one of fact, and not of convenience. Suppose I state that the sun will not rise to-morrow. Then, when to-morrow comes and the sun rises, my statement will be shown false. And it is not equally true to say either that the sun will rise or that it will not rise. One of the two statements will turn out to be false. That the justification of my assumption lies in the facts, and not in convenience, is what places this assumption in a different category from all constructions.

That the principle of the uniformity of nature is an assumption is at present accepted, so far as I know, only by some of the pragmatists. But they usually make the fatal mistake of calling it a *methodological* assumption.[1] This is a mistake because it is not an assumption regarding method, but regarding facts. This is merely repeating what has been said in the last paragraph. But it may be made clearer by a comparison. Suppose I guess, without any reasons at all, that the horse X will win the Derby. This would be a pure assumption, since there are no logical grounds for it. But it would be sheer confusion of thought

[1] Cf. Schiller, *Logic for Use*, pp. 162–3.

to call it a methodological assumption. It has nothing to do with any question of method. And exactly the same is true of the principle of the uniformity of nature, or of any of its applications such as that the sun will rise to-morrow.

Methodological assumptions are always assumptions regarding which we have a *choice*. We can choose one method or another. We can make one assumption or its opposite. The results of our choice will be greater or less convenience of working. And that is all. But we have no choice as regards the uniformity of nature. We have a choice, of course, in the sense that, since there are no logical grounds for believing that the sun will rise to-morrow, we can, if we like, believe that it will not. But when to-morrow comes the belief will (I hope) turn out to be false. This is not the kind of choice which exists in the case of methodological assumptions. In their case I may choose which I like because both will be right. Only one will be more convenient than the other. But the choice as regards the uniformity of nature is a choice between two beliefs one of which will turn out to be true, the other false.

One of the most extraordinary delusions of the philosophic mind consists in supposing that, if we frankly admit that the principle of the uniformity of nature is an unprovable assumption, we are thereby committing ourselves to 'scepticism'. It is this bogy of scepticism which is chiefly responsible for making logicians and philosophers cling desperately to the belief that they will some day discover a way of showing that the uniformity of nature can be proved or shown to be in some way logically valid. But scepticism, if it means anything, means the belief that we have no knowledge, or that the human mind is incapable of knowledge, or that our knowledge is not truth. Now all that our view of the uniformity of nature as an assumption commits us to is an admission that, when I say 'The sun will rise to-morrow', I cannot have any logically binding grounds for the statement, or in other words that I cannot *prove* that it is true. But the statement

LOGICAL KNOWLEDGE

may be in fact true although I cannot prove it. And if it is true, then it contains true knowledge. We may in general have true knowledge without being able to give any logical reason for it. An assumption may contain true knowledge. It does so if the assumption turns out to be correct. The fact that we cannot, at the time we make the assumption, prove that it is going to turn out true, has absolutely nothing to do with the matter. It in no way makes our knowledge false, or misleading, or in any way unsatisfactory. 'The sun will rise to-morrow' is true, and therefore knowledge, if to-morrow the sun does rise. So long as the world continues in its old grooves, so long as the present uniformities of nature persist, we have and shall have true knowledge, and there is, therefore, no ground for scepticism. If ever the world deserts these grooves and uniformities (as it may to-morrow for all I know), then—since we shall all presumably perish immediately—it will not matter to any one whether there is any ground for scepticism or not. We may, therefore, safely reject the view that to admit that the uniformity of nature is an unprovable assumption involves us in scepticism.

It follows from what has been said that inductive reasoning, like deductive reasoning, *proves nothing*. The syllogism about mortality does not prove the mortality of Smith. It shows that you cannot believe *both* that all men are mortal and that Smith is not mortal. It proves that Smith is mortal, *if* we first know that all men are mortal. But how do we know this? We cannot prove it by induction unless we admit the universal truth of the principle of the uniformity of nature. But that principle is a pure assumption. So that in the end all reasoning, deductive and inductive, goes back to an unprovable assumption. And this is another way of saying that *no reasoning, inductive or deductive, ever proves anything, and that no proposition can ever be proved*.

It does not follow from this that logic is a fraud, or that reasoning is a fallacy. What follows is that we have all along expected reason to do something which is not within its function. We have all along been mistaken in supposing that the function of reason is to prove the truth of propositions.

Two questions at once arise. (1) If reason never proves anything, how do we know the truth of truths, and where do we get them from? (2) If proof is not the function of reason, what is?

The answer to the first question is that we arrive at truths, or at least at those truths which are general principles as distinguished from particular facts, by inductive reasoning in much the way usually described in the logic books. We believe that all men are mortal because (1) all men have so far died, and because (2) we also believe in the principles of causation and of the uniformity of nature. It would be inconsistent to accept these two positions and yet to deny that all men are mortal. Therefore we accept that proposition. That is the way in which we *arrive at* that truth. But the process of *arriving at* a belief is not a valid *proof* of it, and does not, or ought not, to profess to be such. We attain to truth by a suitable manipulation of assumptions, constructions, and observed facts (givens). The methods of doing this are described (or misdescribed) in books on inductive logic. But there is no such thing anywhere in the universe as *proof*. The delusion that there is such a thing has very likely arisen, as Doctor Schiller has urged,[1] by reason of the fact that the Greeks, among whom logic as a science originated, were disputatious controversialists who desired above all things an instrument for compelling their opponents to admit the truth of their assertions. The syllogism was supposed—erroneously as we now know—to supply this need. Proof was compulsion applied to your opponent. The mistake of supposing that reasoning proves propositions has persisted all down the ages.

How, then, do we distinguish between a true belief and a false one? If we cannot prove that a proposition is true, how do we ever know that it is true? We need not make this inquiry as regards propositions which only state what

[1] *Logic for Use*, pp. 269-70.

is immediately perceived, such as 'This is red'. Our question refers, of course, to general propositions which go beyond the given, and which make assertions about what is not observed. And the answer appears to be that we cannot ever be certain of the truth of a proposition until observation verifies it. 'The sun will rise to-morrow' is doubtless true. And it is accepted because it satisfies the conditions of inductive logic. But we cannot actually be certain of it until to-morrow. It must also be remembered that although in strict theory logic proves nothing, yet for practical purposes it is not unnaturally credited with the power of proof. For a logical argument does prove its conclusion *if* the premisses are true. When, therefore, we find a conclusion which follows from another proposition which is universally accepted as true; or when the conclusion is a deduction from a whole body of knowledge; then we either have to accept the conclusion or throw overboard accepted truths or perhaps a whole science of painfully elaborated knowledge. Usually in such cases the alternative of rejecting the premisses is a practical impossibility, and never even comes before our minds. In such cases reasoning is not unnaturally regarded as proving conclusions. When we are asked, therefore, how we know that any proposition is true, the answer is that we know it through the ordinary methods laid down in logic, but that this knowledge, so far as it goes beyond the given, never amounts to certainty.

The second question we had to answer concerned the function of reasoning. If proof is not its function, what is? The function of inductive reasoning is to arrive at, i.e. to *discover* truths, but not to *prove* them. The function of deductive reasoning is simply to ensure consistency among the beliefs which we thus arrive at.

Properly speaking, however, induction is not a form of *reasoning* at all. It is, or is supposed to be, a set of rules for observing, experimenting, and making *de*ductions from what is observed. It is a method of discovery, but it is not a form of reasoning distinct from deductive reasoning.

For immediately we attempt to throw our inductions into the form of reasonings we find that they at once exhibit themselves as deductive. Mill's famous 'methods' simply applied the general principles of causation to particular cases in order to discover which phenomenon is the cause of which. They are plainly deductive. Mill first defines a cause as the invariable and unconditional antecedent of a phenomenon. His methods then tell us how to manipulate our data in such a manner as to show that in the particular case before us A is the invariable and unconditional antecedent of B. From this it is plainly a *deduc*tion that A is the cause of B. Moreover, as has often been remarked, all induction is really a syllogism with the uniformity of nature as a major premiss. The whole of the *reasoning* involved in induction is deductive. The rest of what goes by the name of inductive logic consists in the analysis of scientific (and other) methods, not of reasoning, but of observing and experimenting. It is not logic, but methodology. It consists of rules for selecting or discovering the relevant data from which we can *deduce* our conclusions. We are told, for example, that the great rule is to *vary the circumstances one at a time and observe the results*.[1] But this obviously is not a rule of *reasoning*. It has nothing to do with reasoning. It is a rule which purports to tell us what are the relevant things to observe before we begin to reason. Immediately we begin to reason from the data so obtained our reasoning is necessarily deductive.

To argue from general principles to particular cases, from 'All S is P' to 'Some S is P' or to 'This S is P', is considered valid reasoning, and it is deductive. To argue from 'Some S is P' to 'All S is P' is the method of induction and it is not valid, or in other words it is not a piece of reasoning at all. We may throw it into the form of reasoning by saying: 'Nature acts uniformly, so that if we are sure that the same set of circumstances recurs, the same propositions will be true of it each time it recurs. Therefore, since we have found in all observed cases that when

[1] See *A Modern Introduction to Logic*, by Miss L. S. Stebbing, p. 339.

the set of circumstances S occurs we also get the circumstance P, it follows that this will also be true of unobserved cases, so we may conclude that *all S is P*.' This is certainly reasoning, but the reasoning is simply a syllogism.

It follows that *all reasoning is deductive*. All reasoning proceeds from the general to the particular. The idea that there is another kind of reasoning, called inductive, which proceeds from the particular to the general, is the veriest superstition. From this superstition have proceeded all the empty and futile argumentations about how it can be valid to reason from the particular to the general. No one would have asked the absurd question how induction can be valid if he had not proceeded on the false assumption that induction is a kind of reasoning.

Since all reasoning is deductive; and since the function of deduction is, not proof, but to ensure consistency among our beliefs; it follows that to ensure consistency is the function of all reasoning.

We now see how it was that Descartes so lamentably failed in building up the system of our beliefs by reasoning, i.e. by deductions from the foundation of experienced certainty. Nothing can be built up in that way. Reason is powerless to advance us one step from the starting-point of our knowledge. Knowledge advances, not by reasoning, but by means of constructions, assumptions, and observations of the given. It is by these means that we arrive at truths.

Nevertheless the function of reason is of vast importance. Its commands are negative. But these commands are absolute law. It never says 'Thou shalt believe the proposition P'. It is powerless to do that. But it says 'Thou shalt not believe both the propositions P and Q, since they are inconsistent with one another'. It gives us the choice between P and Q. It does not indicate which we are to choose. But it forbids us to accept both.

We have already seen reason at work in the earlier stages of human knowledge, and if we look back we shall see that the description just given of its working is correct.

For example, the second construction of Chapter VI laid it down that there are not many private worlds, but one public world, and that the table which I am now seeing is identical with the table which is seen by some one standing beside me. From this follows the third construction, which lays it down that the table which I perceive continues to exist when I am not looking at it, provided that some other mind is still aware of it. Thus the third construction is a deduction from the second. But this does not mean that the third is *proved* by means of the second. It is not proved at all. The reasoning merely lays it down that we cannot at the same time accept the second and reject the third. If we do not wish to accept the third we must go back on our tracks and give up the second. If we wish to retain the second, then we have to admit the third. Reason gave us this choice. It could not instruct us which alternative to choose. The choice in the case of these constructions was determined by convenience.

Human knowledge is like a mosaic. Our various beliefs are the pieces which have to be fitted into one another. Reason does not supply the pieces, but it is the set of rules which tells us how to fit them together and to reject those which do not fit.

When, as has now happened with the human race, a vast body of knowledge has been built up and accepted, reason may often appear practically to prove a new proposition by showing that we must either accept it or give up the whole, or at least a very large part, of the accepted system of knowledge. We still theoretically have the choice between the two alternatives which reason always gives us. But the alternative of giving up a whole systematic body of knowledge may be practically unthinkable. So we accept the new proposition and consider that it has been conclusively 'proved'. It is as a result of cases of this sort that the delusion has been fostered that reason can prove truths, and that to do so is its function.

The function of reasoning having now been made clear, we must pass on to the second big division of the subject

LOGICAL KNOWLEDGE

of this chapter, the question, namely, of the alleged *necessity* of reason.

We have found that 'necessary truth' does not reside either in mathematical or in categorial knowledge, except in so far as these kinds of knowledge are necessitated by logic. Certain of the axioms of geometry may be necessary, but only because they are analytical propositions whose truth is guaranteed by the logical law of contradiction. The same remark is true of those categories of which necessity can in any sense be predicated. Consequently the claim that necessary truth exists has not been substantiated by our examination of mathematics and of the categories. Such necessity as they possess is not in their own right, but is derivative. It is derived from logic. Consequently, if any necessary truth exists, we must now seek for it in the sphere of logical knowledge.

Necessity, having been pushed back out of mathematics and categorial knowledge, into logic, cannot now be pushed back any farther. It turns at bay here, and we have to meet it and settle final accounts with it. We have to decide what we are to think of necessity. We have either to admit it or explain it away. The necessity of logic, if it is a reality, is something absolute and ultimate for the reason that it cannot be pushed back any farther, but remains here 'in itself'.

The necessity of logic can be seen both in the fundamental logical laws, such as the law of contradiction, and in any valid inferences on any subject. That S cannot be both P and not-P appears necessary. That if Smith is a man, he cannot be a tiger may be expressed in the syllogism

>No men are tigers.
>Smith is a man.
>Therefore Smith is not a tiger.

The conclusion *necessarily* follows from the premises. And it is the same necessity as that which appears in the law of contradiction. For the syllogism is merely the application of the laws of thought. To admit its premises and deny its conclusion is inconsistent, i.e. breaks the law of contradiction. And it is the necessity of that law which compels us, if we have admitted the premisses of the syllogism, to admit the conclusion. It is the same if we consider any deductive argument which cannot be reduced to the syllogism. The truth that if $A > B$, and $B > C$, then $A > C$, possesses exactly the same necessity as does the syllogism, and for the same reason, namely that to admit the premisses and deny the conclusion would be inconsistent.

This, then, is the case for the necessity of logic. It appears as self-evident.

We must now inquire whether this necessity can be, or has been, reasonably disputed. Those who would deny it or explain it away appear to fall into three groups according as they assert one or other of the following opinions:

(1) That the laws of logic are not laws of *thought* at all, but that they are laws of *things*, and that they do not therefore differ epistemologically from other empirically known laws. Their apparent necessity must then be explained away as a delusion due to their extreme familiarity and to the fact that we know of no instances which contradict them. This seems to be the view adopted by some realists.

(2) That the laws of thought may be *subjectively* necessary, i.e. they may be necessary ways of our thinking, but that it does not follow that they are necessarily true of things outside us.

(3) That the laws of logic are similar to the rules of a game. They are conventions which we choose to adopt because they serve our purposes. We might, however, have adopted other conventions, if we had wished, and therefore there is no necessity in those which we have adopted. This opinion is supported by pragmatists.

We will briefly discuss these three types of opinion.

(1) Those realists who adopt this view assert that the so-called laws of thought are not in fact laws of thought at all, but that they are laws of things. And we come to know their truth in the same way as we come to know other laws of things, that is to say, through experience. The law of contradiction is just as much an empirically

learned law as Kepler's laws of the planetary motions. We find in experience that nothing is ever both white and not-white at the same time and place, and that nothing is ever both beef and not-beef, and so on. We generalize these experiences into the law that nothing is ever both X and not-X, and formulate it as the law of contradiction. And similarly with the other so-called laws of thought.

This view is compelled, of course, to deny the existence of any true necessity in logic. For necessity cannot be found in experience. Experience gives us the 'is' of things, but cannot give any 'must'. Hume showed this once for all, and no instructed person can now dispute it. If we adopt the realist explanation of the laws of thought, then we must give up belief in their necessity. We must regard them as merely facts, not necessities. We may say that it is as a matter of fact true that my meat is not both beef and not-beef. But we cannot say that it is impossible that it should be both beef and not-beef. For if the laws of logic, instead of being necessary truths, are merely empirical generalizations, they may become false to-morrow.

This opinion cannot explain the necessity, but has to explain it away. It has to be represented as a delusion which is bred in us by the fact that we have always seen the laws of logic obeyed and never disobeyed. When we invariably see a thing happen in a certain way, we come to think that it *must* happen in that way. Necessity of thought is really the product of lack of imagination and of that kind of stupidity which, according to Mr. Bernard Shaw, makes Englishmen think that their tribal customs are the laws of God and man.

This is a weak position. It draws what little plausibility it has from cases in which beliefs have been supposed to be necessary truths and have afterwards turned out to be either false or at least open to alternatives and so not necessary. Euclid's axiom of parallels is, of course, the stock example. Other examples are usually not so clear. Some philosophers have believed that the law of causation or the principle of the uniformity of nature is a necessary truth, whereas that is not now the general view. Possibly some people long ago may have thought 'the earth is flat' to be a necessary truth—though so far as I know there is no evidence that any one ever did think so.

But it does not follow, because human beings have made mistakes about *what* particular truths are necessary, that the whole conception of necessity is a delusion.

Nor does the attempted psychological explanation of the feeling of necessity seem at all convincing. If it were true that our feeling of the necessity of the law of contradiction is merely the result of the fact that we do not happen to have come across a case in which events did not follow that law, then we should expect that the feeling of necessity would attach to any empirical law of long standing which we have never seen disobeyed. Men must have believed, long before they ever thought about the axioms of Euclid, that all human beings die. Yet the mere fact that belief in human mortality has always existed, and has admitted of no exceptions, has never caused us to regard it as a necessary truth. It certainly seems to me that if the suggested explanation of the feeling of necessity were the true explanation we should expect that feeling to have attached to *all* ancient and uncontradicted beliefs, or at least to far more than those to which it has actually attached. Or at least the supporters of the view which we are discussing should produce as evidence of the correctness of their view a *large number* of undoubted instances in which propositions, other than the laws of thought, have come to be regarded as necessary simply because they were familiar and uncontradicted by experience. The actual evidence adduced is wretchedly meagre. The axioms of Euclid. But the necessity of those axioms which are analytic is derived from logic, and cannot therefore be given as an example of the necessity of propositions *other than* the laws of thought. To adduce this evidence is simply to adduce the laws of thought themselves. And as to the axiom of parallels, if it was mistakenly regarded as necessary, this was probably owing to the accident that it was found in the company of the other axioms which were necessary because they were analytic. The mistake of treating it as a necessary truth is thus quite simply and naturally explained without resorting to the unconvincing and artificial explanation which we are discussing. And what other evidence is there? The law of causation? This was treated as necessary by Kant, because he thought that its being so regarded would alone save knowledge from scepticism, and not for the reasons supposed by the realists. This is about all the evidence there is. And it is plainly insufficient to bear the weight put upon it.

But the best reason for rejecting the realist opinion is that it renders all discussion on any subject futile. It in fact abolishes reason altogether. All argument, all discussion—including that on which the realist contention itself is based—assumes, not merely the truth, but the necessity of the laws of logic. Any reasoned argument assumes that, if certain propositions are granted, certain other propositions follow, and that if you admit the first propositions you *must* admit those which follow, and that you have no choice. To regard the necessity of logic as a delusion is thus to regard all reasoning and discussion as delusion, and in fact to render all thinking futile.

Moreover it may reasonably be doubted whether even those who profess this opinion really believe—as they assert—that to-morrow a thing might be both what it is and what it is not. It may reasonably be asserted that no one really can maintain such a proposition, since it is simply meaningless. It appears to be an impossibility to believe in what is recognized by the believer himself as a sheer self-contradiction.

Connected with the opinion which we are discussing, however, is a question which has caused a good deal of perplexity. How are we to distinguish, it is asked, between logical necessity and the mere psychological *feeling* (which may be false) that a proposition is necessary. Many propositions, now known to be false or at least not necessary, were once considered self-evident and necessary truths. The feeling of self-evidence or necessity is, after all, nothing more than a psychological fact. What guarantee have we that this mere feeling is not misleading us now in regard to the laws of logic as it has in the past in regard to other propositions?

Now in the first place it is not so easy to produce examples of these *other* propositions to which the argument appeals. We have already noted this fact. The axioms of Euclid and the law of causation. Perhaps a few others might be raked out of the rag-bag of the history of philosophy. But in most cases the only mistake has been to suppose that the necessity which the proposition exhibits is in itself, instead of being derivative from logic. This is the case with the analytic axioms of Euclid. And in other cases it is easy to show how the mistake arose and where the mind has gone wrong. These mistakes have been gradually eliminated. We no longer believe that there is a special mathematical necessity, a special categorial necessity, and so on. We see that these apparent necessities are only the shadows cast by the necessity of logic. We assert that there is no necessity anywhere in thought except that of the laws of logic. It is reasonable to suppose that we have reached bed-rock in the matter in logic, and that this necessity is genuine. But even if this is not admitted, the various eliminations from the list of supposed necessary truths give us hope that, if we are mistaken in thinking that logic is necessary, the mistake will be discovered, as the others have been. But this has not been done yet. And we are entitled to continue to assert the necessity of logic until some one proves the contrary, until some one shows that the laws of logic are false, or at least admit of alternatives, *and tells us what the alternatives are.* And for my part I shall be quite content with this position, for I fancy that we shall be allowed to rest in our beliefs for ever!

If any one persists in disbelieving in the necessity of the laws of thought on the ground that they might some day be proved false, he certainly cannot be dislodged from that position by any logic. For if he does not admit the necessity of logic, it is clear that no logical argument can convince him, and that it is useless to argue with him. But this should surely be, to those of us who are sane, a

LOGICAL KNOWLEDGE

sufficient refutation of his opinion, since it is plain that such an opinion reduces all thinking to a futility.

(2) With some hesitation I attribute the opinion that the laws of thought may be subjective necessities which bind our thinking but do not necessarily apply to things outside us to Miss L. S. Stebbing. The hesitation is due to the fact that the meaning of the following passage is not entirely clear to me (which is doubtless my fault and not that of the distinguished authoress).

It might be thought that the principles of logic provide an instance of propositions that are necessarily true.... But this would be a mistake.... The necessity of logical principles is nothing but the necessity of constructing systems. The construction of such systems may be the expression of the thinking of rational beings. But this would not *establish* the necessity. We do not intend to dispute this necessity but to deny that any significance can be attributed to the notion of absolutely necessary principles.[1]

I may be wrong in my interpretation of these sentences. But it appears to me that there are two thoughts intended to be expressed here, viz. (1) that logic is necessary *if* we are going to construct deductive systems, not otherwise; and (2) that its necessity for thought does not establish its necessity for things.

The first of these propositions may certainly be admitted. We are only under the compulsion of logic if we are going to construct systems. But to think at all is to link up experiences into systems or partial systems. So that what the proposition amounts to is that we can avoid the necessity of reason *by not thinking at all*. This is undoubtedly true. It is likewise true that we can avoid the necessity of reason by the simple expedient of being dead. But this does not touch the doctrine of necessity as understood in any rational sense.

The second of the two thoughts which we extracted from the passage quoted asserts that the necessity of logical thinking does not prove that the same necessity applies to things objectively. This, however, rests upon a confusion.

[1] *A Modern Introduction to Logic*, p. 176.

It supposes that we have first (1) a necessary thought, and then (2) that it has to 'apply to' things, and that the doctrine of logical necessity invalidly assumes that it does so. The error here consists in the false abstraction or separation of the two stages. It is false to suppose that there is *first of all* a necessary thought existing in a vacuum, all by itself, apart from things; and that it is then 'applied' to things. This sort of misunderstanding arises from the wooden and unintelligent use of metaphors, or from taking metaphors literally. It is supposed that a thought is like a metal cast or mould which applies, i.e. fits on to, the material that is put into it. It is forgotten that any thought, and therefore a logical law such as the law of contradiction, is from the first a *thought of things*. This thought of things is not twofold and divisible into the thought and the thing, but inseparably one. If the thing is eliminated, the thought too disappears. Thus it is impossible in any manner to think the law of contradiction *without thinking of it as applying to things*. You can only express it in the form 'A thing cannot be both white and not-white, hot and not-hot, &c.' It is true that logicians substitute their S, M, and P for 'thing', 'white', 'hot', and so on. But S, M, and P are merely symbols which stand for things. They indicate that it does not matter *what* things are thought of under the law, that any things will do equally well. But they do not indicate that the law can be thought without things at all. Thus the fact that the law of contradiction is formal does not mean that the thought of it can be framed in the mind without thinking of the things to which it applies. That would be a logical and a psychological impossibility. To think the law at all is to think it as applying to things, not any particular things, but things in general. To suppose that the law can first exist or be thought by itself as a pure thought without reference to things, and that it is afterwards externally applied to things, is simply to be misled by materialistic metaphors. It is therefore meaningless to suggest that a thought might be necessary as a thought, i.e. for us subjectively, but not apply to things. A necessity of thought *is* a necessity of things. And if you admit a necessity of thought, you admit that it necessarily applies to the things of which it is the thought.

(3) The third opinion which we are to discuss is that usually put forward by pragmatist writers. For them, all knowledge derives its validity from its success as an instrument of action. Logic too will be judged in this way. Its rules will have no absolute sanction. They will be no more than the rules of the game, to be altered at will if they do not lead to success, if they do not 'work'.

This view of logic has recently been expressed with great clearness and vigour by Mr. C. I. Lewis in his book *Mind and the World-Order*. Mr. Lewis's views are not merely his own, but are representative of a large volume of opinion. And I shall therefore make no apology for quoting and criticizing them at some length.

'The laws of logic,' says Mr. Lewis, 'are purely formal: they forbid nothing but what concerns the use of terms and the corresponding modes of classification and analysis. The law of contradiction tells us that nothing can be both white and not white, but it does not and cannot tell us whether black is not white or soft or square is not white.... Similarly the law of excluded middle formulates our decision that whatever is not designated by a certain term shall be designated by its negative. It declares our purpose to make, for every name, a complete dichotomy of experience, instead—as we might choose—of classifying on the basis of a tripartite division into opposites and a middle ground between the two.... Further laws of logic are of like significance. They are principles of procedure, the parliamentary rules of intelligent thought and action. Such laws are independent of the given because they impose no limitations whatever upon it. They are legislative because they are addressed to ourselves—because definition, classification, and inference represent no operation in the world of things, but only our categorical attitudes of mind.

'Furthermore, the ultimate criteria of the laws of logic are pragmatic. Indeed, how could they be anything else? The truth of logic is not material truth but a truth about the modes of self-consistency.'[1]

On this I would make the following criticisms:

[1] *Mind and the World-Order*, pp. 246–7.

(1) We have already seen that in spite of logic being purely formal—a fact which we must admit—it is not true that its laws are not laws of things, but only of words or thought. Form, after all, must be the form of something, of some matter. And the fallacy of Mr. Lewis's reasoning consists in supposing that the form is indifferent to the matter. The truth is the very opposite. To legislate for the form is to legislate for the matter. Whatever affects the form of anything affects the matter. The laws of logic are forms whose matter can be nothing but the things in the real world. They are no doubt forms of thought, but that thought is *about* things. For example, it is quite untrue to say that the laws of thought 'are independent of the given because they impose no limitations whatever upon it'. They do impose limitations upon it. Thus the law of contradiction prevents this paper from being both black and white at the same time. It is true that it does not use the terms 'paper', 'black', and 'white'. It generalizes. It lays it down that a thing cannot have at the same time incompatible qualities. That it does not tell us *what* qualities are incompatible has nothing to do with the matter. The law of the land lays it down that I shall not kill. It does not inform me what particular classes of actions on my part will result in killing. Unless I know from experience that to point a loaded pistol at a man's head and pull the trigger will result in his death, the law will not prevent me from doing so. But it would be absurd to say that the law imposes no limitations upon me. Similarly unless I know from experience that black is not white, that the two colours are incompatible, the law of contradiction will not prevent me from thinking that the paper may be both black and white. But as soon as experience has given me that knowledge I see, not merely that I cannot *think* that it is both black and white at the same time, but that the paper itself cannot *be* both black and white. The law thus legislates for the paper, and in general, for things in the world. It must surely be admitted that, quite apart from what I think, things in the world cannot possess contradictory characters. This is

most certainly a limitation imposed by the laws of logic on objective realities.

Mr. Lewis's views imply an utter and irreconcilable dualism. Thought has to be conceived as floating about in a vacuum, as empty of all content, sundered from even the thinnest wisp of reality by an impassable chasm. It seems a simple reflection that if logic governs only words, and has nothing to do with things, which need not obey it, then the thought which the words express must be a completely idle play of the mind working independently of and out of touch with reality.

Logic may be compared with mathematics, which is likewise entirely formal. In spite of its completely formal character, mathematics, as we saw, does apply to things, and has no meaning without them. We had to resist the mathematician's desire to fly off into the blue, to leave the earth behind, to set up a mathematical paradise of his own, and thereafter to ignore the common things on the earth and to pretend that he knows nothing about them. And just as there are not two universes, one earthly and the other mathematical; so there are not two universes, one material and the other logical. If mathematics has any meaning at all, that meaning arises from the fact that it applies to *things*. The same with logic. Mathematics and logic either both apply to things, or they apply to nothing and are wholly meaningless and worthless.

(2) Mr. Lewis tells us that the laws of logic 'forbid nothing but what concerns the use of terms'. Terms, however, stand for things. And the only reason why we cannot use terms inconsistently (which is what the laws of logic enjoin) is because the nature of the real world forbids us to do so. We are not allowed to think that the things for which words stand are both what they are and what they are not, because the world is so constructed that things never are what they are and also what they are not. If I define a horse as an animal with four legs (and other equine qualities), then I cannot use the word horse for an animal with five legs, because in the actual world it is and always must be true that an animal with five legs is not an

animal with four legs. Consistency of language and thought is only necessary *because* the real world is governed by the laws of logic.

(3) Mr. Lewis calls these laws '*our* decisions'. The law of excluded middle is '*our* decision that whatever is not designated by a certain term shall be designated by its negative. It declares *our* purpose to make for every name a complete dichotomy of experience, instead—*as we might choose*—of classifying on the basis of a tripartite division into opposites and a middle ground between them.' (The italics are mine.) This passage is completely fallacious. It implies that instead of the laws of logic which we have adopted we might at will have chosen some other set. So that the set we have chosen are not really necessary. This is simply untrue, and it would be surprising that any competent philosopher should put forward such a farrago of confused ideas, if one did not know by sad experience of what muddle and confusion philosophers are capable. We can, of course, arrange the material of our experience as we please, in dichotomies, trichotomies, or any other kind of division. *But whatever kind of arrangement we choose for the classification or division of experience, all the laws of logic still remain the same and still remain valid.* The colours which happen to confront my eye at this moment may be divided into white and not-white. They may also be divided into white, grey, and black. But whichever way I classify them, the laws still hold that they (and everything else in the world) must be either white or not-white, either grey or not-grey, either black or not-black; that they cannot be both white and not-white, &c. The laws of contradiction, identity, and excluded middle are not in the slightest degree affected by the various methods of classification we may adopt, and methods of classification are totally irrelevant to the problem we are discussing.

Nor is there any sense in which we can *choose* what logical laws we shall use. Nothing can be both white and not-white. You may say this is trivial, or otherwise cast abuse at it. But you *cannot* deny it. And you cannot choose an alternative law. It is sheer confusion of thought to suggest that a tripartite division, such as white–grey–black, implies or follows a logical law alternative to the law of excluded middle. The tripartite division is not an alternative to that law since material arranged in such a division continues to obey that law. The only alternative to the proposition that everything must be either white or not-white would be the proposition that some things may be neither white nor not-white. That proposition would be simply false, and we *cannot* choose it. The necessity of the law of excluded middle is real, cannot be pooh-poohed out of existence as 'a matter of words', and cannot be made a matter of choice between alternatives, for there are no possible alternatives.

(4) Mr. Lewis compares the laws of thought to 'parliamentary rules'. This carries on the same fallacy as that which has just been exposed. Rules of debate can be altered at will and are to a large extent matters of convention. Logical laws cannot be altered at will. They are necessary and binding. Nor are they in any sense matters of convention.

(5) The conclusion of the whole matter is that you cannot, however you twist or turn, explain away the necessity of logic. No doubt it is formal. No doubt it is a matter of 'mere consistency'. Our thoughts may be consistently false. Logic, as we saw, does not guarantee truth, but only consistency. It is in itself nothing but the law of consistency. But is it not an absurdity to suppose that, because of this, one has got rid of the necessity of logic, or in some way whittled it down? It is still there. It is not the necessity of believing this or that material proposition. *What* we believe is not dictated by logic. To think that it is so is the old delusion of thinking that the function of reasoning is to 'prove' truths. But the necessity of logic is simply the necessity of being consistent. Why should I be consistent? I *must* be, because logic *compels* it. This compulsion is necessity. And this necessity cannot be got round or explained away.

If a man of science is endeavouring to construct a

theory—be it a theory of light, of electricity, of palaeontology, or what not—logic lays it down that he cannot in one part of his theory assert that S is P and in another part that S is not-P. If he disobeys this law, one or other part of his theory will be false, though logic cannot tell him which. And it is trifling with philosophical truth to say that we can *choose* whether we shall obey the laws of logic or not, and that if we do not obey them we can still keep within the limits of truth by inventing and obeying some other alternative laws.

Let us take stock of the actual position as we have discovered it to be. We began, in Chapter XI, by inquiring whether knowledge, as well as being tied at its lower end by the given, is also tied in any way at its upper or conceptual end, whether, in other words, there is any necessity in conceptual thought. We have now brought that part of our inquiry to an end. We have examined the claimants to the position of necessary truth, namely mathematics, the categories, and logic. We have found that mathematical knowledge and some of the categories are indeed necessary, but that their necessity is that of analytic propositions, and is not in themselves but is derived from logic. We then examined the position as regards logical laws. And the result of our investigations is to uphold the claim of logic to an absolute necessity, which cannot be explained away, and which cannot be dispersed over the boundaries of logic into some other science. The necessity of logic is in itself, self-determined, absolute, and ultimate.

From an epistemological point of view this result is of importance since it indicates that knowledge, tied to the given, is also tied conceptually at this point by logical laws. There are thus two points at which the line of knowledge is tied, though it perhaps hangs free between them.

CHAPTER XIV
SCIENTIFIC KNOWLEDGE

WILL the same features which we have found in everyday common knowledge be found also to characterize that kind of knowledge which is commonly called 'scientific'? Shall we be able to trace the same structure in the specialized kinds of knowledge associated with such names as those of Newton, Darwin, or Einstein, as we have traced in the knowledge of the common man and even of the savage?

We shall find—as might be expected—that knowledge is of a piece all through, that the same structure appears in the lowest kinds of knowledge and in the most advanced discoveries of science. This will accord with the common remark, the truth of which there seems no reason to doubt, that science is no more than an extension of common sense brought about by its more elaborate organization and increased efficiency.

It is naturally impossible for us to do more than touch the fringe of so vast a subject. A complete survey of the epistemology of science cannot be looked for here. All that I can attempt is very briefly to consider a few of the more famous scientific theories, selected partly because of their intrinsic importance and partly because of their epistemological interest.

1. EVOLUTION

I take the concept of evolution first because, however complex it may be considered as a scientific subject, it is epistemologically extremely simple.

It is important to understand the cause of this simplicity. We are not, of course, concerned with any of the details of the evolutionary theory, much less with any disputed points. In broad outline the concept of evolution may be taken to mean simply that organic species have developed from one another in time, beginning with elementary forms of life, advancing through intermediate species, and going on to such highly organized beings as men.

It is clear that we have here no more than a collection of alleged facts about animals and vegetables and about their changes. The theory purports to be no more than a statement of the facts which have occurred during the history of life on the planet. It is a story about 'things' and their changes. It thus involves nothing epistemologically different from what would be contained in any other history or statement of facts. It is on a par with the statements that Brutus murdered Caesar, that Jack and Jill went up the hill, or that my lawn-mower has just cut a worm in half. Only it is more complicated, remote, and vast, and instead of referring to two people or a worm it refers to billions of organic beings in all ages. These differences are irrelevant. The point is that the theory of evolution is a mere statement of alleged 'facts' about 'things'.

This being so, we have nothing here except concepts of kinds already studied, concepts of the given and concepts of things. The truth of such concepts means, chiefly, their 'correspondence' with the facts, or, more accurately, the correspondence of the concepts with the percepts. The concept contains, in conceptual form, the same substance of knowledge as is given in perception, or as it is supposed would have been given in perception if any mind had been present and watching on the earth throughout the ages. Nothing is added by the mind to these perceptions or possible perceptions. There is no constructive element.

There are, of course, the constructions of independent existence, of continuous public space and continuous public time, &c. These are taken for granted by all science and all common sense. They are the stage on which the whole drama of human knowledge is enacted. We have already settled our account with them. And it would clearly be wrong to describe evolution as a constructive concept on account of them. That would be to include them twice over in our accounts. The point is that there

SCIENTIFIC KNOWLEDGE 377

is in the theory of evolution no *new* construction. We shall be right to call evolution a *factual* concept.

Thus evolution presents no specially interesting features to the epistemologist. It is a straightforward factual concept which does not differ epistemologically from concepts of the given, such as 'red' or 'loud', or concepts of things, such as 'house' or 'steamer', except in the irrelevant fact that it is more complicated. The principle is the same. Its truth consists in the correspondence of the concept with the percept or with what it is believed would have been perceived if any mind had been suitably situated.

2. THE ATOMIC AND ELECTRIC THEORIES OF MATTER

Until recently the old atomic theory of matter held the field. Matter, it was thought, is not infinitely divisible. There must come a limit in the process of division when further division is impossible. You have then reached the atom, the ultimate indivisible constituent of matter. Each element has its own qualitatively peculiar atoms. An atom, therefore, was just a small lump of matter. And matter was entirely composed of these little indivisible lumps. This was the old atomic theory.

But the atom is no longer regarded as indivisible. The first change in outlook came with the view that the atom consists of a nucleus of protons and electrons and a number of electrons circling in orbits around it. The atom so conceived could be compared with perfect correctness to the solar system. The electrons were supposed to whiz round the nucleus just as the planets whiz round the sun.

There are two points to be noted here. Firstly, it was still possible at this stage to make, or at least to imagine, a *model* of the atom. The nucleus with its circling satellites could still quite easily be pictured in imagination. Secondly, we still had before us a theory of *particles*. The early electronic theory of physics still regarded matter as composed of ultimate little bits or particles of stuff. On both points these simple views have now disappeared. Newer and far less simple views hold the field. But it will be profitable for us first to consider the early stages of the atomic and electronic theories in which matter was still conceived as composed of picturable particles.

Now the question in which the epistemologist is interested is this. What is meant (or what was meant when the theory was in vogue) by saying that the theory of particles is 'true'? What, in the first place, did the theories actually mean to assert? Were atoms and electrons supposed to be really existent, or were they merely some kind of a scientific dodge?

If I correctly understand the physicists, they undoubtedly meant to assert that atoms and electrons really exist. And this is still, I believe, the position. The simple view of the electrons as a lot of little bullets or tiny pills has given way to more complicated theories. But I am not aware that physics has abandoned the view that the electron is an actual existent.

But what does it mean to say that atoms or electrons exist? They cannot be perceived. It is inconceivable that human senses will ever perceive them. Nor could any imaginable degree of magnification by the microscope ever bring them within view. No doubt we may be able to perceive their effects. Beautiful laboratory experiments have been devised by means of which it is possible to perceive the effects of a single moving electron. But this is not perceiving the electron itself.

To say that the atom exists unperceived is, for us, on exactly the same level as the assertion that the table exists when no one is aware of it. The latter statement can only mean that *if* some one were looking he would perceive the table. The belief in the existence of atoms can only mean that *if* the human senses could be rendered subtle enough, or instruments refined enough, the atoms would be perceived. Any assertion of existence must, on our view, be understood in terms of perception, and must refer to some perceptual experience conceived as possible. The fact that it is really inconceivable that any senses could ever perceive atoms or electrons proves nothing to the contrary. What it proves is that the existence of the atom is an existential construction. For it is characteristic of such

SCIENTIFIC KNOWLEDGE

constructions that they can only be exhibited by hypothetical propositions having antecedents expressing impossible conditions.

The existence of atoms is, for us as epistemologists, clearly a mental device for making the appearances of matter intelligible to us. On the other hand the existence of atoms is no more unreal than the existence of the table when no one is aware of it. The two are on exactly the same footing. In both cases it is assumed that something can exist unperceived. The lack of perception in one case is supposed to be due to the accident that one is not looking, and in the other to the essential infirmity of human senses. The difference between the two cases is thus unimportant.

Thus the physicist is apt to insist that the atoms are no device of his, no convention which happens to 'work' and to produce results, but that they 'really exist'. We may entirely agree that they really exist. But the question is: what does 'really exist' mean? This real existence is itself nothing but a device of the mind, not the mind of the physicist, but the mind of primordial man. There is no contradiction between our view and that of the physicist. Or if there is any difference, it is not as to the meaning of the theory of atoms (on which the physicist alone is competent to pronounce), but as to the meaning of 'existence'. Physicist and philosopher can both agree that the atom or the electron really exists. The physicist is perhaps apt to take the plain, unreflective man's view that existence is a given fact, whereas the philosopher will view it as a mental construction. But this is quite as it should be. It is the physicist's business, and not the philosopher's, to expound the atomic theory. And it is the philosopher's business, and not the physicist's, to expound the meaning of 'existence'.

The atomic and electronic theories carry the hypothesis of unperceived existence a little further than we have so far seen it carried in our studies of pre-scientific knowledge. The table, after all, is sometimes perceived. The atom never has been and never will be. The constructions which we studied in Chapter VI only went to the extent of assuming that the things which we see, hear, touch, &c., go on existing when no mind is perceiving them. Science now with the atom pushes this idea to the length of assuming that there are existences which never are or can be perceived. The atoms, the electrons, the ether, are examples of this. We have here, therefore, a *new* element of construction for which science, and not common knowledge, is responsible. We shall, therefore, be right to classify all such concepts as constructive, and not factual, concepts.

But an important principle comes to light at this point. When the mind supposes something to exist unperceived, of what materials does it construct this existence? Clearly, of materials taken from the given. It must always suppose that what is not given is constructed of the same materials and in a similar manner to what is given. The best example of this is that the time-gap between the two appearances of the same object, say the table, is filled up in imagination by the continuation of the same table across the gap. The green patch, when I am not looking, is supposed still to be green. Whenever and wherever the mind creates existence by constructive concepts it must necessarily conceive this created existence by means of analogies from actual perception. *For the mind has no other material at its disposal.* This is a universal rule regarding existential constructions.

How does this apply to the atomic theory? The table which is supposed to exist unseen is conceived as exactly like the seen table. But we cannot suppose that the unseen atoms are like seen ones, because atoms have never been seen. What do we do then? We think of them after the analogy of tiny pellets or pills. We think of them after the analogy of small pieces of matter which we have actually seen. This means that we construct for the mind a picture or model of the atom, and this was quite easy so long as the atom or electron was still thought of by physicists as a particle.

But recent developments of physics raise difficulties.

We are told that we must not expect the constitution of matter to be such that any model can conceivably or possibly be made of it. The electron is not a particle after all. In some respects it is now supposed to behave as if it were a particle, but in other respects as if it were a wave. For this new conception Eddington has invented the clever word 'wavicle'. We cannot form a picture of a 'wavicle' because the images of wave and particle cannot be combined, because in fact they possess *contradictory properties*.

This same self-contradictory character of the present-day atom is further brought out very vividly in what is known as Heisenberg's Principle of Indeterminacy. This principle lays it down that an electron may have a determinate position or a determinate velocity, *but not both*. If its velocity is determined, then it cannot be said to be present at any precise position in space. If its exact position is determined, then it cannot be said to have any determinate velocity.

It is clearly impossible to picture such an electron or to make a model of it. For the only materials we have for such a picture are the characters of *perceived* motions. But any perceived moving object must have both determinate position and velocity. The assertion that a particle is moving with a certain determinate velocity *means* that it moves from *this* determinate position to *that* determinate position in a given time. It therefore appears to be self-contradictory and *meaningless* to ascribe to a particle a determinate velocity and to deny it a determinate series of positions. Certainly no picture or model of such a motion can be framed, because no analogies from perceived motion will help us.

Now to say that anything exists of which no model or picture can possibly be made is a definite challenge to the whole philosophy which we are here advocating. The fundamental position of that philosophy is that all truth goes back in the end to what is given, i.e. to images seen, heard, felt, &c. To exist, for us, means nothing more than to be a possible object of perception. Whatever can be perceived, however, can be pictured in imagination, and a model could be made of it. To say that something is incapable of being pictured or modelled is to say that it is incapable of being perceived. And this is to say that it does not exist.

We must distinguish, of course, between the allegation that a thing cannot be perceived owing to some accidental circumstance and the allegation that it is inherently and in itself incapable of being perceived or pictured. The old particle-atom could not be perceived because it was too small. This was an accidental circumstance. We could easily picture the particle in imagination. This kind of imperceptibility is not incompatible with existence. The existence of the particle means that if our eyes were more powerful magnifiers (a physical impossibility, no doubt, but not a logical one) we should see it. But the statement of the modern physicist that no model of the 'wavicle' atom can be made seems to mean much more than this. It seems to mean that the inner nature of the atom is such that the framing of a model or picture would be inherently and logically impossible.

My contention is that this is inconsistent with the very meaning of existence. For to assert that anything exists unperceived can only mean that *if* certain conditions (perhaps impossible ones) were fulfilled, the thing would be perceived. And whatever could be perceived by the senses could be pictured or modelled.

There undoubtedly exist *concepts* the corresponding perceptual objects of which cannot be pictured or modelled. It will be helpful briefly to examine some of these. We will take as our examples the fourth dimension of space, the concept of colour in the mind of the man born blind, and the concept of a square circle.

By the fourth dimension of space I do not refer to the relativist conception of time as a fourth dimension of space-time. I refer to the notion of a fourth *spatial* dimension, i.e. to a supposed direction in space at right angles to the three known dimensions.

It is possible to form a concept of such a dimension. It

SCIENTIFIC KNOWLEDGE

is possible even to work out four-dimensional, five-dimensional, or n-dimensional geometries. But we cannot form a picture or model of the fourth dimension, much less of the fifth or nth.

The blind man's concept of colour is a more homely illustration of the same thing. Assuming that he was born blind, he may use the word colour, and attach some meaning to it, so that he must be considered as having a concept of it. But he has absolutely no *image* of it, and cannot possibly form one (except perhaps a wholly incorrect image based upon the data of the other senses).

But in both these cases the only reason why no picture can be formed is simply that the mind lacks the requisite perceptual experience. It has not the necessary sensuous materials, and it cannot make bricks without straw. There is nothing *self-contradictory* in the ideas of colour and the fourth dimension which prevents the formation of the image or model.

But now consider the case of the square circle. The reason why we cannot picture that, is that it is a flat self-contradiction. And this means, not merely that we cannot picture it, but that *we cannot believe in its existence.*

We must carefully distinguish, then, between these two kinds of cases. In some cases, such as the fourth dimension and the blind man's idea of colour, the reason why the mind is unable to form any picture is simply that it is without that particular kind of perceptual experience which is required as material for the image. The same is true of radiations outside the range of our senses. There is no reason why, in such a case, we should not believe in the existence of the object. But in other cases, such as that of the square circle, the reason why no picture can be formed is that the idea is self-contradictory. And in such cases we cannot believe in the existence of the object.

Now what do the physicists mean when they tell us that the atom is such that no model can be made of it? If they mean merely that we have not the requisite experience, then we need raise no objection. A mind which had the requisite experience could make the model. And the assertion that such an atom exists means only that *if* we had certain faculties which we do not possess, or *if* there actually are any minds with those faculties, then both we and those minds could both perceive and picture the atom. But I am very much afraid that the contention of the physicists involves more than this; involves that the 'wavicle' is like the square circle. And in that case we must pronounce their conceptions erroneous and due to confused thinking.

For the difficulty seems to be that the wave and the particle possess mutually inconsistent properties, like the square and the circle. If so, we must believe that the wavicle theory is not final, is due to a partial understanding of the problem, and that it will be replaced some day by a self-consistent theory. I think it must be clear to any impartial observer that the physics of the atom is to-day in a transitional state, and that it cannot be claimed that any satisfactory theory has been reached. New theories are succeeding each other with bewildering rapidity, and there seems not the slightest reason to suppose that the 'wavicle' theory will stay with us in its present form for very long. In these circumstances I do not think that physicists ought to dogmatize too much about whether a picture or model of the real atom will be possible when its nature is discovered.[1]

I do not think that anything in the present state of physics need deter us from holding to our main doctrine; which is that the assertion of the existence of atoms, whether particles or wavicles or whatever else, means only that *if* . . ., the mind would perceive atoms.

One of the lessons for epistemology here is this. If the 'wavicle' theory is really self-contradictory, it cannot be true. If it is true, it cannot really be self-contradictory, and further research is certain to result in a reconciliation

---

[1] How any one can dare to found upon the present uncertainty in physics such doctrines as free will and the spiritual nature of inner reality passes my comprehension. Philosophers have often been accused of building idle speculations upon insufficient data. But some of our men of science completely outdo the philosophers in this.

SCIENTIFIC KNOWLEDGE

of the apparent contradiction. Truth cannot be self-contradictory. This is the lesson we learnt from the conclusion that logical laws possess necessity, and that truth is tied by these laws.

Present-day theories of the constitution of matter illustrate very well, then, the procedure of the mind in its search for knowledge. Knowledge is fixed at two points. It is tied by the given, and it is tied by the laws of logic. Its attachment to the given means (1) that the truth about the atom must be conceived in terms of perception, and (2) that no deduction from the theory must conflict with given facts. The condition that the atom must be conceived in terms of perception means that it must be possible to picture a model of it. Whatever theory is ultimately established will mean that *if* . . ., then we should perceive the atom in such and such a way, i.e. in accordance with such and such a picture or model. The 'if' clause will of course state an impossible condition, and therefore the concept will be that of an existential construction.

3. THE GEOLOGICAL AND ASTRONOMICAL PAST

The scientific concept which I wish to discuss in this section is that of a past which extends back millions of years before any minds were in existence to perceive anything. As regards its epistemological character there is no difficulty and very little to be said. It is concerned, like evolution, merely with facts which are said to have occurred. It is historical. It involves, of course, the fundamental construction of an independently existing world. But this construction belongs to common sense. Science adds nothing in principle. The concept, therefore, is factual.

But I bring up this subject here for another reason. The theory which is advocated in this book, when it comes to deal with the question of the past, is likely to find itself opposed by violent and obstinate popular prejudices. It will be said that the theory abolishes the past, or renders it a farce. And since the past in geological and astronomical ages, not to mention the past within human memory, is solid unshakable fact, our theory cannot be said to be even plausible. If our theory comes into opposition with the solid past, it is our theory, and not the past, which will look silly.

We shall find, however, that there is no such opposition. What is meant, on our theory, by the past? Let us consider first the recent past which is within human history. What do we mean, for example, by saying that Caesar was murdered two thousand years ago?

Now duration-spread is a quality of that which is given within the solitary solipsist mind. There exists, therefore, even for the solitary mind, a past. But that past will stretch back only so far as the private memory of the individual mind goes. This brief private past is not constructed, —except so far as explained in Chapter IX—but given.

Suppose that two such solitary minds get into communication and compare notes. Suppose that their pasts have run parallel, and that they have been to the same places, at the same times, have seen the same things, &c. They pursue comparison of notes backwards along these parallel private pasts. A's earliest memory is the presentation X. But B, who is ten years older than A, remembers X and also a series of presentations *previous* to X. Now A's series of memories were originally in a different world from B's series. Each of the two minds had his own private world. But, with the development of a public external world, A identifies his series of memories with B's. But B's series goes back beyond A's. Thereupon A discovers that there was, in the now established public world, *a past which existed before his own private world began.*

This would establish the idea of a past having existed so long as there was some mind to perceive it. The extension of this into a past which existed before there was any mind at all to perceive it is merely a deduction which follows as a matter of course from the general belief, the construction of which has been fully described, that things have an independent existence and persist when no one is perceiving them. So the remote past is constructed. The strands in the fabric of our common experience pass backwards out of sight. We naturally continue them and extend them indefinitely. The network of causal and other relations is also extended back into the unknown past.

On archaean sandstones we find pock-marks which look like the imprints of raindrops. We explain these marks by supposing that a rain storm passed over these sands hundreds of millions of years ago. There seems to be no doubt that this theory is *true*. That is what actually happened. Each of us finds in his own experience a series of causes and effects. This is projected into an independent and external world in which there is a series of causes and effects, public, external, and independent, existing whether any one is aware of it or not, and having existed before any mind was aware of anything. Into this causal series the rain drops of the Precambrian age fit with certainty. Leave them out, and there is an inexplicable gap in our world.

The story of the archaean raindrops is just as much true and solid fact as the existence of the atoms. And the meaning of truth is the same in both cases. The statement that atoms exist means that if suitably microscopic eyes could be developed, atoms would be seen. The statement that there was a storm of rain so many hundred million years ago means that if any mind had been present it would have perceived the storm.

And *why* need we assume that these marks on the rocks have been caused in this manner? Why should the mind make any assumption to explain them at all? In the last resort it will be found that the answer to such questions is always as follows. We have *begun* by constructing the world along certain lines. And now we are compelled by the laws of logic to carry on the same work. We are compelled to make new assumptions to fit in with the old. Even in the earliest stages of knowledge we saw how, when a construction had been set up, it came up against *facts* which rendered it necessary either to abandon the construction or to invent a new construction to make the old one square with the facts. This is how the game of knowledge is carried on.

We could have refused to construct a world at all. Each of us could have remained content in his private world of phantasms. Or at least, there would have been nothing *illogical* in doing so. But we did not do this. We began to build. And, having once begun, we cannot stop. It would be illogical to stop arbitrarily anywhere. Somehow or in some way, if we did so, we should come up against inconsistency and self-contradiction in our world-view, or against facts which contradict our world-view and have to be reconciled with it either by modifying our world-view or by adding to it new assumptions and constructions. We began by inventing a permanently existing world, independent of minds, which is 'there' even when we know nothing about it. Having invented this world we cannot control it. It persists in going back into an eternity in the past and forward into another eternity in the future. We invented the independent world. Next we discovered regular sequences in the given, and we set up the idea of causation. The marks on the rock, therefore, must have a cause, and it can only be this cause which geology asserts. Any other assumption will be in some way inconsistent with the world-picture which we have ourselves painted. Thus we go on spinning a network of knowledge across the void. Every strand leads to, and necessitates, the next.

We might have made similar reflections regarding the theories of atoms and electrons. We have a lump of matter before us. It is hard, coloured, shining, pungent-scented, &c. This is all that is actually *given* in experience. Why do we not leave it at that? What necessity is there to go beyond these plain announcements of experience? Why should we go and divide this up into atoms and electrons which we cannot possibly experience? What is the use of this proceeding? And the answer to these questions is as follows. If only we had remained in our private phantasmal world, we might have taken everything that appeared to us, the colour patches, the resistances, the sounds, at their face value and asked no questions. We might have led the simple life pasturing peacefully on floating colours and sounds. But we were not content to do this. We sought the society of other minds, and for purposes of our intercourse with them we built up a solid, permanent, public world. Now we have to pay the price. We are caught in a vast network of assumptions, hypotheses, and explanations, of which we can never free ourselves, and which goes on elaborating itself for ever. Originally logic compelled us to suppose that we could go on dividing up a piece of matter into invisible small bits. But then the idea of the infinitely divisible was supposed to lead to a contradiction and to break the laws of logic. So the indivisible particle, the atom, was assumed. Once that step was taken, all the rest had to follow down to the very latest hypotheses of physics.

But still the old question persists. Under the theory here advocated did the remote astronomical and geological past *really* exist or did it not? If it did not, then the philosophical theory here advocated had better put its head in a sack and drown itself. The reply is quite clear. Certainly the past really existed, and the assertions of geology and astronomy on the matter are true. But real existence is itself the mind's own construction, and the truth likewise. Nor is the universe, its past, its present, and its future, any less solid, real, and permanent on our theory than on any other. But solidity, reality, and permanence are themselves mental constructions.

4. EINSTEIN'S SPACE-TIME

We have seen that the common space and time of our everyday knowledge are themselves constructions. But they are solid constructs, completed long ago, and having become through many ages consolidated and taken for granted, have now the appearance of being given. Just as a platform constructed on the ground, if it is solidly built, may be treated, for the purposes of walking about, as if it were the ground, as if it had always been there; so I shall now, for the sake of shortness, treat time and space practically as if they were given. They are *there*. They are what we start with when we begin to elaborate the further construction of the space-time of modern relativity mechanics.

And we may, without danger, speak of them in this argument as if they were given in experience. They are *relatively* our starting-point. Thus do the constructions of the mind proceed in the manner of the building of a house— one story upon another.

I do not propose to discuss relativity in general, but only the particular idea of space-time. That idea is arrived at as follows. We start with space and time as quite separate entities. It has always been evident, however, that they were closely connected, and indeed necessary to each other. For the apprehension of things in space is successive, i.e. involves time; and the measurement of time is primarily obtained through the perception of the changes of things in space. There seems at any rate sufficient ground for saying that time and space are closely interconnected.

The first discovery which led to the space-time theory was that space measures and time measures vary according to the circumstances of the observer; and that if we are given the variations in the one, the variations in the other can be predicted, so that they are connected by a law. Suppose that we are standing on the earth and regard ourselves as stationary. If an aeroplane, which we have previously measured while it lay on the ground and found to be forty feet long, flashes past; and if its speed is sufficiently enormous (we need not trouble about the figures, but the speed would have to be many thousands of miles per second to make the effect noticeable); then, if we could measure it as it passes us, i.e. if we measured the distance between two points on the earth which we judged to be opposite the two ends of the aeroplane, we should find that it has become shorter along the line of flight. The faster it goes the shorter it would appear to us; until, when it attains the velocity of light, its length disappears altogether and becomes equal to 0. But this change of measures is relative. The man in the aeroplane is not aware of any change in his machine, and when he measures it while it is in motion he finds it still forty feet long. It is we, and the things around us on the earth, which have, in

SCIENTIFIC KNOWLEDGE

the opinion of the man in the aeroplane, changed our sizes. He can regard himself as stationary and us as moving past him. When he measures us he finds that *we* have contracted in the line of our flight past him.

Not only space measures vary according to relative motions in the manner described, but time measures also. What appears as one hour to one observer will be measured as half an hour by another observer, and as two hours by a third.

Thus neither the space-interval nor the time-interval between two events are—as was hitherto assumed—absolute or constant quantities. They vary according to the relative motions of the observers. It happens, however, that an absolute and invariable interval between the two events can be obtained if we combine the ideas of space and time and regard time as a fourth dimension of space-time.

Let us, first of all, imagine a space of only one dimension, a space consisting of a single straight line. Let us suppose that a particle is moving along it with uniform velocity. We can then represent the movement of the particle by means of a graph:

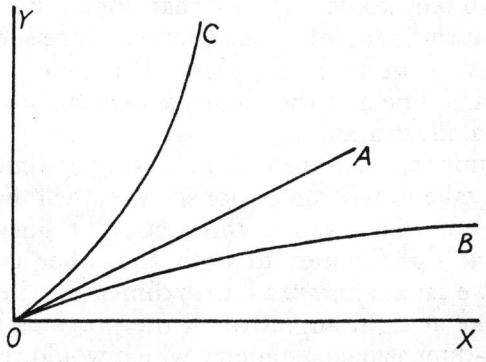

Let OX represent distance in the one-dimensional space, and let OY represent time. If the particle travels uniformly two units of space in one unit of time, the graph of its motion will be the straight line OA. Now suppose that its motion, instead of being uniform, is accelerated.

The graph will then have to be curved. If the acceleration is positive, i.e. if the velocity is increasing, the graph will bend towards the space co-ordinate as in the line OB. If the acceleration is negative, it will bend towards the time co-ordinate as in the line OC.

In this illustration the time line and the space line are placed at right angles to one another as if they were two dimensions in space; and the lines OA, OB, OC, are obtained representing the space *and* time measures of the motion of the particle. It will be realized that this is purely a mathematical device and nothing more. The time and the single space dimension which we have chosen for the illustration are not really at right angles to one another in nature, nor are there any lines in the actual world corresponding to OA, OB, and OC.

We can with equal ease make a graph showing how population increases with the years. We make OY represent years, while OX represents population. OA will then represent a population increasing at an even speed. The curved line OB will represent an accelerating increase of population. OC will represent a slowing down of the increase of population. This would be obviously only a device. No one would suppose that population and time are really at right angles to one another, since such a statement would be quite meaningless. It is exactly the same with the time line and the single-dimension space line in the original illustration.

Next suppose that instead of a single dimension of space we take three dimensions. We then have three Cartesian co-ordinates, i.e. three straight lines each of which is at right angles to both the other two. Now although we cannot *picture* a fourth dimension, i.e. a fourth straight line at right angles to all the previous three, yet the fourth-dimensional geometry which would result from supposing that there is such a straight line can easily be worked out by a mathematician. Let us then imagine a graph constructed exactly on the model of the one already given, except that instead of having a single co-ordinate representing a single space dimension we now introduce

SCIENTIFIC KNOWLEDGE

the three co-ordinates representing the three dimensions of space. And let us, in accordance with the rules of four-dimensional geometry, suppose a fourth straight line at right angles to all three of these co-ordinates. This fourth straight line may be made, for the purposes of our graph, to represent time. We shall by this means be able to get the motion of the particle we are studying represented as a line in a four-dimensional continuum. This line may be called the 'world-line' of the particle. The combination of space and time into a single four-dimensional continuum may be called space-time.

This is just as much a dodge as the graph of the increase of population. People are often puzzled by the idea of time as a fourth dimension which seems to be involved in relativity. This appears to them to be nonsense, because a fourth dimension means a fourth straight line at right angles to the three ordinary co-ordinates. And to say that time is at right angles to a line in space appears to be as meaningless as it would be to say that a scent or an emotion or the number three is at right angles to a line in space. It it true that we all of us think of time on the analogy of a straight line, and we tend to picture it as such. Why we do so is a big question. But it is at any rate certain that such thinking is purely metaphorical, and that in fact time is no more a line in space than a scent or an emotion is. It is for this reason that it appears, and in fact *is*, absurd and meaningless to suppose that time can be a fourth dimension in a continuum of which the other three dimensions are spatial.

The explanation is perfectly simple. The relativist is simply using the dodge with which we became familiar in our childhood as a graph. Time cannot be at right angles to a line in space any more than population can be. But a useful picture can be drawn of the relation of population to time by the graph method. The same can be done, as we have seen, for a moving particle, placing the time interval along one co-ordinate and the one-dimensional space-interval along the other. And there is no geometrical difficulty in making a graph with four co-ordinates instead of two, three being spatial and the fourth representing time (just as it might represent population or anything else). This is what the relativist does. And he does it because it happens to give certain very useful results.

Among these useful results is the following. We ordinarily measure two intervals between two events, namely, a time interval and a space interval. For example, suppose that the two events are (1) an earthquake which occurred in Calabria yesterday, and (2) the striking of a clock in London to-day. Then the space-interval between these two events is the distance between London and Calabria; the time-interval between them may be twenty-four hours. But these two intervals are not invariable for all observers. An observer on the earth may find the time-interval to be t and the space-interval s. But an observer situated on a body travelling at a high velocity relatively to the earth may find the time-interval to be t' and the space-interval s'. But it has been found that if we make a graph of the movement between event and event, in the manner above indicated, taking three co-ordinates to represent the three space dimensions and a fourth co-ordinate (which has, of course, to be imagined as in the fourth dimension) to represent time;[1] then the interval between the two events so obtained along this graph or 'world-line' is constant, i.e. the same for all observers. For example, the space-interval and the time-interval between the earthquake in Calabria and the striking of the clock in London vary according to the motions of the bodies from which they are measured. *But the interval along the 'world-line' in the four-dimensional continuum will be the same whatever the motions of the observer.* It is therefore called the 'absolute interval'.

Space-time, therefore, seems to represent an unchanging reality. Space and time measures fluctuate with the motions of different observers, but space-time measures remain always the same, and are independent of the

---

[1] This is not absolutely accurate because time enters into the equation with a minus instead of a plus sign. But this is neglected in the text because it does not affect our argument.

observers. Hence there is a tendency to hypostatize space-time as a *reality* of which space and time are only appearances or at best abstractions. This tendency, it may be remarked, is based upon the metaphysical view that what is independent of us is more real than what is dependent. It has no scientific value at all.

It is not entirely clear to me whether relativists mean to assert the real existence of space-time or not. From the strictly scientific point of view the question does not appear to be of any importance. It is ontological rather than physical. Physicists find that the conception of space-time gives results, and they therefore rightly use it. They need not concern themselves with anything further. But it would certainly seem, in spite of this, that there is a tendency among men of science to assert real existence of space-time. We may quote the well-known words of Minkowski: 'From now onwards space and time sink to the position of mere shadows, and only a sort of union of both can claim an independent or absolute existence.' In truth this statement goes beyond what physics has a right to declare. It introduces metaphysics, and even allows itself to be coloured by poetical feeling. But I think that passages which imply the real existence of space-time could be quoted from the majority of scientific writers on the subject.

Perhaps the sense of doubt and hesitation which we feel on this point at present is due to the fact that mind is now in process of creating a new existence. Before creation is complete there will be hesitancy. But in the future it may be that the existence of space-time will be taken for granted just as the existence of a public space and a public time, both constructions which must have given pause and hesitation to the mind in ages long past, are now taken for granted. At any rate it is clear that the existence of space-time, if it is asserted, is a creation or construction of the mind, a creation which rests upon the fiction involved in supposing that the mathematical device of the graph represents something real.

To assert the existence of space-time can only mean

that space-time is a possible experience. Yet we have, and can have, no experience of it. We have experience only of space and of time, or more strictly of private extension-spreads and duration-spreads. And to suppose that we could ever experience space-time is as much a fiction as to suppose that we could experience time and increase of population at right angles to one another, or that we could perceive the table when it is not being perceived.

And yet the lesson we learn from our investigations is this. There is no reason why the existence of space-time should not be asserted, if the assertion of it seems necessary to science. And the assertion may prove to be 'true'. It will be true if it is found that the phenomena of nature cannot be explained without it, and if in the long run it fits in with the entire scheme of things which knowledge discloses, and if its results are in accordance with the given and do not contradict any other part of knowledge. The procedure of the mind here amounts to the erection of a fiction to the dignity of existence. But what we have learnt from the beginning of our studies is that 'independent existence' and 'reality' are themselves fictions. To erect the mathematical device of space-time into an independent entity is of a piece with the general procedure of knowledge, and is a perfectly justifiable work of mental construction.

Space-time is, of course, a construction of the existential type. It is not unificatory because it does not *identify* space with time, or abolish an unnecessary existence, as is always the case with unificatory constructions. It creates a new existence. It is therefore expressible in the hypothetical proposition. 'If . . ., we should perceive space-time.' The blank may be filled up how we please.

5. GRAVITATION—NEWTON AND EINSTEIN

Newton's theory of gravitation was that there exists an attractive *force* operating between all particles of matter, the force varying directly as the product of the masses and inversely as the square of the distance between them. If there were no forces acting on a body, then it was supposed that the body would move with uniform velocity in a straight line. That was Newton's first law of motion. But if a force, such as that supposed to be exerted by the sun on the planets, acted on the body, it would be deflected from the straight and its path would be deducible from the law stated in the first sentence of this paragraph, which we will call for short the law of the inverse square.

Einstein's theory of gravitation cannot be so simply formulated, but it may be said to be based on the notion that the movements of bodies, e.g. the planets, are governed, not by 'forces', but by the configuration of the space-time in which they move. The important point to get hold of is that the law of gravitation is thus reduced to a law of *geometry*.

In order to understand this we have, first of all, to replace Newton's first law of motion. Since our new view dispenses altogether with the idea of forces and explains motions by means of geometrical concepts, our first need will be a new law of motion. This law is as follows:

If a body is moving freely, and if X *and* Y *are two events in its history, then the series of events which constitutes its history between* X *and* Y *is such that the 'absolute interval' of* Y *from* X *measured along that path is a maximum.*

This means in effect that a body always takes the longest possible space-time path between two events. It follows that if you know *which* is the longest space-time path you can always predict the movements of any body. But in order to do this all that you require is to know the geometry of the space-time in which the body is moving. *Which* is the longest space-time path is obviously a purely geometrical question. Einstein's law of gravitation is simply a formula which tells us what kind of geometry to expect in different parts of space-time. When we know that, we can deduce which of all possible paths between two events is the longest, and that will be the path of our planet or other heavenly body.

The details of the geometrical formulae required are, of course, very complicated. But we may say at least that in portions of space very remote from any matter space-time has a Euclidean geometry; whereas near heavy masses such as the sun its geometry is non-Euclidean. In remote spaces the longest space-time path will be a straight line. Near the sun it will be a curved line. It will be in fact the orbit which the planet actually takes. Thus the reason why the planets move in the orbits they do is simply that those orbits represent the longest possible space-time paths in the particular kind of space-time which exists at that place. Elsewhere, in another kind of space-time, i.e. in a space-time with a different geometry, different paths would be followed. Thus the orbits chosen are determined solely by geometry.

Given (1) the law of motion as above stated, i.e. the law of the longest path, and (2) suitable formulae for the geometry of space-time, we can deduce the orbits, positions, and times of all bodies in space.

Now if any one finds all this very puzzling (as is the common experience) the reason probably is this. We have got into the habit of thinking that Newton's forces 'explained' the motions of the planets, i.e. gave us an intelligible reason *why* the planets move as they do. But Einstein's law does not seem to give us any reason. That motions should be governed by forces seems understandable. But that they should be governed by geometry seems unintelligible. Why for example should bodies take the longest space-time path? It seemed 'natural' that freely moving bodies acted on by no forces should move in straight lines. But why bodies should go zigzagging about in order to obey this eccentric new law of motion seems inexplicable.

But this supposed difference between Newton's and Einstein's laws in respect of intelligibility is solely the result of our greater familiarity with the former. In reality neither of them give any *reasons* why things move as they do. No explanation can be given of Einstein's law of motion. Neither Einstein nor any one else can tell you *why* bodies move in the way they do. They might, for all any one could tell to the contrary, move in any other way. But it happens that they move in this way. It is a brute fact, and there is no more to be said about it. It is a mistake, therefore, to think that it is difficult to understand. For beyond the fact that it *is* so there is nothing to understand.

Newton deduced the movements of bodies from his formula about forces. Einstein deduces them from formulae about the geometry of space-time. Both the forces and the space-time and its geometry are fictions which are adopted because they are useful for predicting the positions and movements of the heavenly bodies. But we falsely imagine that Newton's formula gives us a *reason why* bodies move as they do, whereas Einstein's does not. And we make this erroneous discrimination because we are more familiar with Newtonian ideas, and more especially because the notion of 'force', being of anthropomorphic origin, appeals to our incorrigible animism.

For a 'force' means primarily a *sensation* of pressure. When some one pushes me from behind I feel the pressure sensation of his hands on my back. When I hold between my fingers a piece of string with a weight hanging from the end of it, the force appears in my consciousness as a pressure sensation in my finger tips and a sense of muscular strain in my arm. Let us suppose a disembodied intelligence suspended in mid space, neither operating on bodies, nor in any way operated on by them. Its entire life consists in inactively watching the motions of the universe, while remaining itself motionless. Such a consciousness, because it would be without experience of sensations of pressure and strain, could not possibly frame or understand the notion of force. Suppose that this intelligence, looking down with telescope-like eyes upon our earth, watched a billiard match in progress. It would not think that one ball striking another 'pushes' it this way or that. But it could perfectly well conclude that when moving solid bodies meet at such and such angles and speeds, their directions and motions are altered in such and such ways. Watching the planets, it would neither suppose any force in existence nor see the necessity for any. It could, however, quite easily frame satisfactory laws of motion and gravitation. But they would be based solely upon the concept of *succession*, and not at all on the concept of *compulsion*. They would be of the form 'when A happens, B happens', not of the form 'A exerts a force which makes B happen'. It would perceive that when bodies move in remote enough empty spaces they move in straight lines, but that when they move in the neighbourhood of other bodies their paths are functions of such factors as velocity, distance, and mass.

The notion of force is as completely otiose in science as that conception of causation which regards a cause as compelling its effect. Both notions, in fact, spring from the same anthropomorphic root; or, more accurately, the concept of force is a particular case of the concept of compulsory causation.

Now it is quite possible to restate the Newtonian law without using the concept of force at all. It then becomes simply a mathematical equation for calculating the paths of moving bodies. The position of the body at any moment will appear as a function of the three variables, velocity, mass, and distance. Such a law makes no pretence of *explaining* (by means of forces or any other anthropomorphic conceptions) why bodies *must* move in such and such a way. It merely states that as a matter of fact they do move in that way, and it provides a formula for the calculation of their positions at any moment.

Unfortunately, however, the Newtonian law, even when purged of the irrelevant concept of force, has not proved to be precisely correct. It is very nearly correct. But it fails to predict with sufficient accuracy certain well-known astronomical phenomena such as the curvature of starlight rays passing the limb of the sun, and the movements of the perihelion of Mercury. This means, of course, that it fails to predict with absolute accuracy the motions of *any* of the heavenly bodies. But it is only in a few cases, such as that of Mercury, that the difference between calculated and observed positions is large enough to be noticeable or important. It is not that the law is correct

SCIENTIFIC KNOWLEDGE

for other heavenly bodies and incorrect for Mercury. It is incorrect for all bodies in greater or less degree.

Now there would be no insuperable difficulty in working out, along Newtonian lines, on the assumptions of Euclidean geometry, without any reference to curved or humped spaces or to any of the familiar paraphernalia of Einsteinian mechanics, a corrected law of gravitation, a law which would correctly predict the movements of the perihelion of Mercury and all the other motions of bodies. It is true that among the factors of Newton's law are distances and times, which are assumed by Newton to be constants, whereas we now know them to vary with the motions of the observer. But allowance could be made for this in our corrected law. This law might be simply an equation or set of equations in terms of velocities, intervals, &c. Such a formula could be worked out. We will call it the corrected Newtonian law. The only trouble about it is that *to make it correct we have to make it enormously complicated.*

To work out such a law would have been one way of meeting the difficulties created by the inaccuracies of Newton's law. Einstein, however, found that a simpler procedure could be introduced by framing a set of formulae in terms of a four-dimensional geometry. These formulae constitute Einstein's law of gravitation.

Thus neither Newton's nor Einstein's laws 'explain' anything. To suppose that they do so would be exactly on a par with supposing that the nautical almanac 'explains' the movements of the stars. Newton's law, Einstein's law, and the nautical almanac are all alike no more than abbreviated statements of what happens, short memoranda or keys which we can apply to any particular case to ascertain the motions, positions, and times of any particular moving body.

There is at the present day a danger of the geometrical properties of space-time becoming an anthropomorphic superstition in the same way as 'force' did. This superstition is being created by those popular writers who talk about bent and curved spaces and who tell us, for example, that around the sun there is a hill or hump in space-time, so that the planets have to run around it instead of running straight. The truth which these metaphors represent is that, if we choose to adopt the assumptions of non-Euclidean geometry, we can deduce from them and from the new law of motion the movements of the planets. We need not adopt these assumptions, and if we adopt Euclidean axioms instead we can equally work out the motions of the planets. The only point is that our calculations are easier and simpler if we adopt a non-Euclidean geometry. Pure space itself, the space which is *given*, is neither Euclidean nor non-Euclidean. It has no geometry at all. It is nothing but the extension-spread of private sense-data. We invented Euclidean space. And the human mind has later invented various kinds of non-Euclidean spaces. And it is found more convenient to use the fiction of non-Euclidean space or space-time in the formula for working out the motions of the heavenly bodies than to use the fiction of Euclidean space. But these popular writers speak as if the hills and the humps in space-time were actual physical things which push the planets about. The image inevitably created in the mind by their metaphors is that of a planet being pushed out of a straight course by hitting up against a bump. This encourages the mind once more to believe that space-time in some mysterious way *compels* the planets in their courses.

But there no more exists any compulsion by the geometry of space-time than there exists any compulsion by 'forces'. All that scientific laws, if properly framed and understood, should ever attempt to do is to state in a generalized form *what as a matter of fact happens*. What they should above all avoid is to attempt to give *reasons* why things happen as they do, for all such reasons turn out to be errors and anthropomorphic superstitions. Newton's law was primarily a formula which enabled any one, given the necessary data, to work out the path of any freely moving body. But over and above this there was foisted in the conception of 'forces'. This was not essential to the law. The law merely stated how bodies move. The addition of 'forces' was supposed to explain *why* bodies move as they do. The ideas of pushing and pulling were supposed to make us understand the reasons why the planets do not move in straight lines. They were a pandering to the human mind which feels happier and more satisfied if the operations of the universe can be ascribed to anthropomorphically conceived agencies.

Einstein's law, if stated in purely mathematical terms, is merely a generalized statement of how bodies move, which turns out to be more accurate than Newton's. But the human craving for an answer, in anthropomorphic terms, to the question why they move as they do, causes popular writers to foist in the idea of compulsion by the humps and curves in space-time. Since we are not allowed to have forces to push the planets about we must have bumps in space-time. Such is the weakness of the human mind.

Newton's law is often credited with having given the 'explanation' of Kepler's laws. But in the light of what has been said it will be evident that it does not explain either Kepler's laws or anything else. The only superiority of Newton's law over Kepler's three laws resides in the facts that it reduces three laws to one and is therefore simpler, and that it is of wider application than Kepler's laws, extending as it does to the whole universe and not merely to the solar system.

It happens that Einstein's law is presented in terms of geometry. But it must not be supposed from this that geometry is the cause of anything. The law would be just as true if it were presented in terms of arithmetic, chemistry, eugenics, heraldry, or cookery, provided that it correctly predicted the positions of moving bodies. Geometry is not a cause, or explanation, or reason, why bodies move as they do. It is a mental construction which happens to provide a satisfactory method of procedure in predicting the facts of experience.

It follows also from what has been said that the corrected Newtonian law and the law of Einstein are both equally 'true'. They are *alternative truths*. Science chooses the law of Einstein purely because it is simpler and easier to manipulate. 'Forces' and non-Euclidean space-time are both alike existential constructions. Einstein has not discovered a single new *fact* about nature. For the only real facts are our experiences of the given, colour patches, sounds, and the like. What he has done is to invent a new fiction or construction which is superior to the Newtonian construction because it agrees better with the facts (e.g. our light sensations from Mercury), and is superior to the corrected Newtonian law because it is simpler.

This throws light upon the difference between valid and invalid constructions. The three requirements of a valid construction are (1) that it shall be internally self-consistent; (2) that it shall be consistent with all other constructions which form a permanent part of 'knowledge'; and (3) that it shall agree with the facts. The meaning of the last condition will be more fully discussed in the next chapter. Newton's uncorrected law fulfils the first two conditions, but not the third. It is therefore invalid. Newton's corrected law would fulfil all three conditions, and would therefore be valid. Einstein's law fulfils, so far as is at present known, all three conditions. It is therefore valid. Thus because they are both valid constructions Einstein's law and the corrected Newtonian law are both 'true'. They are, as we said, alternative truths. But Einstein's law is now being embodied into 'knowledge', and the corrected law of Newton rejected because the former is simpler than the latter.

6. PTOLEMAIC AND COPERNICAN ASTRONOMY

Both Ptolemaic and Copernican astronomy assumed, until the advent of Einstein, the truth of absolute rest and motion. In one sense, therefore, they have both been superseded and rendered untrue by Einstein's views. But it does not appear that the theory of absolute motion is essential to either of them. For, granted the truth of the relativist doctrine, we can work out the motions of the heavenly bodies either by taking the earth as relatively at rest and the sun and planets as revolving round it (the

SCIENTIFIC KNOWLEDGE

Ptolemaic method of procedure), or by taking the sun as relatively at rest and the planets as revolving round it (the Copernican method of procedure).

Understood in this way the Copernican hypothesis is now generally supposed to be true and the Ptolemaic hypothesis false. But the more correct way of viewing the matter would appear to be to think of the two hypotheses as alternative *methodological assumptions*. Neither of them is, strictly speaking, true. It is false that the earth is at rest and that the sun and planets move round it. It is false that sun is at rest and that the planets revolve about it. The truth is that all these bodies move relatively to one another. But we may, for the purposes of calculation of their paths and positions, treat the facts either *as if* the sun were at rest or *as if* the earth were at rest. Either assumption will, if properly handled, lead to true predictions and correct results. But the Ptolemaic hypothesis with its cycles and epicycles is so complicated that it has been abandoned in favour of the other method which is simpler.

Thus the two hypotheses, properly understood, do not either of them now claim truth. They are not judgements which state any facts about the universe. What they affirm is simply that this method or that method will give us truths about the universe. Their subject-matter is not anything in the external world at all but only our *methods* of dealing with things. It is for that reason that they should be classed as methodological assumptions.

This is the first occasion on which we have come across the methodological assumption in the course of our inquiries. This is natural because such assumptions are mostly confined to that kind of knowledge which we commonly call scientific. And since we shall not, in the limited space now left at our disposal, be able to make any fuller study of them, it will be well forthwith to fix their epistemological character and determine their functions in knowledge.

A methodological assumption may be defined as *a proposition, not known to be true, and the truth or falsehood of which is, for the limited purposes for which the assumption is used in knowledge, a matter of indifference; but from which it is known that true propositions can be deduced within a limited area of knowledge.*

It must not be known to be true. For if it is, then it ceases to be purely methodological and becomes a substantive truth about the universe. For example, the concept of purpose may be used as a methodological assumption in biology. We may up to a certain point and with certain reservations treat the facts *as if* it were true that every organ has been designed by a mind seeking to adapt means to ends. Whether such a mind or such a purpose actually exists is, from the purely biological point of view, a matter of indifference. For the biologist, as such, it is unknown whether it is true or not, and it is for him, therefore, a methodological assumption. The theologian presumably will not regard it as merely a methodological assumption. For him it will be a substantive truth. Which shows, of course, that a proposition which is at one time a methodological assumption, treated as if true within certain limits but not known to be true, may in the light of advancing knowledge come to be recognized as substantive truth. On the other hand, propositions once regarded as true may be degraded to the level of methodological assumptions. This is what has now happened to the Copernican hypothesis.

The methodological assumption must not be known to be true, but it may be known to be false. Even if it were known to be false that there is a purposive mind governing the development of organisms, the teleological concept might still be used in biological researches exactly as if it were true, and with equally good results. The Ptolemaic and Copernican hypotheses in astronomy are actual examples of methodological assumptions which are known to be false. For, as we have already had occasion to point out, it is false that either the sun or the earth is absolutely at rest in space.

The existence and nature of methodological assumptions should not be surprising to any one who has learnt the lesson of the logic books that an hypothesis may lead to

SCIENTIFIC KNOWLEDGE

true deductions and yet be false. As is well known, there may be several hypotheses all of which cover the facts, and the problem of science then is to find a crucial experiment to decide between them. Any hypothesis which covers the facts within a certain area of knowledge, and which is not known to be true, may be used as a methodological assumption, provided there are proper safeguards against its misuse.

In fitting the methodological assumption into its proper place in the scheme of epistemology it may be felt that there is a difficulty in distinguishing it from certain kinds of construction. It is essential that they should be distinguished. For valid constructions, we have declared, are 'true', and give actual knowledge about the world. Methodological assumptions are propositions the truth of which is indifferent, and which may be definitely false. But now, take the case of our belief in the existence of a single public world. We have represented this as a construction, and therefore as essentially true. But is it not equally capable of being represented as a methodological assumption? And is there not, therefore, some confusion here? We believe in a single world. We believe, for example, that there is only one ink-pot on my table which I and any other persons who are in the room see. Might it not be said that the *truth* is that there are as many private ink-pots as there are people seeing them, and that the view that there is only one ink-pot is a methodological assumption? For it may be argued that it is strictly speaking untrue (the real truth being that there are many private ink-pots), but that it is an assumption which leads to true results. This, of course, would fit in with the definition of the methodological assumption but not with that of the construction. It is therefore necessary that we should make clear the difference between the two.

The nature of the difference is indicated in the wording of our definition of the methodological assumption. It is defined as a proposition 'from which it is known that true propositions can be deduced *within a limited area of knowledge*'. This implies that whereas the construction is true throughout the entire field of knowledge and all deductions made from it are true, the methodological assumption, on the other hand, only yields true deductions within a certain restricted area. If it is used outside that area it comes, or may come, into conflict with other parts of knowledge, and leads to false results. Thus the construction of the public external world yields results which are recognized as true over the whole field of knowledge. It is true for all purposes. To assume one universe instead of millions of private ones makes no difference to any of the facts in the universe. But the proposition that the sun is at rest and that the planets revolve round it can only be regarded as if it were true for the limited purpose of calculating the positions of the planets. If we try to treat it as always and unconditionally true it comes into conflict with the fundamental principles of modern mechanics which are relativistic. Again the teleological assumption in biology is valid as a method if confined within narrow limits. But if we extend it outside those limits, if we assume that it is true generally, and outside biology, then it will have to be taken as asserting an actual factual existence, namely the existence of an overruling mind. This may come into conflict with facts, and it will actually do so if there is in fact no such mind.

Thus an assumption is true if it is true for all purposes, unconditionally, in all branches of knowledge, and in all contexts. In that case we call it a construction. It yields substantive truth about the universe. An assumption which can be treated as if it were true within certain limited areas and within a limited context, but which would conflict with other propositions which are known to be true if it were asserted outside that area and that context, is methodological. It does not contain substantive truth about the universe, although the deductions which follow from it within its proper area will contain substantive truth.

If we now understand the nature of methodological assumptions we can see more clearly the fallacy, already exposed, of the pragmatist suggestion that the principle

SCIENTIFIC KNOWLEDGE

of 'the uniformity of nature' is a methodological assumption. An assumption it is, for its truth cannot be proved and no reason or ground can be given for it. But it is not methodological. If it is true at all it is unconditionally true in all contexts. For its absolute universality is its very essence, and if exceptions were allowed to it, it would cease to be the principle of the uniformity of nature. It is either a substantive truth about the universe or it is nothing.

7. THE ETHER OF SPACE

At the present day it appears that physicists are divided as to whether ether exists or not. The more recent view is that the ether is no longer necessary, that empty space or space-time is sufficient to explain the facts, and in fact that ether may be identified with empty space. The older view, of course, was that ether is a continuous something —are we to call it a substance?—pervading all space. We need not concern ourselves with the dispute as to which view is correct. The only question of interest to us is whether the concept of the ether—be it true or false—throws any light upon epistemological problems.

The assertion of the existence of ether—if it is asserted —means, of course, that *if* . . ., then we should perceive the ether. The conditions with which the blank in the antecedent clause might be filled in are inconceivable and unimaginable. The hypothesis of the ether deliberately robbed it of any qualities by means of which it could be perceived, since it was conceived as possessing only those qualities which would make it a wave bearer. But most minds, I imagine, must have helped themselves out with some kind of vague picture of a thin mist throughout space, or of something like the invisible air but infinitely finer. Of course the mind was well aware that these images were inadequate and even misleading if taken too seriously. But they show that the mind, in conceiving of any supposed existence, attempts to imagine how it could *perceive* that existence. The pictorial habit of the mind bears witness to the deep-seated feeling that whatever exists must be somehow or other perceptible, i.e. that existence must be conceived in terms of perception.

The ether hypothesis illustrates very well the procedure of the mind in filling up gaps in knowledge. To fill up gaps is one of the functions of the existential construction. We desire a continuous world in time and space and circumstance, and where we find holes and crevasses in the given we stop them up with new existences invented by ourselves. The gap between the two appearances of the table in perception is filled up by the fiction of the unperceived table. The ether performs a similar function. In the world which the mind has constructed out of the given it finds itself confronted by a number of truths of which the following are well-known examples: that the distance of the earth from the sun is about ninety-three million miles; that light travels with a velocity of about three hundred thousand kilometres per second; and that it travels in waves or vibrations. These truths are themselves, of course, not given. They are constructions out of far simpler elements of the given. This means that innumerable gaps have already been filled up. But there is obviously one left. Light is stated to consist of waves or vibrations which race across space at an enormous velocity. But waves or vibrations of *what*? Everything which is supposed to exist must be supposed to be in some way perceptible or picturable or conceived in terms of perception. Can we conceive or picture waves without their being waves either of water or of air or of some kind of substance? It was this necessity of the mind for thinking all existence in terms of perception which compelled us to insist that if there are waves they must be waves *of something*. Here then is the gap in knowledge. An existence has to be invented to stop it up. It has to be invented because it cannot be found. There is not the slightest trace of such a wave-bearing medium in space. It is not perceptible, and the subtlest experiments have failed to reveal its presence. There is thus no evidence of its existence whatever. But it is wanted to fill up a hole in our world-picture. The mind, therefore, asserted its existence.

SCIENTIFIC KNOWLEDGE

But what are its qualities? It cannot be given such crass qualities as ponderability, colour, odour, and taste; for these would render it perceptible, and it is entirely imperceptible. It is therefore endowed with only those qualities which are the minimum required by the mathematician and the physicist for transmitting waves. These minimal properties were *assumed* by the physicists, without any positive evidence, solely because they fitted in with the wave theory.

Thus the ether bears everywhere the marks of being a creation of the mind, a stop-gap in a very literal sense, something made to fit into an awkward hole in knowledge. And now that, with relativity physics, it is apparently no longer needed by the mind which gave it birth, it is quietly being relegated to the limbo of non-existence, to the annoyance of Sir Oliver Lodge, who wants to retain it as the seat and special residence of spirits. Very clearly the question whether it exists or not is simply the question whether the mind has need of it. Existence is nothing else but what the mind needs to build its world.

8. THE SUBCONSCIOUS

Our examples of scientific knowledge have so far been taken from the sciences of external reality. I will take my final example from the science of internal reality or mind, namely psychology. The concept of the subconscious has of late years been specially emphasized by the psychoanalysts, though it was, of course, known to psychology long before their day. The essence of it is the assumption that mental phenomena can take place unknown to the mind in which they occur, that we may think, feel, and will without being conscious of our thoughts, feelings, and conations.

This, as is obvious, is a formal self-contradiction. An unconscious thought appears to be a contradiction in terms, since thought is a kind of consciousness. An unconscious feeling is similarly a contradiction, since it implies that we have a feeling which we do not feel. And yet the concept has been successfully introduced into the science of psychology and is used with telling effect. How is this?

The contradiction is resolved if we take the view that the assertion of the existence of the subconscious is a fiction, an assumption which the mind makes for the purpose of filling up gaps in its experience. Consider an unconscious train of thought or reasoning. Let us assume that there is a train of reasoning of which the consecutive steps are a, b, c, d, e, f, g. In order to get from a to g I have to pass through all the intermediate steps. This may be true both logically and psychologically. It will be true in the logical sense if all the steps are necessary to make the argument valid. It will be true psychologically if it is unlikely that the thought g would enter my mind unless led up to by the train of associated ideas b, c, d, &c. Now suppose I actually think the consecutive steps a, b, c, and that for the moment I can get no further with my problem. I give it up and think about other things or go to sleep for the night. Later on—on waking in the morning, it may be—the proposition g suddenly flashes into my mind as the solution of the problem set by the thoughts of the previous day a, b, c. My mind appears to have skipped the intermediate links d, e, f. We account for this by saying that the thoughts d, e, f have been worked through *unconsciously* during the night or during the period when I was thinking of other things.

But what is *given* in internal experience here is simply $a, b, c, \ldots g$. We have the beginning and the end of the process and a gap between them. That is absolutely all that my experience contains. I have no warrant whatever for assuming that anything exists between c and g. The very fact that I am said to be unconscious of the intermediate links means that I have no warrant for postulating them. But I invent the concept of the subconscious (or unconscious, as the case may be) to fill up the gap.

The position of the subconscious links in a train of thought is exactly parallel to the position of the changing states of a material object when no one is aware of it. We assume that the material object projects itself unseen across the gap which lies between its appearances to mind. We assume that process, change, and causality continue in it when it is unperceived. Exactly the same assumption, when it is made in regard to mind instead of to matter, is the concept of the subconscious. In only one important respect is there a difference. The material world, both when perceived and when not perceived, is further assumed to be public. The world of mind remains always private.

The subconscious is, of course, an existential construction. And subconscious thoughts, emotions, and conations have a constructive, and not a factual, existence. This does not make them the less real. They really exist. They are, as the Freudians tell us, the causes of many of our conscious actions, of our dreams, &c.

Will it not follow that the mind itself, the very ego, has a factual existence only while it is conscious, and that its continued existence through periods of total unconsciousness (if there are any such periods) is a construction? In view of the purely empirical character of our undertaking, I have purposely avoided all such transcendental questions as the nature of the ego itself. Nor do I propose to discuss them now. But I see no reason why we should seek to avoid the inference just suggested. It is certainly important that the mind, while it is functioning, should be regarded as a factual existence. But I do not see any reason why we should insist that, if it is convenient to regard it as continuing to exist during unconsciousness, such existence must be anything more than a construction of the conscious mind. We like to regard ourselves as the 'same' persons to-day, yesterday, and throughout our lives. But this appears to be very little more than a convenience of speech. If it became the custom to regard ourselves as 'different' from day to day, and as having changed our egos after every period of unconsciousness, I think we should very soon adapt ourselves to the change so long as every one was treated alike.

CHAPTER XV
HISTORICAL KNOWLEDGE. PHILOSOPHICAL KNOWLEDGE. THE PROBLEM OF TRUTH AND ERROR

WE have endeavoured to trace the evolution of knowledge from its lowest to its highest manifestations, and have taken at least a bird's-eye view of the majority of its forms. Notable exceptions, it may be pointed out, are historical and philosophical knowledge, to which we have not given any special treatment. Nor is it worth while, in my opinion, to devote separate chapters to them. What little I have to say will be said here. As to historical knowledge, there is indeed little to say which would throw light upon our particular problems. For historical truths do not differ, from our point of view, from any other statements of fact. That Brutus stabbed Caesar is a proposition of the same epistemological kind as that some roses are red, or that there are lions in Africa, or that Jones beat Smith at golf. In pure history there is no constructive element over and above the constructions of the external world, and of space and time, which are common to all forms of knowledge above the most rudimentary. What has been said in Chapter XIV, section 3, on the nature of the past, and in section 1 of the same chapter on biological evolution, contains in principle all that we need say in this book on historical knowledge. Apart from the constructions of space, time, and the external world, it is purely factual in type, and presents no further features of interest. Its truth or falsity will be of the same character as the truth or falsity of other kinds of factual knowledge, the nature of which will receive their final definition in this chapter.

Philosophical knowledge might indeed form the subject of a special epistemological study. But I shall content myself here with recording my opinion that philosophical knowledge will not be found to differ epistemologically from other forms of knowledge already analysed. Special

PHILOSOPHICAL KNOWLEDGE

claims have from time to time been put forward on behalf of philosophy. It has been supposed to possess its own peculiar method of knowing, different both from the methods of common knowledge and from the methods of the sciences. The philosophy of Hegel is the most notable example of this claim. Regarding such claims I have here only two remarks to make. The first is that their validity is exceedingly dubious, and that it is more probable that philosophy will have in the end to recognize that its methods must be simply those of the other sciences, suitably modified, no doubt, to meet its special subject-matter. The second is that, even if the claims put forward to special philosophical methods were allowed, they would never amount, so far as I know, to new epistemological *types* of knowledge. For example, the novelty in Hegel was his special method of deduction by means of thesis, antithesis, and synthesis. Whether this kind of deduction was or was not sound is a question for logic, not for epistemology. Epistemologically it is merely a kind of inference, and the place of inference in knowledge has already been determined. It is true that, even as epistemologists, we should be compelled to disallow the claim to be able to develop the whole world out of nothing by the mere process of inference. As we have seen, inferences lead us nowhere, never give rise to anything new, and merely ensure consistency in our knowledge. But this is really irrelevant to the issue we are discussing. The point is that, whether or not the Hegelian method is valid, it does not imply the existence of any new epistemological type of knowledge. Similar remarks will apply to all the other special claims of philosophers to methods different from those of ordinary knowledge.

For philosophies, too, in so far as they go beyond the facts of experience, are mental constructions, and can be nothing else. Consider, for example, the great philosophical concept of the Absolute. The Absolute may be regarded by some as a being—an infinite mind perhaps—which factually exists and experiences itself or is even experienced by other minds. This, or something like it, would be the special note of a definitely theistic idealism.

If the Absolute is so regarded, then we can place it without difficulty in our epistemological scheme. It is a factual existence similar in kind, though greater in degree, to our own minds. But if this view be not taken, then the Absolute must be regarded as a mental construction, a creation of the human intellect, an attempt to frame a single concept in which all the differences and contradictions in the universe can be merged in harmony. I need hardly say, at this late stage in our inquiry, that to call the Absolute a mental construction, is in no way to cast doubt upon its genuineness and reality. For if we have not yet learnt that the majority of real existences are constructions, we have learnt nothing. And to regard the Absolute as a construction, rather than as a factual existence, is, I think the more reasonable view. The question whether it 'exists' or not then becomes simply the question whether it is a valid construction, whether the conception of it is internally self-consistent, agrees with the facts of the world, and is valuable in the scheme of knowledge and for the purposes of thought. Those who attack it will do so, not on the ground that it cannot be found in experience (which is the way one would attack theism), but on the grounds that it is self-contradictory, that it is inconsistent with known facts, or that it is valueless as an instrument of knowledge. They will attempt to prove that it is an *in*valid construction.

Thus the Absolute must be regarded either as a factual existence or as a constructive existence. In either case it fits without difficulty into the epistemological scheme which has been developed, and presents no new characters. Nor is it likely that a detailed examination of the history of different philosophical conceptions—however interesting in itself—would throw any further light upon the special problems we are attempting to solve.

Before leaving the subject, however, I cannot refrain from one reflection. If, as I conceive, most philosophies are mental constructions, and not mere assertions of fact, then it will follow that there may be more than one true philosophy, and that rival systems of philosophy may be alternative systems of truth. For, as we have time after time seen, even two formally incompatible propositions may both be true, provided that we choose one or the other and do not attempt to combine them in the same context. It is true that there are as many universes as there are minds. It is also true that there is only one single universe. These two propositions are logically inconsistent with one another. But they are alternative truths. Their logical inconsistency does not condemn one of them to falsehood. It means merely that the two truths cannot be both asserted at the same time, in the same context, and in the same system of truths. We have here then at least a suggestion that pluralistic and monistic philosophies may both be true. And perhaps even realism and idealism may be regarded as alternative mental constructions.

I now leave the topic of philosophical knowledge and pass to the more proper subject of this chapter, the problem of the nature of truth and error. We have to gather together, into a single theory or definition, the various threads of our discussion.

The first point to note is the familiar one that truth is a character of judgements. No doubt there are usages of the word truth which seem to import something different. We speak of a true friend or of a true artist. We say that 'God is Truth'. Some philosophers say that the Absolute is the Truth. I think that these uses of the word are mere metaphors which will mislead us if we take them literally. But whether this is so or not, the problem of this book, at any rate, is concerned with truth and error as characters of judgements, and not with any transcendental Truth with a capital T. What we want to know is simply what is meant by saying that any statement, such as 'Horses are useful', 'Trees are green', or 'Electrons exist', is true or false. We are concerned, therefore, with very lowly matters, and do not presume to pry into the Absolute, which is too high for us.

If it is accepted, then, that truth is concerned solely with judgements, the next point is that *all judgements either assert or deny something about particular existents.* These existents may be either physical or psychical. Judgements may be about either cabbages or souls. But they must in the end refer, directly or indirectly, to particular realities. The point of this statement is to eliminate any notion that universal or abstract propositions do not refer to concrete things. It is, of course, obvious that if we say 'This rose is red', we are talking about a particular existent, namely, this rose. Even if we say 'All roses are pretty' this judgement, though it is universal, yet refers to particular existents, namely all the individual members of the class of things called roses. But even if we take pure abstractions, such as those of mathematics, it is still true that all propositions about them, or containing them, are statements the import of which is to assert or deny something about particular existents. Mathematical propositions are simply generalized statements of facts in the world. The judgement that $2+2 = 4$ is just as much a statement about particular existents as any other. It means that two apples and two apples are four apples, that two thoughts and two emotions are four mental states, &c. I am aware that mathematicians are apt to take a different view, to suppose that their science has nothing to do with 'things', that it is about 'pure numbers', and so forth. But we thrashed this question out in our chapter on mathematical knowledge. We saw that the mathematician's attempt to live in a vacuum, cut off from reality—though it may be an amusing game or pose for professors—cannot be successful, and that the only meaning and truth which mathematics can claim lies in its applicability to the concrete world of things. It is either true of those things or it is not true at all. We saw that there is no harm in mathematics regarding itself as self-enclosed, and as apart from the world, so long as this was recognized as an abstraction which may be useful to the mathematician, but is not actually the full concrete truth. And it is not necessary again to agitate these matters. I shall assert without further ado that mathematical propositions, like all others, assert or deny something about particular existents.

What has been said of mathematics will apply *a fortiori* to all lesser abstractions. It is admitted that mathematics is among the most abstract branches of knowledge. But if we take any other abstractions, such for example as Newton's law of gravitation, it will be equally true of them that their truth or falsity depends upon whether they correctly apply to things in the concrete world. The law of gravitation is 'about' the positions at different times of the earth, of the planet Mars, and so on. This is evident from the fact that if it predicts their positions wrongly it is said to be false. Enough has been said, I think, to prove our contention that all judgements of whatever kind assert or deny facts about particular existents, and will be true or false according as those particular assertions or denials are true or false.

Perhaps it is desirable briefly to consider one kind of judgement which might be alleged to be an exception. It might be said that judgements about Platonic Ideas, forms, or universals, are plainly not about particulars. The judgement 'the Idea of the Good is higher than all other Ideas' might be given as an example. But this is not really an exception. For we are in that case talking about *particular* universals, namely, the Idea of the Good and other particular Ideas.

The truth of judgements, therefore, is bound to be concerned with their application to the concrete. In other words, every judgement, in order to be true, must in some sense exhibit an 'agreement with the facts'. This is the same as saying that truth is tied by the given. And our first step must be to consider what this means.

We may begin by considering the simplest and lowest kind of perceptual knowledge such as is expressed in the proposition 'This is red'. I assume that the assertor of this judgement is himself experiencing the red sensation when he makes the judgement. Now the proposition is true if the 'this' is in fact red. If it is not red, the judgement is false. This statement is correct whether the assertor is experiencing what we call an hallucination or what we call a reality. For all that the judgement means is that the presentation which is appearing to him is a presentation of red. Whether there really is a red *object* present or not is irrelevant. And we must not import into the proposition any implications that there exists a public external world, that there are 'realities' and 'unrealities', or other such. If we do so, then the proposition ceases to be of that elementary kind which we wish to consider first. Further and more elaborate considerations regarding the conditions which make for the validity of mental constructions will then have to be brought in. And it is our purpose to keep these till later.

The 'this', therefore, is not a thing or an object in the public external world. It is a mere colour patch. It is nothing but a presentation. The truth of the judgement, in that case, consists in the agreement between the presentation and the judgement, or between the percept and the concept. (Both expressions mean the same thing. It will be noted that I here use the word percept as equivalent to bare presentation, which may not be in accordance with strict usage, but will, I hope, not be misunderstood now that I have noted it.) 'This is red' is true if it agrees with the presentation, i.e. if the 'this' is in fact red. But if the 'this' were green, the judgement would be false.

To say this is so simple and obvious that one may well run the risk of being asked what necessity there is to write a book to say it. And one may be expected to say something more difficult and profound. And in particular one may be expected to explain what is meant by such agreement and disagreement, or how agreement and disagreement between concept and percept are possible. But to these questions there is, in my opinion, no answer, for the reason that we have reached rock bottom. These conceptions are ultimate facts of consciousness. They cannot be analysed into anything simpler (or more learned and elaborate, if that is what is demanded). They cannot be further explained in terms of anything other than themselves. That my judgement 'This is red' may either agree or not agree with my percept; that when I have a sensation, I may either make a judgement which does correspond with it or one which does not; that if I see green, but say 'This is red', there is then a failure of my judgement to correspond with my percept; these are ultimate facts. If they are not admitted and understood, nothing further can be done to prove them or make them intelligible. We can no more say *why* there should exist such correspondence and lack of it than we can say why presentations exist, or why minds exist, or why one presentation bears the relation of resemblance to another, or why there are concepts in the mind.

In the judgement 'This is red' it is clear, of course, that 'red' is a concept. No doubt 'this' may also be represented as a concept. But in the example we are considering it is to be thought of rather as the verbal equivalent of the act of pointing. We may therefore concentrate on the fact that 'red' is a concept. This implies that the judgement 'This is red' really asserts the existence of the relation of resemblance between 'this' and other presentations which have previously been called red. If this is true, i.e. if this resemblance actually exists, then we have applied the right concept. If it is not true, then we have applied the wrong concept. Hence if we say that the truth of the judgement consists in the application of the right concepts to the facts, or to the percepts, this will mean exactly the same thing as saying that the truth consists in a correspondence between the concept and the percept.

It is obvious, I think, that in the kind of 'correspondence' here asserted to constitute the truth of these elementary kinds of judgement there is not that fatal fallacy which has so often been noted in most correspondence theories of truth. The essence of these theories consisted in supposing that truth lies in the correspondence of our perceptions with things which were believed to lie outside our perceptions in the external world. And it was evident that whether or not our perceptions agreed with outside things could never be known since we can inspect only our percepts and not things as they exist outside our percepts. That was the fallacy of the old correspondence theory of truth. It was a legacy of the absurd view that things have a factual existence outside our perceptions. That it led to such a fallacy is in itself enough to condemn that view. But in the theory now presented no such fallacy occurs. A correspondence is alleged to exist between our percepts and our concepts, *both of which are open to our inspection and comparison*.

So far the only kind of judgement which we have considered is one framed in the present tense, 'This *is* red'. But whether the percepts concerned in the judgement are present, future, or past, makes no difference to the theory of truth. Suppose that the judgement were 'This will be red to-morrow'. (We will agree to ignore the fact that a mind at the extremely low level which we are studying could not yet have framed the construction of continuous time, and could scarcely, therefore, understand the idea of 'to-morrow'.) The judgement 'This will be red to-morrow' is true if to-morrow's percept corresponds with to-day's judgement. Similarly the judgement 'This was red yesterday' is true if the judgement agrees with yesterday's percept. No doubt there are difficult problems involved here regarding the nature of memory and imagination. But they are not the problems with which we are concerned. It is just as much a fact—however we try to explain it—that a concept of to-day may agree with a percept of yesterday or to-morrow as that a present concept may agree with a present percept. The formula of the correspondence of concept and percept as the essence of the truth of these kinds of elementary perceptual propositions is thus equally correct whether the propositions refer to the present, the past, or the future.

Now suppose that we advance to a very slightly higher level of knowledge. The kind of judgement which we have been considering was one which applied to the presentation before the mind *a concept of the given*, such as 'red', i.e. the lowest kind of concept in the gamut of knowledge. We will advance one step higher, and apply one of *the concepts of things*. Instead of 'This is red' we will say 'This is an apple', and we will ask ourselves wherein the truth of this judgement lies.

Concepts of things are, as we have seen, essentially predictive of future possible experience. I see a red round patch and I say 'This is an apple'. The meaning of this is: if I bite the red patch, I shall experience a certain sweet taste; if I feel it, it will be soft; if I cut it open, it will appear whitish; and so on. The judgement, it is evident, will be true if these various predictions are true. The predictions, however, when analysed into their simplest elements, are merely judgements in the future tense which apply concepts of the given to the presentation. They say 'If I bite it, this will be *sweet*', or 'if . . . this will be *white*, this will be *soft*', and so on. It is true that the 'if' clause introduces the construction of possibility, and other constructions connected with thinghood, a public world, &c., may be involved. These, of course, would take the judgement into a much higher sphere of knowledge than that which we are now considering. We can for the present neglect these constructive elements of the judgement, since we shall be considering the whole question of the truth of constructions a little later. And if we thus neglect these constructive elements, it is clear that the truth of the judgement 'This is an apple' consists solely once more in the correspondence of the judgement with the percepts. The judgement is true if it turns out correct that the inside of the apple is white, sweet, and the rest. We do not need, therefore, as yet to go beyond the simple formula of the correspondence of concepts with percepts to find the essence of the truth or falsity of this kind of judgement.

It is at this point that we can solve the problem of *illusion*, so far as it is a problem of epistemology. An illusion occurs when we interpret a presentation wrongly, i.e. when we apply to it the wrong concept of things. I see a faint object in the distance, and take it for a man. On going nearer I find that it is a tree stump. Why I make this mistake is not a question for epistemology, but for psychology. It may be due to carelessness, lack of clear vision, mental confusion of one kind or another. With that we are not concerned. The epistemological character of the illusion consists in the fact that we have applied the wrong predictive concepts to the presentation. There is a lack of agreement between the concepts and the future percepts. There is, therefore, nothing new here to be investigated.

If the judgement whose truth is under consideration is, say, 'This apple is red', it is clear that the epistemological analysis already made of such propositions as 'This is an apple' will apply with merely the necessary minor modifications. There will be no change in principle. The entire truth of the judgement, apart from its constructive elements, will reside in the correspondence of concepts with percepts. For the judgement 'This apple is red' tells us that 'this is an apple' and that 'it is red'. The first of these two statements is identical with the judgement whose truth we found in the paragraph before the last to consist solely in the agreement of concept with percept; and the second 'it is red' also plainly requires no further analysis.

We may now advance one step further to general and abstract propositions. For 'This apple is red' we substitute judgements such as 'All apples are pleasant-coloured', or 'All matter is heavy', or 'Most Englishmen are fair-skinned'. The truth of all general and abstract judgements lies in their applicability to particular cases. We have seen that once and for all in connexion with the case of mathematics. So that, if we still ignore the constructive elements, the truth of these general judgements lies in nothing but the correspondence of concepts with percepts.

Let us take as an example a very highly abstract judgement, namely Newton's law of gravitation. We will consider it purged of the concept of force. For force is, in the first place, a construction, and in the second place an invalid construction. So that it would complicate our inquiry from every point of view for us to take it into account. Instead, we will think of Newton's law as no more than a formula stated in terms of its essential factors, such as time, mass, distance. Now although Newton's law makes no direct assertions about particular percepts—as it would do if it said, for example, 'This planet is now visible at this spot'—although it is abstract, yet its whole meaning and truth reside in the end in its applicability to percepts. It is a general formula or recipe from which can be drawn particular statements about particular facts of perception. That is its sole function and use. We can deduce from it the position of Mars at midnight on 1 January 1950, the times and dates of solar and lunar eclipses or of a transit of Venus, and so on. The correctness of these deductions consists in the agreement of them with what is actually perceived, i.e. in the correspondence of the concepts with the percepts, and the truth of the law *is* nothing but the correctness of the deductions made from it.

It is true, of course, that we get cases in which it is said that true deductions follow from a false law. It is a commonplace of the logic books that a hypothesis may cover all the known facts and yet be false. But it will be found in all such cases that the law is not a mere generalized statement of what happens, containing nothing except the very deductions which are made from it wrapped up in pill form, but that there is always in the law which is thus found false some other element, usually a constructive element, which is false, and which poisons the supposed law with its falsehood. Very likely 'phlogiston' in its time explained the then known facts. If it had been nothing but a generalized statement of those facts, it would have been true. But it contained also the assertion of a new existence, an element called 'phlogiston'. This was plainly an existential construction. For reasons which we need not at the moment discuss it was an invalid construction. Again, if it is true that the ether of space, so long believed in, is not a real existence at all—as appears to be nowadays thought—we have another example of the same thing. Elaborate laws were discovered for the propagation of radiation through space by the medium of the ether. The laws explained the facts, and in so far as they resulted in an agreement of concepts with percepts, were true. If there was any untrue element, it lay in the invalid existential construction of the ether.

It begins plainly to emerge that in most judgements

there are two elements, the factual and the constructive. A statement may be wholly factual, such as 'This is red'. Or it may be wholly constructive, such as 'ether exists'. Or, by far the commonest case, it may be a mixture of the factual and the constructive. Practically all ordinary judgements belong to this mixed class. This will be evident when we consider that the very existence of a public world of 'things' is a construction, so that all judgements which rise above the level of mere statements that we have some particular sensation such as redness contain a constructive element.

It is also becoming plain that the truth of the factual part of a judgement always depends solely upon the correspondence of concepts with percepts. We may generalize and say that all judgements about the external world are judgements whose truth resides in the correspondence of concepts and percepts, so long as we ignore the constructive element. What are the conditions of the truth of mental constructions is a question which we have still to discuss.

But before leaving the present topic I will give one or two more examples to make matters clearer. No one has ever seen an electron. But if we assume the existence of electrons and of the laws which are believed to govern their activities we can then make deductions which agree with our actual perceptions. These perceptions may consist in the visual readings of the position of a pointer on a dial, or in feelings of heat, or in the readings of a thermometer, or in the perceived behaviour of any material object. If the deductions are correct, then we have a correspondence between concepts and percepts. This correspondence does not alone prove the truth of the theory, for as we already noted, there may be constructive elements in the theory, and owing to this fact correct deductions may always follow from false theories.

Again the truth of the judgement 'All men are mortal' —if it means only that the presentations which make up what we call human bodies all come in the end to be perceived as cold, motionless, rigid, &c., i.e. if we ignore all constructive elements—depends solely upon whether it agrees with all actual past, present, and future perceptions in regard to human bodies.

The judgement $2+2 = 4$, though it is highly abstract, contains no construction, and its truth therefore consists solely in correspondence. It means that any two percepts and any two percepts make four percepts. And it can only be shown false if in some case there turn out to be two percepts and two percepts which make three, five, or a dozen percepts, i.e. if the percepts do not agree with the judgement.

We have so far had in mind only judgements about the physical world. And it is for that reason that we have made 'percepts' the basis of our argument. Now if we turn to judgements about non-physical things, we have of course to substitute for physical percepts the internal awarenesses by the mind of its own states. To use the word percept for our awarenesses of our own states would not be incorrect; but it is apt to mislead owing to the fact that it is more usually confined to the physical sphere. Moreover, as already noted, philosophers have rightly distinguished between mere presentations and perceptions, whereas our use of the word percept has not kept that fact in view because it was not relevant to our discussion here. It will be better, however, in the final statement of the theory to substitute for the word 'percept' the word 'given'. The 'given' covers both the internal and the external worlds. My emotions, thoughts, &c., in so far as I am aware of them, are as much givens as are the red patches and sounds of the physical world. Moreover, if we use the word 'given,' this will make it clear that all constructive elements are excluded. We may therefore sum up this part of our theory by saying that *all judgements are either factual or constructive or both; and in regard to all factual judgements, and all factual elements in mixed judgements, their truth consists solely in a correspondence between concept and given.*

Before passing to the question of the validity of constructions—which is the next main point on our programme—it will be convenient here shortly to consider the place of logic in the theory. Nothing can be true, it will be admitted, if it involves a breach of the laws of logic. A single judgement cannot by itself, however, involve such a breach. For every illogicality must in the end boil down to a contradiction or inconsistency between *two* judgements. Therefore there must be at least two judgements to make an illogicality. Examples such as 'This is both red and not-red' do not, of course, prove the contrary. For such a judgement is compound, and may be analysed into two judgements which contradict each other. Hence questions of logic do not arise for single truths, but only for systems of truths, a system being constituted by at least two judgements. Where the question is whether a certain judgement shall be admitted into a given system of supposed truths, logic may decide whether it can or not. If it is consistent with all the judgements which already make up the system, then the new judgement can be admitted to membership of the system. If it is inconsistent with any of them, it cannot. In that case either the new judgement must be rejected from this system—though it might perhaps fit into another—or the system itself must be modified to make it consistent with the new judgement, and then the new judgement accepted into it.

We have already seen many times that two incompatible judgements may be alternative truths. Euclid's axiom of parallels and the corresponding axioms of non-Euclidean geometry are a case in point. Another example is the following pair of propositions, which formally contradict each other but are both true: (1) that there exist as many worlds as there are minds; (2) that there is only one world.

The truth that there are many worlds does not fit into the system of truths which the human race happens to have adopted and which constitutes its body of knowledge. But it would have been quite possible to build up another system of truths into which this would have fitted, and of which it would have been the foundation.

This does not signify, however, that we are entitled to

break the laws of logic. Nor is it to be made the basis of one of those shallow quibbling attacks on the laws of logic by means of which a reputation for brilliance is nowadays to be made. The substance of the old law of contradiction is essentially valid. But the recognition of alternative truths may indicate that some slight modification is necessary in the traditional mode of expressing or presenting that law. Two contradictory propositions may both be true, but not in the same system of truths. The precise modification of the law required, the precise definition of the law, must be left to the logicians. I am, however, indicating the lines on which the modification must proceed. We can accept the truth that there is only one world, but in that case we must consistently stick to that view and to all that it implies throughout the system of truths in which we are moving. A system based on the opposite truth is possible and may be adopted if desired. But that too must be consistently held by. We cannot mix up the two systems. In the same way we may adopt Euclidean or one of the non-Euclidean geometries. They are all true. And in studying, say, a problem of astronomy we can adopt whichever is most convenient. But having once adopted one we must stick to it consistently throughout the consideration of that problem.

It will now be convenient to consider the problem of the validity of mental constructions. A construction is a fiction, a judgement invented by the mind without any foundation in fact (i.e. in the given). That being so, it is evident that, unless strict conditions are laid down as to precisely what constructions are to be allowed within the fold of truth, we shall be reduced to the pass of allowing any wild figments of a diseased imagination to pose as truths. We might be compelled to believe in salamanders and goblins, in magic, in charms, in the man in the moon. These are all certainly in a sense 'mental constructions'. But they cannot be accepted as truths. We have therefore somehow to distinguish between those constructions which are true and those which are false. In other words we have to find the criteria of the validity of mental constructions.

It is clear, in the first place, that constructive truths, like those which are factual, are subject to the laws of logic. A *single* constructive judgement cannot, for reasons pointed out in the last section, be either logical or illogical. But not only are systems of constructions common, but even what would ordinarily pass as a single construction can usually be analysed into several judgements. We may therefore lay it down (1) that a construction must be internally self-consistent, and (2) that it must be consistent with the system of truths into which it is sought to embody it. These conditions will serve to eliminate a vast number of otherwise possible constructions. They will invalidate belief in the man in the moon because such a belief is inconsistent with many accepted truths such as that there is no atmosphere in the moon which men could breathe.

Our next step must be to investigate the relation of constructions to the given, i.e. to facts, to actual percepts, and so on. We laid it down very early that all truth is tied to the given. We shall find that this applies as much to constructions as to factual truths. But it cannot mean, in the case of constructions, that there is an actual correspondence of the judgement with the given, for the very essence of the construction is that it is not a fact and that no given corresponds to it. We judge that the table exists unperceived, and we consider this to be a truth. But the unperceived table can never be given. In other words there is no given which corresponds to the construction of the unperceived table. Constructions, however, are tied to the given in the sense that if any deductions from them *disagree* with the given, the constructions must be false. For it commonly happens that the very purpose of a construction is that we may be able to deduce from it judgements which are not themselves constructions but factual propositions. This is practically always the case with the constructions of science. It is not the case with all constructions. From the existence of the unperceived table, for example, we cannot deduce anything whatever regarding

TRUTH AND ERROR

the perceived facts of the world. They would all be exactly the same if the table went out of existence when we ceased to perceive it and came into existence again when perception of it began again. We do not invent the unperceived table in order to make deductions from it which will enable us to predict future experience. We invent it for certain other reasons of convenience which have been examined in their proper place. But in the case of scientific constructions, although their logical structure and characters are the same as those of the ordinary constructions such as the unperceived table, their purpose is somewhat different. Their purpose is to 'explain' actual facts, and to predict future ones. The 'explanation', it need hardly be said, does not aim at telling us the 'why' of anything, but only the 'how'. It consists only in being able to deduce the many facts from one concept, i.e. to subsume the particulars under a universal, to discover a law. The universal concept which is assumed as the explanation of the facts may be a construction. And it is then a condition of the validity of the construction that the deductions from it shall agree with the facts, i.e. that in them there shall be a correspondence between the concepts and the given. For example, an electron is a construction. But the theory of the electron agrees with the facts in the sense that deductions from it agree with our actual perceptions. If deductions from it clashed with the facts of perception, we should have to conclude that the construction is false.

If we express this relationship of constructions to the given by saying that *if any deduction from a construction clashes with the given, that construction is invalid*, this will be found to be a universal condition of the validity of constructions and to apply, not only to scientific constructions, but to all. Take the construction of the unperceived table. As already pointed out, we do not make elaborate deductions and predictions from it. That is not its purpose. But still it is nevertheless the case that, if any deduction from this or any other such construction were found somehow to clash with actual perceptions, we should have to reject the construction. We are enabled to believe in the unperceived table precisely because to do so *makes no difference to the facts*, i.e. does not clash with them.

Hence all constructions are limited by the two conditions that they are bound (1) by the given, and (2) by the laws of logic. These are not, however, the sole conditions of their validity. For we might invent all kinds of fanciful figments of the imagination which would be logically feasible and also not clash with any known facts. Therefore there must be some other condition of the truth of a construction. This further condition is that the construction must be *necessary for the purposes of knowledge*. That is to say, we cannot admit as valid any constructions which are unnecessary and superfluous. Under this canon we shall refuse to allow the mind to multiply all kinds of fantastic agencies and existences which may perhaps not clash with the laws of logic nor with the given, but which we should nevertheless declare unreal.

We will analyse more carefully in a moment the nature of this condition. But we will first remark that it is the logical foundation of the famous principle of Occam's razor. That principle has not up till now been understood in its true light. It could not be, because the nature and function of mental constructions has not been understood. It has been assumed that the principle of Occam's razor is merely a methodological one. But what we have now to see is that it is much more than this. It is a constitutive principle of reality. It was supposed to be no more than a rule for guiding research, for avoiding unnecessary complexity, for attaining economy and simplicity, and also for seeing that we do not go beyond the evidence. This would be all that could be said so long as the mental construction was not recognized as *creating* existence. Now that this is recognized, now that such creation by thought is seen to be one of the constitutive elements of real existence, it follows that the question whether an entity actually exists or not may depend solely upon whether it satisfies the conditions of a valid construction. It may depend, therefore, upon whether the construction is necessary for the purposes of knowledge. Its being necessary for the purposes of knowledge brings it into existence, creates it, constitutes its existence. Its being superfluous prevents its existence, constitutes its non-existence, if such a phrase may be allowed. Hence Occam's razor serves, not only to guide thought into economical methods, but to prevent unnecessary existences from being created.

But it must not be supposed that the condition of the validity of constructions which we are here examining, i.e. that of necessity for knowledge, can be *identified* with Occam's razor. It is, on the contrary, much wider than the latter. It is the logical foundation of the razor, and the razor is merely one example of it. Occam's principle is that we must not suppose superfluous existences. Our principle is that we must not invent superfluous constructions of any kind. It thus applies just as much to unificatory as to existential constructions. The principle would invalidate the construction of a single world in place of the many private worlds, or the assumption that the continuing appearances of the table constitute the 'same' thing, if it could be shown that these fictions are not necessary to thought.

But what is meant by the phrase 'necessary for the purposes of knowledge'? It is clearly essential that it should not be left vague. The question resolves itself into two: (1) What kind of 'necessity' is intended? (2) What are 'the purposes of knowledge'?

As to the first question, it is clearly not logical necessity that is meant. There was no logical necessity to reduce the many worlds to one public world, to assume the resemblance of your red to my red, to invent the third visual dimension of space, or to suppose that the table goes on existing when no one is aware of it. That it is not logical necessity that is involved follows indeed from the very definition of a construction. For a construction is, among other things, an assumption which cannot be proved, i.e. cannot be shown to be logically necessary. It is true, as we have seen, that earlier constructions do often logically necessitate later constructions. We saw many examples of this in earlier chapters. Having invented one construction, we are often compelled by sheer logic to invent another for the sake of consistency. But the original motivation of such a series or system of constructions is not any logical necessity. In such a case the members of the system may be related to each other by bonds of logical necessity, but the system as a whole is a pure assumption, i.e. is not logically necessitated by anything.

The 'necessary' here means simply what is *required*. It is the simple and homely notion of what we *need* for our purposes, i.e. for the purposes of knowledge. We assumed the single public world because it was convenient, because it helped thought, because we needed it for the purposes of thought. The same will be found true of any construction whatever. This will, I think, suffice as an explication of the kind of 'necessity' involved in constructions.

Next we have to inquire what are 'the purposes of knowledge'. I cannot see that any single all-inclusive answer can be given to this question. Philosophers are too much in love with such simple answers. One school emphasizes the practical necessities of the physical organism, another the spiritual ideal of pure knowledge. Why it should be supposed that the truth can be summed up in a single concept I do not know. And it seems clear in the present case that both of the answers just mentioned are partial truths.

At the beginning of the evolution of mind practical needs will hold exclusive sway. The crocodile has no ideal of knowledge for its own sake. Even the average uneducated human being has very little, and thought for him is mostly practically conditioned. It may be taken as certain that the main necessities which led to the early development of knowledge, and therefore of mental constructions, were strictly practical. A single world was originally assumed, not as a truth for its own sake, but because it rendered communication and co-operation between organisms easier, and because minds hungered for the society of their fellows. Communication could have been carried on, as we have shown in an earlier chapter, on the basis of a multitude of private worlds. A single world was assumed because it was easier and simpler. In the last resort, ease and simplicity of thought are preferred to labour and complexity because the mind's energy is limited, because, if you like, the mind is lazy. Similar considerations apply to all the early constructions of the human mind.

Later constructions, such as those of science, are similarly conditioned, because of two possible constructions we prefer the simpler. But the elaboration of such constructions is undertaken for two reasons. Firstly, they are forced on us by logic, by the fact that, having once created constructions, we are compelled to invent others in order to maintain consistency. This process has been fully illustrated in previous chapters. When once we have invented the idea of the atom, logic, together with new facts (i.e. new perceptions) which appear inconsistent with the older forms of the theory of the atom, will force us on to later forms of the theory, to the construction of the electron, &c. Secondly, there grows up a desire for knowledge for its own sake. *Curiosity* is aroused. This forces us to carry on the process of constructing new truths to fit in with the old.

The statement that some truths, namely, for the most part, the earlier constructions of the mind, are created to meet practical needs, is not an admission of the pragmatist position. It is indeed the element of truth which that position contains. But the pragmatist position as a whole is false because (1) all truth, whether factual or constructive, is tied by the given, and because (2) it is tied by the laws of logic. Both the given and the laws of logic are absolute, are forced upon us *ab extra*, whether we like it or not, whether it suits our convenience or no. This is true whether we interpret convenience as meaning convenience for the purposes of practical action or of theoretical thought. Truth, therefore, is not whatever we will to believe. Nor is the will the sole arbiter, as the name 'voluntarism' would seem to imply. Truth is compelled both by facts and by logic.

The elements of truth in pragmatism are as follows: A *part* of truth is constructive, and constructions may be moulded by the will, i.e. by considerations of either practical or theoretical needs, within the limits laid down by fact and logic. But the truth of purely factual judgements, and of the factual elements in mixed judgements, is entirely independent of pragmatic considerations. It is also to be admitted, however, that even among factual truths the mind *selects* those which are useful or convenient to it. And as between two or more alternative truths it chooses the simpler for reasons of convenience. The pragmatic elements in knowledge are, therefore, threefold, (1) free construction within fixed limits, (2) selectiveness, and (3) simplification for ease and convenience.

The element of truth in the 'correspondence' theory is that all factual truths are in fact true by virtue of a correspondence. Not the correspondence, however, between external thing and perception, but between concept and given. Moreover even in constructive truths correspondence is involved in that a *dis*agreement between the implications of, or deductions from, the construction and the given renders the construction false.

The element of truth in the 'coherence' theory is that knowledge constitutes a system of judgements which must be logically coherent, which must be consistent with one another, which must obey the laws of logic.

Any judgement, therefore, is true
  (1) if it is a bare statement of what is given, and if in such statement the concepts correspond with the given;
  or (2) if it is a valid construction, i.e. a construction which (a) involves no implications which are contradicted by the given, and (b) is required or necessary for the practical or theoretical purposes of knowledge;
  or (3) if it is a combination of the above two.

This is the definition of the truth of single judgements. If more than one judgement is in question a further condition is involved, namely (4) *in systems of truths the laws of logic must be obeyed*. This includes the condition that a complex construction, i.e. a construction which is a compound of more than one judgement, must be internally self-consistent.

It will be observed that no special mention is made of universal, general, or abstract judgements. This is because they are regarded merely as a multitude of individual judgements telescoped into one. The same conditions of truth, therefore, apply to them as to individual judgements.

The majority of judgements come under head (3). They are combinations of factual and constructive elements.

The definition of *error* is the opposite of that of truth. Any proposition which does not conform to the above conditions is *false*.

It may rightly be asked whether this definition implies belief in 'absolute' truth, i.e. whether it involves that a judgement once true is always true, that if it is true at all, it is true at all times and for all purposes. Or does our theory, on the contrary, imply the pragmatist doctrine that a judgement may be true for the purposes we have in hand, but false when our purpose changes; or true in one age and false in another?

The answer is plainly that our theory implies belief in absolute truth, and is therefore in agreement with the view always taken in the past by common sense. It will be best to make the issue clear by thinking in terms of a specific example. Suppose that there is one theory of the atom which is accepted in 1932 because it explains all the known facts. We will call this theory A. Suppose that in 1942 a new set of facts is discovered which definitely clashes with theory A and necessitates the elaboration of a new theory B. In 1952 this may again be upset by the discovery of new facts and the establishment of a third theory C; and so on.

What are we to say regarding this series of theories? The pragmatist will say apparently that theory A was true in 1932, but became false in 1942. Common sense and the theory of 'absolute' truth say, on the contrary, that if theory A was proved false in 1942, it must have been false in 1932, and will always have been false at all times. This latter is the view with which we agree. For the falsity of the theory in 1942 was due to the fact that it clashed with certain givens or certain percepts. In ordinary parlance we should say that it clashed with certain facts. Now those facts were also facts in 1932, only they were not then known. That they existed unperceived in 1932 is, of course, a construction. But it is a construction which has long ago been accepted as true by the human mind. Hence the issue is quite clear. When we say that a judgement is false if it disagrees with the given facts, do we mean to refer to the then known facts or to all facts known and unknown? It seems to me that the former view introduces chaos into the theory of truth. For suppose that I believe that horse X won the Derby yesterday, when in fact horse Y won it. We should surely say that my belief was false. But, if we adopt the view against which I am arguing, we shall have to say that, as my belief did not clash with any facts which were known to me, it was true. Which is absurd.

Or we may put the matter thus. Let the proposition which asserts the existence of the new facts discovered in 1942 be called P. P, it is admitted, is true in 1942. Was it true in 1932? If the newly discovered facts existed in 1932, then P was true, if not, it was false. But by construction long admitted those facts did exist in 1932. (I am assuming, of course, that they are not the kind of facts which come newly into existence, in which case they would hardly be of a nature which could be relevant to the problem of the constitution of matter.) Therefore P was true in 1932. But P is inconsistent with theory A. For it asserts precisely those facts which rendered A obsolete. Hence if we assert with the pragmatists that A was true in 1932, then we shall have to admit that A and P, which are logically inconsistent, were both true at the same time. For these reasons we reject the pragmatist view, and adopt that of common sense. This is what one would have expected. For common sense proceeds upon a crude form of the 'correspondence' theory of truth. Our theory is also essentially a form of the correspondence theory, though it is hoped that it is less crude. Both for us and for common sense truth is tied by the facts, and does not change Proteus-like from day to day, according to our wishes, as the pragmatists would have us think.

No doubt this means that we can never be certain, in regard to complicated scientific theories, that we have reached any measure of truth. We can never be certain until we know *all* the facts, i.e. until we are omniscient. But I see no objection to admitting this. It does not render science hopeless or vain. For although we can never attain certainty, there is a growing probability that our theories are true the more we come to know of the facts. Moreover it must be remembered that theories are complex, i.e. they consist of a large number of judgements some of which may be true, some false. When theory A is superseded by theory B, it is not usual to find that the whole of theory A is false. We are more likely to find that a very few of the judgements of which it was composed are inconsistent with the new facts, but that most of them are still left standing as true. In this way theories A, B, and C may be regarded as increasing approximations to the truth. And lastly, theory A, though false or partly false, was useful in its time since it explained the then known facts and yielded true predictions of experience. Even in 1942, when it has been superseded, it may still be used *within certain defined limits* to explain and predict. This means that it has become a methodological assumption.

There is one fact regarding the nature of existential constructions which may, if its implications are not discussed and cleared up, give rise to difficulties. This is the fact that such constructions are only expressible in hypothetical propositions whose antecedents contain impossible conditions. This appears so far as a strange peculiarity, a sort of eccentricity on the part of the existential construction. We have stressed it throughout, but made no attempt to explain it. The time has now come when we must endeavour to do so.

The difficulty which it seems to create is that it appears to involve the construction in a logical contradiction. And since it is one of the conditions of the validity of a construction that it shall be internally self-consistent, any such admission would be fatal to the validity of all existential constructions. The difficulty will be most easily examined if we take a concrete case. We assume the existence of the unperceived table. This means 'if any one were now looking, he would perceive the table'. But by hypothesis no one is looking. The belief in the unperceived table therefore attempts to combine the hypothesis that no one is looking with the supposition that some one is looking. This is what renders the condition which is contained in the antecedent an impossibility. This is, in fact, a logical contradiction. The point may be put otherwise by considering that since, in its ultimate meaning, *esse* is simply *percipi*, the hypothesis of the unperceived table amounts to believing in an unperceived percept, a non-existent existence. The same kind of contradiction may be found in every existential construction. And it may therefore be argued with some show of plausibility that no existential construction is ever valid.

The first point to notice here is that, although every existential construction contains an apparent logical contradiction, it is always one and the same contradiction which appears in them all. The assertion of the existence of the atom means 'if . . ., then we should perceive atoms'. The assertion of the existence of the invisible side of the moon means 'if we were on the other side, we should see it'. Every existential construction supposes an existence which we should perceive *if* . . . . The contradiction in all cases resides in the fact that we suppose something to be perceived while at the same time asserting that it is not perceived. It arises from the attempt which we are always making to get away from the fundamental identity of *esse* and *percipi*. It is, in short, the contradiction of the *unperceived percept*.

This primitive contradictory assumption is a kind of original sin which the human mind committed when man first began to eat of the fruit of the tree of knowledge. It keeps breaking out afresh everywhere in knowledge, in the case of the ether or the atoms as much as in our common sense beliefs about tables and chairs. But we have at least only one contradiction to deal with in all cases, not a distinct contradiction for each existential construction.

We have thus only one problem to solve, and it does not seem difficult of solution when we come to examine it. There is in truth a contradiction involved, and the mind accepted it once and for all when it undertook the great adventure of admitting that, although *esse* is *percipi*, yet things can exist unperceived. There is only one possible way of reconciling the contradiction, and that consists in pointing out that this admission is, after all, only a supposal, a make-belief, a pretence which has been entered into for the purpose of enriching life and knowledge. The contradiction is reconciled, in fact, by pointing out that the unperceived object has not factual but only constructive existence. If it were supposed that the unperceived object has factual existence, then the contradiction would be final and insoluble. This is, in fact, the contradiction which lies at the root of all forms of the theory of representative ideas, and which has broken out perpetually in the history of philosophy in one form or another. If we persist in asserting it, we shall then either have to give up the doctrine that *esse* is *percipi*, or the doctrine that things exist unperceived. Realists follow the former course and deny to existence its essential relativity to perception. Phenomenalists, I suppose, would follow the latter alternative, and deny that anything exists unless it is actually perceived. Our theory is enabled to grasp together both sides of the dilemma and to reconcile them. The theory of constructive existence resolves the contradiction.

It is the character of knowledge as constructive which has given rise to the category of 'possibility'. Presumably every proposition asserts or denies something. Now what is asserted or denied by the proposition 'if it had rained to-day, the ground would have been wet'? It did not rain, and the ground was not wet. Yet most people would say that the proposition is nevertheless true. What is it that is true? What is it that is asserted or denied to be true? Not any *actual fact* about the universe. What is asserted is a *possibility*. But what is the possible? By definition it is not anything actual. It is not anything that exists or is real. Is it then an absolute non-entity? And if so, how is it that it can be meaningfully asserted? Here is a flat self-contradiction which is yet admitted every day as a valid part of knowledge. The world of possibility, it seems, is neither an existence nor a non-existence. For what exists is the actual and not the merely possible. And what does not exist is nothing, and cannot be truthfully asserted about the universe. That is the contradiction involved in the notion of the possible.

The solution of the puzzle is that the contradiction involved here is the very same contradiction which we have been considering in existential constructions. It is the same 'if . . ., then we should perceive'. 'If it had rained, we should have perceived wet ground.' And it ceases to be a contradiction when it is recognized as a supposal, a realm set up and brought into existence by the mind for its own purposes, a realm which is not factual. It is neither existent (factual) nor non-existent (non-entity). It is constructive existence. If we believe that in asserting the possible, in asserting hypothetical propositions generally, we are asserting a factual or actual existence, then indeed we are involved in hopeless contradictions. But if we admit that the world of possibility is a world supposed or constructed by the mind, the contradiction vanishes.

This, then, is the explanation of the strange 'if' clause which dogs the steps of the existential construction.

CHAPTER XVI
CONCLUSION

THE picture of the universe which is presented to us at the conclusion of our inquiries may be briefly sketched. The universe is fundamentally a colony of multitudes of minds. I hold back from saying that the ultimate stuff or reality of the universe is mind. For I do not know, or at least I have not inquired in this book, what is meant by 'ultimate' reality. Inquiries of that kind belong to the sphere of transcendental philosophy, which I have here and for the moment forsworn. Moreover, in addition to minds there are givens, floating colours and sounds, relations between these, mental states as themselves intuited and given. Each monadic mind possesses and dwells in its own self-enclosed world of givens. But to say that mind is the ultimate reality of the universe would imply, I think, that it is more real than the givens, that it is in some way more 'fundamental' than they are (whatever that may mean), that it is prior to them, perhaps even that it produces them. Any of these propositions may, for all I know, be true. But they do not result from anything that is asserted in this book. I have not inquired regarding them, because in my opinion they would take me beyond the empirical standpoint which I have adopted. They would take me into the sphere of transcendental metaphysics, into questions of the purpose and rationality of things, into the *why* of the universe.

For the same reasons I forbear to inquire whether the parallelism of private worlds, which is a fact, and which—as was noted in Chapter VII—lies at the basis of our whole theory, is evidence of a designing mind overruling the universe; or whether the universality and necessity of logical laws, the fact that they are not personal but overpersonal, does not point to some deeper universal mind of which our own minds are but individualizations or manifestations. These suggestions lie outside the scope of our limited empirical investigations. And I will only say that there is nothing in any of these views which is inconsistent with the epistemology here advocated.

For us at the close of our inquiries all we can say is (1) that minds exist and (2) that givens exist and are perceived by minds. The minds and the givens are facts, brute facts. I do not know how or why they come into existence. To make any inquiry into this is no part of my undertaking. Nor do I inquire 'what minds are' or 'what givens are' or what the 'ultimate nature' of either of them is. I do not even know what the meaning of these questions is. For to ask 'what mind is' seems to imply that it can be described or defined in terms of something else which is not mind. And I have no idea what that something else could be. Either it must be some transcendental reality, in which case we leave it to transcendental philosophers. Or else it must be some other factual existent. The only other factual existents are the givens. And it does not seem a very hopeful line to suggest that minds are wholly explicable in terms of colour patches, sounds, odours, and the like. Moreover this solution would leave us still asking 'what the givens are'. If we do not accept them as ultimate facts, then they will have to be explained either in terms of a transcendental reality or in terms of the only other known existents, namely minds. And the process of explanation would in the latter case be obviously circular. So that, if I am asked 'what minds are' or 'what givens are', I can get no further in replying than to say that minds are minds, and givens are givens. I do not know how to answer the question 'what is the ultimate nature of a red patch?' except by saying that a red patch is a red patch. For me at this empirical standpoint minds and givens are simply ultimate facts of which no further account can be given. And it is at least questionable whether to ask for a further account of them has any real meaning.

Multitudes of minds perceiving multitudes of colour patches, sounds, tactile presentations, and other givens. These are the raw material, the ultimate constituents, of the universe. These are the only *factual* existents. These are the only pure facts. In this arena of primitive being the

CONCLUSION

givens of each mind constitute its own private universe. There are as many universes as there are minds. And each such universe is internally disconnected, full of gaps, holes, and chasms. There are gaps between the presentations of the different senses. A sight is in a different world from a sound. There are gaps in time when the mind is asleep or unconscious and when therefore its universe simply ceases to exist. There is a gap between the table (or the colour patch which later becomes the table) which I see now and the one I saw yesterday. They are not the 'same' table and between their two existences there is a dark blank in the picture. The whole of each private world is patchy and disconnected.

Such is the picture of the 'beginning of the world', the crude material out of which the universe has been constructed. It is in itself orderly, in that it contains regularities of sequence (which later become causal laws) and the parallelism of private worlds. It is not true to say, as is sometimes said, that it is mind which introduces all order into the universe. There are the rudiments of order there at the beginning. But otherwise the world in the beginning is patchy, disconnected, unsolid, a jumble of discrete scraps of private worlds and multitudinous bits of universes. All the rest of the universe as we know it, perduring through connected time, extending through a single space, solid, permanent, continuous, and independent of mind, all this has been built up by thousands of generations of minds labouring together.

It is quite conceivable that if there are other minds with which we are not in communication they may have built up worlds totally different from ours. If there are minds on Mars, their system of knowledge may be so unlike ours that language or communication between us might be now practically impossible, even if we could overcome the distance and the physical obstacles. For on the road of knowledge, as we have seen, there are many forks at which the human mind may choose between different paths. These different paths are alternative truths. At most of these forks the human mind has chosen one route and has left the others unexplored. How are we to know that the Martian mind, or any other in the universe (if there be any), has taken the same turns as we have? Those other minds may have built up universes in which the multitude of private worlds, rather than the singleness of a public world, is the basic feature; in which there are two disconnected spaces, visual and tactile; in which visual space has only two dimensions; in which empty visual space does not exist; in which the motion of solid visual bodies is unknown; in which what we call motion is explained as simply change of colour on a flat world; in which the notions of substance, self-identity, thinghood, solidity, permanence, have no application, or are applied quite differently from the way in which we apply them. And it must be remembered that if these strange minds have taken turnings of the road different from those taken by us, they will have had to follow them out, diverging farther and farther from our route at every step, until they may have entered fields of knowledge which we cannot imagine. Suppose for example that, instead of inventing a third spatial dimension as we did, they built their world on the basis of a flat plane in which motions were explained as merely changes of colour. Thus far we can follow their proceeding. But as a result of this all their subsequent constructions, the whole of their physical science, will have to be quite different from ours. What vast adjustments and reconstructions of our knowledge would be necessary before it could come into line with theirs?

It may be that the human race is only one group of minds; that there are many groups; and that there exist as many different systems of knowledge as there are groups of minds; and that none of these groups could now in any wise understand one another if brought into contact.

These suggestions are not put forward for the sake of idle speculation about the men in Mars, or in remoter bodies, as is the case with those newspaper descriptions of the 'marvels' of 'science' at which the credulous are accustomed to be set a-gaping. I do not know whether there actually are any other groups of minds in the universe or not. So far as I know, there is not the slightest evidence of it. And to speculate on the point is altogether beside my purpose. My purpose is to emphasize, by means of this *picture*, the fact that, owing to the existence of alternative truths, other systems of knowledge than ours are possible and would be equally 'true'.

For the building up of the world by mind, as it is conceived in our philosophy, is in no way parallel to that world-construction by Mind which was a feature of such systems as those of Kant and Hegel. For them the world was built once and for all, in some single necessary way, by some vast non-human transcendental cosmic universal Mind. But in our view it has been the work of billions of individual human and perhaps pre-human minds, working ant-like through the aeons, each contributing its morsel. It has been governed, not primarily by logical necessity, but by human, and perhaps pre-human, *needs*. And it might have been built quite differently.

Logically speaking, each individual mind might have adopted its own system of knowledge, and your world might be quite different from mine. I might have adopted one alternative truth, you another. There are never any logical grounds which compel us to adopt one rather than the other. If there were, they would not be alternative truths. The only reasons why the human race has developed a single common system of knowledge are (1) that men's minds are similar. For example, all minds will in general prefer the simpler and easier of two possible routes. And (2) they have laboured together in common, with a common end, and each mind influencing all the others. Their guiding aim has been a common world for the sake of fellowship. If we could discover some other group of minds in some other planet, we might find their system of knowledge different from ours. But it is to be expected that they would share a single common system among themselves.

INDEX

Absolute, the, 30, 152, 417; as a construction, 415-16.
— Interval, 391, 394.
Abstraction, 28, 42.
Action, relation of knowledge to, 1-13, 46-7, 58-64, 243, 245-6, 434, 435, 436.
Activity, as characteristic of the I, 42-4, 81, 82, 89, 99.
Alexander, S., 170, 172, 173; on our knowledge of other minds, 176-86, 194; on the categories, 290, 293; on causation, 321.
Algebra, 271.
Alternative truths, 46, 105-6, 113, 114, 119, 122, 146, 201, 225, 281-4, 309, 310, 311, 315, 403, 417, 445-7.
Andrade, E. N. de C., 116, 167.
Animal faith, see Instinctive Belief.
— psychology, 247-8.
Antecedent, in hypothetical judgements expressing existential constructions, 107, 108, 111, 132-3, 140, 210, 222, 314-15, 320-1, 378-9, 387, 409, 439-42.
Archaean rocks, 387.
Aristotle, 1, 293, 311, 313.
Arithmetic, necessary truth in, 268; nature of truth in, 269.
Assumptions, mental constructions as, 105, 111, 115, 121, 131, 139, 146, 157; methodological, 353-4, 405-9, 439.
Astronomy, 18; Ptolemaic and Copernican, 404-9.
Atomic Theory, 377-85, 388-9.
Atoms, 166, 167, 168; as a construction, 378-80; as a fiction, 116; as particles, 377; as 'wavicles', 381, 382, 384; meaning of existence of, 378-80; models of, 132, 133, 377, 380-4.
Attention, 42, 43.
Awareness, is originally identical with presentation, 79-88; not an activity of mind, 81-3, 87.
Axiom, as construction, 281-4, 288; as basis of deduction, 342-3; as disguised definition, 265-7; geometrical, 16, 87, 238, 270, 272; of parallels, 70, 263, 264, 265, 340, 343, 350, 364, 428; question of necessity of, 260, 262, 366.

Bacon, Francis, 256.
Balfour, Lord, on solipsism, 65.
Being, The category of, 294-7; distinguished from existence and reality, 294-5.
Beltrami, 265, 350.
Bergson, 1, 2.
Berkeley, 1, 39, 214; and use of the word 'idea', 91; on vision, 35; on visual depth, 216, 219, 222.
Body, the human, not given as body, 37-8, 188; how we become aware of, 187-90.
Bolyai, 263.
Brahma, 7.
Broad, C. D. x, 84, 85, 214, 263, 264; on inductive logic, 347; on visual depth, 217.

Categorical judgement, *see under* Judgement.
Categories vii, 289-339; factual and constructive, 296; exclude constructive concepts, 336; exclude non-necessary factual concepts, 336-337; Kant on, 261, 290-1, 292, 293, 294, 295; necessity of, 290, 291, 292, 338.
Causality, 127, 139, 154, 155; as compulsion, 322-3, 400; S. Alexander on, 321; the category of, 321-5; Kant on, 323, 365; J. S. Mill on, 321; not a true category, 337-8; Bertrand Russell on, 321-2; L. S. Stebbing on, 321-2.
Causal sequences, 125, 126, 127, 128.
Change, of position, 220; of quality, 138-9; of state, 220.
Classes, based on resemblances, 59; singular and nil-classes, 50-1.
Classification, guided by purpose, 244.
Coherence, 436.
Colour-blindness, 104.
Concepts, as facts, 49; as given, 49; equivalent to judgements, 57; evolu-

tion of, 246, 248-52; founded on resemblances, 50-1, 59; free and submerged, 246-8; necessary for knowledge, 48; pyramidal arrangement of, 53, 54.

Concepts of the Given, 21, 46, 48-64, 68, 99; as beginning of knowledge, 51-2, 55-6; are not constructions, 50, 51, 53; factual categories are, 296; not predictive, 61-3; are possible to the solitary mind, 51, 57, 68.

— of Things, 241-56; are predictive, 245, 252, 254; are subsequent to concepts of the given, 52, 56.

Consistency, in constructions, 120, 158, 159; in logic, 340-1, 359, 373.

Construction, 21, 22, 27, 28, 45, 77; as assumption, 105, 111, 115, 121, 131, 139; as part of truth, 80, 83, 86, 161-3, 429-37; as tied by the given, 430-2; as tied by logic, 430; as tied by needs, 432-5; as unconscious, 97-8; contradiction in existential, 439-42; criteria of validity of, 162-3, 404, 429-35; distinguished from hypothesis, 163-8; distinguished from methodological assumption, 407-8; existential, 157-9; imagination in, 110, 111, 115, 133, 157; logical characters of, 111, 114-15, 120-2, 131-3, 139-42, 146, 156, 439-42; of the Absolute, 415-16; of the atom, 378-80; of categories, viz. (1) of existence, 296-7; (2) of identity, 306-10; (3) of possibility, 318-19; (4) of substance 314-15; of ether, 409-11; of the external world, 95-148; viz. (1) of resemblance between presentations of different minds, 101-111; (2) of the identity of such presentations, and of the one universe, 111-16; (3) of unperceived presentations perceived by other minds, 116-22; (4) of wholly unperceived presentations, 122-33; (5) of 'things' and 'qualities', 133-42; (6) of the equivalence of the senses, 142-6; of geometrical axioms, 281-4, 288; of the past, 386-8, 389; of space and time, 199-240; viz. (1) of continuous private spaces, 203-10; (2) of continuous private times, 210-11; (3) of the identity of visual and tactile spaces, 211-12; (4) of public space and time, 212-14; (5) of the third visual dimension, 214-22; (6) of empty visual space, 222-7; (7) of the measurability of space, 227-35; (8) of the measurability of time, 235-7; of space-time, 395-6; of the subconscious, 412-13; the subsidiary, 118-19, 121-2, 138, 146; systems of, 157, 209; unificatory, 156-7.

Constructional character of science, 115-16, 134, 162, 164-8.

Continuity of Space, 207-8.

Contradiction, see Law of Contradiction.

Correspondence theory of Truth, 255, 419-27, 436, 438-9.

Cosmos, 155.

Creative Evolution, 1.

Croce, B., 289.

Curiosity, 435.

Darwin, Charles, 375.

Deduction, 340-7; all reasoning is, 359; infinite regress in, 342, 345; not an instrument of proof, 344-5, 355-6.

Definitions, as analytic propositions, 266; as necessary truths, 266.

Dependence, causal, logical, and part-whole, 93.

Depth, visual, 35-6, 38, 214-22; Berkeley on, 216, 219, 222; Broad on, 217; William James on, 216.

Descartes, viii, 17, 20, 21, 22, 33, 311, 359.

De Sitter, 200.

Differences between parallel universes, 112-13, 116, 117, 118, 134, 135, 158, 159.

Dimension, fourth, fifth, etc., 239-40; of extension-spreads, 202; the third tactile, 214-16; the third visual, 214-22; time as fourth, 392-4.

Distance, visual. See Depth.

Diversity, The category of, 304-11.

Dream, 34, 44, 45, 52; distinguished from veridical perception, 89-90, 326-33.

INDEX

Dualism, The Revolt against, 125–8, 153.
Duration-spread, 36, 38, 45; distinguished from time, 38, 52.

Eddington, Sir Arthur, 167, 227, 270, 381.
Ego, the, 17, 20, 41, 413.
Egocentric Predicament, 124.
Einstein, ix, 11, 165, 166, 200, 235, 262, 263, 279, 375, 389–404.
Electric theory of Matter, 377–85.
Empiricism, v, vi, 29–30, 151, 152.
Encyclopaedia Britannica, 40.
Equality, in space, 227–35, 265; in time, 235–7.
Equivalence of the Senses, 142–6.
Error, 90, 437.
Esse, and *percipi*, ix, 72–3, 74, 75, 77–88, 92, 94, 108–9, 119, 120, 131, 198.
Ether, 137, 164, 409–11, 425.
Euclid, 38, 70, 87, 203, 227, 260, 263, 264, 265, 270, 272, 274, 278, 279, 283, 285, 288, 323, 340, 350, 364, 366, 428.
Evolution, 1, 24, 58; of concepts, 245, 248–52; creative, 1; emergent, 1; epistemological character of, 375–7; factual character of, 376–7.
Excluded Middle, *see* Law of Excluded Middle.
Existence, the category of, 297–300; distinguished from being and reality, 294–5, 297; factual and constructive, 159–63; relation to perception, 109–10, 381, 382.
Existential Construction, *see* Construction.
Experience, as starting-point of philosophy, 14, 15, 17; as an abstraction, 14–15, 67.
Explanation, of facts, 154; by laws, 398, 401, 403.
Extension-spread, 36, 37, 45, 201–3; distinguished from space, 36, 52, 201–2.
External World, as public, 69–70; common to different senses, 71; construction of, 95–148; independence of, 21, 42, 69–70, 94–5, 130, 147; unknown to the solitary mind, 57.

Fact, identified with given, 46; mind as a, 168; position of, in our theory, 149–55, 168, 444; pragmatism and, 47.
Fichte, 152.
Fiction, vii; the atom as a, 116, 167.
Force, ix, 396, 397, 398, 399–400, 402–3, 404.
Fourth Dimension, 239–40; time as a, 392–4.
Freud, 97.

Geology, 385–9.
Geometry, 36, 203, 221, 227, 237; abstract character of, 273, 281; as deductive, 29; as empirical, 29; as ideal limit, 275–8; axioms in, *see* Axiom; constructive character of, 281–4; deals with non-existent objects, 272–3; Euclidean, 106; extension-spread and, 36, 52; generalization of, 271; Kant on, 261, 262, 266–7, 273; necessity in, 262–8; non-Euclidean, 106, 262–5, 281–4; of Lobachevsky, 263–4, 283; of Riemann, 264, 283; of space-time, 165, 166, 397–8, 399, 401–2; Poincaré on, 280–1; self-consistency of, 271, 288; truth of, 272, 278–81, 288.
Given, the, 17, 18, 19, 20, 31–47; as an abstraction, 31, 46; concepts of, *see* Concepts of the Given; identified with fact, 46; the internal, 40–4; knowledge tied to, 47, 254, 269, 281, 288; the logical, 32–3, 39; the metaphysical, 32–3, 39.
Gravitation, 396–404; does not involve compulsion, 400; dependent on geometry, 397 et seq.; Einstein's law of, 279; Newton's law of, 396–7; refers to particulars, 424–5.

Hallucination, 34, 44, 45, 52; distinguished from veridical perception, 326–33.
Hearing, 38.
Hegel, 30, 293, 338, 447; method of, 415; on quality, 301, 302; on unity and plurality, 303.
Heisenberg, viii, 381.
Hereditary tendencies to belief, 98.
Historical knowledge, 414.

Historical order, relation of to logical order, 19–20, 23–7, 56, 96–8.
Hume, David, 1, 41, 323, 349, 363.
Huxley, Julian, 247.
Hypothesis, nature of, 163–8; distinguished from construction, 163–168.
Hypothetical character of science, *see* Science.
Hypothetical judgement, *see* Judgement.

I, the, 44, 82, 89, 99.
Idea, as intermediate between mind and object, 82–3; Berkeley's use of the word, 91.
Idealism versus realism, 39–40, 73–94, 417.
Ideas, Platonic, 152, 419.
Identity, personal, 413; the category of, 304–11; two meanings of, 304–5.
Illusion, 423–4.
Imagination, in constructions, 110, 111, 115, 133, 157.
Impossibility, in existential constructions, 107, 108, 111, 439–42.
Independence, of external given, 43, 44; of external world, 21, 42, 69, 94–5, 130, 147; of presentations, 74–5, 92–4, 100.
Indeterminacy, Principle of, viii, ix, 381.
Indian Thought, 7.
Induction, 342, 343–4, 347–59; depends on deduction, 358–9; involves illicit process, 347–8; not a form of reasoning, 357–9; not an instrument of proof, 355–6. *See also* Uniformity of Nature.
Infant psychology, 56, 97–8.
Inference, 21, 22, 28, 77. *See also* Deduction, Logic, Induction, Syllogism.
Infinity of space, 203, 237–9.
Innate Ideas, 86.
Instinct, 27; and belief in other minds, 180–6, 194–6; directed to action, 183–4, 194.
Instinctive belief in external world, 27–8, 84–7, 88, 97, 123, 125.
Interval, The Absolute, 391, 394.
Intuition, 26, 28, 59.

Irrationalism, 181, 183, 185.
Irreversibility of time, 268.

James, William, 1, 214; on visual depth, 216–17.
Jeans, Sir James, ix.
Judgement, and concepts of the given, 57; categorical, and unificatory constructions, 115, 122; equivalent to concept, 57; hypothetical, and existential constructions, 107–10, 111, 122, 131, 140, 157, 439–42; refers to particulars, 417–19.
Jurisprudence, 277.

Kant, 1, 16, 30, 32, 33, 39, 271, 447; on categories, 261, 290–1, 292, 293, 294, 295; on causation, 323, 365; on geometry, 261, 262, 266–7, 273; on necessary truth, 261; on space, 261, 262, 266–7.
Kepler's laws, 403.
Knowledge of Other Minds, 169–98; Alexander on, 176–86; direct knowledge theory of, 169, 170, 174–86; how related to knowledge of external world, 100, 169, 170; inferential theory of, 170, 186–92, 196–7; logical and psychological base of, 172–4, 180–1, 192–6; not a construction, 169, 197–8; not a datum, 66, 69.

Law of Contradiction, and non-Euclidean geometry, 287; C. I. Lewis on, 369; modifications needed in, 287, 429; necessity of, 361–2.
Law of Excluded Middle, 369, 372–3.
Lewis, C. I., 61; on logic, 369–74.
Light, bending of, 400.
Lobachevsky, 263, 270, 278, 283, 285, 288.
Locke, John, 144, 235.
Lodge, Sir Oliver, 411.
Logic, 340–74; deductive, 340–7; deductive, gives only negative commands, 345–6; inductive, 342, 343–4, 347–59; inductive, involves illicit process, 347–8; Miss Stebbing's view of, 367–9; pragmatist view of, 369–74; realist view of, 362–7; *see also* Deduction, Induction.

INDEX

Logical order, relation of to historical order, 19–20; 23–7, 56, 96–8.
Lovejoy, Professor, 125–8, 153.

Materialism, 87.
Mathematics, 257–88, 418.
Measurement, fundamental to science, 227; of astronomical triangles, 264, 265, 278–9; of space, 227–35; of time, 235–7.
Memory, 34, 55.
Meno, The, 260.
Mental, as equivalent to private, 89 et seq.; whether the not-I is, 44–5; whether presentations are, 74, 88–92, 100.
Mental Constructions, *see* Construction.
Mercury, orbit of, 165–6, 400, 401, 404.
Method, 14–30, 258; empirical, 29–30; of Descartes, 16–17, 20; of Hegel, 415.
Methodological assumption, 353–4, 405–9, 439.
Mill, J. S., inductive methods of, 358; on causation, 321.
Minds, as factual, 168, 169, 197–8. *See also* Knowledge of Other Minds.
Minkowski, 395.
Models of the atom, 132, 133, 377, 380–4.
Motion, absolute and relative, 404; and empty space, 224–5; as change of state, 224–5, 284–5, 446; Einstein's law of, 397; Newton's first law of, 396–7.
Multiplicity of universes, 111–13.

Necessary truth, 87, 259; in the categories, *see* Necessity; Kant on, 261; in logic, *see* Necessity; in mathematics, 260–8.
Necessity, logical, 268, 293; categories and, 290, 291, 292, 335–9, viz. (1) being, 295–6; (2) causality, 322–4; (3) diversity, 305–6; (4) existence, 297–9; (5) identity, 305–6; (6) plurality, 303–4; (7) possibility, 318; (8) quality, 300–2; (9) reality, 333; (10) relation, 334; (11) substance, 313–14; (12) unity, 303–4; constructive concepts do not possess, 335; distinguished from practical, 298, 299, 323; Miss Stebbing's view of, 367–9; pragmatist view of, 362, 369–74; psychological feeling of, 365–6; realist view of, 362–7.
Neptune, discovery of, 165, 167.
Newton, ix, 38, 375, 396, 397, 398, 399, 401, 424.
Niels Bohr, 235.
Nirvana, 7.
Not-I, 41, 44, 89, 99.
Nought as a number, 51.

Object, construction of, 133–42; distinguished from presentation, 21, 28, 34–5, 37, 49, 69–73.
Occam's razor, 28, 432–3.
One, the, 311.
Optics, 279.

Parallelism of private worlds, 112, 117, 134, 149–55, 443.
Particles, 377, 381, 384.
Passivity of the not-I, 43, 44, 82, 89, 99.
Past, the, 385–9.
Percipi. See *Esse*.
Permanence, 138–9, 312–13, 316.
Philosophical knowledge, 413–17.
Phlogiston, 425.
Platner, 206.
Plato, 1, 30, 260, 261.
Plurality, of worlds, *see* Multiplicity; the category of, 303–4.
Poincaré, H., vi, vii; on geometry, 280–1, 288.
Possibility, the category of, 316–21, 441–2.
Pragmatism, 1–13, 59–64, 114, 252–4, 256, 362, 369–74, 435–6, 437–8.
Pre-Cambrian rocks, 387.
Predictivity of concepts, 61–3, 245, 252, 254.
Pre-established Harmony, 149, 155.
Presentations, are private, 69; as existing unperceived, 116–33; as given, 34, 45; become 'qualities', 133–42; belong to one sense, 69; dependence or independence of, 74–5, 92–4; distinguished from objects, 34–5, 37, 49, 69–73, 133–

42; identity of, in different minds, 111–16; include non-veridical images, 34, 45; non-existence of, when unperceived, 69–71, 73, 74–7; resemblance between, in different minds, 31–2, 101–11.
Primitive belief, *see* Instinctive Belief.
Proof, reasoning is not, 344–5, 355–6.
Psychology, of animals, 247–8; of infants, 56, 96–8.
Pythagoras, Theorem of, 19, 23, 271, 275, 277.

Quality, as a concept of the given, 55, 60; different meanings of, 300; of 'things', 133, 137, 139, 141, 142; Hegel on, 301, 302; the category of, 300–3.

Rationalism, 66, 85, 124–5.
Rattray, R. F., 98.
Real, the, 90, 92.
Realism, and parallelism of worlds, 150–4; on distinction between presentation and awareness, 79–88; on 'egocentric predicament', 124; on instinctive belief in external world, 27–8, 84–7, 88, 123; on logic, 362–7; versus idealism, 39–40, 73–94, 417.
Realism, The New, 124, 128.
Reality, and external stimulus, 328–9, 331–2, 333; as sharability, 332–3; distinguished from being and existence, 294–5, 297; not a true category, 337–8; the category of, 325–34.
Reason, in animals, 25, 247; subconscious, 24–7.
Reasoning, *see* Deduction, Induction, Logic, Syllogism.
Recognition of objects, 25, 243, 248–52.
Reed, H. L., x.
Relation, as constructed, 40; as given, 38, 39, 40; as the work of thought, 39; the category of, 334–5.
Relativity, gravitation in, 396–404; non-Euclidean geometry in, 106, 265–6, 279; space-time in, 389–96.
Resemblance, as basis of concepts, 50–1, 59; as concept of the given, 52; as given, 39, 40, 45; of presentations in different minds, 31–2, 101–11; relative to possible comparison, 106–7.
Riemann, 264, 270, 278, 279, 283, 285, 288.
Russell, Bertrand, 123, 270; on causation, 321–2.

'Same', Concept of the, 76, 96, 118–19, 138, 142, 156, 307.
Scepticism, 354–5, 365.
Schiller, F. C. S., 307, 312, 353, 356.
Science, 375–413; hypothetical or constructional character of, 115–16, 134, 162, 164–8.
Self-consciousness, 25.
Self-knowledge, 40–4.
Sensa, 74, 85, 86, 87, 88.
Sensation, 18, 19, 20, 31–2.
Senses, equivalence of the, 142–6.
Shape, as given, 36.
Shaw, G. B., 363.
Sight, 35–8, 202; relation of, to touch, 143–5. *See also* Depth, Vision.
Simplification, as a factor in knowledge, 105, 106, 113, 114, 119, 120, 122, 128–9, 145–6, 158, 436.
Simultaneity of Space, 208–9.
Socrates, 18, 19.
Solipsism, 65–7, 171, 197.
Solitary Mind, the, can form concepts of the given, 51, 57, 68; can know distinction between I and not-I, 89; can know extension-spread and duration-spread, but not space and time, 201–3; cannot know distinction between *esse* and *percipi*, 73, 77–88; cannot know permanent objects, 74, 88; cannot know that presentations persist unperceived, 73, 74–7; cannot know 'things', 57, 69, 133–42; the world of, 65–94.
Space, continuity of, 207–8; construction of, *see* Construction; curved, 401–2, 403; empty, 36, 202–3, 222–7; empty, not necessary to explain motion, 224–5; finite, 237–9; fourth and further dimensions of, 239–40; identification of tactile with visual, 211–12; infinite,

203, 237–9; Kant on, 261, 262, 266–7; measurability of, 227–35; primarily an intensive magnitude, 228–30; simultaneity of, 208–9; tactile, not identical with time, 38, 206–7.

Space-time, ix, 201; as a construction, 395–6, 404; as a real existence, 395–6; Einstein's theory of, 389–96; geometry of, 165–6; Minkowski on, 395.

Spinoza, on substance, 311, 312.

Stebbing, Miss L. S., on causation, 321–2; on induction, 358; on necessity in logic, 367–9.

Subconsciousness, 411–13.

Subconscious reasoning, 24–7.

Substance, as development of the 'thing' and its 'properties', 312; definition of, 312; Spinoza on, 311, 312; the category of, 307, 311–16, 336.

Syllogism, The, infinite regress in, 342, 345, 346–7; necessity in, 361; not an instrument of proof, 344–5; *petitio principii* in, 344, 345, 346.

Taylor, A. E., 170.

Teleology, 152, 155; in biology, 406.

Telepathy, 15, 16, 176.

Theism, 152, 155, 415–16.

Thing-in-itself, Kant's, 32, 33.

Things, concepts of, 52, 56–7, 241–56; construction of, 133–42; contradictions in the notion of, 136–7, 140–2; distinguished from presentations, 49, 69–73; how carved out of the sense-manifold, 241–3; unknown to solitary mind, 57, 69, 133–42.

Thought, The laws of, their necessity, 362–74; *see also* Law of Contradiction, Law of Excluded Middle.

Time, as fourth dimension, 392–4; construction of, *see* Construction; distinguished from duration-spread, 38, 52; future, 38, 388; irreversibility of, 268.

Touch, 38; relation of, to sight, 143–5.

Transcendentalism, v, 28–9, 261, 443.

Truth, absoluteness of, 437–9; coherence theory of, 436; correspondence theory of, 255, 419–27, 436, 438–9; definition of, 436; includes constructions, 80, 83, 86, 161–3, 429, 436; includes fictions, 116; involves correspondence of concept with given, 419–27; in mathematics, 259, 260–8, 288; is a character of judgements, 417; nature of arithmetical, 269; nature of geometrical, 269–81, 288; necessary, *see* Necessary truth; pragmatist theory of, *see* Pragmatism; the problem of, 417–37.

Unconscious constructions, 79–98.

— reasoning, 24–7.

Unificatory constructions, *see* Construction.

Uniformity of Nature, the, 154, 348–55; an unprovable assumption, 350; justification of, 352–3; not a construction, 350–3; not a methodological assumption, 350.

Unity, the category of, 303–4.

Universality, of categories, 290, 291, 292.

Universe, construction of a single, 111–16; difference between parallel universes, 112–13, 116, 117, 118, 134, 135, 158, 159; parallel universes, 112, 117, 134, 149–55, 443.

Unreal, the, 90; how distinguished from reality, 326–33.

Useful, the, distinguished from the true, 61, 63, 64; in pragmatism, 10, 11, 12.

Vaihinger, vi, vii, 1.

Value, knowledge as a, 1–13.

Veridical Perception, 89, 90, 91, 92, 326.

Villey, Pierre, 144, 206.

Vision, logical operations in, 25, 98.

'Wavicles', 381, 382, 384.

Webb, C. C. J., on knowledge of other minds, 170, 172–3, 187, 190; on solipsism, 65.

'Working', the meaning of, in pragmatism, 10, 12.

World-line, 393, 394.

Yoga, 7.